MW00378314

A History of the
Moravian Church

By J. E. Hutton

Layout and Cover Copyright ©2014
All Rights Reserved
Printed in the USA

Table of Contents

Preface

FOR assistance in the preparation of this second edition, I desire herewith to express my obligations to several friends:—To the late Rev. L. G. Hasse, B.D., whose knowledge of Moravian history was profound, and who guided me safely in many matters of detail; to the Rev. N. Libbey, M.A., Principal of the Moravian Theological College, Fairfield, for the loan of valuable books; to the Rev. J. T. Mueller, D.D., Archivist at Herrnhut, for revising part of the MS., and for many helpful suggestions; to Mr. W. T. Waugh, M.A., for assistance in correcting the proof-sheets, and for much valuable criticism; to the members of the Moravian Governing Board, not only for the loan of books and documents from the Fetter Lane archives, but also for carefully reading through the MS.; to the ministers who kindly supplied my pulpit for three months; and last, but not least, to the members of my own congregation, who relieved me from some pastoral duties to enable me to make good speed with my task.

MORAVIAN MANSE,
HECKMONDWIKE.

Book 1:

The Bohemian Brethren

Chapter 1: The Rising Storm

WHEN an ordinary Englishman, in the course of his reading, sees mention made of Moravians, he thinks forthwith of a foreign land, a foreign people and a foreign Church. He wonders who these Moravians may be, and wonders, as a rule, in vain. We have all heard of the Protestant Reformation; we know its principles and admire its heroes; and the famous names of Luther, Calvin, Melancthon, Latimer, Cranmer, Knox and other great men are familiar in our ears as household words. But few people in this country are aware of the fact that long before Luther had burned the Pope's bull, and long before Cranmer died at the stake, there had begun an earlier Reformation, and flourished a Reforming Church. It is to tell the story of that Church—the Church of the Brethren—that this little book is written.

For her cradle and her earliest home we turn to the distressful land of Bohemia, and the people called Bohemians, or Czechs. To us English readers Bohemia has many charms. As we call to mind our days at school, we remember, in a dim and hazy way, how famous Bohemians in days of yore have played some part in our national story. We have sung the praises at Christmas time of the Bohemian Monarch, "Good King Wenceslaus." We have read how John, the blind King of Bohemia, fell mortally wounded at the Battle of Crecy, how he died in the tent of King Edward III., and how his generous conqueror exclaimed: "The crown of chivalry has fallen today; never was the like of this King of Bohemia." We have all read, too, how Richard II. married Princess Anne of Bohemia; how the Princess, so the story goes, brought a Bohemian Bible to England; how Bohemian scholars, a few years later, came to study at Oxford; how there they read the writings of Wycliffe, the "Morning Star of the Reformation"; and how, finally, copies of Wycliffe's books were carried to Bohemia, and there gave rise to a religious revival of world-wide importance. We have struck the trail of our journey. For one person that Wycliffe stirred in England, he stirred hundreds in Bohemia. In England his influence was fleeting; in Bohemia it was deep and abiding. In England his followers were speedily suppressed by law; in Bohemia they became a great national force, and prepared the way for the foundation of the Church of the Brethren.

For this startling fact there was a very powerful reason. In many ways the history of Bohemia is very like the history of Ireland, and the best way to understand the character of the people is to think of our Irish friends as we know them to-day. They sprang from the old Slavonic stock, and the Slavonic is very like the Keltic in nature. They had fiery Slavonic blood in their veins, and Slavonic hearts beat high with hope in their bosoms. They had all the delightful Slavonic zeal, the Slavonic dash, the Slavonic imagination. They were easy to stir, they were swift in action, they were witty in speech, they were mystic and poetic in soul, and, like the Irish of the present day, they revelled in the joy of party politics, and discussed religious questions with the keenest zest. With them religion came first and foremost. All their poetry was religious; all their legends were religious; and thus the message of Wycliffe fell on hearts prepared to give it a kindly welcome.

Again, Bohemia, like Ireland, was the home of two rival populations. The one was the native Czech, the other was the intruding German; and the two had not yet learned to love each other. From all sides except one these German invaders had come. If the reader will consult a map of Europe he will see that, except on the south-east frontier, where the sister country, Moravia, lies, Bohemia is surrounded by German-speaking States. On the north-east is Silesia, on the north-west Saxony, on the west Bavaria and the Upper Palatinate, and thus Bohemia was flooded with Germans from three sides at once. For years these Germans had been increasing in power, and the whole early history of Bohemia is one dreary succession of bloody wars against German Emperors and Kings. Sometimes the land had been ravaged by German soldiers, sometimes a German King had sat on the Bohemian throne. But now the German settlers in Bohemia had become more powerful than ever. They had settled in large numbers in the city of Prague, and had there obtained special privileges for themselves. They had introduced hundreds of German clergymen, who preached in the German language. They had married their daughters into noble Bohemian families. They had tried to make German the language of the court, had spoken with contempt of the Bohemian language, and had said that it was only fit for slaves. They had introduced German laws into many a town, and German customs into family life; and, worse than all, they had overwhelming power in that pride of the country, the University of Prague. For these Germans the hatred of the people was intense. "It is better," said one of their popular writers, "for the land to be a desert than to be held by Germans; it is better to marry a Bohemian peasant girl than to marry a German queen." And Judas Iscariot himself, said a popular poet, was in all probability a German.

Again, as in Ireland, these national feuds were mixed up with religious differences. The seeds of future strife were early sown. Christianity came from two opposite sources. On the one hand, two preachers, Cyril and Methodius, had come from the Greek Church in Constantinople, had received the blessing of the Pope, and had preached to the people in the Bohemian language; on the other, the German Archbishop of Salzburg had brought in hosts of German priests, and had tried in vain to persuade the Pope to condemn the two preachers as heretics. And the people loved the Bohemian preachers, and hated the German priests. The old feud was raging still. If the preacher spoke in German, he was hated; if he spoke in Bohemian, he was beloved; and Gregory VII. had made matters worse by forbidding preaching in the language of the people.

The result can be imagined. It is admitted now by all historians—Catholic and Protestant alike—that about the time when our story opens the Church in Bohemia had lost her hold upon the affections of the people. It is admitted that sermons the people could understand were rare. It is admitted that the Bible was known to few, that the services held in the parish churches had become mere senseless shows, and that most of the clergy never preached at all. No longer were the clergy examples to their flocks. They hunted, they gambled, they caroused, they committed adultery, and the suggestion was actually solemnly made that they should be provided with concubines.

For some years a number of pious teachers had made gallant but vain attempts to cleanse the stables. The first was Conrad of Waldhausen, an Augustinian Friar (1364-9). As this man was a German and spoke in German, it is not likely that he had much effect on the common people, but he created quite a sensation in Prague, denounced alike the vices of the clergy and the idle habits of the rich, persuaded the ladies of high degree to give up their fine dresses and jewels, and even caused certain well-known sinners to come and do penance in public.

The next was Milic of Kremsir (1363-74). He was a Bohemian, and preached in the Bohemian language. His whole life was one of noble self-sacrifice. For the sake of the poor he renounced his position as Canon, and devoted himself entirely to good works. He rescued thousands of fallen women, and built them a number of homes. He was so disgusted with the evils of his days that he thought the end of the world was close at hand, declared that the Emperor, Charles IV., was Anti-Christ, went to Rome to expound his views to the Pope, and posted up a notice on the door of St. Peter's, declaring that Anti-Christ had come.

The next was that beautiful writer, Thomas of Stitny (1370-1401). He exalted the Holy Scriptures as the standard of faith, wrote several beautiful devotional books, and denounced the immorality of the monks. "They have fallen away from love," he said; "they have not the peace of God in their hearts; they quarrel, condemn and fight each other; they have forsaken God for money."

In some ways these three Reformers were all alike. They were all men of lofty character; they all attacked the vices of the clergy and the luxury of the rich; and they were all loyal to the Church of Rome, and looked to the Pope to carry out the needed reform.

But the next Reformer, Matthew of Janow, carried the movement further (1381-93). The cause was the famous schism in the Papacy. For the long period of nearly forty years (1378-1415) the whole Catholic world was shocked by the scandal of two, and sometimes three, rival Popes, who spent their time abusing and fighting each other. As long as this schism lasted it was hard for men to look up to the Pope as a true spiritual guide. How could men call the Pope the Head of the Church when no one knew which was the true Pope? How could men respect the Popes when some of the Popes were men of bad moral character? Pope Urban VI. was a ferocious brute, who had five of his enemies secretly murdered; Pope Clement VII., his clever rival, was a scheming politician; and Pope John XXIII. was a man whose character will scarcely bear describing in print. Of all the scandals in the Catholic Church, this disgraceful quarrel between rival Popes did most to upset the minds of good men and to prepare the way for the Reformation. It aroused the scorn of John Wycliffe in England, and of Matthew of Janow in Bohemia. "This schism," he wrote, "has not arisen because the priests loved Jesus Christ and His Church, but rather because they loved themselves and the world."

But Matthew went even further than this. As he did not attack any Catholic dogma—except the worship of pictures and images—it has been contended by some writers that he was not so very radical in his views after all; but the whole tone of his writings shows that he had lost his confidence in the Catholic Church, and desired to revive the simple Christianity of Christ and the Apostles. "I consider it essential," he wrote, "to root out all weeds, to restore the word of God on earth, to bring back the Church of Christ to its original, healthy, condensed condition, and to keep only such regulations as date from the time of the Apostles." "All the works of men," he added, "their ceremonies and traditions, shall soon be totally destroyed; the Lord Jesus shall alone be exalted, and His Word shall stand for ever." Back to Christ! Back to the Apostles! Such was the message of Matthew of Janow.

At this point, when the minds of men were stirred, the writings of Wycliffe were brought to Bohemia, and added fuel to the fire. He had asserted that the Pope was capable of committing a sin. He had declared that the Pope was not to be obeyed unless his commands were in accordance with Scripture, and thus had placed the authority of the Bible above the authority of the Pope. He had attacked the Doctrine of Transubstantiation, and had thus denied the power of the priests "to make the Body of Christ." Above all, in his volume, "De Ecclesia," he had denounced the whole Catholic sacerdotal system, and had laid down the Protestant doctrine that men could come into contact with God without the aid of priests. Thus step by step the way was prepared for the coming revolution in Bohemia. There was strong patriotic national feeling; there was hatred of the German priests; there was a growing love for the Bible; there was lack of respect for the immoral clergy, and lack of belief in the Popes; there was a vague desire to return to Primitive Christianity; and all that was needed now was a man to gather these straggling beams together, and focus them all in one white burning light.

Chapter 2: The Burning of Hus

ON Saturday, July 6th, 1415, there was great excitement in the city of Constance. For the last half-year the city had presented a brilliant and gorgeous scene. The great Catholic Council of Constance had met at last. From all parts of the Western World distinguished men had come. The streets were a blaze of colour. The Cardinals rode by in their scarlet hats; the monks in their cowls were telling their beads; the revellers sipped their wine and sang; and the rumbling carts from the country-side bore bottles of wine, cheeses, butter, honey, venison, cakes and fine confections. King Sigismund was there in all his pride, his flaxen hair falling in curls about his shoulders; there were a thousand Bishops, over two thousand Doctors and Masters, about two thousand Counts, Barons and Knights, vast hosts of Dukes, Princes and Ambassadors—in all over 50,000 strangers.

And now, after months of hot debate, the Council met in the great Cathedral to settle once for all the question, What to do with John Hus? King Sigismund sat on the throne, Princes flanking him on either side. In the middle of the Cathedral floor was a scaffold; on the scaffold a table and a block of wood; on the block of wood some priestly robes. The Mass was said. John Hus was led in. He mounted the scaffold. He breathed a prayer. The awful proceedings began.

But why was John Hus there? What had he done to offend both Pope and Emperor? For the last twelve years John Hus had been the boldest reformer, the finest preacher, the most fiery patriot, the most powerful writer, and the most popular hero in Bohemia. At first he was nothing more than a child of his times. He was born on July 6th, 1369, in a humble cottage at Husinec, in South Bohemia; earned coppers in his youth, like Luther, by chanting hymns; studied at Prague University; and entered the ministry, not because he wanted to do good, but because he wanted to enjoy a comfortable living. He began, of course, as an orthodox Catholic. He was Rector first of Prague University, and then of the Bethlehem Chapel, which had been built by John of Milheim for services in the Bohemian language. For some years he confined himself almost entirely, like Milic and Stitny before him, to preaching of an almost purely moral character. He attacked the sins and vices of all classes; he spoke in the Bohemian language, and the Bethlehem Chapel was packed. He began by attacking the vices of the idle rich. A noble lady complained to the King. The King told the Archbishop of Prague that he must warn Hus to be more cautious in his language.

"No, your Majesty," replied the Archbishop, "Hus is bound by his ordination oath to speak the truth without respect of persons."

John Hus went on to attack the vices of the clergy. The Archbishop now complained to the King. He admitted that the clergy were in need of improvement, but he thought that

Hus's language was rash, and would do more harm than good. "Nay," said the King, "that will not do. Hus is bound by his ordination oath to speak the truth without respect of persons."

And Hus continued his attacks. His preaching had two results. It fanned the people's desire for reform, and it taught them to despise the clergy more than ever.

At the same time, when opportunity offered, John Hus made a practice of preaching on the burning topics of the day; and the most popular topic then was the detested power of Germans in Bohemia. German soldiers ravaged the land; German nobles held offices of state; and German scholars, in Prague University, had three-fourths of the voting power. The Bohemian people were furious. John Hus fanned the flame. "We Bohemians," he declared in a fiery sermon, "are more wretched than dogs or snakes. A dog defends the couch on which he lies. If another dog tries to drive him off, he fights him. A snake does the same. But us the Germans oppress. They seize the offices of state, and we are dumb. In France the French are foremost. In Germany the Germans are foremost. What use would a Bohemian bishop or priest, who did not know the German language, be in Germany? He would be as useful as a dumb dog, who cannot bark, to a flock of sheep. Of exactly the same use are German priests to us. It is against the law of God! I pronounce it illegal." At last a regulation was made by King Wenceslaus that the Bohemians should be more fairly represented at Prague University. They had now three votes out of four. John Hus was credited by the people with bringing about the change. He became more popular than ever.

If Hus had only halted here, it is probable that he would have been allowed to die in peace in his bed in a good old age, and his name would be found enrolled to-day in the long list of Catholic saints. However wicked the clergy may have been, they could hardly call a man a heretic for telling them plainly about the blots in their lives. But Hus soon stepped outside these narrow bounds. The more closely he studied the works of Wycliffe, the more convinced he became that, on the whole, the great English Reformer was right; and before long, in the boldest possible way, he began to preach Wycliffe's doctrines in his sermons, and to publish them in his books. He knew precisely what he was doing. He knew that Wycliffe's doctrines had been condemned by the English Church Council at Black-Friars. He knew that these very same doctrines had been condemned at a meeting of the Prague University Masters. He knew that no fewer than two hundred volumes of Wycliffe's works had been publicly burned at Prague, in the courtyard of the Archbishop's Palace. He knew, in a word, that Wycliffe was regarded as a heretic; and yet he deliberately defended Wycliffe's teaching. It is this that justifies us in calling him a Protestant, and this that caused the Catholics to call him a heretic.

John Hus, moreover, knew what the end would be. If he stood to his guns they would burn him, and burned he longed to be. The Archbishop forbade him to preach in the Bethlehem Chapel. John Hus, defiant, went on preaching. At one service he actually read to the people a letter he had received from Richard Wyche, one of Wycliffe's followers. As the years rolled on he became more "heterodox" than ever. At this period there were

13

still two rival Popes, and the great question arose in Bohemia which Pope the clergy there were to recognise. John Hus refused to recognise either. At last one of the rival Popes, the immoral John XXIII., sent a number of preachers to Prague on a very remarkable errand. He wanted money to raise an army to go to war with the King of Naples; the King of Naples had supported the other Pope, Gregory XII., and now Pope John sent his preachers to Prague to sell indulgences at popular prices. They entered the city preceded by drummers, and posted themselves in the market place. They had a curious message to deliver. If the good people, said they, would buy these indulgences, they would be doing two good things: they would obtain the full forgiveness of their sins, and support the one lawful Pope in his holy campaign. John Hus was hot with anger. What vulgar traffic in holy things was this? He believed neither in Pope John nor in his indulgences.

"Let who will," he thundered, "proclaim the contrary; let the Pope, or a Bishop, or a Priest say, I forgive thee thy sins; I free thee from the pains of Hell.' It is all vain, and helps thee nothing. God alone, I repeat, can forgive sins through Christ."

The excitement in Prague was furious. From this moment onwards Hus became the leader of a national religious movement. The preachers went on selling indulgences (1409). At one and the same time, in three different churches, three young artisans sang out: "Priest, thou liest! The indulgences are a fraud." For this crime the three young men were beheaded in a corner near Green Street. Fond women—sentimental, as usual—dipped their handkerchiefs in the blood of the martyrs, and a noble lady spread fine linen over their corpses. The University students picked up the gauntlet. They seized the bodies of the three young men, and carried them to be buried in the Bethlehem Chapel. At the head of the procession was Hus himself, and Hus conducted the funeral. The whole city was in an uproar.

As the life of Hus was now in danger, and his presence in the city might lead to riots, he retired for a while from Prague to the castle of Kradonec, in the country; and there, besides preaching to vast crowds in the fields, he wrote the two books which did the most to bring him to the stake. The first was his treatise "On Traffic in Holy Things"; the second his great, elaborate work, "The Church." [1] In the first he denounced the sale of indulgences, and declared that even the Pope himself could be guilty of the sin of simony. In the second, following Wycliffe's lead, he criticised the whole orthodox conception of the day of the "Holy Catholic Church." What was, asked Hus, the true Church of Christ? According to the popular ideas of the day, the true Church of Christ was a visible body of men on this earth. Its head was the Pope; its officers were the cardinals, the bishops, the priests, and other ecclesiastics; and its members were those who had been baptized and who kept true to the orthodox faith. The idea of Hus was different. His conception of the nature of the true Church was very similar to that held by many Non-conformists of to-day. He was a great believer in predestination. All men, he said, from Adam onwards, were divided into two classes: first, those predestined by God to eternal bliss; second, those fore-doomed to eternal damnation. The true Church of Christ consisted of those predestined to eternal bliss, and no one but God Himself knew to which class any man belonged. From this position a remarkable consequence followed. For anything the Pope knew to the contrary, he might belong himself to the number of the damned. He could not, therefore, be the true Head of the Church; he could not be the Vicar of Christ; and the only Head of the Church was Christ Himself. The same argument applied to Cardinals, Bishops and Priests. For anything he knew to the contrary, any Cardinal, Bishop or Priest in the Church might belong to the number of the damned; he might be a servant, not of Christ, but of Anti-Christ; and, therefore, said Hus, it was utterly absurd to look to men of such doubtful character as infallible spiritual guides. What right, asked Hus, had the Pope to claim the "power of the keys?" What right had the Pope to say who might be admitted to the Church? He had no right, as Pope, at all. Some of the Popes were heretics; some of the clergy were villains, foredoomed to torment in Hell; and, therefore, all in search of the truth must turn, not to the Pope and the clergy, but to the Bible and the law of Christ. God alone had the power of the keys; God alone must be obeyed; and the Holy Catholic Church consisted, not of the Pope, the Cardinals, the Priests, and so many baptized members, but "of all those that had been chosen by God." It is hard to imagine a doctrine more Protestant than this. It struck at the root of the whole Papal conception. It undermined the authority of the Catholic Church, and no one could say to what, ere long, it might lead. It was time, said many, to take decisive action.

For this purpose Sigismund, King of the Romans and of Hungary, persuaded Pope John XXIII. to summon a general Church Council at Constance; and at the same time he invited Hus to attend the Council in person, and there expound his views. John Hus set out for Constance. As soon as he arrived in the city, he received from Sigismund that famous letter of "safe conduct" on which whole volumes have been written. The King's promise was as clear as day. He promised Hus, in the plainest terms, three things: first, that he should come unharmed to the city; second, that he should have a free hearing; and third, that if he did not submit to the decision of the Council he should be allowed to go home. Of those promises only the first was ever fulfilled. John Hus soon found himself caught in a trap. He was imprisoned by order of the Pope. He was placed in a dungeon on an island in the Rhine, and lay next to a sewer; and Sigismund either would not or could not lift a finger to help him. For three and a-half mouths he lay in his dungeon; and then he was removed to the draughty tower of a castle on Lake Geneva. His opinions were examined and condemned by the Council; and at last, when he was called to appear in person, he found that he had been condemned as a heretic already. As soon as he opened his month to speak he was interrupted; and when he closed it they roared, "He has admitted his guilt." He had one chance of life, and one chance only. He must recant his heretical Wycliffite opinions, especially those set forth in his treatise on the "Church." What need, said the Council, could there be of any further trial? The man was a heretic. His own books convicted him, and justice must be done.

And now, on the last day of the trial, John Hus stood before the great Council. The scene was appalling. For some weeks this gallant son of the morning had been tormented by neuralgia. The marks of suffering were on his brow. His face was pale; his cheeks were sunken; his limbs were weak and trembling. But his eye flashed with a holy fire, and his words rang clear and true. Around him gleamed the purple and gold and the scarlet robes. Before him sat King Sigismund on the throne. The two men looked each other in the face. As the articles were rapidly read out against him, John Hus endeavoured to speak in his own defence. He was told to hold his tongue. Let him answer the charges all at once at the close.

"How can I do that," said Hus, "when I cannot even bear them all in mind?"

He made another attempt.

"Hold your tongue," said Cardinal Zabarella; "we have already given you a sufficient hearing."

With clasped hands, and in ringing tones, Hus begged in vain for a hearing. Again he was told to hold his peace, and silently he raised his eyes to heaven in prayer. He was accused of denying the Catholic doctrine of transubstantiation. He sprang to his feet in anger. Zabarella tried to shout him down. The voice of Hus rang out above the babel.

"I have never held, taught or preached," he cried, "that in the sacrament of the altar material bread remains after consecration."

The trial was short and sharp. The verdict had been given beforehand. He was now accused of another horrible crime. He had actually described himself as the fourth person in the Godhead! The charge was monstrous.

"Let that doctor be named," said Hus, "who has given this evidence against me."

But the name of his false accuser was never given. He was now accused of a still more dangerous error. He had appealed to God instead of appealing to the Church.

"O Lord God," he exclaimed, "this Council now condemns Thy action and law as an error! I affirm that there is no safer appeal than that to the Lord Jesus Christ."

With those brave words he signed his own death warrant. For all his orthodoxy on certain points, he made it clearer now than ever that he set the authority of his own conscience above the authority of the Council; and, therefore, according to the standard of the day, he had to be treated as a heretic.

"Moreover," he said, with his eye on the King, "I came here freely to this Council, with a safe-conduct from my Lord the King here present, with the desire to prove my innocence and to explain my beliefs."

At those words, said the story in later years, King Sigismund blushed. If he did, the blush is the most famous in the annals of history; if he did not, some think he ought to have done. For Hus the last ordeal had now arrived; and the Bishop of Concordia, in solemn tones, read out the dreadful articles of condemnation. For heretics the Church had then but little mercy. His books were all to be burned; his priestly office must be taken from him; and he himself, expelled from the Church, must be handed over to the civil power. In vain, with a last appeal for justice, he protested that he had never been obstinate in error. In vain he contended that his proud accusers had not even taken the trouble to read some of his books. As the sentence against himself was read, and the vision of death rose up before him, he fell once more on his knees and prayed, not for himself, but for his enemies.

"Lord Jesus Christ," he said, "pardon all my enemies, I pray thee, for the sake of Thy great mercy! Thou knowest that they have falsely accused me, brought forward false witnesses and false articles against me. O! pardon them for Thine infinite mercies'sake."

At this beautiful prayer the priests and bishops jeered. He was ordered now to mount the scaffold, to put on the priestly garments, and to recant his heretical opinions. The first two commands he obeyed; the third he treated with scorn. As he drew the alb over his shoulders, he appealed once more to Christ.

"My Lord Jesus Christ," he said, "was mocked in a white robe, when led from Herod to Pilate."

There on the scaffold he stood, with his long white robe upon him and the Communion Cup in his hand; and there, in immortal burning words, he refused to recant a single word that he had written.

"Behold," he cried, "these Bishops demand that I recant and abjure. I dare not do it. If I did, I should be false to God, and sin against my conscience and Divine truth."

The Bishops were furious. They swarmed around him. They snatched the Cup from his hand.

"Thou cursed Judas!" they roared. "Thou hast forsaken the council of peace. Thou hast become one of the Jews. We take from thee this Cup of Salvation."

"But I trust," replied Hus, "in God Almighty, and shall drink this Cup this day in His Kingdom."

The ceremony of degradation now took place. As soon as his robes had been taken from him, the Bishops began a hot discussion about the proper way of cutting his hair. Some clamoured for a razor, others were all for scissors.

"See," said Hus to the King, "these Bishops cannot agree in their blasphemy."

At last the scissors won the victory. His tonsure was cut in four directions, and a fool's cap, a yard high, with a picture of devils tearing his soul, was placed upon that hero's head.

"So," said the Bishops, "we deliver your soul to the devil."

"Most joyfully," said Hus, "will I wear this crown of shame for thy sake, O Jesus! who for me didst wear a crown of thorns."

"Go, take him," said the King. And Hus was led to his death. As he passed along he saw the bonfire in which his books were being burned. He smiled. Along the streets of the city he strode, with fetters clanking on his feet, a thousand soldiers for his escort, and crowds of admirers surging on every hand. Full soon the fatal spot was reached. It was a quiet meadow among the gardens, outside the city gates. At the stake he knelt once more in prayer, and the fool's cap fell from his head. Again he smiled. It ought to be burned along with him, said a watcher, that he and the devils might be together. He was bound to the stake with seven moist thongs and an old rusty chain, and faggots of wood and straw were piled round him to the chin. For the last time the Marshal approached to give him a fair chance of abjuring.

"What errors," he retorted, "shall I renounce? I know myself guilty of none. I call God to witness that all that I have written and preached has been with the view of rescuing souls from sin and perdition, and therefore most joyfully will I confirm with my blood the truth I have written and preached."

As the flame arose and the wood crackled, he chanted the Catholic burial prayer, "Jesu, Son of David, have mercy upon me." From the west a gentle breeze was blowing, and a gust dashed the smoke and sparks in his face. At the words "Who was born of the Virgin Mary" he ceased; his lips moved faintly in silent prayer; and a few moments later the martyr breathed no more. At last the cruel fire died down, and the soldiers wrenched his remains from the post, hacked his skull in pieces, and ground his bones to powder. As they prodded about among the glowing embers to see how much of Hus was left, they found, to their surprise, that his heart was still unburned. One fixed it on the point of his spear, thrust it back into the fire, and watched it frizzle away; and finally, by the Marshal's orders, they gathered all the ashes together, and tossed them into the Rhine.

He had died, says a Catholic writer, for the noblest of all causes. He had died for the faith which he believed to be true.

Chapter 3: The Welter (1415-1434)

THE excitement in Bohemia was intense. As the ashes of Hus floated down the Rhine, the news of his death spread over the civilized world, and in every Bohemian town and hamlet the people felt that their greatest man had been unjustly murdered. He had become the national hero and the national saint, and now the people swore to avenge his death. A Hussite League was formed by his followers, a Catholic League was formed by his enemies. The Hussite Wars began. It is important to note with exactness what took place. As we study the history of men and nations, we are apt to fancy that the rank and file of a country can easily be united in one by common adherence to a common cause. It is not so. For one man who will steadily follow a principle, there are hundreds who would rather follow a leader. As long as Hus was alive in the flesh, he was able to command the loyalty of the people; but now that his tongue was silent for ever, his followers split into many contending factions. For all his eloquence he had never been able to strike one clear commanding note. In some of his views he was a Catholic, in others a Protestant. To some he was merely the fiery patriot, to others the champion of Church Reform, to others the high-souled moral teacher, to others the enemy of the Pope. If the people had only been united they might now have gained their long-lost freedom. But unity was the very quality they lacked the most. They had no clear notion of what they wanted; they had no definite scheme of church reform; they had no great leader to show them the way through the jungle, and thus, instead of closing their ranks against the common foe, they split up into jangling sects and parties, and made the confusion worse confounded.

First in rank and first in power came the Utraquists or Calixtines. [2] For some reason these men laid all the stress on a doctrine taught by Hus in his later years. As he lay in his gloomy dungeon near Constance, he had written letters contending that laymen should be permitted to take the wine at the Communion. For this doctrine the Utraquists now fought tooth and nail. They emblazoned the Cup on their banners. They were the aristocrats of the movement; they were led by the University dons; they were political rather than religious in their aims; they regarded Hus as a patriot; and, on the whole, they did not care much for moral and spiritual reforms.

Next came the Taborites, the red-hot Radicals, with Socialist ideas of property and loose ideals of morals. They built themselves a fort on Mount Tabor, and held great open-air meetings. They rejected purgatory, masses and the worship of saints. They condemned incense, images, bells, relics and fasting. They declared that priests were an unnecessary nuisance. They celebrated the Holy Communion in barns, and baptized their babies in ponds and brooks. They held that every man had the right to his own interpretation of the Bible; they despised learning and art; and they revelled in pulling churches down and burning monks to death.

Next came the Chiliasts, who fondly believed that the end of all things was at hand, that the millennial reign of Christ would soon begin, and that all the righteous—that is, they themselves—would have to hold the world at bay in Five Cities of Refuge. For some years these mad fanatics regarded themselves as the chosen instruments of the Divine displeasure, and only awaited a signal from heaven to commence a general massacre of their fellow men. As that signal never came, however, they were grievously disappointed.

Next in folly came the Adamites, so called because, in shameless wise, they dressed like Adam and Eve before the fall. They made their head-quarters on an island on the River Nesarka, and survived even after Ziska had destroyed their camp.

But of all the heretical bodies in Bohemia the most influential were the Waldenses. As the history of the Waldenses is still obscure, we cannot say for certain what views they held when they first came from Italy some fifty or sixty years before. At first they seem to have been almost Catholics, but as the Hussite Wars went on they fell, it is said, under the influence of the Taborites, and adopted many radical Taborite opinions. They held that prayer should be addressed, not to the Virgin Mary and the Saints, but to God alone, and spoke with scorn of the popular doctrine that the Virgin in heaven showed her breast when interceding for sinners. As they did not wish to create a disturbance, they attended the public services of the Church of Rome; but they did not believe in those services themselves, and are said to have employed their time at Church in picking holes in the logic of the speaker. They believed neither in building churches, nor in saying masses, nor in the adoration of pictures, nor in the singing of hymns at public worship. For all practical intents and purposes they rejected entirely the orthodox Catholic distinction between things secular and things sacred, and held that a man could worship God just as well in a field as in a church, and that it did not matter in the least whether a man's body was buried in consecrated or unconsecrated ground. What use, they asked, were holy water, holy oil, holy palms, roots, crosses, holy splinters from the Cross of Christ? They rejected the doctrine of purgatory, and said that all men must go either to heaven or to hell. They rejected the doctrine of Transubstantiation, and said that the wine and bread remained wine and bread. For us, however, the chief point of interest lies in the attitude they adopted towards the priests of the Church of Rome. At that time there was spread all over Europe a legend that the Emperor, Constantine the Great, had made a so-called "Donation" to Pope Sylvester; and the Waldenses held that the Church of Rome, by thus consenting to be endowed by the State, had become morally corrupt, and no longer possessed the keys of the Kingdom of Heaven. For this reason they utterly despised the Roman priests; and contended that, being worldly men of bad character, they were qualified neither to administer the sacraments nor to hear confessions. At this point we lay our finger on the principle which led to the foundation of the Moravian Church. What ideal, we ask, did the Waldenses now set before them? We can answer the question in a sentence. The whole object the Waldenses had now in view was to return to the simple teaching of Christ and the Apostles. They wished to revive what they regarded as true primitive Christianity. For this reason they brushed aside with scorn the bulls of Popes and the decrees of Councils, and appealed to the command of the New Testament Scriptures. For them the law of Christ was supreme and final; and, appealing to His teaching in the Sermon on the Mount, they declared that oaths were wicked, and that war was no better than murder. If the law of Christ were obeyed, said they, what need would there be of government? How long they had held these views we do not know. Some think they had held them for centuries; some think they had learned them recently from the Taborites. If scholars insist on this latter view, we are forced back on the further question: Where did the Taborites get their advanced opinions? If the Taborites taught the Waldenses, who taught the Taborites? We do not know. For the present all we call say is that the Waldenses in a quiet way were fast becoming a mighty force in the country. They addressed each other as brother and sister; they are said to have had their own translations of the Bible; they claimed a descent from the Apostles; and they are even held by some (though here we tread on very thin ice) to have possessed their own episcopal succession.

But the method of the Taborites was different. If the Kingdom of God was to come at all, it must come, they held, by force, by fire, by the sword, by pillage and by famine. What need to tell here the blood-curdling story of the Hussite Wars? What need to tell here how Pope Martin V. summoned the whole Catholic world to a grand crusade against the Bohemian people? What need to tell how the people of Prague attacked the Town Hall, and pitched the burgomaster and several aldermen out of the windows? For twenty years the whole land was one boiling welter of confusion; and John Ziska, the famous blind general, took the lead of the Taborite army, and, standing on a wagon, with the banner above him emblazoned with the Hussite Cup, he swept the country from end to end like a devouring prairie fire. It is held now by military experts that Ziska was the greatest military genius of the age. If military genius could have saved Bohemia, Bohemia would now have been saved. For some years he managed to hold at bay the finest chivalry of Europe; and he certainly saved the Hussite cause from being crushed in its birth. For faith and freedom he fought—the faith of Hus and the freedom of Bohemia. He formed the rough Bohemian peasantry into a disciplined army. He armed his men with lances, slings, iron-pointed flails and clubs. He formed his barricades of iron-clad wagons, and whirled them in murderous mazes round the field. He made a special study of gunpowder, and taught his men the art of shooting straight. He has often been compared to Oliver Cromwell, and like our Oliver he was in many ways. He was stern in dealing with his enemies, and once had fifty Adamites burned to death. He was sure that God was on his side in the war. "Be it known," he wrote to his supporters, "that we are collecting men from all parts of the country against these enemies of God and devastators of our Bohemian land." He composed a stirring battle song, and taught his men to sing it in chorus when they marched to meet the foe.

Therefore, manfully cry out:

"At them! rush at them."
Wield bravely your arms!
Pray to your Lord God.
Strike and kill! spare none!

What a combination of piety and fury! It was all in vain. The great general died of a fever. The thunderbolt fell. At a meeting in Prague the Utraquists and Catholics at last came to terms, and drew up a compromise known as the "Compactata of Basle" (1433). For nearly two hundred years after this these "Compactata" were regarded as the law of the land; and the Utraquist Church was recognised by the Pope as the national self-governing Church of Bohemia. The terms of the Compactata were four in number. The Communion was to be given to laymen in both kinds; all mortal sins were to be punished by the proper authorities; the Word of God was to be freely preached by faithful priests and deacons; and no priests were to have any worldly possessions. For practical purposes this agreement meant the defeat of the advanced reforming movement. One point the Utraquists had gained, and one alone; they were allowed to take the wine at the Communion. For the rest these Utraquist followers of Hus were as Catholic as the Pope himself. They adored the Host, read the masses, kept the fasts, and said the prayers as their fathers had done before them. From that moment the fate of the Taborite party was sealed. At the battle of Lipan they were defeated, routed, crushed out of existence. The battle became a massacre. The slaughter continued all the night and part of the following day, and hundreds were burned to death in their huts.

Was this to be the end of Hus's strivings? What was it in Hus that was destined to survive? What was it that worked like a silent leaven amid the clamours of war? We shall see. Amid these charred and smoking ruins the Moravian Church arose.

Chapter 4: Peter of Chelcic (1419-1450)

MEANWHILE a mighty prophet had arisen, with a clear and startling message. His name was Peter, and he lived down south, in the little village of Chelcic. [3] As the historian rummages among the ancient records, he discovers to his sorrow that scarcely anything is known of the life of this great man; but, on the other hand, it is a joy to know that while his story is wrapped in mystery, his teaching has been preserved, and that some of the wonderful books he wrote are treasured still in his native land as gems of Bohemian literature. In later years it was commonly said that he began life as a cobbler; but that story, at least, may be dismissed as a legend. He enlisted, we are told, in the army. He then discovered that a soldier's life was wicked; he then thought of entering a monastery, but was shocked by what he heard of the immoralities committed within the holy walls; and finally, having some means of his own, retired to his little estate at Chelcic, and spent his time in writing pamphlets about the troubles of his country. He had picked up a smattering of education in Prague. He had studied the writings of Wycliffe and of Hus, and often appealed to Wycliffe in his works. He could quote, when he liked, from the great Church Fathers. He had a fair working knowledge of the Bible; and, above all, he had the teaching of Christ and the Apostles engraved upon his conscience and his heart. As he was not a priest, he could afford to be independent; as he knew but little Latin, he wrote in Bohemian; and thus, like Stitny and Hus before him, he appealed to the people in language they could all understand. Of all the leaders of men in Bohemia, this Peter was the most original and daring. As he pondered on the woes of his native land, he came to the firm but sad conclusion that the whole system of religion and politics was rotten to the core. Not one of the jangling sects was in the right. Not one was true to the spirit of Christ. Not one was free from the dark red stain of murder. His chief works were his Net of Faith, his Reply to Nicholas of Pilgram, his Reply to Rockycana, his Image of the Beast, his theological treatise On the Body of Christ, his tract The Foundation of Worldly Laws, his devotional commentary, Exposition of the Passion according to St. John, and, last, though not least, his volume of discourses on the Gospel lessons for the year, entitled Postillia. Of these works the most famous was his masterly Net of Faith. He explained the title himself. "Through His disciples," said Peter, "Christ caught the world in the net of His faith, but the bigger fishes, breaking the net, escaped. Then others followed through these same holes made by the big fishes, and the net was left almost empty." His meaning was clear to all. The net was the true Church of Christ; the two whales who broke it were the Emperor and the Pope; the big fishes were the mighty "learned persons, heretics and offenders"; and the little fishes were the true followers of Christ.

He opened his bold campaign in dramatic style. When John Ziska and Nicholas of Husinec declared at Prague that the time had come for the faithful to take up arms in their own defence, Peter was present at the debate, and contended that for Christians war was a crime. (1419)

"What is war?" he asked. "It is a breach of the laws of God! All soldiers are violent men, murderers, a godless mob!"

He hated war like a Quaker, and soldiers like Tolstoy himself. He regarded the terrible Hussite Wars as a disgrace to both sides. As the fiery Ziska swept the land with his waggons, this Apostle of peace was sick with horror. "Where," he asked, in his Reply to Rockycana, "has God recalled His commands, Thou shalt not kill,' Thou shalt not steal,' Thou shalt not take thy neighbour's goods'? If God has not repealed these commands, they ought still to be obeyed to-day in Prague and Tabor. I have learned from Christ, and by Christ I stand; and if the Apostle Peter himself were to come down from Heaven and say that it was right for us to take up arms to defend the truth, I should not believe him."

For Peter the teaching of Christ and the Apostles was enough. It was supreme, final, perfect. If a king made a new law, he was spoiling the teaching of Christ. If the Pope issued a bull, he was spoiling the teaching of Christ. If a Council of Bishops drew up a decree, they were spoiling the teaching of Christ. As God, said Peter, had revealed His will to full perfection in Jesus Christ, there was no need for laws made by men. "Is the law of God sufficient, without worldly laws, to guide and direct us in the path of the true Christian religion? With trembling, I answer, it is. It was sufficient for Christ Himself, and it was sufficient for His disciples." And, therefore, the duty of all true Christians was as clear as the noon-day sun. He never said that Christian people should break the law of the land. He admitted that God might use the law for good purposes; and therefore, as Christ had submitted to Pilate, so Christians must submit to Government. But there their connection with Government must end. For heathens the State was a necessary evil; for Christians it was an unclean thing, and the less they had to do with it the better. They must never allow the State to interfere in matters within the Church. They must never drag each other before the law courts. They must never act as judges or magistrates. They must never take any part whatever in municipal or national government. They must never, if possible, live in a town at all. If Christians, said Peter, lived in a town, and paid the usual rates and taxes, they were simply helping to support a system which existed for the protection of robbers. He regarded towns as the abodes of vice, and citizens as rogues and knaves. The first town, he said, was built by the murderer, Cain. He first murdered his brother Abel; he then gathered his followers together; he then built a city, surrounded by walls; and thus, by robbery and violence, he became a well-to-do man. And modern towns, said Peter, were no whit better. At that time the citizens of some towns in Bohemia enjoyed certain special rights and privileges; and this, to Peter, seemed grossly unfair. He condemned those citizens as thieves. "They are," he said, "the strength of Anti-Christ; they are adversaries to Christ; they are an evil rabble; they are bold in wickedness; and though they pretend to follow the truth, they will sit at tables with wicked people and knavish followers of Judas." For true Christians, therefore, there was only one course open. Instead of living in godless towns, they should try to settle in country places, earn their living as farmers or gardeners, and thus keep as clear of the State as possible. They were not to try to support the law at all. If they did, they were supporting a wicked thing, which never tried to make men better, but only crushed them with cruel and useless punishments. They must never try to make big profits in business. If they did, they were simply robbing and cheating their neighbours. They must never take an oath, for oaths were invented by the devil. They must never, in a word, have any connection with that unchristian institution called the State.

And here Peter waxed vigorous and eloquent. He objected, like Wycliffe, to the union of Church and State. Of all the bargains ever struck, the most wicked, ruinous and pernicious was the bargain struck between Church and State, when Constantine the Great first took the Christians under the shadow of his wing. For three hundred years, said Peter, the Church of Christ had remained true to her Master; and then this disgusting heathen Emperor, who had not repented of a single sin, came in with his vile "Donation," and poisoned all the springs of her life. If the Emperor, said Peter, wanted to be a Christian, he ought first to have laid down his crown. He was a ravenous beast; he was a wolf in the fold; he was a lion squatting at the table; and at that fatal moment in history, when he gave his "Donation" to the Pope, an angel in heaven had spoken the words: "This day has poison entered the blood of the Church." [4]

"Since that time," said Peter, "these two powers, Imperial and Papal, have clung together. They have turned everything to account in Church and in Christendom for their own impious purposes. Theologians, professors, and priests are the satraps of the Emperor. They ask the Emperor to protect them, so that they may sleep as long as possible, and they create war so that they may have everything under their thumb."

If Peter lashed the Church with whips, he lashed her priests with scorpions. He accused them of various vices. They were immoral; they were superstitious; they were vain, ignorant and empty-headed; and, instead of feeding the Church of God, they had almost starved her to death. He loathed these "honourable men, who sit in great houses, these purple men, with their beautiful mantles, their high caps, their fat stomachs." He accused them of fawning on the rich and despising the poor. "As for love of pleasure," he said, "immorality, laziness, greediness, uncharitableness and cruelty—as for these things, the priests do not hold them as sins when committed by princes, nobles and rich commoners. They do not tell them plainly, "You will go to hell if you live on the fat of the poor, and live a bestial life," although they know that the rich are condemned to eternal death by such behaviour. Oh, no! They prefer to give them a grand funeral. A crowd of priests, clergy, and other folk make a long procession. The bells are rung. There are masses, singings, candles and offerings. The virtues of the dead man are proclaimed from the pulpit. They enter his soul in the books of their cloisters and churches to be continually prayed for, and if what they say be true, that soul cannot possibly perish, for he has been so kind to the Church, and must, indeed, be well cared for."

He accused them, further, of laziness and gluttony. "They pretend to follow Christ," he said, "and have plenty to eat every day. They have fish, spices, brawn, herrings, figs, almonds, Greek wine and other luxuries. They generally drink good wine and rich beer in large quantities, and so they go to sleep. When they cannot get luxuries they fill themselves with vulgar puddings till they nearly burst. And this is the way the priests fast." He wrote in a similar strain of the mendicant friars. He had no belief in their profession of poverty, and accused them of gathering as much money as they could. They pocketed more money by begging, he declared, than honest folk could earn by working; they despised plain beef, fat bacon and peas, and they wagged their tails with joy when they sat down to game and other luxuries. "Many citizens," said Peter, "would readily welcome this kind of poverty."

He accused the priests of loose teaching and shameless winking at sin. "They prepare Jesus," he said, "as a sweet sauce for the world, so that the world may not have to shape its course after Jesus and His heavy Cross, but that Jesus may conform to the world; and they make Him softer than oil, so that every wound may be soothed, and the violent, thieves, murderers and adulterers may have an easy entrance into heaven."

He accused them of degrading the Seven Sacraments. They baptized sinners, young and old, without demanding repentance. They sold the Communion to rascals and rogues, like a huckstress offering her wares. They abused Confession by pardoning men who never intended to amend their evil ways. They allowed men of the vilest character to be ordained as priests. They degraded marriage by preaching the doctrine that it was less holy than celibacy. They distorted the original design of Extreme Unction, for instead of using it to heal the sick they used it to line their own pockets. And all these blasphemies, sins and follies were the offspring of that adulterous union between the Church and the State, which began in the days of Constantine the Great. For of all the evils under Heaven, the greatest, said Peter, was that contradiction in terms—a State Church.

He attacked the great theologians and scholars. Instead of using their mental powers in the search for truth, these college men, said Peter, had done their best to suppress the truth; and at the two great Councils of Constance and Basle, they had actually obtained the help of the temporal power to crush all who dared to hold different views from theirs. What use, asked Peter, were these learned pundits? They were no use at all. They never instructed anybody. "I do not know," he said, "a single person whom they have helped with their learning." Had they instructed Hus? No. Hus had the faith in himself; Hus was instructed by God; and all that these ravens did for Hus was to flock together against him.

Again, Peter denounced the Bohemian nobles. As we read his biting, satirical phrases we can see that he was no respecter of persons and no believer in artificial distinctions of rank. For him the only distinction worth anything was the moral distinction between those who followed the crucified Jesus and those who rioted in selfish pleasures.

He had no belief in blue blood and noble birth. He was almost, though not quite, a Socialist. He had no definite, constructive social policy. He was rather a champion of the rights of the poor, and an apostle of the simple life. "The whole value of noble birth," he said, "is founded on a wicked invention of the heathen, who obtained coats of arms from emperors or kings as a reward for some deed of valour." If a man could only buy a coat of arms—a stag, a gate, a wolf's head, or a sausage—he became thereby a nobleman, boasted of his high descent, and was regarded by the public as a saint. For such "nobility" Peter had a withering contempt. He declared that nobles of this stamp had no right to belong to the Christian Church. They lived, he said, in flat opposition to the spirit of Jesus Christ. They devoured the poor. They were a burden to the country. They did harm to all men. They set their minds on worldly glory, and spent their money on extravagant dress. "The men," said he, "wear capes reaching down to the ground, and their long hair falls down to their shoulders; and the women wear so many petticoats that they can hardly drag themselves along, and strut about like the Pope's courtezans, to the surprise and disgust of the whole world." What right had these selfish fops to call themselves Christians? They did more harm to the cause of Christ than all the Turks and heathens in the world.

Thus Peter, belonging to none of the sects, found grievous faults in them all. As he always mentions the Waldenses with respect, it has been suggested that he was a Waldensian himself. But of that there is no real proof. He had, apparently, no organizing skill; he never attempted to form a new sect or party, and his mission in the world was to throw out hints and leave it to others to carry these hints into practice. He condemned the Utraquists because they used the sword. "If a man," he said, "eats a black pudding on Friday, you blame him; but if he sheds his brother's blood on the scaffold or on the field of battle you praise him." He condemned the Taborites because they made light of the Sacraments. "You have called the Holy Bread," he said, "a butterfly, a bat, an idol. You have even told the people that it is better to kneel to the devil than to kneel at the altar; and thus you have taught them to despise religion and wallow in unholy lusts." He condemned the King for being a King at all; for no intelligent man, said Peter, could possibly be a King and a Christian at the same time. And finally he condemned the Pope as Antichrist and the enemy of God.

Yet Peter was something more than a caustic critic. For the terrible ills of his age and country he had one plain and homely remedy, and that for all true Christians to leave the Church of Rome and return to the simple teaching of Christ and His Apostles. If the reader goes to Peter for systematic theology, he will be grievously disappointed; but if he goes for moral vigour, he will find a well-spread table.

He did not reason his positions out like Wycliffe; he was a suggestive essayist rather than a constructive philosopher; and, radical though he was in some of his views, he held firm to what he regarded as the fundamental articles of the Christian faith. He believed in the redemptive value of the death of Christ. He believed that man must build his hopes, not so much on his own good works, but rather on the grace of God. He believed, all the same, that good works were needed and would receive their due reward. He believed, further, in the real bodily presence of Christ in the Sacrament; and on this topic he held a doctrine very similar to Luther's doctrine of Consubstantiation. But, over and above all these beliefs, he insisted, in season and out of season, that men could partake of spiritual blessings without the aid of Roman priests. Some fruit of his labours he saw. As the fire of the Hussite Wars died down, a few men in different parts of the country—especially at Chelcic, Wilenow and Divischau—began to take Peter as their spiritual guide. They read his pamphlets with delight, became known as the "Brethren of Chelcic," and wore a distinctive dress, a grey cloak with a cord tied round the waist. The movement spread, the societies multiplied, and thus, in a way no records tell, were laid the foundations of the Church of the Brethren. Did Peter see that Church? We do not know. No one knows when Peter was born, and no one knows when he died. He delivered his message; he showed the way; he flashed his lantern in the darkness; and thus, whether he knew it or not, he was the literary founder of the Brethren's Church. He fired the hope. He drew the plans. It was left to another man to erect the building.

Chapter 5: Gregory the Patriarch (1457-1473)

A BRILLIANT idea is an excellent thing. A man to work it out is still better. At the very time when Peter's followers were marshalling their forces, John Rockycana, [5] Archbishop-elect of Prague (since 1448), was making a mighty stir in that drunken city. What Peter had done with his pen, Rockycana was doing with his tongue. He preached Peter's doctrines in the great Thein Church; he corresponded with him on the burning topics of the day; he went to see him at his estate; he recommended his works to his hearers; and week by week, in fiery language, he denounced the Church of Rome as Babylon, and the Pope as Antichrist himself. His style was vivid and picturesque, his language cutting and clear. One day he compared the Church of Rome to a burned and ruined city, wherein the beasts of the forests made their lairs; and, again, he compared her to a storm-tossed ship, which sank beneath the howling waves because the sailors were fighting each other. "It is better," he said, "to tie a dog to a pulpit than allow a priest to defile it. It is better, oh, women! for your sons to be hangmen than to be priests; for the hangman only kills the body, while the priest kills the soul. Look there," he suddenly exclaimed one Sunday, pointing to a picture of St. Peter on the wall, "there is as much difference between the priests of to-day and the twelve apostles as there is between that old painting and the living St. Peter in heaven. [6] For the priests have put the devil into the sacraments themselves, and are leading you straight to the fires of Hell."

If an eloquent speaker attacks the clergy, he is sure to draw a crowd. No wonder the Thein Church was crammed. No wonder the people listened with delight as he backed up his hot attack with texts from the prophet Jeremiah. No wonder they cried in their simple zeal: "Behold, a second John Hus has arisen."

But John Rockycana was no second John Hus. For all his fire in the pulpit, he was only a craven at heart. "If a true Christian," said he to a friend, "were to turn up now in Prague, he would be gaped at like a stag with golden horns." But he was not a stag with golden horns himself. As he thundered against the Church of Rome, he was seeking, not the Kingdom of God, but his own fame and glory. His followers soon discovered his weakness. Among those who thronged to hear his sermons were certain quiet men of action, who were not content to paw the ground for ever. They were followers of Peter of Chelcic; they passed his pamphlets in secret from hand to hand; they took down notes of Rockycana's sermons; and now they resolved to practise what they heard. If Peter had taught them nothing else, he had at least convinced them all that the first duty of Christian men was to quit the Church of Rome. Again and again they appealed to Rockycana to be their head, to act up to his words, and to lead them out to the promised land. The great orator hemmed and hawed, put them off with excuses, and told them, after the manner of cowards, that they were too hasty and reckless. "I know you are right," said he, "but if I joined your ranks I should be reviled on every hand." [7] But these listeners were not to be cowed. The more they studied Peter's writings, the more they lost faith in Rockycana. As Rockycana refused to lead them, they left his church in a body, and found a braver leader among themselves. His name was Gregory; he was known as Gregory the Patriarch; and in due time, as we shall see, he became the founder of the Church of the Brethren. He was already a middle-aged man. He was the son of a Bohemian knight, and was nephew to Rockycana himself. He had spent his youth in the Slaven cloister at Prague as a bare-footed monk, had found the cloister not so moral as he had expected, had left it in disgust, and was now well known in Bohemia as a man of sterling character, pious and sensible, humble and strict, active and spirited, a good writer and a good speaker. He was a personal friend of Peter, had studied his works with care, and is said to have been particularly fond of a little essay entitled "The Image of the Beast," which he had borrowed from a blacksmith in Wachovia. As time went on he lost patience with Rockycana, came into touch with the little societies at Wilenow and Divischau, visited Peter on his estate, and gradually formed the plan of founding an independent society, and thus doing himself what Rockycana was afraid to do. As soldiers desert a cowardly general and rally round the standard of a brave one, so these listeners in the old Thein Church fell away from halting Rockycana, and rallied round Gregory the Patriarch. From all parts of Bohemia, from all ranks of society, from all whom Peter's writings had touched, from all who were disgusted with the Church of Rome, and who wished to see the True Church of the Apostles bloom in purity and beauty again, from all especially who desired the ministration of priests of moral character—from all these was his little band recruited. How it all happened we know not; but slowly the numbers swelled. At last the terrible question arose: How and where must they live? The question was one of life and death. Not always could they worship in secret; not always be scattered in little groups. It was time, they said, to close their ranks and form an army that should last. "After us," Rockycana had said in a sermon, "shall a people come well-pleasing unto God and right healthy for men; they shall follow the Scriptures, and the example of Christ and the footsteps of the Apostles." And these stern men felt called to the holy task.

In the year 1457, Uladislaus Postumus, King of Bohemia, died, and George Podiebrad reigned in his stead; and about the same time it came to the ears of Gregory the Patriarch that in the barony of Senftenberg, on the north-east border of Bohemia, there lay a village that would serve as a home for him and his trusty followers. And the village was called Kunwald, and the old castle hard by was called Lititz. The village was almost deserted, and only a few simple folk, of the same mind as Gregory, lived there now. What better refuge could be found? Gregory the Patriarch laid the scheme before his uncle Rockycana; Rockycana, who sympathized with their views and wished to help them, brought the matter before King George; the King, who owned the estate, gave his gracious permission; and Gregory and his faithful friends wended their way to Kunwald, and there began to form the first settlement of the Church of the Brethren. And now many others from far and wide came to make Kunwald their home. Some came from the Thein Church in Prague, some across the Glatz Hills from Moravia, some from Wilenow, Divischau and Chelcic, some from the Utraquist Church at Koeniggratz, [8] some, clothed and in their right minds, from those queer folk, the Adamites, and some from little Waldensian groups that lay dotted here and there about the land. There were citizens from Prague and other cities. There were bachelors and masters from the great University. There were peasants and nobles, learned and simple, rich and poor, with their wives and children; and thus did many, who longed to be pure and follow the Master and Him alone, find a Bethany of Peace in the smiling little valley of Kunwald.

Here, then, in the valley of Kunwald, did these pioneers lay the foundation stones of the Moravian Church (1457 or 1458). [9] They were all of one heart and one mind. They honoured Christ alone as King; they confessed His laws alone as binding. They were not driven from the Church of Rome; they left of their own free will. They were men of deep religious experience. As they mustered their forces in that quiet dale, they knew that they were parting company from Church and State alike. They had sought the guidance of God in prayer, and declared that their prayers were answered. They had met to seek the truth of God, not from priests, but from God Himself. "As we knew not where to turn," they wrote to Rockycana, "we turned in prayer to God Himself, and besought Him to reveal to us His gracious will in all things. We wanted to walk in His ways; we wanted instruction in His wisdom; and in His mercy He answered our prayers." They would rather, they said, spend weeks in gaol than take the oath as councillors. They built cottages, tilled the land, opened workshops, and passed their time in peace and quietness. For a law and a testimony they had the Bible and the writings of Peter of Chelcic. In Michael Bradacius, a Utraquist priest, they found a faithful pastor. They made their own laws and appointed a body of twenty-eight elders to enforce them. They divided themselves into three classes, the Beginners, the Learners and the Perfect; [10] and the Perfect gave up their private property for the good of the common cause. They had overseers to care for the poor. They had priests to administer the sacraments, They had godly laymen to teach the Scriptures. They had visitors to see to the purity of family life. They were shut off from the madding crowd by a narrow gorge, with the Glatz Mountains towering on the one side and the hoary old castle of Lititz, a few miles off, on the other; and there in that fruitful valley, where orchards smiled and gardens bloomed, and neat little cottages peeped out from the woodland, they plied their trades and read their Bibles, and kept themselves pure and unspotted from the world under the eye of God Almighty. [11]

But it was not long before these Brethren had to show of what metal they were made. With each other they were at peace, but in Bohemia the sea still rolled from the storm. It is curious how people reasoned in those days. As the Brethren used bread instead of wafer at the Holy Communion, a rumour reached the ears of the King that they were dangerous conspirators, and held secret meetings of a mysterious and unholy nature. And

King George held himself an orthodox King, and had sworn to allow no heretics in his kingdom. As soon therefore, as he heard that Gregory the Patriarch had come on a visit to Prague, and was actually holding a meeting of University students in the New Town, he came down upon them like a wolf on the fold, and gave orders to arrest them on the spot. He was sure they were hatching a villainous plot of some kind. In vain some friends sent warning to the students. They resolved, with a few exceptions, to await their fate and stand to their guns. "Come what may," said they, in their fiery zeal, "let the rack be our breakfast and the funeral pile our dinner!" The door of the room flew open. The magistrate and his bailiffs appeared. "All," said the magistrate, as he stood at the threshold, "who wish to live godly in Christ Jesus must suffer persecution. Follow me to prison." They followed him, and were at once stretched upon the rack. As soon as the students felt the pain of torture their courage melted like April snow. After they had tasted the breakfast they had no appetite for the dinner. They went in a body to the Thein Church, mounted the pulpit one by one, pleaded guilty to the charges brought against them, and confessed, before an admiring crowd, their full belief in all the dogmas of the Holy Church of Rome. But for Gregory the Patriarch, who was now growing old, the pain was too severe. His wrists cracked; he swooned, and was thought to be dead, and in his swoon he dreamed a dream which seemed to him like the dreams of the prophets of old. He saw, in a lovely meadow, a tree laden with fruit; the fruit was being plucked by birds; the flights of the birds were guided by a youth of heavenly beauty, and the tree was guarded by three men whose faces he seemed to know. What meant that dream to Gregory and his Brethren? It was a vision of the good time coming. The tree was the Church of the Brethren. The fruit was her Bible teaching. The birds were her ministers and helpers. The youth of radiant beauty was the Divine Master Himself. And the three men who stood on guard were the three men who were afterwards chosen as the first three Elders of the Brethren's Church.

While Gregory lay in his swoon, his old teacher, his uncle, his sometime friend, John Rockycana, hearing that he was dying, came to see him. His conscience was stricken, his heart bled, and, wringing his hands in agony, he moaned: "Oh, my Gregory, my Gregory, would I were where thou art." When Gregory recovered, Rockycana pleaded for him, and the King allowed the good old Patriarch to return in peace to Kunwald.

Meanwhile, the first persecution of the Brethren had begun in deadly earnest (1461). King George Podiebrad was furious. He issued an order that all his subjects were to join either the Utraquist or the Roman Catholic Church. He issued another order that all priests who conducted the Communion in the blasphemous manner of the Brethren should forthwith be put to death. The priest, old Michael, was cast into a dungeon; four leading Brethren were burned alive; the peaceful home in Kunwald was broken; and the Brethren fled to the woods and mountains. For two full years they lived the life of hunted deer in the forest. As they durst not light a fire by day, they cooked their meals by night; and then, while the enemy dreamed and slept, they read their Bibles by the watch-fires' glare, and prayed till the blood was dripping from their knees. If provisions ran short, they formed a procession, and marched in single file to the nearest village; and when the snow lay on the ground they trailed behind them a pine-tree branch, so that folk would think a wild beast had been prowling around. We can see them gathering in those Bohemian glades. As the sentinel stars set their watch in the sky, and the night wind kissed the pine trees, they read to each other the golden promise that where two or three were gathered together in His name He would be in the midst of them; [12] and rejoiced that they, the chosen of God, had been called to suffer for the truth and the Church that was yet to be.

In vain they appealed to Rockycana; he had done with them for ever. "Thou art of the world," they wrote, "and wilt perish with the world." They were said to have made a covenant with the devil, and were commonly dubbed "Pitmen" because they lived in pits and caves. Yet not for a moment did they lose hope. At the very time when the king in his folly thought they were crushed beneath his foot, they were in reality increasing in numbers every day. As their watch-fires shone in the darkness of the forests, so their pure lives shone among a darkened people. No weapon did they use except the pen. They never retaliated, never rebelled, never took up arms in their own defence, never even appealed to the arm of justice. When smitten on one cheek, they turned the other; and from ill-report they went to good report, till the King for very shame had to let them be. Well aware was he that brutal force could never stamp out spiritual life. "I advise you," said a certain Bishop, "to shed no more blood. Martyrdom is somewhat like a half-roasted joint of meat, apt to breed maggots."

And now the time drew near for Gregory's dream to come true. When the Brethren settled in the valley of Kunwald they had only done half their work. They had quitted the "benighted" Church of Rome; they had not yet put a better Church in her place. They had settled on a Utraquist estate; they were under the protection of a Utraquist King; they attended services conducted by Utraquist priests. But this black-and-white policy could not last for ever. If they wished to be godly men themselves, they must have godly men in the pulpits. What right had they, the chosen of God (as they called themselves) to listen to sermons from men in league with the State? What right had they to take the Holy Bread and Wine from the tainted hands of Utraquist priests? What right had they to confess their sins to men with the brand of Rome upon their foreheads? If they were to have any priests at all, those priests, like Caesar's wife, must be above suspicion. They must be pastors after God's own heart, who should feed the people with knowledge and understanding (Jer. iii. 15). They must be clear of any connection with the State. They must be descended from the twelve Apostles. They must be innocent of the crime of simony. They must work with their hands for their living, and be willing to spend their money on the poor. But where could such clean vessels of the Lord be found? For a while the Brethren were almost in despair; for a while they were even half inclined to do without priests at all. In vain they searched the country round; in vain they inquired about priests in foreign lands. When they asked about the pure Nestorian Church supposed to exist in India, they received the answer that that Church was now as corrupt as the

Romish. When they asked about the Greek Church in Russia, they received the answer that the Russian Bishops were willing to consecrate any man, good or bad, so long as he paid the fees. The question was pressing. If they did without good priests much longer, they would lose their standing in the country. "You must," said Brother Martin Lupac, a Utraquist priest, who had joined their ranks, "you must establish a proper order of priests from among yourselves. If you don't, the whole cause will be ruined. To do without priests is no sin against God; but it is a sin against your fellow-men." As they pondered on the fateful question, the very light of Heaven itself seemed to flash upon their souls. It was they who possessed the unity of the spirit; and therefore it was they who were called to renew the Church of the Apostles. They had now become a powerful body; they were founding settlements all over the land; they stood, they said, for the truth as it was in Jesus; they had all one faith, one hope, one aim, one sense of the Spirit leading them onward; and they perceived that if they were to weather the gale in those stormy times they must cut the chains that bound them to Rome, and fly their own colours in the breeze.

And so, in 1467, about ten years after the foundation of Kunwald, there met at Lhota a Synod of the Brethren to settle the momentous question (1467), "Is it God's will that we separate entirely from the power of the Papacy, and hence from its priesthood? Is it God's will that we institute, according to the model of the Primitive Church, a ministerial order of our own?" For weeks they had prayed and fasted day and night. About sixty Brethren arrived. The Synod was held in a tanner's cottage, under a cedar tree; and the guiding spirit Gregory the Patriarch, for his dream was haunting him still. The cottage has long since gone; but the tree is living yet.

The fateful day arrived. As the morning broke, those sixty men were all on their knees in prayer. If that prayer had been omitted the whole proceedings would have been invalid. As the Master, said they, had prayed on the Mount before he chose His twelve disciples, so they must spend the night in prayer before they chose the elders of the Church. And strange, indeed, their manner of choosing was. First the Synod nominated by ballot nine men of blameless life, from whom were to be chosen, should God so will, the first Pastors of the New Church. Next twelve slips of paper were folded and put into a vase. Of these slips nine were blank, and three were marked "Jest," the Bohemian for "is." Then a boy named Procop entered the room, drew out nine slips, and handed them round to the nine nominated Brethren.

There was a hush, a deep hush, in that humble room. All waited for God to speak. The fate of the infant Church seemed to hang in the balance. For the moment the whole great issue at stake depended on the three papers left in the vase. It had been agreed that the three Brethren who received the three inscribed papers should be ordained to the ministry. The situation was curious. As the Brethren rose from their knees that morning they were all as sure as men could be that God desired them to have Pastors of their own; and yet they deliberately ran the risk that the lot might decide against them. [13] What slips were those now lying in the vase? Perhaps the three inscribed ones. But it turned out otherwise. All three were drawn, and Matthias of Kunwald, Thomas of Prelouic, and Elias of Chrenouic, are known to history as the first three ministers of the Brethren's Church. And then Gregory the Patriarch stepped forward, and announced with trembling voice that these three men were the very three that he had seen in his trance in the torture-chamber at Prague. Not a man in the room was surprised; not a man doubted that here again their prayers had been plainly answered. Together the members of the Synod arose and saluted the chosen three. Together, next day, they sang in a hymn written for the occasion:—

We needed faithful men, and He
Granted us such. Most earnestly,
We Pray, Lord, let Thy gifts descend,
That blessing may Thy work attend. [14]

But the battle was not won even yet. If these three good men, now chosen by Christ, were to be acknowledged as priests in Bohemia, they must be ordained in the orthodox way by a Bishop of pure descent from the Apostles. For this purpose they applied to Stephen, a Bishop of the Waldenses. He was just the man they needed. He was a man of noble character. He was a man whose word could be trusted. He had often given them information about the Waldensian line of Bishops. He had told them how that line ran back to the days of the early Church. He had told them how the Waldensian Bishops had kept the ancient faith unsullied, and had never broken the law of Christ by uniting with the wicked State. To that line of Bishops he himself belonged. He had no connection with the Church of Rome, and no connection with the State. What purer orders, thought the Brethren, could they desire? They believed his statements; they trusted his honour; they admired his personal character; and now they sent old Michael Bradacius to see him in South Moravia and to lay their case before him. The old Bishop shed tears of joy. "He laid his hand on my head," says Michael, "and consecrated me a Bishop." Forthwith the new Bishop returned to Lhota, ordained the chosen three as Priests, and consecrated Matthias of Kunwald a Bishop. And thus arose those Episcopal Orders which have been maintained in the Church of the Brethren down to the present day.

The goal was reached; the Church was founded; the work of Gregory was done. For twenty years he had taught his Brethren to study the mind of Christ in the Scriptures and to seek the guidance of God in united prayer, and now he saw them joined as one to face the rising storm.

"Henceforth," he wrote gladly to King George Podiebrad, "we have done with the Church of Rome." As he saw the evening of life draw near, he urged his Brethren more and more to hold fast the teaching of Peter of Chelcic, and to regulate their daily conduct by the law of Christ; and by that law of Christ he probably meant the "Six Commandments" of the Sermon on the Mount. [15] He took these Commandments literally, and enforced them with a rod of iron. No Brother could be a judge or magistrate or councillor. No Brother could take an oath or keep an inn, or trade beyond the barest needs of life. No noble, unless he laid down his rank, could become a Brother at all. No peasant could render military service or act as a bailiff on a farm. No Brother could ever divorce his wife or take an action at law. As long as Gregory remained in their midst, the Brethren held true to him as their leader. He had not, says Gindely, a single trace of personal ambition in his nature; and, though he might have become a Bishop, he remained a layman to the end. Full of years he died, and his bones repose in a cleft where tufts of forget-me-not grow, at Brandeis-on-the-Adler, hard by the Moravian frontier (Sept.13th, 1473).

Chapter 6: Luke of Prague (1473-1530)

OF the Brethren who settled in the valley of Kunwald the greater number were country peasants and tradesmen of humble rank. But already the noble and mighty were pressing in. As the eyes of Gregory closed in death, a new party was rising to power. Already the Brethren were strong in numbers, and already they were longing to snap the fetters that Gregory had placed upon their feet. From Neustadt in the North to Skutch in the South, and from Chlumec in the West to Kunwald in the East, they now lay thickly sprinkled; and in all the principal towns of that district, an area of nine hundred square miles, they were winning rich and influential members. In came the University dons; in came the aldermen and knights. In came, above all, a large colony of Waldenses, who had immigrated from the Margravate of Brandenburg (1480). Some settled at Fulneck, in Moravia, others at Landskron, in Bohemia; and now, by their own request, they were admitted to the Brethren's Church. [16] For a while the Brethren held to the rule that if a nobleman joined their Church he must first lay down his rank. But now that rule was beginning to gall and chafe. They were winning golden opinions on every hand; they were becoming known as the best men for positions of trust in the State; they were just the men to make the best magistrates and aldermen; and thus they felt forced by their very virtues to renounce the narrow ideas of Peter and to play their part in national and city life.

At this moment, when new ideas were budding, there entered the service of the Church a young man who is known as Luke of Prague. He was born about 1460, was a Bachelor of Prague University, was a well-read theological scholar, and for fifty years was the trusted leader of the Brethren. Forthwith he read the signs of the times, and took the tide at the flood. In Procop of Neuhaus, another graduate, he found a warm supporter. The two scholars led the van of the new movement. The struggle was fierce. On the one side was the "great party" of culture, led by Luke of Prague and Procop of Neuhaus; on the other the so-called "little party," the old-fashioned rigid Radicals, led by two farmers, Amos and Jacob. "Ah, Matthias," said Gregory the Patriarch, on his death-bed, "beware of the educated Brethren!" But, despite this warning, the educated Brethren won the day. For once and for ever the Brethren resolved that the writings of Peter and Gregory should no longer be regarded as binding. At a Synod held at Reichenau they rejected the authority of Peter entirely (1494). They agreed that nobles might join the Church without laying down their rank; they agreed that if a man's business were honest he might make profits therein; they agreed that Brethren might enter the service of the State; and they even agreed that oaths might be taken in cases of special need. [17] And then, next year, they made their position still clearer (1495). Instead of taking Peter as their guide, they now took the Bible and the Bible alone. "We content ourselves," they solemnly declared, at another Synod held at Reichenau, "with those sacred books which have been accepted from of old by all Christians, and are found in the Bible"; and thus, forty years before John Calvin, and eighty years before the Lutherans, they declared that the words of Holy Scripture, apart from any disputed interpretation, should be their only standard of faith and practice. No longer did they honour the memory of Peter; no longer did they appeal to him in their writings; no longer, in a word, can we call the Brethren the true followers of Peter of Chelcic. Instead, henceforward, of regarding Peter as the founder of their Church, they began now to regard themselves as the disciples of Hus. In days gone by they had spoken of Hus as a "causer of war." Now they held his name and memory sacred; and from this time onward the real followers of Peter were, not the Brethren, but the "little party" led by Amos and Jacob. [18] 18

But the scholars led the Brethren further still. If the reader will kindly refer to the chapter on Peter, he will see that that racy pamphleteer had far more to say about good works than about the merits of saving faith; but now, after years of keen discussion, Procop of Neuhaus put to the Council of Elders the momentous question: "By what is a man justified?" The answer given was clear: "By the merits of Jesus Christ." The great doctrine of justification by grace was taught; the old doctrine of justification by works was modified; and thus the Brethren's Church became the first organized Evangelical Church in Europe. [19]

And Luke designed to make her the strongest, too. His energy never seemed to flag. As he wished to establish the ministry more firmly, he had the number of Bishops enlarged, and became a Bishop himself. He enlarged the governing Council, with his friend Procop of Neuhaus as Ecclesiastical Judge. He beautified the Church Services, and made the ritual more ornate. He introduced golden communion cups and delicately embroidered corporals, and some of the Brethren actually thought that he was leading them back to Rome. He gave an impulse to Church music, encouraged reading both in Priests and in people, and made a use of the printing press which in those days was astounding. Of the five printing presses in all Bohemia, three belonged to the Brethren; of sixty printed works that appeared between 1500 and 1510, no fewer than fifty were published by the Brethren; and of all the scribes of the sixteenth century, Luke was the most prolific. He wrote a "Catechism for Children." He edited the first Brethren's hymn book (1501), the first Church hymnal in history. He published a commentary on the Psalms, another on the Gospel of St. John, and another on the eleventh chapter of 1 Corinthians; he drew up "Confessions of Faith," and sent them to the King; and thus, for the first time in the history of Bohemia, he made the newly invented press a mighty power in the land.

And even with this the good Bishop was not content (1491). If the Brethren, thought he, were true to their name, they must surely long for fellowship with others of like mind with themselves. For this purpose Luke and his friends set off to search for Brethren in other lands. Away went one to find the pure Nestorian Church that was said to exist in

India, got as far as Antioch, Jerusalem and Egypt, and, being misled somehow by a Jew, returned home with the wonderful notion that the River Nile flowed from the Garden of Eden, but with no more knowledge of the Church in India than when he first set out. Another explored the South of Russia, and the third sought Christians in Turkey. And Luke himself had little more success. He explored a number of Monasteries in Greece, came on to Rome (1498), saw the streets of the city littered with corpses of men murdered by Caesar Borgia, picked up some useful information about the private character of the Pope, saw Savonarola put to death in Florence, fell in with a few Waldenses in the Savoy, and then, having sought for pearls in vain, returned home in a state of disgust, and convinced that, besides the Brethren, there was not to be found a true Christian Church on the face of God's fair earth. He even found fault with the Waldenses.

It was time, indeed, for Luke to return, for trouble was brewing at home. For some years there dwelt in the town of Jungbunzlau, the headquarters of the Brethren's Church, a smart young man, by name John Lezek. He began life as a brewer's apprentice; he then entered the service of a Brother, and learned a good deal of the Brethren's manners and customs; and now he saw the chance of turning his knowledge to good account. If only he told a good tale against the Brethren, he would be sure to be a popular hero. For this purpose he visited the parish priest, and confessed to a number of abominations committed by him while among the wicked Brethren. The parish priest was delighted; the penitent was taken to the Church; and there he told the assembled crowd the story of his guilty past. Of all the bad men in the country, he said, these Brethren were the worst. He had even robbed his own father with their consent and approval. They blasphemed. They took the Communion bread to their houses, and there hacked it in pieces. They were thieves, and he himself had committed many a burglary for them. They murdered men and kidnapped their wives. They had tried to blow up Rockycana in the Thein Church with gunpowder. They swarmed naked up pillars like Adam and Eve, and handed each other apples. They prepared poisonous drinks, and put poisonous smelling powders in their letters. They were skilled in witchcraft, worshipped Beelzebub, and were wont irreverently to say that the way to Hell was paved with the bald heads of priests. As this story was both alarming and lively, the parish priest had it taken down, sealed and signed by witnesses, copied out, and scattered broadcast through the land. In vain John Lezek confessed soon after, when brought by the Brethren before a Magistrate, that his whole story was a vile invention. If a man tells a falsehood and then denies it, he does not thereby prevent the falsehood from spreading.

For now a more powerful foe than Lezek made himself felt in the land. Of all the Popes that ever donned the tiara, Alexander VI. is said to have presented the most successful image of the devil. [20] He was the father of the prince of poisoners, Caesar Borgia; he was greedy, immoral, fond of ease and pleasure; he was even said to be a poisoner himself. If a well-known man died suddenly in Rome, the common people took it for granted that the Pope had poisoned his supper. For all that he was pious enough in a way of his own; and now, in his zeal for the Catholic cause, he took stern measures against the Church of the Brethren. He had heard some terrible tales about them. He heard that Peter's pamphlet, "The Antichrist," [21] was read all over the country. He heard that the number of the Brethren now was over 100,000. He resolved to crush them to powder (Papal Bull, Feb. 4th, 1500). He sent an agent, the Dominican, Dr. Henry Institoris, as censor of the press. As soon as Institoris arrived on the scene, he heard, to his horror, that most of the Brethren could read; and thereupon he informed the Pope that they had learned this art from the devil. He revived the stories of Lezek, the popular feeling was fanned to fury, and wire-pullers worked on the tender heart of the King.

"Hunt out and destroy these shameless vagabonds," wrote Dr. Augustin Kaesebrot to King Uladislaus, "they are not even good enough to be burnt at the stake. They ought to have their bodies torn by wild beasts and their blood licked up by dogs." For the last five years there had grown in the land a small sect known as Amosites. They were followers of old Farmer Amos; they had once belonged to the Brethren; they had broken off when the scholars had won the day, and now they sent word to the King to say that the Brethren were planning to defend their cause with the sword. "What!" said the King, "do they mean to play Ziska? Well, well! We know how to stop that!" They were worse than Turks, he declared; they believed neither in God nor in the Communion; they were a set of lazy vagabonds. He would soon pay them out for their devilish craft, and sweep them off the face of the earth. And to this end he summoned the Diet, and, by the consent of all three Estates, issued the famous Edict of St. James (July 25th, 1508). [22] The decree was sweeping and thorough. The meetings of the Brethren, public and private, were forbidden. The books and writings of the Brethren must be burnt. All in Bohemia who refused to join the Utraquist or Roman Catholic Church were to be expelled from the country; all nobles harbouring Brethren were to be fined, and all their priests and teachers were to be imprisoned.

The persecution began. In the village of Kuttenburg lived a brother, by name Andrew Poliwka. As Kuttenburg was a Romanist village, he fled for refuge to the Brethren's settlement at Leitomischl. But his wife betrayed him. He returned to the village, and, desiring to please her, he attended the parish Church.

The occasion was an installation service. As the sermon ended and the host was raised, he could hold his tongue no longer. "Silence, Parson Jacob," he cried to the priest, "you have babbled enough! Mine hour is come; I will speak. Dear friends," he continued, turning to the people, "what are you doing? What are you adoring? An idol made of bread! Oh! Adore the living God in heaven! He is blessed for evermore!" The priest ordered him to hold his peace. He only shrieked the louder. He was seized, his head was dashed against the pillar, and he was dragged bleeding to prison. Next day he was tried, and asked to explain why he had interrupted the service.

"Who caused Abram," he answered, "to forsake his idolatry and adore the living God? Who induced Daniel to flee from idols?" In vain was he stretched upon the rack. No further answer would he give. He was burnt to death at the stake. As the flames began to lick his face, he prayed aloud: "Jesus, Thou Son of the living God, have mercy upon me, miserable sinner."

At Strakonic dwelt the Brother George Wolinsky, a dependent of Baron John of Rosenberg (1509). The Baron was a mighty man. He was Grand Prior of the Knights of Malta; he was an orthodox subject of the King, and he determined that on his estate no villainous Picards [23] should live. "See," he said one day to George, "I have made you a servant in the Church. You must go to Church. You are a Picard, and I have received instructions from Prague that all men on my estate must be either Utraquists or Catholics."

The Brother refused; the Baron insisted; and the Prior of Strakonic was brought to convert the heretic. "No one," said the Prior, "should ever be tortured into faith. The right method is reasonable instruction, and innocent blood always cries to Heaven, Lord, Lord, when wilt Thou avenge me.'"

But this common sense was lost on the furious Baron. As Brother George refused to yield, the Baron cast him into the deepest dungeon of his castle. The bread and meat he had secreted in his pockets were removed. The door of the dungeon was barred, and all that was left for the comfort of his soul was a heap of straw whereon to die and a comb to do his hair. For five days he lay in the dark, and then the Baron came to see him. The prisoner was almost dead. His teeth were closed; his mouth was rigid; the last spark of life was feebly glimmering. The Baron was aghast. The mouth was forced open, hot soup was poured in, the prisoner revived, and the Baron burst into tears.

"Ah," he exclaimed, "I am glad he is living"; and allowed George to return to his Brethren.

Amid scenes like this, Bishop Luke was a tower of strength to his Brethren. For six years the manses were closed, the Churches empty, the Pastors homeless, the people scattered; and the Bishop hurried from glen to glen, held services in the woods and gorges, sent letters to the parishes he could not visit, and pleaded the cause of his Brethren in woe in letter after letter to the King. As the storm of persecution raged, he found time to write a stirring treatise, entitled, "The Renewal of the Church," and thus by pen and by cheery word he revived the flagging hope of all.

For a while the Brethren were robbed of this morsel of comfort. As the Bishop was hastening on a pastoral visit, he was captured by Peter von Suda, the brigand, "the prince and master of all thieves," was loaded with chains, cast into a dungeon, and threatened with torture and the stake. At that moment destruction complete and final seemed to threaten the Brethren. Never had the billows rolled so high; never had the breakers roared so loud; and bitterly the hiding Brethren complained that their leaders had steered them on the rocks.

Yet sunshine gleamed amid the gathering clouds. For some time there had been spreading among the common people a conviction that the Brethren were under the special protection of God, and that any man who tried to harm them would come to a tragic end. It was just while the Brethren were sunk in despair that several of their enemies suddenly died, and people said that God Himself had struck a blow for the persecuted "Pitmen." The great Dr. Augustin, their fiercest foe, fell dead from his chair at dinner. Baron Colditz, the Chancellor, fell ill of a carbuncle in his foot, and died. Baron Henry von Neuhaus, who had boasted to the King how many Brethren he had starved to death, went driving in his sleigh, was upset, and was skewered on his own hunting knife. Baron Puta von Swihow was found dead in his cellar. Bishop John of Grosswardein fell from his carriage, was caught on a sharp nail, had his bowels torn out, and miserably perished. And the people, struck with awe, exclaimed: "Let him that is tired of life persecute the Brethren, for he is sure not to live another year."

Thus the Brethren possessed their souls in patience till the persecution ended. The King of Bohemia, Uladislaus II., died (March 13th, 1516). His successor was only a boy. The Utraquists and Catholics began to quarrel with each other. The robber, von Suda, set Luke at liberty. The great Bishop became chief Elder of the Church. The whole land was soon in a state of disorder. The barons and knights were fighting each other, and, in the general stress and storm, the quiet Brethren were almost forgotten and allowed to live in peace.

And just at this juncture came news from afar that seemed to the Brethren like glad tidings from Heaven (1517). No longer were the Brethren to be alone, no longer to be a solitary voice crying in the wilderness. As the Brethren returned from the woods and mountains, and worshipped once again by the light of day, they heard, with amazement and joy, how Martin Luther, on Hallows Eve, had pinned his famous ninety-five Theses to the Church door at Wittenberg. The excitement in Bohemia was intense. For a while it seemed as though Martin Luther would wield as great an influence there as ever he had in Germany. For a while the Utraquist priests themselves, like Rockycana of yore, thundered in a hundred pulpits against the Church of Rome; and Luther, taking the keenest interest in the growing movement, wrote a letter to the Bohemian Diet, and urged the ecclesiastical leaders in Prague to break the last fetters that bound them to Rome.

For a while his agent, Gallus Cahera, a butcher's son, who had studied at Wittenberg, was actually pastor of the Thein Church (1523-9), referred in his sermons to the "celebrated Dr. Martin Luther," and openly urged the people to pray for that "great man of God." For a while even a preacher of the Brethren, named Martin, was allowed to stand where Hus had stood, and preach in the Bethlehem Church. For a while, in a word, it seemed to the Brethren that the Reformation now spreading in Germany would conquer Bohemia at a rush. The great Luther was loved by many classes. He was loved by the Utraquists because he had burned the Pope's Bull. He was loved by the young because he favoured learning. He was loved by the Brethren because he upheld the Bible as the standard of faith (1522). As soon as Luther had left the Wartburg, the Brethren boldly held out to him the right hand of fellowship; sent two German Brethren, John Horn and Michael Weiss, to see him; presented him with a copy of their Confession and Catechism; began a friendly correspondence on various points of doctrine and discipline, and thus opened their hearts to hear with respect what the great Reformer had to say.

Amid these bright prospects Luke of Prague breathed his last (Dec. 11th, 1528). As Gregory the Patriarch had gone to his rest when a new party was rising among the Brethren, so Luke of Prague crossed the cold river of death when new ideas from Germany were stirring the hearts of his friends. He was never quite easy in his mind about Martin Luther. He still believed in the Seven Sacraments. He still believed in the Brethren's system of stern moral discipline. He still believed, for practical reasons, in the celibacy of the clergy. "This eating," he wrote, "this drinking, this self-indulgence, this marrying, this living to the world—what a poor preparation it is for men who are leaving Babylon. If a man does this he is yoking himself with strangers. Marriage never made anyone holy yet. It is a hindrance to the higher life, and causes endless trouble." Above all, he objected to Luther's way of teaching the great doctrine of justification by faith.

"Never, never," he said, in a letter to Luther, "can you ascribe a man's salvation to faith alone. The Scriptures are against you. You think that in this you are doing a good work, but you are really fighting against Christ Himself and clinging to an error." He regarded Luther's teaching as extreme and one-sided. He was shocked by what he heard of the jovial life led by Luther's students at Wittenberg, and could never understand how a rollicking youth could be a preparation for a holy ministry. As Gregory the Patriarch had warned Matthias against "the learned Brethren," so Luke, in his turn, now warned the Brethren against the loose lives of Luther's merry-hearted students; and, in order to preserve the Brethren's discipline, he now issued a comprehensive treatise, divided into two parts—the first entitled "Instructions for Priests," and the second "Instructions and Admonitions for all occupations, all ages in life, all ranks and all sorts of characters." As he lay on his death-bed at Jungbunzlau, his heart was stirred by mingled feelings. There was land in sight—ah, yes!—but what grew upon the enchanting island? He would rather see his Church alone and pure than swept away in the Protestant current. Happy was he in the day of his death. So far he had steered the Church safely. He must now resign his post to another pilot who knew well the coming waters.

Chapter 7: The Brethren at Home

AS we have now arrived at that bend in the lane, when the Brethren, no longer marching alone, became a regiment in the conquering Protestant army, it will be convenient to halt in our story and look at the Brethren a little more closely—at their homes, their trades, their principles, their doctrines, their forms of service, and their life from day to day. After all, what were these Brethren, and how did they live?

They called themselves Jednota Bratrska—i.e., the Church of the Brethren. As this word "Jednota" means union, and is used in this sense in Bohemia at the present day, it is possible that the reader may think that instead of calling the Brethren a Church, we ought rather to call them the Union or Unity of the Brethren. If he does, however, he will be mistaken. We have no right to call the Brethren a mere Brotherhood or Unity. They regarded themselves as a true apostolic Church. They believed that their episcopal orders were valid. They called the Church of Rome a Jednota; [24] they called the Lutheran Church a Jednota; [25] they called themselves a Jednota; and, therefore, if the word Jednota means Church when applied to Lutherans and Roman Catholics, it must also mean Church when applied to the Bohemian Brethren. It is not correct to call them the Unitas Fratrum. The term is misleading. It suggests a Brotherhood rather than an organized Church. We have no right to call them a sect; the term is a needless insult to their memory. [26] As the Brethren settled in the Valley of Kunwald, the great object which they set before them was to recall to vigorous life the true Catholic Church of the Apostles; and as soon as they were challenged by their enemies to justify their existence, they replied in good set terms.

"Above all things," declared the Brethren, at a Synod held in 1464, "we are one in this purpose. We hold fast the faith of the Lord Christ. We will abide in the righteousness and love of God. We will trust in the living God. We will do good works. We will serve each other in the spirit of love. We will lead a virtuous, humble, gentle, sober, patient and pure life; and thereby shall we know that we hold the faith in truth, and that a home is prepared for us in heaven. We will show obedience to one another, as the Holy Scriptures command. We will take from each other instruction, reproof and punishment, and thus shall we keep the covenant established by God through the Lord Christ." [27] To this purpose the Brethren held firm. In every detail of their lives—in business, in pleasure, in civil duties—they took the Sermon on the Mount as the lamp unto their feet. From the child to the old man, from the serf to the lord, from the acoluth to the bishop, the same strict law held good. What made the Brethren's Church shine so brightly in Bohemia before Luther's days was not their doctrine, but their lives; not their theory, but their practice; not their opinions, but their discipline. Without that discipline they would have been a shell without a kernel. It called forth the admiration of Calvin, and drove Luther to despair. It was, in truth, the jewel of the Church, her charm against foes within and without; and so great a part did it play in their lives that in later years they were known to some as "Brethren of the Law of Christ."

No portion of the Church was more carefully watched than the ministers. As the chief object which the Brethren set before them was obedience to the Law of Christ, it followed, as the night the day, that the chief quality required in a minister was not theological learning, but personal character. When a man came forward as a candidate for the ministry he knew that he would have to stand a most searching examination. His character and conduct were thoroughly sifted. He must have a working knowledge of the Bible, a blameless record, and a living faith in God. For classical learning the Brethren had an honest contempt. It smacked too much of Rome and monkery. As long as the candidate was a holy man, and could teach the people the plain truths of the Christian faith, they felt that nothing more was required, and did not expect him to know Greek and Hebrew. In vain Luther, in a friendly letter, urged them to cultivate more knowledge. "We have no need," they replied, "of teachers who understand other tongues, such as Greek and Hebrew. It is not our custom to appoint ministers who have been trained at advanced schools in languages and fine arts. We prefer Bohemians and Germans who have come to a knowledge of the truth through personal experience and practical service, and who are therefore qualified to impart to others the piety they have first acquired themselves. And here we are true to the law of God and the practice of the early Church." [28] Instead of regarding learning as an aid to faith, they regarded it as an hindrance and a snare. It led, they declared, to wordy battles, to quarrels, to splits, to uncertainties, to doubts, to corruptions. As long, they said, as the ministers of the Church of Christ were simple and unlettered men, so long was the Church a united body of believers; but as soon as the parsons began to be scholars, all sorts of evils arose. What good, they argued, had learning done in the past? It had caused the translation of the Bible into Latin, and had thus hidden its truths from the common people. "And therefore," they insisted, "we despise the learning of tongues."

For this narrow attitude they had also another reason. In order to be true to the practice of the early Christian Church, they laid down the strict rule that all ministers should earn their living by manual labour; and the result was that even if a minister wished to study he could not find time to do so. For his work as a minister he never received a penny. If a man among the Brethren entered the ministry, he did so for the pure love of the work. He had no chance of becoming rich. He was not allowed to engage in a business that brought in large profits. If he earned any more in the sweat of his brow than he needed to make ends meet, he was compelled to hand the surplus over to the general funds of the Church; and if some one kindly left him some money, that money was treated in the same way. He was to be as moderate as possible in eating and drinking; he was to avoid all gaudy show in dress and house; he was not to go to fairs and banquets; and, above all, he was not to marry except with the consent and approval of the Elders. Of marriage the Brethren had rather a poor opinion. They clung still to the old Catholic view that it was less holy than celibacy. "It is," they said, "a good thing if two people find that they cannot live continent without it." If a minister married he was not regarded with favour; he was supposed to have been guilty of a fleshly weakness; and it is rather sarcastically recorded in the old "Book of the Dead" that in every case in which a minister failed in his duties, or was convicted of immorality, the culprit was a married man.

And yet, for all his humble style, the minister was held in honour. As the solemn time of ordination drew near there were consultations of ministers with closed doors, and days set apart for fasting and prayer throughout the whole Church. His duties were many and various. He was commonly spoken of, not as a priest, but as the "servant" of the Church. He was not a priest in the Romish sense of the word. He had no distinctive sacerdotal powers. He had no more power to consecrate the Sacrament than any godly layman. Of priests as a separate class the Brethren knew nothing. All true believers in Christ, said they, were priests. We can see this from one of their regulations. As the times were stormy, and persecution might break out at any moment, the Brethren (at a Synod in 1504) laid down the rule that when their meetings at Church were forbidden they should be held in private houses, and then, if a minister was not available, any godly layman was authorised to conduct the Holy Communion. [29] And thus the minister was simply a useful "servant." He gave instruction in Christian doctrine. He heard confessions. He expelled sinners. He welcomed penitents. He administered the Sacraments. He trained theological students. If he had the needful gift, he preached; if not, he read printed sermons. He was not a ruler lording it over the flock; he was rather a "servant" bound by rigid rules. He was not allowed to select his own topics for sermons; he had to preach from the Scripture lesson appointed for the day. He was bound to visit every member of his congregation at least once a quarter; he was bound to undertake any journey or mission, however dangerous, at the command of the Elders; and he was bound, for a fairly obvious reason, to take a companion with him when he called at the houses of the sick. If he went alone he might practise as a doctor, and give dangerous medical advice; and that, said the Brethren, was not his proper business. He was not allowed to visit single women or widows. If he did, there might be scandals about him, as there were about the Catholic priests. For the spiritual needs of all unmarried women the Brethren made special provision. They were visited by a special "Committee of Women," and the minister was not allowed to interfere.

The good man did not even possess a home of his own. Instead of living in a private manse he occupied a set of rooms in a large building known as the Brethren's House; and the minister, as the name implies, was not the only Brother in it. "As Eli had trained Samuel, as Elijah had trained Elisha, as Christ had trained His disciples, as St. Paul trained Timothy and Titus," so a minister of the Brethren had young men under his charge. There, under the minister's eye, the candidates for service in the Church were trained. Neither now nor at any period of their history had the Bohemian Brethren any theological colleges. If a boy desired to become a minister he entered the Brethren's

House at an early age, and was there taught a useful trade. Let us look at the inmates of the House.

First in order, next to the Priest himself, were the Deacons. They occupied a double position. They were in the first stage of priesthood, and in the last stage of preparation for it. Their duties were manifold. They supplied the out-preaching places. They repeated the pastor's sermon to those who had not been able to attend the Sunday service. They assisted at the Holy Communion in the distribution of the bread and wine. They preached now and then in the village Church to give their superior an opportunity for criticism and correction. They managed the domestic affairs of the house. They acted as sacristans or churchwardens. They assisted in the distribution of alms, and took their share with the minister in manual labour; and then, in the intervals between these trifling duties, they devoted their time to Bible study and preparation for the ministry proper. No wonder they never became very scholarly pundits; and no wonder that when they went off to preach their sermons had first to be submitted to the head of the house for approval.

Next to the Deacons came the Acoluths, young men or boys living in the same building and preparing to be Deacons. They were trained by the minister, very often from childhood upwards. They rang the bell and lighted the candles in the Church, helped the Deacons in household arrangements, and took turns in conducting the household worship. Occasionally they were allowed to deliver a short address in the Church, and the congregation "listened with kindly forbearance." When they were accepted by the Synod as Acoluths they generally received some Biblical name, which was intended to express some feature in the character. It is thus that we account for such names as Jacob Bilek and Amos Comenius.

Inside this busy industrial hive the rules were rigid. The whole place was like a boarding-school or college. At the sound of a bell all rose, and then came united prayer and Scripture reading; an hour later a service, and then morning study. As the afternoon was not considered a good time for brain work, the Brethren employed it in manual labour, such as weaving, gardening and tailoring. In the evening there was sacred music and singing. At meal times the Acoluths recited passages of Scripture, or read discourses, or took part in theological discussions.

No one could leave the house without the pastor's permission, and the pastor himself could not leave his parish without the Bishop's permission. If he travelled at all he did so on official business, and then he lodged at other Brethren's Houses, when the Acoluths washed his feet and attended to his personal comforts.

The Brethren's rules struck deeper still. As the Brethren despised University education, it is natural to draw the plain conclusion that among them the common people were the most benighted and ignorant in the land. The very opposite was the case. Among them the common people were the most enlightened in the country. Of the Bohemian people, in those days, there were few who could read or write; of the Brethren there was scarcely one who could not. If the Brethren taught the people nothing else, they at least taught them to read their native tongue; and their object in this was to spread the knowledge of the Bible, and thus make the people good Protestants. But in those days a man who could read was regarded as a prodigy of learning. The result was widespread alarm. As the report gained ground that among the Brethren the humblest people could read as well as the priest, the good folk in Bohemia felt compelled to concoct some explanation, and the only explanation they could imagine was that the Brethren had the special assistance of the devil. [30] If a man, said they, joined the ranks of the Brethren, the devil immediately taught him the art of reading, and if, on the other hand, he deserted the Brethren, the devil promptly robbed him of the power, and reduced him again to a wholesome benighted condition. "Is it really true," said Baron Rosenberg to his dependant George Wolinsky, "that the devil teaches all who become Picards to read, and that if a peasant leaves the Brethren he is able to read no longer?"

In this instance, however, the devil was innocent. The real culprit was Bishop Luke of Prague. Of all the services rendered by Luke to the cause of popular education and moral and spiritual instruction, the greatest was his publication of his "Catechism for Children," commonly known as "The Children's Questions." It was a masterly and comprehensive treatise. It was published first, of course, in the Bohemian language (1502). It was published again in a German edition for the benefit of the German members of the Church (1522). It was published again, with some alterations, by a Lutheran at Magdeburg (1524). It was published again, with more alterations, by another Lutheran, at Wittenberg (1525). It was published again, in abridged form, at Zuerich, and was recommended as a manual of instruction for the children at St. Gallen (1527). And thus it exercised a profound influence on the whole course of the Reformation, both in Germany and in Switzerland. For us, however, the point of interest is its influence in Bohemia and Moravia. It was not a book for the priests. It was a book for the fathers of families. It was a book found in every Brother's home. It was the children's "Reader." As the boys and girls grew up in the Brethren's Church, they learned to read, not in national schools, but in their own homes; and thus the Brethren did for the children what ought to have been done by the State. Among them the duties of a father were clearly defined. He was both a schoolmaster and a religious instructor. He was the priest in his own family. He was to bring his children up in the Christian faith. He was not to allow them to roam at pleasure, or play with the wicked children of the world. He was to see that they were devout at prayers, respectful in speech, and noble and upright in conduct. He was not to allow brothers and sisters to sleep in the same room, or boys and girls to roam the daisied fields together. He was not to strike his children with a stick or with his fists. If he struck them at all, he must do so with a cane. Above all, he had to teach his children the Catechism. They were taught by their parents until they were twelve years old; they were then taken in hand by their sponsors; and thus they were prepared for Confirmation, not as in the Anglican Church, by a clergyman only, but partly by their own parents and friends.

The Brethren's rules struck deeper still. For law and order the Brethren had a passion. Each congregation was divided into three classes: the Beginners, those who were learning the "Questions" and the first elements of religion; the Proficients, the steady members of the Church; and the Perfect, those so established in faith, hope and love as to be able to enlighten others. For each class a separate Catechism was prepared. At the head, too, of each congregation was a body of civil Elders. They were elected by the congregation from the Perfect. They assisted the pastor in his parochial duties. They looked after his support in case he were in special need. They acted as poor-law guardians, lawyers, magistrates and umpires, and thus they tried to keep the people at peace and prevent them from going to law. Every three months they visited the houses of the Brethren, and inquired whether business were honestly conducted, whether family worship were held, whether the children were properly trained. For example, it was one of the duties of a father to talk with his children at the Sunday dinner-table on what they had heard at the morning service; and when the Elder paid his quarterly visit he soon discovered, by examining the children, how far this duty had been fulfilled.

The Brethren's rules struck deeper still. For the labourer in the field, for the artizan in the workshop, for the tradesman with his wares, for the baron and his tenants, for the master and his servants, there were laws and codes to suit each case, and make every trade and walk in life serve in some way to the glory of God. Among the Brethren all work was sacred. If a man was not able to show that his trade was according to the law of Christ and of direct service to His holy cause, he was not allowed to carry it on at all. He must either change his calling or leave the Church. In the Brethren's Church there were no dice makers, no actors, no painters, no professional musicians, no wizards or seers, no alchemists, no astrologers, no courtezans or panderers. The whole tone was stern and puritanic. For art, for music, for letters and for pleasure the Brethren had only contempt, and the fathers were warned against staying out at night and frequenting the card-room and the liquor-saloon. And yet, withal, these stern Brethren were kind and tender-hearted. If the accounts handed down are to be believed, the villages where the Brethren settled were the homes of happiness and peace. As the Brethren had no definite social policy, they did not, of course, make any attempt to break down the distinctions of rank; and yet, in their own way, they endeavoured to teach all classes to respect each other. They enjoined the barons to allow their servants to worship with them round the family altar. They urged the rich to spend their money on the poor instead of on dainties and fine clothes. They forbade the poor to wear silk, urged them to be patient, cheerful and industrious, and reminded them that in the better land their troubles would vanish like dew before the rising sun. For the poorest of all, those in actual need, they had special collections several times a year. The fund was called the Korbona, and was managed by three officials. The first kept the box, the second the key, the third the accounts. And the rich and poor had all to bow to the same system of discipline. There were three degrees of punishment. For the first offence the sinner was privately admonished. For the second he was rebuked before the Elders, and excluded from the Holy Communion until he repented. For the third he was denounced in the Church before the whole congregation, and the loud "Amen" of the assembled members proclaimed his banishment from the Brethren's Church.

The system of government was Presbyterian. At the head of the whole Brethren's Church was a board, called the "Inner Council," elected by the Synod. Next came the Bishops, elected also by the Synod. The supreme authority was this General Synod. It consisted of all the ministers. As long as the Inner Council held office they were, of course, empowered to enforce their will; but the final court of appeal was the Synod, and by the Synod all questions of doctrine and policy were settled.

The doctrine was simple and broad. As the Brethren never had a formal creed, and never used their "Confessions of Faith" as tests, it may seem a rather vain endeavour to inquire too closely into their theological beliefs. And yet, on the other hand, we know enough to enable the historian to paint a life-like picture. For us the important question is, what did the Brethren teach their children? If we know what the Brethren taught their children we know what they valued most; and this we have set before us in the Catechism drawn up by Luke of Prague and used as an authorised manual of instruction in the private homes of the Brethren. It contained no fewer than seventy-six questions. The answers are remarkably full, and therefore we may safely conclude that, though it was not an exhaustive treatise, it gives us a wonderfully clear idea of the doctrines which the Brethren prized most highly. It is remarkable both for what it contains and for what it does not contain. It has no distinct and definite reference to St. Paul's doctrine of justification by faith. It is Johannine rather than Pauline in its tone. It contains a great deal of the teaching of Christ and a very little of the teaching of St. Paul. It has more to say about the Sermon on the Mount than about any system of dogmatic theology. For one sentence out of St. Paul's Epistles it has ten out of the Gospel of St. Matthew. As we read the answers in this popular treatise, we are able to see in what way the Brethren differed from the Lutheran Protestants in Germany. They approached the whole subject of Christian life from a different point of view. They were less dogmatic, less theological, less concerned about accurate definition, and they used their theological terms in a broader and freer way. For example, take their definition of faith. We all know the definition given by Luther. "There are," said Luther, "two kinds of believing: first, a believing about God which means that I believe that what is said of God is true. This faith is rather a form of knowledge than a faith. There is, secondly, a believing in God which means that I put my trust in Him, give myself up to thinking that I can have dealings with Him, and believe without any doubt that He will be and do to me according to the things said of Him. Such faith, which throws itself upon God, whether in life or in death, alone makes a Christian man." But the Brethren gave the word faith a richer meaning. They made it signify more than trust in God. They made it include both hope and love. They made it include obedience to the Law of Christ.

"What is faith in the Lord God?" was one question in the Catechism.

"It is to know God, to know His word; above all, to love Him, to do His commandments, and to submit to His will."

"What is faith in Christ?"

"It is to listen to His word, to know Him, to honour Him, to love Him and to join the company of His followers." [31]

And this is the tone all through the Catechism and in all the early writings of the Brethren. As a ship, said Luke, is not made of one plank, so a Christian cannot live on one religious doctrine. The Brethren had no pet doctrines whatever. They had none of the distinctive marks of a sect. They taught their children the Apostles' Creed, the Ten Commandments, the Lord's Prayer, the Eight Beatitudes, and the "Six Commandments" of the Sermon on the Mount. They taught the orthodox Catholic doctrines of the Holy Trinity and the Virgin Birth. They held, they said, the universal Christian faith. They enjoined the children to honour, but not worship, the Virgin Mary and the Saints, and they warned them against the adoration of pictures. If the Brethren had any peculiarity at all, it was not any distinctive doctrine, but rather their insistence on the practical duties of the believer. With Luther, St. Paul's theology was foremost; with the Brethren (though not denied) it fell into the background. With Luther the favourite court of appeal was St. Paul's Epistle to the Galatians; with the Brethren it was rather the Sermon on the Mount and the tender Epistles of St. John.

Again the Brethren differed from Luther in their doctrine of the Lord's Supper. As this subject was then the fruitful source of much discussion and bloodshed, the Brethren at first endeavoured to avoid the issue at stake by siding with neither of the two great parties and falling back on the simple words of Scripture. "Some say," they said, "it is only a memorial feast, that Christ simply gave the bread as a memorial. Others say that the bread is really the body of Christ, who is seated at the right hand of God. We reject both these views; they were not taught by Christ Himself. And if anyone asks us to say in what way Christ is present in the sacrament, we reply that we have nothing to say on the subject. We simply believe what He Himself said, and enjoy what He has given." [32]

But this attitude could not last for ever. As the storms of persecution raged against them, the Brethren grew more and more radical in their views. They denied the doctrine of Transubstantiation; they denied also the Lutheran doctrine of Consubstantiation; they denied that the words in St. John's Gospel about eating the flesh and drinking the blood of Christ had any reference to the Lord's Supper. They took the whole passage in a purely spiritual sense. If those words, said Bishop Luke, referred to the Sacrament, then all Catholics, except the priests, would be lost; for Catholics only ate the flesh and did not drink the blood, and could, therefore, not possess eternal life. They denied, in a word, that the Holy Communion had any value apart from the faith of the believer; they denounced the adoration of the host as idolatry; and thus they adopted much the same position as Wycliffe in England nearly two hundred years before. The Lord Christ, they said, had three modes of existence. He was present bodily at the right hand of God; He was present spiritually in the heart of every believer; He was present sacramentally, but not personally, in the bread and wine; and, therefore, when the believer knelt in prayer, he must kneel, not to the bread and wine, but only to the exalted Lord in Heaven.

Again, the Brethren differed from Luther in their doctrine of Infant Baptism. If a child, said Luther, was prayed for by the Church, he was thereby cleansed from his unbelief, delivered from the power of the devil, and endowed with faith; and therefore the child was baptised as a believer. [33] The Brethren rejected this teaching. They called it Romish. They held that no child could be a believer until he had been instructed in the faith. They had no belief in baptismal regeneration. With them Infant Baptism had quite a different meaning. It was simply the outward and visible sign of admission to the Church. As soon as the child had been baptised, he belonged to the class of the Beginners, and then, when he was twelve years old, he was taken by his godfather to the minister, examined in his "Questions," and asked if he would hold true to the faith he had been taught. If he said "Yes!" the minister struck him in the face, to teach him that he would have to suffer for Christ; and then, after further instruction, he was confirmed by the minister, admitted to the communion, and entered the ranks of the Proficient.

Such, then, was the life, and such were the views, of the Bohemian Brethren. What sort of picture does all this bring before us? It is the picture of a body of earnest men, united, not by a common creed, but rather by a common devotion to Christ, a common reverence for Holy Scripture, and a common desire to revive the customs of the early Christian Church. [34] In some of their views they were narrow, in others remarkably broad. In some points they had still much to learn; in others they were far in advance of their times, and anticipated the charitable teaching of the present day.

Chapter 8: John Augusta (1531-1548)

AS the great Bishop Luke lay dying at Jungbunzlau, there was rising to fame among the Brethren the most brilliant and powerful leader they had ever known. Again we turn to the old Thein Church; again the preacher is denouncing the priests; and again in the pew is an eager listener with soul aflame with zeal. His name was John Augusta. He was born, in 1500, at Prague. His father was a hatter, and in all probability he learned the trade himself. He was brought up in the Utraquist Faith; he took the sacrament every Sunday in the famous old Thein Church; and there he heard the preacher declare that the priests in Prague cared for nothing but comfort, and that the average Christians of the day were no better than crack-brained heathen sprinkled with holy water. The young man was staggered; he consulted other priests, and the others told him the same dismal tale. One lent him a pamphlet, entitled "The Antichrist"; another lent him a treatise by Hus; and a third said solemnly: "My son, I see that God has more in store for you than I can understand." But the strangest event of all was still to come. As he rode one day in a covered waggon with two priests of high rank, it so happened that one of them turned to Augusta and urged him to leave the Utraquist Church and join the ranks of the Brethren at Jungbunzlau. Augusta was horrified.

Again he consulted the learned priest; again he received the same strange counsel; and one day the priest ran after him, called him back, and said: "Listen, dear brother! I beseech you, leave us. You will get no good among us. Go to the Brethren at Bunzlau, and there your soul will find rest." Augusta was shocked beyond measure. He hated the Brethren, regarded them as beasts, and had often warned others against them. But now he went to see them himself, and found to his joy that they followed the Scriptures, obeyed the Gospel and enforced their rules without respect of persons. For a while he was in a quandary. His conscience drew him to the Brethren, his honour held him to the Utraquists, and finally his own father confessor settled the question for him.

"Dear friend," said the holy man, "entrust your soul to the Brethren. Never mind if some of them are hypocrites, who do not obey their own rules. It is your business to obey the rules yourself. What more do you want? If you return to us in Prague, you will meet with none but sinners and sodomites."

And so, by the advice of Utraquist priests, this ardent young man joined the ranks of the Brethren, was probably trained in the Brethren's House at Jungbunzlau, and was soon ordained as a minister. Forthwith he rose to fame and power in the pulpit. His manner was dignified and noble. His brow was lofty, his eye flashing, his bearing the bearing of a commanding king. He was a splendid speaker, a ready debater, a ruler of men, an inspirer of action; he was known ere long as the Bohemian Luther; and he spread the fame of the

Brethren's Church throughout the Protestant world. Full soon, in truth, he began his great campaign. As he entered on his work as a preacher of the Gospel, he found that among the younger Brethren there were quite a number who did not feel at all disposed to be bound by the warning words of Luke of Prague. They had been to the great Wittenberg University; they had mingled with Luther's students; they had listened to the talk of Michael Weiss, who had been a monk at Breslau, and had brought Lutheran opinions with him; they admired both Luther and Melancthon; and they now resolved, with one consent, that if the candlestick of the Brethren's Church was not to be moved from out its place, they must step shoulder to shoulder with Luther, become a regiment in the conquering Protestant army, and march with him to the goodly land where the flower of the glad free Gospel bloomed in purity and sweet perfume. At the first opportunity Augusta, their leader, brought forward their views. At a Synod held at Brandeis-on-the-Adler, summoned by Augusta's friend, John Horn, the senior Bishop of the Church, for the purpose of electing some new Bishops, Augusta rose to address the assembly. He spoke in the name of the younger clergy, and immediately commenced an attack upon the old Executive Council. He accused them of listlessness and sloth; he said that they could not understand the spirit of the age, and he ended his speech by proposing himself and four other broad-minded men as members of the Council. The old men were shocked; the young were entranced; and Augusta was elected and consecrated a Bishop, and thus, at the age of thirty-two, became the leader of the Brethren's Church. He had three great schemes in view; first, friendly relations with Protestants in other countries; second, legal recognition of the Brethren in Bohemia; third, the union of all Bohemian Protestants.

First, then, with Augusta to lead them on, the Brethren enlisted in the Protestant army, and held the banner of their faith aloft that all the world might see. As the Protestants in Germany had issued the Confession of Augsburg, and had it read in solemn style before the face of the Emperor, Charles V., so now the Brethren issued a new and full "Confession of Faith," to be sent first to George, Margrave of Brandenburg, and then laid in due time before Ferdinand, King of Bohemia. It was a characteristic Brethren's production. [35] It is perfectly clear from this Confession that the Brethren had separated from Rome for practical rather than dogmatic reasons. It is true the Brethren realised the value of faith; it is true the Confession contained the sentence, "He is the Lamb that taketh away the sins of the world; and whosoever believeth in Him and calleth on His name shall be saved"; but even now the Brethren did not, like Luther, lay stress on the doctrine of justification by faith alone. And yet Luther had no fault to find with this Confession. It was addressed to him, was printed at Wittenberg, was issued with his consent and approval, and was praised by him in a preface. It was read and approved by John Calvin, by Martin Bucer, by Philip Melancthon, by pious old George, Margrave of Brandenburg, and by John Frederick, Elector of Saxony. Again and again the Brethren sent deputies to see the great Protestant leaders. At Wittenberg, Augusta discussed good morals with Luther and Melancthon; and at Strasburg, Cerwenka, the Brethren's historian, held friendly counsel with Martin Bucer and Calvin. Never had the Brethren been so widely known, and never had they received so many compliments. Formerly Luther, who liked plain speech, had called the Brethren "sour-looking hypocrites and self-grown saints, who believe in nothing but what they themselves teach." But now he was all good humour. "There never have been any Christians," he said, in a lecture to his students, "so like the apostles in doctrine and constitution as these Bohemian Brethren."

"Tell your Brethren," he said to their deputies, "to hold fast what God has given them, and never give up their constitution and discipline. Let them take no heed of revilements. The world will behave foolishly. If you in Bohemia were to live as we do, what is said of us would be said of you, and if we were to live as you do, what is said of you would be said of us." "We have never," he added, in a letter to the Brethren, "attained to such a discipline and holy life as is found among you, but in the future we shall make it our aim to attain it."

The other great Reformers were just as enthusiastic. "How shall I," said Bucer, "instruct those whom God Himself has instructed! You alone, in all the world, combine a wholesome discipline with a pure faith." "We," said Calvin, "have long since recognised the value of such a system, but cannot, in any way, attain to it." "I am pleased," said Melancthon, "with the strict discipline enforced in your congregations. I wish we could have a stricter discipline in ours." It is clear what all this means. It means that the Brethren, in their humble way, had taught the famous Protestant leaders the value of a system of Church discipline and the need of good works as the proper fruit of faith.

Meanwhile Augusta pushed his second plan. The task before him was gigantic. A great event had taken place in Bohemia. At the battle of Mohacz, in a war with the Turks, Louis, King of Bohemia, fell from his horse when crossing a stream, and was drowned (1526). The old line of Bohemian Kings had come to an end. The crown fell into the hands of the Hapsburgs; the Hapsburgs were the mightiest supporters of the Church of Rome; and the King of Bohemia, Ferdinand I., was likewise King of Hungary, Archduke of Austria, King of the Romans, and brother of the Emperor Charles V., the head of the Holy Roman Empire.

For the Brethren the situation was momentous. As Augusta scanned the widening view, he saw that the time was coming fast when the Brethren, whether they would or no, would be called to play their part like men in a vast European conflict. Already the Emperor Charles V. had threatened to crush the Reformation by force; already (1530) the Protestant princes in Germany had formed the Smalkald League; and Augusta, scenting the battle from afar, resolved to build a fortress for the Brethren. His policy was clear and simple. If the King of Bohemia joined forces with the Emperor, the days of the Brethren's Church would soon be over. He would make the King of Bohemia their friend, and thus save the Brethren from the horrors of war. For this purpose Augusta now instructed the powerful Baron, Conrad Krajek, the richest member of the Brethren's Church, to present the Brethren's Confession of Faith to King Ferdinand. The Baron undertook the task. He was the leader of a group of Barons who had recently joined the Church; he had built the great Zbor of the Brethren in Jungbunzlau, known as "Mount Carmel"; he had been the first to suggest a Confession of Faith, and now, having signed the Confession himself, he sought out the King at Vienna, and was admitted to a private interview (Nov. 11th, 1535). The scene was stormy. "We would like to know," said the King, "how you Brethren came to adopt this faith. The devil has persuaded you."

"Not the devil, gracious liege," replied the Baron, "but Christ the Lord through the Holy Scriptures. If Christ was a Picard, then I am one too."

The King was beside himself with rage.

"What business," he shouted, "have you to meddle with such things? You are neither Pope, nor Emperor, nor King. Believe what you will! We shall not prevent you! If you really want to go to hell, go by all means!"

The Baron was silent. The King paused.

"Yes, yes," he continued, "you may believe what you like and we shall not prevent you; but all the same, I give you warning that we shall put a stop to your meetings, where you carry on your hocus-pocus."

The Baron was almost weeping.

"Your Majesty," he protested, "should not be so hard on me and my noble friends. We are the most loyal subjects in your kingdom."

The King softened, spoke more gently, but still held to his point.

"I swore," he said, "at my coronation to give justice to the Utraquists and Catholics, and I know what the statute says."

As the King spoke those ominous words, he was referring, as the Baron knew full well, to the terrible Edict of St. James. The interview ended; the Baron withdrew; the issue still hung doubtful.

And yet the Baron had not spoken in vain. For three days the King was left undisturbed; and then two other Barons appeared and presented the Confession, signed by twelve nobles and thirty-three knights, in due form (Nov. 14th}.

"Do you really think," they humbly said, "that it helps the unity of the kingdom when priests are allowed to say in the pulpit that it is less sinful to kill a Picard than it is to kill a dog."

The King was touched; his anger was gone, and a week later he promised the Barons that as long as the Brethren were loyal subjects he would allow them to worship as they pleased. For some years the new policy worked very well, and the King kept his promise. The Brethren were extending on every hand. They had now at least four hundred churches and two hundred thousand members. They printed and published translations of Luther's works. They had a church in the city of Prague itself. They enjoyed the favour of the leading nobles in the land; and Augusta, in a famous sermon, expressed the hope that before very long the Brethren and Utraquists would be united and form one National Protestant Church. [36]

At this point a beautiful incident occurred. As the Brethren were now so friendly with Luther, there was a danger that they would abandon their discipline, become ashamed of their own little Church, and try to imitate the teaching and practice of their powerful

Protestant friends. For some years after Luke's death they actually gave way to this temptation, and Luke's last treatise, "Regulations for Priests," was scornfully cast aside. But the Brethren soon returned to their senses. As John Augusta and John Horn travelled in Germany, they made the strange and startling discovery that, after all, the Brethren's Church was the best Church they knew. For a while they were dazzled by the brilliance of the Lutheran preachers; but in the end they came to the conclusion that though these preachers were clever men they had not so firm a grip on Divine truth as the Brethren. At last, in 1546, the Brethren met in a Synod at Jungbunzlau to discuss the whole situation. With tears in his eyes John Horn addressed the assembly. "I have never understood till now," he said, "what a costly treasure our Church is. I have been blinded by the reading of German books! I have never found any thing so good in those books as we have in the books of the Brethren. You have no need, beloved Brethren, to seek for instruction from others. You have enough at home. I exhort you to study what you have already; you will find there all you need." Again the discipline was revived in all its vigour; again, by Augusta's advice, the Catechism of Luke was put into common use, and the Brethren began to open schools and teach their principles to others.

But now their fondest hopes were doomed to be blasted. For the last time Augusta went to Wittenberg to discuss the value of discipline with Luther, and as his stay drew to a close he warned the great man that if the German theologians spent so much time in spinning doctrines and so little time in teaching morals, there was danger brewing ahead. The warning soon came true. The Reformer died. The gathering clouds in Germany burst, and the Smalkald War broke out. The storm swept on to Bohemia. As the Emperor gathered his forces in Germany to crush the Protestant Princes to powder, so Ferdinand in Bohemia summoned his subjects to rally round his standard at Leitmeritz and defend the kingdom and the throne against the Protestant rebels. For the first time in their history the Bohemian Brethren were ordered to take sides in a civil war. The situation was delicate. If they fought for Ferdinand they would be untrue to their faith; if they fought against him they would be disloyal to their country. In this dilemma they did the best they could.

As soon as they could possibly do so, the Elders issued a form of prayer to be used in all their churches. It was a prayer for the kingdom and the throne. [37] But meanwhile others were taking definite sides. At Leitmeritz the Catholics and old-fashioned Utraquists mustered to fight for the King; and at Prague the Protestant nobles met to defend the cause of religious liberty. They met in secret at a Brother's House; they formed a Committee of Safety of eight, and of those eight four were Brethren; and they passed a resolution to defy the King, and send help to the German Protestant leader, John Frederick, Elector of Saxony.

And then the retribution fell like a bolt from the blue. The great battle of Muehlberg was fought (April 24th, 1547); the Protestant troops were routed; the Elector of Saxony was captured; the Emperor was master of Germany, and Ferdinand returned to Prague with vengeance written on his brow. He called a council at Prague Castle, summoned the nobles and knights before him, ordered them to deliver up their treasonable papers, came down on many with heavy fines, and condemned the ringleaders to death.

At eight in the morning, August 22nd, four Barons were led out to execution in Prague, and the scaffold was erected in a public place that all the people might see and learn a lesson. Among the Barons was Wenzel Petipesky, a member of the Brethren's Church. He was to be the first to die. As he was led from his cell by the executioner, he called out in a loud voice, which could be heard far and wide: "My dear Brethren, we go happy in the name of the Lord, for we go in the narrow way." He walked to the scaffold with his hands bound before him, and two boys played his dead march on drums. As he reached the scaffold the drums ceased, and the executioner announced that the prisoner was dying because he had tried to dethrone King Ferdinand and put another King in his place.

"That," said Petipesky, "was never the case."

"Never mind, my Lord," roared the executioner, "it will not help you now."

"My God," said Petipesky, "I leave all to Thee;" and his head rolled on the ground.

But the worst was still to come. As Ferdinand came out of the castle church on Sunday morning, September 18th, he was met by a deputation of Utraquists and Catholics, who besought him to protect them against the cruelties inflicted on them by the Picards. The King soon eased their minds. He had heard a rumour that John Augusta was the real leader of the revolt; he regarded the Brethren as traitors; he no longer felt bound by his promise to spare them; and, therefore, reviving the Edict of St. James, he issued an order that all their meetings should be suppressed, all their property be confiscated, all their churches be purified and transformed into Romanist Chapels, and all their priests be captured and brought to the castle in Prague (Oct. 8th, 1547). The Brethren pleaded not guilty. [38] They had not, as a body, taken any part in the conspiracy against the King. Instead of plotting against him, in fact, they had prayed and fasted in every parish for the kingdom and the throne. If the King, they protested, desired to punish the few guilty Brethren, by all means let him do so; but let him not crush the innocent many for the sake of a guilty few. "My word," replied the King, "is final." The Brethren continued to protest. And the King retorted by issuing an order that all Brethren who lived on Royal estates must either accept the Catholic Faith or leave the country before six weeks were over (May, 1548).

And never was King more astounded and staggered than Ferdinand at the result of this decree.

Chapter 9: The Brethren in Poland (1548-1570)

IT is easy to see what Ferdinand expected. He had no desire to shed more blood; he wished to see Bohemia at peace; he knew that the Brethren, with all their skill, could never sell out in six weeks; and therefore he hoped that, like sensible men, they would abandon their Satanic follies, consider the comfort of their wives and children, and nestle snugly in the bosom of the Church of Rome. But the Brethren had never learned the art of dancing to Ferdinand's piping. As the King would not extend the time, they took him at his word. The rich came to the help of the poor, [39] and before the six weeks had flown away a large band of Brethren had bidden a sad farewell to their old familiar haunts and homes, and started on their journey north across the pine-clad hills. From Leitomischl, Chlumitz and Solnic, by way of Frankenstein and Breslau, and from Turnau and Brandeis-on-the-Adler across the Giant Mountains, they marched in two main bodies from Bohemia to Poland. The time was the leafy month of June, and the first part of the journey was pleasant. "We were borne," says one, "on eagles' wings." As they tramped along the country roads, with wagons for the women, old men and children, they made the air ring with the gladsome music of old Brethren's hymns and their march was more like a triumphal procession than the flight of persecuted refugees. They were nearly two thousand in number. They had hundreds with them, both Catholic and Protestant, to protect them against the mountain brigands. They had guards of infantry and cavalry. They were freed from toll at the turn-pikes. They were supplied with meat, bread, milk and eggs by the simple country peasants. They were publicly welcomed and entertained by the Mayor and Council of Glatz. As the news of their approach ran on before, the good folk in the various towns and villages would sweep the streets and clear the road to let them pass with speed and safety to their desired haven far away. For two months they enjoyed themselves at Posen, and the Polish nobles welcomed them as Brothers; but the Bishop regarded them as wolves in the flock, and had them ordered away. From Posen they marched to Polish Prussia, and were ordered away again; and not till the autumn leaves had fallen and the dark long nights had come did they find a home in the town of Koenigsberg, in the Lutheran Duchy of East Prussia.

And even there they were almost worried to death. As they settled down as peaceful citizens in this Protestant land of light and liberty, they found, to their horror and dismay, that Lutherans, when it suited their purpose, could be as bigoted as Catholics. They were forced to accept the Confession of Augsburg. They were forbidden to ordain their own priests or practise their own peculiar customs. They were treated, not as Protestant brothers, but as highly suspicious foreigners; and a priest of the Brethren was not allowed to visit a member of his flock unless he took a Lutheran pastor with him. "If you stay with us," said Speratus, the Superintendent of the East Prussian Lutheran Church, "you must accommodate yourselves to our ways. Nobody sent for you; nobody asked you to come." If the Brethren, in a word, were to stay in East Prussia, they must cease to be Brethren at all, and allow themselves to be absorbed by the conquering Lutherans of the land.

Meanwhile, however, they had a Moses to lead them out of the desert. George Israel is a type of the ancient Brethren. He was the son of a blacksmith, was a close friend of Augusta, had been with him at Wittenberg, and was now the second great leader of the Brethren. When Ferdinand issued his decree, Israel, like many of the Brethren's Ministers, was summoned to Prague to answer for his faith and conduct on pain of a fine of one thousand ducats; and when some of his friends advised him to disobey the summons, and even offered to pay the money, he gave one of those sublime answers which light up the gloom of the time. "No," he replied, "I have been purchased once and for all with the blood of Christ, and will not consent to be ransomed with the gold and silver of my people. Keep what you have, for you will need it in your flight, and pray for me that I may be steadfast in suffering for Jesus." He went to Prague, confessed his faith, and was thrown into the White Tower. But he was loosely guarded, and one day, disguised as a clerk, with a pen behind his ear, and paper and ink-horn in his hand, he walked out of the Tower in broad daylight through the midst of his guards, and joined the Brethren in Prussia. He was just the man to guide the wandering band, and the Council appointed him leader of the emigrants. He was energetic and brave. He could speak the Polish tongue. He had a clear head and strong limbs. For him a cold lodging in Prussia was not enough. He would lead his Brethren to a better land, and give them nobler work to do.

As the Brethren had already been driven from Poland, the task which Israel now undertook appeared an act of folly. But George Israel knew better. For a hundred years the people of Poland had sympathised to some extent with the reforming movement in Bohemia. There Jerome of Prague had taught. There the teaching of Hus had spread. There the people hated the Church of Rome. There the nobles sent their sons to study under Luther at Wittenberg. There the works of Luther and Calvin had been printed and spread in secret. There, above all, the Queen herself had been privately taught the Protestant faith by her own father-confessor. And there, thought Israel, the Brethren in time would find a hearty welcome. And so, while still retaining the oversight of a few parishes in East Prussia, George Israel, by commission of the Council, set out to conduct a mission in Poland (1551). Alone and on horseback, by bad roads and swollen streams, he went on his dangerous journey; and on the fourth Sunday in Lent arrived at the town of Thorn, and rested for the day. Here occurred the famous incident on the ice which made his name remembered in Thorn for many a year to come. As he was walking on the frozen river to try whether the ice was strong enough to bear his horse, the ice broke up with a crash. George Israel was left on a solitary lump, and was swept whirling down the river; and then, as the ice blocks cracked and banged and splintered into thousands of fragments, he sprang like a deer from block to block, and sang with loud exulting voice: "Praise the Lord from the earth, ye dragons and all deeps; fire and hail, snow and vapour, stormy wind fulfilling his word." There was a great crowd on the bank. The people watched the thrilling sight with awe, and when at last he reached firm ground they welcomed him with shouts of joy. We marvel not that such a man was like the sword of Gideon in the conflict. He rode on to Posen, the capital of Great Poland, began holding secret meetings, and established the first evangelical church in the country. The Roman Catholic Bishop heard of his arrival, and put forty assassins on his track. But Israel was a man of many wiles as well as a man of God. He assumed disguises, and changed his clothes so as to baffle pursuit, appearing now as an officer, now as a coachman, now as a cook. He presented himself at the castle of the noble family of the Ostrorogs, was warmly welcomed by the Countess, and held a service in her rooms. The Count was absent, heard the news, and came in a state of fury. He seized a whip. "I will drag my wife out of this conventicle," he exclaimed; and burst into the room while the service was proceeding, his eyes flashing fire and the whip swinging in his hand. The preacher, Cerwenka, calmly went on preaching. "Sir," said George Israel, pointing to an empty seat "sit down there." The Count of Ostrorog meekly obeyed, listened quietly to the discourse, became a convert that very day, turned out his own Lutheran Court Chaplain, installed George Israel in his place, and made a present to the Brethren of his great estate on the outskirts of the town.

For the Brethren the gain was enormous. As the news of the Count's conversion spread, other nobles quickly followed suit. The town of Ostrorog became the centre of a swiftly growing movement; the poor Brethren in Prussia returned to Poland, and found churches ready for their use; and before seven years had passed away the Brethren had founded forty congregations in this their first land of exile.

They had, however, another great mission to fulfil. As the Brethren spread from town to town, they discovered that the other Protestant bodies—the Lutherans, Zwinglians and Calvinists—were almost as fond of fighting with each other as of denouncing the Church of Rome; and therefore the people, longing for peace, were disgusted more or less with them all. But the Brethren stood on a rather different footing. They were cousins to the Poles in blood; they had no fixed and definite creed; they thought far more of brotherly love than of orthodoxy in doctrine; and therefore the idea was early broached that the Church of the Brethren should be established as the National Church of Poland. The idea grew. The Lutherans, Zwinglians, Calvinists and Brethren drew closer and closer together. They exchanged confessions, discussed each other's doctrines, met in learned consultations, and held united synods again and again. For fifteen years the glorious vision of a union of all the Protestants in Poland hung like glittering fruit just out of reach. There were many walls in the way. Each church wanted to be the leading church in Poland; each wanted its own confession to be the bond of union; each wanted its own form of service, its own form of government, to be accepted by all. But soon one and all began to see that the time had come for wranglings to cease. The Jesuits were gaining ground in Poland. The Protestant Kingdom must no longer be divided against itself.

At last the Brethren, the real movers of the scheme, persuaded all to assemble in the great United Synod of Sendomir, and all Protestants in Poland felt that the fate of the country depended on the issue of the meeting (1570). It was the greatest Synod that had ever been held in Poland. It was an attempt to start a new movement in the history of the Reformation, an attempt to fling out the apple of discord and unite all Protestants in one grand army which should carry the enemy's forts by storm. At first the goal seemed further off than ever. As the Calvinists were the strongest body, they confidently demanded that their Confession should be accepted, and put forward the telling argument that it was already in use in the country. As the Lutherans were the next strongest body, they offered the Augsburg Confession, and both parties turned round upon the Brethren, and accused them of having so many Confessions that no one knew which to take. And then young Turnovius, the representative of the Brethren, rose to speak. The Brethren, he said, had only one Confession in Poland. They had presented that Confession to the King; they believed that it was suited best to the special needs of the country, and yet they would accept the Calvinists' Confession as long as they might keep their own as well.

There was a deadlock. What was to be done? The Brethren's work seemed about to come to nought. Debates and speeches were in vain. Each party remained firm as a rock. And then, in wondrous mystic wise, the tone of the gathering softened.

"For God's sake, for God's sake," said the Palatine of Sendomir in his speech, "remember what depends upon the result of our deliberations, and incline your hearts to that harmony and love which the Lord has commanded us to follow above all things."

As the Palatine ended his speech he burst into tears. His friend, the Palatine of Cracow, sobbed aloud. Forthwith the angry clouds disparted and revealed the bow of peace, the obstacles to union vanished, and the members of the Synod agreed to draw up a new Confession, which should give expression to the united faith of all. The Confession was prepared (April 14th). It is needless to trouble about the doctrinal details. For us the important point to notice is the spirit of union displayed. For the first, but not for the last, time in the history of Poland the Evangelical Protestants agreed to sink their differences on points of dispute, and unite their forces in common action against alike the power of Rome and the Unitarian [40] sects of the day. The joy was universal. The scene in the hall at Sendomir was inspiring. When the Committee laid the Confession before the Synod all the members arose and sang the Ambrosian Te Deum. With outstretched hands the Lutherans advanced to meet the Brethren, and with outstretched hands the Brethren advanced to meet the Lutherans. The next step was to make the union public. For this purpose the Brethren, a few weeks later, formed a procession one Sunday morning and attended service at the Lutheran Church; and then, in the afternoon, the Lutherans attended service in the Church of the Brethren (May 28th, 1570). It is hard to believe that all this was empty show. And yet the truth must be confessed that this "Union of Sendomir" was by no means the beautiful thing that some writers have imagined. It was the result, to a very large extent, not of any true desire for unity, but rather of an attempt on the part of the Polish nobles to undermine the influence and power of the clergy. It led to no permanent union of the Protestants in Poland. Its interest is sentimental rather than historic. For the time—but for a very short time only—the Brethren had succeeded in teaching others a little charity of spirit, and had thus shown their desire to hasten the day when the Churches of Christ, no longer asunder, shall know "how good and how pleasant it is for Brethren to dwell together in unity."

And all this—this attempt at unity, this second home for the Brethren, this new Evangelical movement in Poland—was the strange result of the edict issued by Ferdinand, King of Bohemia.

Chapter 10: The Matyr-Bishop (1548-1560)

MEANWHILE, John Augusta, the great leader of the Brethren, was passing through the furnace of affliction.

Of all the tools employed by Ferdinand, the most crafty, active and ambitious was a certain officer named Sebastian Schoeneich, who, in the words of the great historian, Gindely, was one of those men fitted by nature for the post of hangman.

For some months this man had distinguished himself by his zeal in the cause of the King. He had seized sixteen heads of families for singing hymns at a baker's funeral, had thrown them into the drain-vaults of the White Tower at Prague, and had left them there to mend their ways in the midst of filth and horrible stenches. And now he occupied the proud position of town-captain of Leitomischl. Never yet had he known such a golden chance of covering himself with glory. For some time Augusta, who was now First Senior of the Church, had been hiding in the neighbouring woods, and only two or three Brethren knew his exact abode. But already persecution had done her work, and treachery now did hers.

Among the inhabitants of Leitomischl were certain renegade Brethren, and these now said to the Royal Commissioners: "If the King could only capture and torture Augusta, he could unearth the whole conspiracy."

"Where is Augusta?" asked the Commissioners.

"He is not at home," replied the traitors, "but if you will ask his friend, Jacob Bilek, he will tell you all you want to know."

The wily Schoeneich laid his plot. If only he could capture Augusta, he would win the favour of the King and fill his own pockets with money. As he strolled one day through the streets of Leitomischl he met a certain innocent Brother Henry, and there and then began his deadly work.

"If you know," he said, "where Augusta is, tell him I desire an interview with him. I will meet him wherever he likes. I have something special to say to him, something good, not only for him, but for the whole Brethren's Church. But breathe not a word of this to anyone else. Not a soul—not even yourself—must know about the matter."

The message to Augusta was sent. He replied that he would grant the interview on condition that Schoeneich would guarantee his personal safety.

"That," replied Schoeneich, "is quite impossible. I cannot give any security whatever. The whole business must be perfectly secret. Not a soul must be present but Augusta and myself. I wouldn't have the King know about this for a thousand groschen. Tell Augusta not to be afraid of me. I have no instructions concerning him. He can come with an easy mind to Leitomischl. If he will not trust me as far as that, let him name the place himself, and I will go though it be a dozen miles away."

But Augusta still returned the same answer, and Schoeneich had to strengthen his plea. Again he met the guileless Brother Henry, and again he stormed him with his eloquent tongue.

"Have you no better answer from Augusta?" he asked.

"No," replied Brother Henry.

"My dear, my only Henry," pleaded Schoeneich, "I do so long for a little chat with Augusta. My heart bleeds with sympathy for you. I am expecting the King's Commissioners. They may be here any moment. It will go hard with you poor folk when they come. If only I could have a talk with Augusta, it would be so much better for you all. But do tell him not to be afraid of me. I have no instructions concerning him. I will wager my neck for that," he said, putting his finger to his throat. "I am willing to give my life for you poor Brethren."

The shot went home. As Augusta lay in his safe retreat he had written stirring letters to the Brethren urging them to be true to their colours; and now, he heard from his friends in Leitomischl that Schoeneich was an evangelical saint, and that if he would only confer with the saint he might render his Brethren signal service, and deliver them from their distresses. He responded nobly to the appeal. For the sake of the Church he had led so long, he would risk his liberty and his life. In vain the voice of prudence said "Stay!"; the voice of love said "Go!"; and Augusta agreed to meet the Captain in a wood three miles from the town. The Captain chuckled. The time was fixed, and, the night before, the artful plotter sent three of his trusty friends to lie in wait. As the morning broke of the fateful day (April 25th, 1548), Augusta, still suspecting a trap, sent his secretary, Jacob Bilek, in advance to spy the land; and the three brave men sprang out upon him and carried him off to Schoeneich. And then, at the appointed hour, came John Augusta himself. He had dressed himself as a country peasant, carried a hoe in is hand, and strolled in the woodland whistling a merry tune. For the moment the hirelings were baffled. They seized him and let him go; they seized him again and let him go again; they seized him, for the third time, searched him, and found a fine handkerchief in his bosom.

"Ah," said one of them, "a country peasant does not use a handkerchief like this."

The game was up. Augusta stood revealed, and Schoeneich, hearing the glorious news, came prancing up on his horse.

"My lord," said Augusta, "is this what you call faith?"

"Did you never hear," said Schoeneich, "that promises made in the night are never binding? Did you never hear of a certain Jew with his red beard and yellow bag? Did you never hear of the mighty power of money? And where have you come from this morning? I hear you have plenty of money in your possession. Where is that money now?"

As they rode next day in a covered waggon on their way to the city of Prague, the Captain pestered Augusta with many questions.

"My dear Johannes," said the jovial wag, "where have you been? With whom? Where are your letters and your clothes? Whose is this cap? Where did you get it? Who lent it to you? What do they call him? Where does he live? Where is your horse? Where is your money? Where are your companions?"

"Why do you ask so many questions?" asked Augusta.

"Because," replied Schoeneich, letting out the murder, "I want to be able to give information about you. I don't want to be called a donkey or a calf."

And now began for John Augusta a time of terrible testing. As the Captain rapped his questions out he was playing his part in a deadly game that involved the fate, not only of the Brethren's Church, but of all evangelicals in the land.

For months King Ferdinand had longed to capture Augusta. He regarded him as the author of the Smalkald League; he regarded him as the deadliest foe of the Catholic faith in Europe; he regarded the peaceful Brethren as rebels of the vilest kind; and now that he had Augusta in his power he determined to make him confess the plot, and then, with the proof he desired in his hands, he would stamp out the Brethren's Church for once and all.

For this purpose Augusta was now imprisoned in the White Tower at Prague. He was placed in the wine vaults below the castle, had heavy fetters on his hands and feet, and sat for days in a crunched position. The historic contest began. For two hours at a stretch the King's examiners riddled Augusta with questions. "Who sent the letter to the King?" [41] they asked. "Where do the Brethren keep their papers and money? To whom did the Brethren turn for help when the King called on his subjects to support him? Who went with you to Wittenberg? For what and for whom did the Brethren pray."

"They prayed," said Augusta, "that God would incline the heart of the King to be gracious to us."

"By what means did the Brethren defend themselves?"

"By patience," replied Augusta.

"To whom did they apply for help?"

Augusta pointed to heaven.

As Augusta's answers to all these questions were not considered satisfactory, they next endeavoured to sharpen his wits by torturing a German coiner in his presence; and when this mode of persuasion failed, they tortured Augusta himself. They stripped him naked. They stretched him face downwards on a ladder. They smeared his hips with boiling pitch. They set the spluttering mess on fire, and drew it off, skin and all, with a pair of tongs. They screwed him tightly in the stocks. They hung him up to the ceiling by a hook, with the point run through his flesh. They laid him flat upon his back and pressed great stones on his stomach. It was all in vain. Again they urged him to confess the part that he and the Brethren had played in the great revolt, and again Augusta bravely replied that the Brethren had taken no such part at all.

At this the King himself intervened. For some months he had been busy enough at Augsburg, assisting the Emperor in his work; but now he sent a letter to Prague, with full instructions how to deal with Augusta. If gentle measures did not succeed, then sterner measures, said he, must be employed. He had three new tortures to suggest. First, he said, let Augusta be watched and deprived of sleep for five or six days. Next, he must be strapped to a shutter, with his head hanging over one end; he must have vinegar rubbed into his nostrils; he must have a beetle fastened on to his stomach; and in this position, with his neck aching, his nostrils smarting, and the beetle working its way to his vitals, he must be kept for two days and two nights. And, third, if these measures did not act, he must be fed with highly seasoned food and allowed nothing to drink.

But these suggestions were never carried out. As the messenger hastened with the King's billet-doux, and the Brethren on the northern frontier were setting out for Poland, Augusta and Bilek were on their way to the famous old castle of Puerglitz. For ages that castle, built on a rock, and hidden away in darkling woods, had been renowned in Bohemian lore. There the mother of Charles IV. had heard the nightingales sing; there the faithful, ran the story, had held John Ziska at bay; there had many a rebel suffered in the terrible "torture-tower"; and there Augusta and his faithful friend were to lie for many a long and weary day.

They were taken to Puerglitz in two separate waggons. They travelled by night and arrived about mid-day; they were placed in two separate cells, and for sixteen years the fortunes of the Brethren centred round Puerglitz Castle.

If the Bishop had been the vilest criminal, he could not have been more grossly insulted. For two years he had to share his cell with a vulgar German coiner; and the coiner, in facetious pastime, often smote him on the head.

His cell was almost pitch-dark. The window was shuttered within and without, and the merest glimmer from the cell next door struggled in through a chink four inches broad. At meals alone he was permitted half a candle. For bedding he had a leather bolster, a coverlet and what Germans call a "bed-sack." For food he was allowed two rations of meat, two hunches of bread, and two jugs of barley-beer a day. His shirt was washed about once a fortnight, his face and hands twice a week, his head twice a year, and the rest of his body never. He was not allowed the use of a knife and fork. He was not allowed to speak to the prison attendants. He had no books, no papers, no ink, no news of the world without; and there for three years he sat in the dark, as lonely as the famous prisoner of Chillon. Again, by the King's command, he was tortured, with a gag in his mouth to stifle his screams and a threat that if he would not confess he should have an interview with the hangman; and again he refused to deny his Brethren, and was flung back into his corner.

The delivering angel came in humble guise. Among the warders who guarded his cell was a daring youth who had lived at Leitomischl. He had been brought up among the Brethren. He regarded the Bishop as a martyr. His wife lived in a cottage near the castle; and now, drunken rascal though he was, he risked his life for Augusta's sake, used his cottage as a secret post office, and handed in to the suffering Bishop letters, books, ink, paper, pens, money and candles.

The Brethren stationed a priest in Puerglitz village. The great Bishop was soon as bright and active as ever. By day he buried his tools in the ground; by night he plugged every chink and cranny, and applied himself to his labours. Not yet was his spirit broken; not yet was his mind unhinged. As his candle burned in that gloomy dungeon in the silent watches of the night, so the fire of his genius shone anew in those darksome days of trial and persecution; and still he urged his afflicted Brethren to be true to the faith of their fathers, to hold fast the Apostles' Creed, and to look onward to the brighter day when once again their pathway would shine as the wings of a dove that are covered with silver and her feathers with yellow gold. He comforted Bilek in his affliction; he published a volume of sermons for the elders to read in secret; he composed a number of stirring and triumphant hymns; and there he penned the noble words still sung in the Brethren's Church:—

Praise God for ever.
Boundless is his favour,
To his Church and chosen flock,
Founded on Christ the Rock.

As he lay in his cell he pondered much on the sad fate of his Brethren. At one time he heard a rumour that the Church was almost extinct. Some, he knew, had fled to Poland. Some had settled in Moravia. Some, robbed of lands and houses, were roaming the country as pedlars or earning a scanty living as farm labourers. And some, alas! had lowered the flag and joined the Church of Rome.

And yet Augusta had never abandoned hope. For ten years, despite a few interruptions, he kept in almost constant touch, not only with his own Brethren, but also with the Protestant world at large. He was still, he thought, the loved and honoured leader; he was still the mightiest religious force in the land; and now, in his dungeon, he sketched a plan to heal his country's woes and form the true disciples of Christ into one grand national Protestant army against which both Pope and Emperor would for ever contend in vain.

Chapter 11: The Last Days of Augusta (1560-1572)

TO Augusta the prospect seemed hopeful. Great changes had taken place in the Protestant world. The Lutherans in Germany had triumphed. The religious peace of Augsburg had been consummated, The German Protestants had now a legal standing. The great Emperor, Charles V., had resigned his throne. His successor was his brother Ferdinand, the late King of Bohemia. The new King of Bohemia was Ferdinand's eldest son, Maximilian I. Maximilian was well disposed towards Protestants, and persecution in Bohemia died away.

And now the Brethren plucked up heart again. They rebuilt their chapel at their headquarters, Jungbunzlau. They presented a copy of their Hymn-book to the King. They divided the Church into three provinces—Bohemia, Moravia and Poland. They appointed George Israel First Senior in Poland, John Czerny First Senior in Bohemia and Moravia, and Cerwenka secretary to the whole Church.

But the Brethren had gone further still. As Augusta was the sole surviving Bishop in the Church, the Brethren were in a difficulty. They must not be without Bishops. But what were they to do? Were they to wait till Augusta was set at liberty, or were they to elect new Bishops without his authority? They chose the latter course, and Augusta was deeply offended. They elected Czerny and Cerwenka to the office of Bishops; they had them consecrated as Bishops by two Brethren in priests' orders; and they actually allowed the two new Bishops to consecrate two further Bishops, George Israel and Blahoslaw, the Church Historian.

And even this was not the worst of the story. As he lay in his dungeon forming plans for the Church he loved so well, it slowly dawned upon Augusta that his Brethren were ceasing to trust him, and that the sun of his power, which had shone so brightly, was now sloping slowly to its setting. He heard of one change after another taking place without his consent. He heard that the Council had condemned his sermons as too learned and dry for the common people, and that they had altered them to suit their own opinions. He heard that his hymns, which he had desired to see in the new Hymn-book, had been mangled in a similar manner. His Brethren did not even tell him what they were doing. They simply left him out in the cold. What he himself heard he heard by chance, and that was the "most unkind cut of all." His authority was gone; his position was lost; his hopes were blasted; and his early guidance, his entreaties, his services, his sufferings were all, he thought, forgotten by an ungrateful Church.

As Augusta heard of all these changes, a glorious vision rose before his mind. At first he was offended, quarrelled with the Brethren, and declared the new Bishops invalid. But at last his better feelings gained the mastery. He would not sulk like a petted child; he would render his Brethren the greatest service in his power. He would fight his way to liberty; he would resume his place on the bridge, and before long he would make the Church the national Church of Bohemia.

The door was opened by a duke. The Archduke Ferdinand, brother of the King, came to reside at Puerglitz (1560). Augusta appealed for liberty to Ferdinand; the Archduke referred the matter to the King; the King referred the matter to the clergy; and the clergy drew up for Augusta's benefit a form of recantation. The issue before him was now perfectly clear. There was one road to freedom and one only. He must sign the form of recantation in full. The form was drastic. He must renounce all his previous religious opinions. He must acknowledge the Holy Catholic Church and submit to her in all things. He must eschew the gatherings of Waldenses, Picards and all other apostates, denounce their teaching as depraved, and recognise the Church of Rome as the one true Church of Christ. He must labour for the unity of the Church and endeavour to bring his Brethren into the fold. He must never again interpret the Scriptures according to his own understanding, but submit rather to the exposition and authority of the Holy Roman Church, which alone was fit to decide on questions of doctrine. He must do his duty by the King, obey him and serve him with zeal as a loyal subject. And finally he must write out the whole recantation with his own hand, take a public oath to keep it, and have it signed and sealed by witnesses. Augusta refused point blank. His hopes of liberty vanished. His heart sank in despair. "They might as well," said Bilek, his friend, "have asked him to walk on his head."

But here Lord Sternberg, Governor of the Castle, suggested another path. If Augusta, said he, would not join the Church of Rome, perhaps he would at least join the Utraquists. He had been a Utraquist in his youth; the Brethren were Utraquists under another name; and all that Augusta had to do was to give himself his proper name, and his dungeon door would fly open. Of all the devices to entrap Augusta, this well-meant trick was the most enticing. The argument was a shameless logical juggle. The Utraquists celebrated the communion in both kinds; the Brethren celebrated the communion in both kinds; therefore the Brethren were Utraquists. [42] At first Augusta himself appeared to be caught.

"I, John Augusta," he wrote, "confess myself a member of the whole Evangelical Church, which, wherever it may be, receives the body and blood of the Lord Jesus Christ in both kinds. I swear that, along with the Holy Catholic Church, I will maintain true submission and obedience to her chief Head, Jesus Christ. I will order my life according to God's holy word and the truth of his pure Gospel. I will be led by Him, obey Him alone, and by no other human thoughts and inventions. I renounce all erroneous and wicked opinions against the holy universal Christian apostolic faith. I will never take any part in the meetings of Picards or other heretics."

If Augusta thought that by language like this he would catch his examiners napping, he was falling into a very grievous error. He had chosen his words with care. He never said what he meant by the Utraquists. He never said whether he would include the

Brethren among the Utraquists or among the Picards and heretics. And he had never made any reference to the Pope.

His examiners were far too clever to be deceived. Instead of recommending that Augusta be now set at liberty, they contended that his recantation was no recantation at all. He had shown no inclination, they said, towards either Rome or Utraquism. His principles were remarkably like those of Martin Luther. He had not acknowledged the supremacy of the Pope, and when he said he would not be led by any human inventions he was plainly repudiating the Church of Rome. What is the good, they asked, of Augusta's promising to resist heretics when he does not acknowledge the Brethren to be heretics? "It is," they said, "as clear as day that John Augusta has no real intention of renouncing his errors." Let the man say straight out to which party he belonged.

Again Augusta tried to fence, and again he met his match. Instead of saying in plain language to which party he belonged, he persisted in his first assertion that he belonged to the Catholic Evangelical Church, which was now split into various sects. But as the old man warmed to his work he threw caution aside.

"I have never," he said, "had anything to do with Waldenses or Picards. I belong to the general Evangelical Church, which enjoys the Communion in both kinds. I renounce entirely the Popish sect known as the Holy Roman Church. I deny that the Pope is the Vicar of Christ. I deny that the Church of Rome alone has authority to interpret the Scriptures. If the Church of Rome claims such authority, she must first show that she is free from the spirit of the world, and possesses the spirit of charity, and until that is done I refuse to bow to her decrees."

He defended the Church of the Brethren with all his might. It was, he said, truly evangelical. It was Catholic. It was apostolic. It was recognised and praised by Luther, Calvin, Melancthon, Bucer, Bullinger and other saints. As long as the moral life of the Church of Rome remained at such a low ebb, so long would there be need for the Brethren's Church.

"If the Church of Rome will mend her ways, the Brethren," said he, "will return to her fold; but till that blessed change takes place they will remain where they are."

He denied being a traitor. "If any one says that I have been disloyal to the Emperor, I denounce that person as a liar. If his Majesty knew how loyal I have been, he would not keep me here another hour. I know why I am suffering. I am suffering, not as an evil-doer, but as a Christian."

The first skirmish was over. The clergy were firm, and Augusta sank back exhausted in his cell. But the kindly Governor was still resolved to smooth the way for his prisoners. "I will not rest," he said, "till I see them at liberty." He suggested that Augusta should have an interview with the Jesuits!

"What would be the good of that?" said Augusta. "I should be like a little dog in the midst of a pack of lions. I pray you, let these negotiations cease. I would rather stay where I am. It is clear there is no escape for me unless I am false to my honour and my conscience. I will never recant nor act against my conscience. May God help me to keep true till death."

At last, however, Augusta gave way, attended Mass, with Bilek, in the castle chapel, and consented to an interview with the Jesuits, on condition that Bilek should go with him, and that he should also be allowed another interview with the Utraquists (1561). The day for the duel arrived. The chosen spot was the new Jesuit College at Prague. As they drove to the city both Augusta and Bilek were allowed to stretch their limbs and even get out of sight of their guards. At Prague they were allowed a dip in the Royal Bath. It was the first bath they had had for fourteen years, and the people came from far and near to gaze upon their scars.

And now, being fresh and clean in body, Augusta, the stubborn heretical Picard, was to be made clean in soul. As the Jesuits were determined to do their work well, they laid down the strict condition that no one but themselves must be allowed to speak with the prisoners. For the rest the prisoners were treated kindly. The bedroom was neat; the food was good; the large, bright dining-room had seven windows. They had wine to dinner, and were waited on by a discreet and silent butler. Not a word did that solemn functionary utter. If the Brethren made a remark to him, he laid his fingers on his lips like the witches in Macbeth.

The great debate began. The Jesuit spokesman was Dr. Henry Blissem. He opened by making a clean breast of the whole purpose of the interview.

"It is well known to you both," said he, "for what purpose you have been handed over to our care, that we, if possible, may help you to a right understanding of the Christian faith."

If the Jesuits could have had their way, they would have had Augusta's answers set down in writing. But here Augusta stood firm as a rock. He knew the game the Jesuits were playing. The interview was of national importance. If his answers were considered satisfactory, the Jesuits would have them printed, sow them broadcast, and boast of his conversion; and if, on the other hand, they were unsatisfactory, they would send them to the Emperor as proof that Augusta was a rebel, demand his instant execution, and start another persecution of the Brethren.

Dr. Henry, made the first pass.

"The Holy Universal Church," he said, "is the true bride of Christ and the true mother of all Christians."

Augusta politely agreed.

"On this is question," he said, "our own party thinks and believes exactly as you do."

"No one," continued the doctor suavely, "can believe in God who does not think correctly of the Holy Church, and regard her as his mother; and without the Church there is no salvation."

Again Augusta politely agreed, and again the learned Jesuit beamed with pleasure. Now came the tug of war.

"This Holy Christian Church," said Blissem, "has never erred and cannot err."

Augusta met this with a flat denial. If he surrendered here he surrendered all, and would be untrue to his Brethren. If he once agreed that the Church was infallible he was swallowing the whole Roman pill. In vain the doctor argued. Augusta held his ground. The Jesuits reported him hard in the head, and had him sent back to his cell.

For two more years he waited in despair, and then he was brought to the White Tower again, and visited by two Utraquist Priests, Mystopol and Martin. His last chance, they told him, had now arrived. They had come as messengers from the Archduke Ferdinand and from the Emperor himself.

"I know," said one of them, "on what you are relying and how you console yourself, but I warn you it will avail you nothing."

"You know no secrets," said Augusta.

"What secrets?" queried Mystopol.

"Neither divine nor mine. My dear administrators, your visit is quite a surprise! With regard to the recantation, however, let me say at once, I shall not sign it! I have never been guilty of any errors, and have nothing to recant. I made my public confession of faith before the lords and knights of Bohemia twenty-eight years ago. It was shown to the Emperor at Vienna, and no one has ever found anything wrong with it."

"How is it," said Mystopol, "you cannot see your error? You know it says in our confession, I believe in the Holy Catholic Church.' You Brethren have fallen away from that Church. You are not true members of the body. You are an ulcer. You are a scab. You have no sacraments. You have written bloodthirsty pamphlets against us. We have a whole box full of your productions."

"We never wrote any tracts," said Augusta, "except to show why we separated from you, but you urged on the Government against us. You likened me to a bastard and to Goliath the Philistine. Your petition read as if it had been written in a brothel."

And now the character of John Augusta shone forth in all its grandeur. The old man was on his mettle.

"Of all Christians known to me," he said, "the Brethren stick closest to Holy Writ. Next to them come the Lutherans; next to the Lutherans the Utraquists; and next to the Utraquists the—!"

But there in common honesty he had to stop. And then he turned the tables on Mystopol, and came out boldly with his scheme. It was no new idea of his. He had already, in 1547, advocated a National Protestant Church composed of Utraquists and Brethren. Instead of the Brethren joining the Utraquists, it was, said Augusta, the plain duty of the Utraquists to break from the Church of Rome and join the Brethren. For the last forty years the Utraquists had been really Lutherans at heart. He wanted them now to be true to their own convictions. He wanted them to carry out in practice the teaching of most of their preachers. He wanted them to run the risk of offending the Emperor and the Pope. He wanted them to ally themselves with the Brethren; and he believed that if they would only do so nearly every soul in Bohemia would join the new Evangelical movement. De Schweinitz says that Augusta betrayed his Brethren, and that when he called himself a Utraquist he was playing with words. I cannot accept this verdict. He explained clearly and precisely what he meant; he was a Utraquist in the same sense as Luther; and the castle he had built in the air was nothing less than a grand international union of all the Evangelical Christians in Europe.

"My lords," he pleaded in golden words, "let us cease this mutual accusation of each other. Let us cease our destructive quarrelling. Let us join in seeking those higher objects which we both have in common, and let us remember that we are both of one origin, one nation, one blood and one spirit. Think of it, dear lords, and try to find some way to union."

The appeal was pathetic and sincere. It fell on adders' ears. His scheme found favour neither with Brethren nor with Utraquists. To the Brethren Augusta was a Jesuitical juggler. To the Utraquists he was a supple athlete trying to dodge his way out of prison.

"You shift about," wrote the Brethren, "in a most remarkable manner. You make out the Utraquist Church to be different from what it really is, in order to keep a door open through which you may go." In their judgment he was nothing less than an ambitious schemer. If his scheme were carried out, they said, he would not only be First Elder of the Brethren's Church, but administrator of the whole united Church.

At last, however, King Maximilian interceded with the Emperor in his favour, and Augusta was set free on the one condition that he would not preach in public (1564). His hair was white; his beard was long; his brow was furrowed; his health was shattered; and he spent his last days amongst the Brethren, a defeated and broken-hearted man. He was restored to his old position as First Elder; he settled down again at Jungbunzlau; and yet somehow the old confidence was never completely restored. In vain he upheld his daring scheme of union. John Blahoslaw opposed him to the teeth. For the time, at least, John Blahoslaw was in the right. Augusta throughout had made one fatal blunder. As the Utraquists were now more Protestant in doctrine he thought that they had begun to love the Brethren. The very contrary was the case. If two people agree in nine points out of ten, and only differ in one, they will often quarrel more fiercely with each other than if they disagreed in all the ten. And that was just what happened in Bohemia. The more Protestant the Utraquists became in doctrine, the more jealous they were of the Brethren. And thus Augusta was honoured by neither party. Despised by friend and foe alike, the old white-haired Bishop tottered to the silent tomb. "He kept out of our way," says the sad old record, "as long as he could; he had been among us long enough." As we think of the noble life he lived, and the bitter gall of his eventide, we may liken him to one of those majestic mountains which tower in grandeur under the noontide sun, but round whose brows the vapours gather as night settles down on the earth. In the whole gallery of Bohemian portraits there is none, says Gindely, so noble in expression as his; and as we gaze on those grand features we see dignity blended with sorrow, and pride with heroic fire. [43]

Chapter 12: The Golden Age (1572-1603)

AS the Emperor Maximilian II. set out from the Royal Castle in Prague for a drive he met a baron famous in all the land (1575). The baron was John von Zerotin, the richest member of the Brethren's Church. He had come to Prague on very important business. His home lay at Namiest, in Moravia. He lived in a stately castle, built on two huge crags, and surrounded by the houses of his retainers and domestics. His estate was twenty-five miles square. He had a lovely park of beeches, pines and old oaks. He held his court in kingly style. He had gentlemen of the chamber of noble birth. He had pages and secretaries, equerries and masters of the chase. He had valets, lackeys, grooms, stable-boys, huntsmen, barbers, watchmen, cooks, tailors, shoemakers, and saddlers. He had sat at the feet of Blahoslaw, the learned Church historian: he kept a Court Chaplain, who was, of course, a pastor of the Brethren's Church; and now he had come to talk things over with the head of the Holy Roman Empire.

The Emperor offered the Baron a seat in his carriage. The Brother and the Emperor drove on side by side.

"I hear," said the Emperor, "that the Picards are giving up their religion and going over to the Utraquists."

The Baron was astounded. He had never, he said, heard the slightest whisper that the Brethren intended to abandon their own Confessions.

"I have heard it," said the Emperor, "as positive fact from Baron Hassenstein himself."

"It is not true," replied Zerotin.

"What, then," said the Emperor, "do the Utraquists mean when they say that they are the true Hussites, and wish me to protect them in their religion?"

"Your gracious Majesty," replied Zerotin, "the Brethren, called Picards, are the true Hussites: they have kept their faith unsullied, as you may see yourself from the Confession they presented to you." [44]

The Emperor looked puzzled. He was waxing old and feeble, and his memory was failing.

"What!" he said, "have the Picards got a Confession?"

He was soon to hear the real truth of the matter. For some months there had sat in Prague a committee of learned divines, who had met for the purpose of drawing up a National Protestant Bohemian Confession. The dream of Augusta seemed to be coming true. The Brethren took their part in the proceedings. "We are striving," said Slawata, one of their deputies, "for peace, love and unity. We have no desire to be censors of dogmas. We leave such matters to theological experts." The Confession [45] was prepared, read out at the Diet, and presented to the Emperor. It was a compromise between the teaching of Luther and the teaching of the Brethren. In its doctrine of justification by faith it followed the teaching of Luther: in its doctrine of the Lord's Supper it inclined to the broader evangelical view of the Brethren. The Emperor attended the Diet in person, and made a notable speech.

"I promise," he said, "on my honour as an Emperor, that I will never oppress or hinder you in the exercise of your religion; and I pledge my word in my own name and also in the name of my successors."

Let us try to grasp the meaning of this performance. As the Edict of St. James was still in force, the Brethren, in the eyes of the law, were still heretics and rebels; they had no legal standing in the country; and at any moment the King in his fury might order them to quit the land once more. But the truth is that the King of Bohemia was now a mere figurehead. The real power lay in the hands of the barons. The barons were Protestant almost to a man.

As the Emperor lay dying a few months later in the castle of Regensburg, he was heard to murmur the words, "The happy time is come." For the Brethren the happy time had come indeed. They knew that the so-called Utraquist Church was Utraquist only in name; they knew that the Bible was read in every village; they knew that Lutheran doctrines were preached in hundreds of Utraquist Churches; they knew that in their own country they had now more friends than foes; and thus, free from the terrors of the law they trod the primrose path of peace and power. We have come to the golden age of the Brethren's Church.

It was the age of material prosperity. As the sun of freedom shone upon their way, the Brethren drifted further still from the old Puritan ascetic ideas of Peter and Gregory the Patriarch. They had now all classes in their ranks. They had seventeen rich and powerful barons, of the stamp of John Zerotin; they had over a hundred and forty knights; they had capitalists, flourishing tradesmen, mayors, and even generals in the Army, and the Lord High Chamberlain now complained that two-thirds of the people in Bohemia were Brethren. [46] Nor was this all. For many years the Brethren had been renowned as the most industrious and prosperous people in the country; and were specially famous for their manufacture of knives. They were noted for their integrity of character, and were able to obtain good situations as managers of estates, houses, wine cellars and mills; and in many of the large settlements, such as Jungbunzlau and Leitomischl, they conducted flourishing business concerns for the benefit of the Church at large. They made their settlements the most prosperous places in the country; they built hospitals; they had a fund for the poor called the Korbona; and on many estates they made themselves so useful that the barons, in their gratitude, set them free from the usual tolls and taxes. To the Brethren business was now a sacred duty. They had seen the evils of poverty, and they did their best to end them. They made no hard and fast distinction between secular and sacred; and the cooks and housemaids in the Brethren's Houses were appointed by the Church, and called from one sphere of service to another, just as much as the presbyters and deacons. The clergy, though still doing manual labour, were now rather better off: the gardens and fields attached to the manses helped to swell their income; and, therefore, we are not surprised to hear that some of them were married.

Again, the Brethren were champions of education. They had seen the evil of their ways. As the exiles banished by Ferdinand I. came into contact with Lutherans in Prussia they heard, rather to their disgust, that they were commonly regarded by the German Protestants as a narrow-minded and benighted set of men; and, therefore, at the special invitation of the Lutheran Bishop Speratus, they began the practice of sending some of their students to foreign universities. It is pathetic to read how the first two students were sent (1549). "We granted them," says the record, "their means of support. We gave them - L-7 10s. a-piece, and sent them off to Basle." We are not informed how long the money was to last. For some years the new policy was fiercely opposed; and the leader of the opposition was John Augusta. He regarded this new policy with horror, condemned it as a falling away from the old simplicity and piety, and predicted that it would bring about the ruin of the Brethren's Church. At the head of the progressive party was John Blahoslaw, the historian. He had been to Wittenberg and Basle himself; he was a master of Greek and Latin; and now he wrote a brilliant philippic, pouring scorn on the fears of the conservative party. "For my part," he said, "I have no fear that learned and pious men will ever ruin the Church. I am far more afraid of the action of those high-minded and stupid schemers, who think more highly of themselves than they ought to think." It is clear to whom these stinging words refer. They are a plain hit at Augusta. "It is absurd," he continued, "to be afraid of learning and culture. As long as our leaders are guided by the Spirit of Christ, all will be well; but when craft and cunning, and worldly prudence creep in, then woe to the Brethren's Church! Let us rather be careful whom we admit to the ministry, and then the Lord will preserve us from destruction." As we read these biting words, we can understand how it came to pass that Augusta, during his last few years, was held in such little honour. The old man was behind the times. The progressive party triumphed. Before long there were forty students at foreign Universities. The whole attitude of the Brethren changed. As the Humanist movement spread in Bohemia, the Brethren began to take an interest in popular education; and now, aided by friendly nobles, they opened a number of free elementary schools. At Eibenschuetz, in Moravia, they had a school for the sons of the nobility, with Esrom Ruedinger as headmaster; both Hebrew and Greek were taught; and the school became so famous that many of the pupils came from Germany. At Holleschau, Leitomischl, Landskron, Gross-Bitesch, Austerlitz, Fulneck, Meseretoch, Chropin, Leipnik, Kaunic, Trebitzch, Paskau, Ungarisch-Brod, Jungbunzlau, and Prerau, they had free schools supported by Protestant nobles and manned with Brethren's teachers. As there is no direct evidence to the contrary, we may take it for granted that in these schools the syllabus was much the same as in the other schools of the country. In most the Latin language was taught, and in some dialectics, rhetoric, physics, astronomy and geometry. The education was largely practical. At most of the Bohemian schools in those days the children were taught, by means of conversation books, how to look after a horse, how to reckon with a landlord, how to buy cloth, how to sell a garment, how to write a letter, how to make terms with a pedlar, how, in a word, to get on in the world. But the Brethren laid the chief stress on religion. Instead of separating the secular and the sacred, they combined the two in a wonderful way, and taught both at the same time. For this purpose, they published, in the first place, a school edition of their Catechism in three languages, Bohemian, German, and Latin; and thus the Catechism became the scholar's chief means of instruction. He learned to read from his Catechism; he learned Latin from his Catechism; he learned German from his Catechism; and thus, while mastering foreign tongues, he was being grounded at the same time in the articles of the Christian faith. He lived, in a word, from morning to night in a Christian atmosphere. For the same purpose a Brother named Matthias Martinus prepared a book containing extracts from the Gospels and Epistles. It was printed in six parallel columns. In the first were grammatical notes; in the second the text in Greek; in the third a translation in Bohemian; in the fourth in German; in the fifth in Latin; and in the sixth a brief exposition.

Second, the Brethren used another text-book called the "Book of Morals." It was based, apparently, on Erasmus's "Civilitas Morum." It was a simple, practical guide to daily conduct. It was written in rhyme, and the children learned it by heart. It was divided into three parts. In the first, the child was taught how to behave from morning to night; in the second, how to treat his elders and masters; in the third, how to be polite at table.

Third, the Brethren, in all their schools, made regular use of hymn-books; and the scholar learnt to sing by singing hymns. Sometimes the hymns were in a separate volume; sometimes a selection was bound up with the Catechism. But in either case the grand result was the same. As we follow the later fortunes of the Brethren we shall find ourselves face to face with a difficult problem. How was it, we ask, that in later years, when their little Church was crushed to powder, these Brethren held the faith for a hundred years? How was it that the "Hidden Seed" had such vitality? How was it that, though forbidden by law, they held the fort till the times of revival came? For answer we turn to their Catechism. They had learned it first in their own homes; they had learned it later at school; they had made it the very marrow of their life; they taught it in turn to their children; and thus in the darkest hours of trial they handed on the torch of faith from one generation to another.

We come now to another secret of their strength. Of all the Protestants in Europe the Bohemian Brethren were the first to publish a Hymn-book; and by this time they had published ten editions. The first three were in Bohemian, and were edited by Luke of Prague, 1501, 1505, 1519; the fourth in German, edited by Michael Weiss, 1531; the fifth in Bohemian, edited by John Horn, 1541; the sixth in German, edited by John Horn, 1544; the seventh in Polish, edited by George Israel, 1554; the eighth in Bohemian, edited by John Blahoslaw, 1561; the ninth in German, 1566; the tenth in Polish, 1569. As they wished here to appeal to all classes, they published hymns both ancient and modern, and tunes both grave and gay. Among the hymn-writers were John Hus, Rockycana, Luke of Prague, Augusta, and Martin Luther; and among the tunes were Gregorian Chants and popular rondels of the day. The hymns and tunes were published in one volume. The chief purpose of the hymns was clear religious instruction. The Brethren had nothing to conceal. They had no mysterious secret doctrines; and no mysterious secret practices. They published their hymn-books, not for themselves only, but for all the people in the country, and for Evangelical Christians in other lands. "It has been our chief aim," they said, "to let everyone fully and clearly understand what our views are with regard to the articles of the Christian faith." And here the hymns were powerful preachers of the faith. They spread the Brethren's creed in all directions. They were clear, orderly, systematic, and Scriptural; and thus they were sung in the family circle, by bands of young men in the Brethren's Houses, by shepherds watching their flocks by night, by sturdy peasants as they trudged to market. And then, on Sunday, in an age when congregational singing was as yet but little known, the Brethren made the rafters ring with the sound of united praise. "Your churches," wrote the learned Esrom Ruedinger, "surpass all others in singing. For where else are songs of praise, of thanksgiving, of prayer and instruction so often heard? Where is there better singing? The newest edition of the Bohemian Hymn-book, with its seven hundred and forty-three hymns, is an evidence of the multitude of your songs. Three hundred and forty-six have been translated into German. In your churches the people can all sing and take part in the worship of God."

But of all the services rendered by the Brethren to the cause of the evangelical faith in Bohemia the noblest and the most enduring was their translation of the Bible into the Bohemian tongue. In the archives of the Brethren's Church at Herrnhut are now to be seen six musty volumes known as the Kralitz Bible (1579-93). The idea was broached by Blahoslaw, the Church historian. The expense was born by Baron John von Zerotin. The actual printing was executed at Zerotin's Castle at Kralitz. The translation was based, not on the Vulgate, but on the original Hebrew and Greek. The work of translating the Old Testament was entrusted to six Hebrew scholars, Aeneas, Cepollo, Streic, Ephraim, Jessen, and Capito. The New Testament was translated by Blahoslaw himself (1565). The work was of national interest. For the first time the Bohemian people possessed the Bible in a translation from the original tongue, with the chapters subdivided into verses, and the Apocrypha separated from the Canonical Books. The work appeared at first in cumbersome form. It was issued in six bulky volumes, with only eight or nine verses to a page, and a running commentary in the margin. The paper was strong, the binding dark brown, the page quarto, the type Latin, the style chaste and idiomatic, and the commentary fairly rich in broad practical theology. But all this was no use to the poor. For the benefit, therefore, of the common people the Brethren published a small thin paper edition in a plain calf binding. It contained an index of quotations from the Old Testament in the New, an index of proper names with their meanings, a lectionary for the Christian Year, references in the margin, and a vignette including the famous Brethren's episcopal seal, "The Lamb and the Flag." The size of the page was only five inches by seven and a half; the number of pages was eleven hundred and sixty; the paper was so remarkably thin that the book was only an inch and a quarter thick; [47] and thus it was suited in every way to hold the same place in the affections of the people that the Geneva Bible held in England in the days of our Puritan fathers. The Kralitz Bible was a masterpiece. It helped to fix and purify the language, and thus completed what Stitny and Hus had begun. It became the model of a chaste and simple style; and its beauty of language was praised by the Jesuits. It is a relic that can never be forgotten, a treasure that can never lose its value. It is issued now, word for word, by the British and Foreign Bible Society; it is read by the people in their own homes, and is used in the Protestant Churches of the country; and thus, as the Catholic, Gindely, says, it will probably endure as long as the Bohemian tongue is spoken.

But even this was not the end of the Brethren's labours. We come to the most amazing fact in their history. On the one hand they were the greatest literary force in the country; [48] on the other they took the smallest part in her theological controversies. For example, take the case of John Blahoslaw. He was one of the most brilliant scholars of his day. He was master of a beautiful literary style. He was a member of the Brethren's Inner Council. He wrote a "History of the Brethren." He translated the New Testament into Bohemian. He prepared a standard Bohemian Grammar. He wrote also a treatise on Music, and other works too many to mention here. And yet, learned Bishop though he was, he wrote only one theological treatise, "Election through Grace," and even here he handled his subject from a practical rather than a theological point of view.

Again, take the case of Jacob Bilek, Augusta's companion in prison. If ever a man had just cause to hate the Church of Rome it was surely this humble friend of the great Augusta; and yet he wrote a full account of their dreary years in prison without saying one bitter word against his persecutors and tormentors. [49] From this point of view his book is delightful. It is full of piety, of trust in God, of vivid dramatic description; it has not a bitter word from cover to cover; and thus it is a beautiful and precious example of the broad and charitable spirit of the Brethren.

Again, it is surely instructive to note what subject most attracted the Brethren's attention. For religious debate they cared but little; for history they had a consuming passion; and now their leading scholars produced the greatest historical works in the language. Brother Jaffet wrote a work on the Brethren's Episcopal Orders, entitled, "The Sword of Goliath." Wenzel Brezan wrote a history of the "House of Rosenberg," containing much interesting information about Bohemian social life. Baron Charles von Zerotin wrote several volumes of memoirs. The whole interest of the Brethren now was broad and national in character. The more learned they grew the less part they took in theological disputes. They regarded such disputes as waste of time; they had no pet doctrines to defend; they were now in line with the other Protestants of the country; and they held that the soul was greater than the mind and good conduct best of all. No longer did they issue "Confessions of Faith" of their own; no longer did they lay much stress on their points of difference with Luther. We come here to a point of great importance. It has been asserted by some historians that the Brethren never taught the doctrine of

Justification by Faith. For answer we turn to their later Catechism prepared (1554) by Jirek Gyrck.

"In what way," ran one question, "can a sinful man obtain salvation?"

"By the pure Grace of God alone, through Faith in Jesus Christ our Lord who of God is made unto us wisdom and righteousness and sanctification and redemption."

What sort of picture does all this bring before us? It is the picture of a body of men who had made remarkable progress. No longer did they despise education; they fostered it more than any men in the country. No longer did they speak with contempt of marriage; they spoke of it as a symbol of holier things. It was time, thought some, for these broad-minded men to have their due reward. It was time to amend the insulting law, and tear the musty Edict of St. James to tatters.

Chapter 13: The Letter of Majesty (1603-1609)

OF all the members of the Brethren's Church, the most powerful and the most discontented was Baron Wenzel von Budowa. He was now fifty-six years of age. He had travelled in Germany, Denmark, Holland, England, France and Italy. He had studied at several famous universities. He had made the acquaintance of many learned men. He had entered the Imperial service, and served as ambassador at Constantinople. He had mastered Turkish and Arabic, had studied the Mohammedan religion, had published the Alcoran in Bohemian, and had written a treatise denouncing the creed and practice of Islam as Satanic in origin and character. He belonged to the Emperor's Privy Council, and also to the Imperial Court of Appeal. He took part in theological controversies, and preached sermons to his tenants. He was the bosom friend of Baron Charles von Zerotin, the leading Brother of Moravia. He corresponded, from time to time, with the struggling Protestants in Hungary, and had now become the recognised leader, not only of the Brethren, but of all evangelicals in Bohemia.

He had one great purpose to attain. As the Brethren had rendered such signal service to the moral welfare of the land, it seemed to him absurd and unfair that they should still be under the ban of the law and still be denounced in Catholic pulpits as children of the devil. He resolved to remedy the evil. The Emperor, Rudolph II., paved the way. He was just the man that Budowa required. He was weak in body and in mind. He had ruined his health, said popular scandal, by indulging in dissolute pleasures. His face was shrivelled, his hair bleached, his back bent, his step tottering. He was too much interested in astrology, gems, pictures, horses, antique relics and similar curiosities to take much interest in government; he suffered from religious mania, and was constantly afraid of being murdered; and his daily hope and prayer was that he might be spared all needless trouble in this vexatious world and have absolutely nothing to do. And now he committed an act of astounding folly. He first revived the Edict of St. James, ordered the nobles throughout the land to turn out all Protestant pastors (1602-3), and sent a body of armed men to close the Brethren's Houses at Jungbunzlau; and then, having disgusted two-thirds of his loyal subjects, he summoned a Diet, and asked for money for a crusade against the Turks. But this was more than Wenzel could endure. He attended the Diet, and made a brilliant speech. He had nothing, he said, to say against the Emperor. He would not blame him for reviving the musty Edict. For that he blamed some secret disturbers of the peace. If the Emperor needed money and men, the loyal knights and nobles of Bohemia would support him. But that support would be given on certain conditions. If the Emperor wished his subjects to be loyal, he must first obey the law of the land himself. "We stand," he said, "one and all by the Confession of 1575, and we do not know a single person who is prepared to submit to the Consistory at Prague." He finished, wept, prepared a petition, and sent it in to the poor invisible Rudolph. And Rudolph replied as Emperors sometimes do. He replied by closing the Diet.

Again, however, six years later, Budowa returned to the attack (1609). He was acting, not merely on behalf of the Brethren, but on behalf of all Protestants in the country. And this fact is the key to the situation. As we follow the dramatic story to its sad and tragic close, we must remember that from this time onward the Brethren, for all intents and purposes, had almost abandoned their position as a separate Church, and had cast in their lot, for good or evil, with the other Protestants in Bohemia. They were striving now for the recognition, not of their own Confession of Faith, but of the general Bohemian Protestant Confession presented to the Emperor, Maximilian II. And thus Budowa became a national hero. He called a meeting of Lutherans and Brethren in the historic "Green Saloon," prepared a resolution demanding that the Protestant Confession be inscribed in the Statute Book, and, followed by a crowd of nobles and knights, was admitted to the sacred presence of the Emperor.

Again the Diet was summoned. The hall was crammed, and knights and nobles jostled each other in the corridors and in the square outside (Jan. 28th, 1609). For some weeks the Emperor, secluded in his cabinet, held to his point like a hero. The debate was conducted in somewhat marvellous fashion. There, in the Green Saloon, sat the Protestants, preparing proposals and petitions. There, in the Archbishop's palace, sat the Catholics, rather few in number, and wondering what to do. And there, in his chamber, sat the grizzly, rickety, imperial Lion, consulting with his councillors, Martinic and Slawata, and dictating his replies. And then, when the king had his answer ready, the Diet met in the Council Chamber to hear it read aloud. His first reply was now as sharp as ever. He declared that the faith of the Church of Rome was the only lawful faith in Bohemia. "And as for these Brethren," he said, "whose teaching has been so often forbidden by royal decrees and decisions of the Diet, I order them, like my predecessors, to fall in with the Utraquists or Catholics, and declare that their meetings shall not be permitted on any pretence whatever."

In vain the Protestants, by way of reply, drew up a monster petition, and set forth their grievances in detail. They suffered, they said, not from actual persecution, but from nasty insults and petty annoyances. They were still described in Catholic pulpits as heretics and children of the devil. They were still forbidden to honour the memory of Hus. They were still forbidden to print books without the consent of the Archbishop. But the King snapped them short. He told the estates to end their babble, and again closed the Diet (March 31st).

The blood of Budowa was up. The debate, thought he, was fast becoming a farce. The King was fooling his subjects. The King must be taught a lesson. As the Diet broke up, he stood at the door, and shouted out in ringing tones: "Let all who love the King and the land, let all who care for unity and love, let all who remember the zeal of our fathers, meet here at six to-morrow morn."

He spent the night with some trusty allies, prepared another declaration, met his friends in the morning, and informed the King, in language clear, that the Protestants had now determined to win their rights by force. And Budowa was soon true to his word. He sent envoys asking for help to the King's brother Matthias, to the Elector of Saxony, to the Duke of Brunswick, and to other Protestant leaders. He called a meeting of nobles and knights in the courtyard of the castle, and there, with heads bared and right hands upraised, they swore to be true to each other and to win their liberty at any price, even at the price of blood. He arranged for an independent meeting in the town hall of the New Town. The King forbade the meeting. What better place, replied Budowa, would His Majesty like to suggest? As he led his men across the long Prague bridge, he was followed by thousands of supporters. He arrived in due time at the square in front of the hall. The Royal Captain appeared and ordered him off. The crowd jeered and whistled the Captain away.

And yet Budowa was no vulgar rebel. He insisted that every session in the hall should be begun and ended with prayer. He informed the King, again and again, that all he wished was liberty of worship for Protestants. He did his best to put an end to the street rows, the drunken brawls, that now disgraced the city.

For the third time the King summoned the Diet (May 25th). The last round in the terrible combat now began. He ordered the estates to appear in civilian's dress. They arrived armed to the teeth. He ordered them to open the proceedings by attending Mass in the Cathedral. The Catholics alone obeyed; the Protestants held a service of their own; and yet, despite these danger signals, the King was as stubborn as ever, and again he sent a message to say that he held to his first decision. The Diet was thunderstruck, furious, desperate.

"We have had enough of useless talk," said Count Matthias Thurn; "it is time to take to arms." The long fight was drawing to a finish. As the King refused to listen to reason, the members of the Diet, one and all, Protestants and Catholics alike, prepared an ultimatum demanding that all evangelical nobles, knights, citizens and peasants should have full and perfect liberty to worship God in their own way, and to build schools and churches on all Royal estates; and, in order that the King might realise the facts of the case, Budowa formed a Board of thirty directors, of whom fourteen were Brethren, raised an army in Prague, and sent the nobles flying through the land to levy money and troops. The country, in fact, was now in open revolt. And thus, at length compelled by brute force, the poor old King gave way, and made his name famous in history by signing the Letter of Majesty and granting full religious liberty to all adherents of the Bohemian National Protestant Confession. All adherents of the Confession could worship as they pleased, and all classes, except the peasantry, could build schools and churches on Royal estates (July 9th). "No decree of any kind," ran one sweeping clause, "shall be issued either by us or by our heirs and succeeding kings against the above established religious peace."

The delight in Prague was boundless. The Letter of Majesty was carried through the streets in grand triumphal procession. The walls were adorned with flaming posters. The bells of the churches were rung. The people met in the Church of the Holy Cross, and there sang jubilant psalms of thanksgiving and praise. The King's couriers posted through the land to tell the gladsome news; the letter was hailed as the heavenly herald of peace and goodwill to men; and Budowa was adored as a national hero, and the redresser of his people's wrongs.

But the work of the Diet was not yet complete. As the Brethren, led by the brave Budowa, had borne the brunt of the battle, we naturally expect to find that now the victory was won, they would have the lion's share of the spoils. But they really occupied a rather modest position. The next duty of the Diet was to make quite sure that the Letter of Majesty would not be broken. For this purpose they elected a Board of Twenty-four Defenders, and of these Defenders only eight were Brethren. Again, the Brethren had now to submit to the rule of a New National Protestant Consistory. Of that Consistory the Administrator was a Utraquist Priest; the next in rank was a Brethren's Bishop; the total number of members was twelve; and of these twelve only three were Brethren. If the Brethren, therefore, were fairly represented, they must have constituted at this time about one-quarter or one-third of the Protestants in Bohemia. [50] They were now a part, in the eyes of the law, of the National Protestant Church. They were known as Utraquist Christians. They accepted the National Confession as their own standard of faith, and though they could still ordain their own priests, their candidates for the priesthood had first to be examined by the national Administrator.

And, further, the Brethren had now weakened their union with the Moravian and Polish branches. No longer did the three parts of the Church stand upon the same footing. In Poland the Brethren were still the leading body; in Moravia they were still independent; in Bohemia alone they bowed to the rule of others. And yet, in some important respects, they were still as independent as ever. They could still hold their own Synods and practise their own ceremonies; they still retained their own Confession of faith; they could still conduct their own schools and teach their Catechism; and they could still, above all, enforce as of old their system of moral discipline. And this they guarded as the apple of their eye.

As soon as the above arrangements were complete they addressed themselves to the important task of defining their own position. And for this purpose they met at a General Synod at Zerawic, and prepared a comprehensive descriptive work, entitled "Ratio Disciplinae" —i.e., Account of Discipline. [51] It was a thorough, exhaustive, orderly code of rules and regulations. It was meant as a guide and a manifesto. It proved to be an epitaph. In the second place, the Brethren now issued (1615) a new edition of their Catechism, with the questions and answers in four parallel columns—Greek, Bohemian, German and Latin; [52] and thus, once more, they shewed their desire to play their part in national education.

Thus, at last, had the Brethren gained their freedom. They had crossed the Red Sea, had traversed the wilderness, had smitten the Midianites hip and thigh, and could now settle down in the land of freedom flowing with milk and honey.

Chapter 14: The Downfall (1616-1621)

THE dream of bliss became a nightmare. As the tide of Protestantism ebbed and flowed in various parts of the Holy Roman Empire, so the fortunes of the Brethren ebbed and flowed in the old home of their fathers. We have seen how the Brethren rose to prosperity and power. We have now to see what brought about their ruin. It was nothing in the moral character of the Brethren themselves. It was purely and simply their geographical position. If Bohemia had only been an island, as Shakespeare seems to have thought it was, it is more than likely that the Church of the Brethren would have flourished there down to the present day. But Bohemia lay in the very heart of European politics; the King was always a member of the House of Austria; the House of Austria was the champion of the Catholic faith, and the Brethren now were crushed to powder in the midst of that mighty European conflict known as the Thirty Years' War. We note briefly the main stages of the process.

The first cause was the rising power of the Jesuits. For the last fifty years these zealous men had been quietly extending their influence in the country. They had built a magnificent college in Prague. They had established a number of schools for the common people. They had obtained positions as tutors in noble families. They went about from village to village, preaching, sometimes in the village churches and sometimes in the open air; and one of their number, Wenzel Sturm, had written an exhaustive treatise denouncing the doctrines of the Brethren. But now these Jesuits used more violent measures. They attacked the Brethren in hot, abusive language. They declared that the wives of Protestant ministers were whores. They denounced their children as bastards. They declared that it was better to have the devil in the house than a Protestant woman. And the more they preached, and the more they wrote, the keener the party feeling in Bohemia grew.

The next cause was the Letter of Majesty itself. As soon as that Letter was closely examined, a flaw was found in the crystal. We come to what has been called the "Church Building Difficulty." It was clearly provided in one clause of the Letter of Majesty that the Protestants should have perfect liberty to build churches on all Royal estates. But now arose the difficult question, what were Royal estates? What about Roman Catholic Church estates? What about estates held by Catholic officials as tenants of the King? Were these Royal estates or were they not? There were two opinions on the subject. According to the Protestants they were; according to the Jesuits they were not; and now the Jesuits used this argument to influence the action of Matthias, the next King of Bohemia. The dispute soon came to blows. At Klostergrab the land belonged to the Catholic Archbishop of Prague; at Brunau it belonged to the Abbot of Brunau; and yet, on each of these estates, the Protestants had churches. They believed, of course, that they were in the right. They regarded those estates as Royal estates. They had no desire to break the law of the land. But now the Catholics began to force the pace. At Brunau the Abbot interfered and turned the Protestants out of the church. At Klostergrab the church was pulled down, and the wood of which it was built was used as firewood; and in each case the new King, Matthias, took the Catholic side. The truth is, Matthias openly broke the Letter. He broke it on unquestioned Royal estates. He expelled Protestant ministers from their pulpits, and put Catholics in their place. His officers burst into Protestant churches and interrupted the services; and, in open defiance of the law of the land, the priests drove Protestants with dogs and scourges to the Mass, and thrust the wafer down their mouths. What right, said the Protestants, had the Catholics to do these things? The Jesuits had an amazing answer ready. For two reasons, they held, the Letter of Majesty was invalid. It was invalid because it had been obtained by force, and invalid because it had not been sanctioned by the Pope. What peace could there be with these conflicting views? It is clear that a storm was brewing.

The third cause was the famous dispute about the Kingship. As Matthias was growing old and feeble, it was time to choose his successor; and Matthias, therefore, summoned a Diet, and informed the Estates, to their great surprise, that all they had to do now was to accept as King his adopted son, Ferdinand Archduke of Styria. At first the Diet was thunderstruck. They had met to choose their own King. They intended to choose a Protestant, and now they were commanded to choose this Ferdinand, the most zealous Catholic in Europe. And yet, for some mysterious reason, the Diet actually yielded. They surrendered their elective rights; they accepted Ferdinand as King, and thus, at the most critical and dangerous point in the whole history of the country, they allowed a Catholic devotee to become the ruler of a Protestant people. For that fatal mistake they had soon to pay in full. Some say they were frightened by threats; some say that the Diet was summoned in a hurry, and that only a few attended. The truth is, they were completely outwitted. At this point the Protestant nobles of Bohemia showed that fatal lack of prompt and united action which was soon to fill the whole land with all the horrors of war. In vain Budowa raised a vehement protest. He found but few to support him. If the Protestants desired peace and good order in Bohemia, they ought to have insisted upon their rights and elected a Protestant King; and now, in Ferdinand, they had accepted a man who was pledged to fight for the Church of Rome with every breath of his body. He was a man of fervent piety. He was a pupil of the Jesuits. He regarded himself as the divinely appointed champion of the Catholic faith. He had already stamped out the Protestants in Styria. He had a strong will and a clear conception of what he regarded as his duty. He would rather, he declared, beg his bread from door to door, with his family clinging affectionately around him, than allow a single Protestant in his dominions. "I would rather," he said, "rule over a wilderness than over heretics." But what about his oath to observe the Letter of Majesty? Should he take the oath or not? If he took it he would be untrue to his conscience; if he refused he could never be crowned King of

Bohemia. He consulted his friends the Jesuits. They soon eased his conscience. It was wicked, they said, of Rudolph II. to sign such a monstrous document; but it was not wicked for the new King to take the oath to keep it. And, therefore, Ferdinand took the oath, and was crowned King of Bohemia. "We shall now see," said a lady at the ceremony, "whether the Protestants are to rule the Catholics or the Catholics the Protestants."

She was right. Forthwith the Protestants realised their blunder, and made desperate efforts to recover the ground they had lost. Now was the time for the Twenty-four Defenders to arise and do their duty; now was the time, now or never, to make the Letter no longer a grinning mockery. They began by acting strictly according to law. They had been empowered to summon representatives of the Protestant Estates. They summoned their assembly, prepared a petition, and sent it off to Matthias. He replied that their assembly was illegal. He refused to remedy their grievances. The Defenders were goaded to fury. At their head was a violent man, Henry Thurn. He resolved on open rebellion. He would have the new King Ferdinand dethroned and have his two councillors, Martinic and Slawata, put to death. It was the 23rd of May, 1618. At an early hour on that fatal day, the Protestant Convention met in the Hradschin, and then, a little later, the fiery Thurn sallied out with a body of armed supporters, arrived at the Royal Castle, and forced his way into the Regent's Chamber, where the King's Councillors were assembled. There, in a corner, by the stove sat Martinic and Slawata. There, in that Regent's Chamber, began the cause of all the woe that followed. There was struck the first blow of the Thirty Years' War. As Thurn and his henchmen stood in the presence of the two men, who, in their opinion, had done the most to poison the mind of Matthias, they felt that the decisive moment had come. The interview was stormy. Voices rang in wild confusion. The Protestant spokesman was Paul von Rican. He accused Martinic and Slawata of two great crimes. They had openly broken the Letter of Majesty, and had dictated King Matthias's last reply. He appealed to his supporters crowded into the corridor outside.

"Aye, aye," shouted the crowd.

"Into the Black Tower with them," said some.

"Nay, nay," said Rupow, a member of the Brethren's Church, "out of the window with them, in the good old Bohemian fashion."

At this signal, agreed upon before, Martinic was dragged to the window. He begged for a father confessor.

"Commend thy soul to God," said someone. "Are we to allow any Jesuit scoundrels here?"

"Jesus! Mary!" he screamed.

He was flung headlong from the window. He clutched at the window-sill. A blow came down on his hands. He had to leave go, and down he fell, seventy feet, into the moat below.

"Let us see," said someone, "whether his Mary will help him."

He fell on a heap of soft rubbish. He scrambled away with only a wound in the head.

"By God," said one of the speakers, "his Mary has helped him."

At this point the conspirators appear to have lost their heads. As Martinic had not been killed by his fall, it was absurd to treat Slawata in the same way; and yet they now flung him out of the window, and his secretary Fabricius after him. Not one of the three was killed, not one was even maimed for life, and through the country the rumour spread that all three had been delivered by the Virgin Mary.

From that moment war was inevitable. As the details of the struggle do not concern us, it will be enough to state here that the Defenders now, in slipshod fashion, began to take a variety of measures to maintain the Protestant cause. They formed a national Board of Thirty Directors. They assessed new taxes to maintain the war, but never took the trouble to collect them. They relied more on outside help than on their own united action. They deposed Ferdinand II.; they elected Frederick, Elector Palatine, and son-in-law of James I. of England, as King of Bohemia; and they ordered the Jesuits out of the kingdom. There was a strange scene in Prague when these Jesuits departed. They formed in procession in the streets, and, clad in black, marched off with bowed heads and loud wailings; and when their houses were examined they were found full of gunpowder and arms. For the moment the Protestants of Prague were wild with joy. In the great Cathedral they pulled off the ornaments and destroyed costly pictures. What part did the Brethren play in these abominations? We do not know. At this tragic point in their fateful story our evidence is so lamentably scanty that it is absolutely impossible to say what part they played in the revolution. But one thing at least we know without a doubt. We know that the Catholics were now united and the Protestants quarrelling with each other; we know that Ferdinand was prompt and vigorous, and the new King Frederick stupid and slack; and we know, finally, that the Catholic army, commanded by the famous general Tilly, was far superior to the Protestant army under Christian of Anhalt. At last the Catholic army appeared before the walls of Prague. The battle of the White Hill was fought (November 8th, 1620). The new King, in the city, was entertaining some ambassadors to dinner. The Protestant army was routed, the new King fled from the country, and once again Bohemia lay crushed under the heel of the conqueror.

At this time the heel of the conqueror consisted in a certain Prince Lichtenstein. He was made regent of Prague, and was entrusted with the duty of restoring the country to order. He set about his work in a cool and methodical manner. He cleared the rabble out of the streets. He recalled the Jesuits. He ordered the Brethren out of the kingdom. He put a Roman Catholic Priest into every church in Prague; and then he made the strange announcement that all the rebels, as they were called, would be freely pardoned, and invited the leading Protestant nobles to appear before him at Prague. They walked into the trap like flies into a cobweb. If the nobles had only cared to do so, they might all have escaped after the battle of the White Hill; for Tilly, the victorious general, had purposely given them time to do so. But for some reason they nearly all preferred to stay. And now Lichtenstein had them in his grasp. He had forty-seven leaders arrested in one night. He imprisoned them in the castle tower, had them tried and condemned, obtained the approval of Ferdinand, and then, while some were pardoned, informed the remaining twenty-seven that they had two days in which to prepare for death. They were to die on June 21st. Among those leaders about a dozen were Brethren. We have arrived at the last act of the tragedy. We have seen the grim drama develop, and when the curtain falls the stage will be covered with corpses and blood.

Chapter 15: The Day of Blood at Prague

THE City of Prague was divided into two parts, the Old Town and the New Town. In the middle of the Old Town was a large open space, called the Great Square. On the west side of the Great Square stood the Council House, on the east the old Thein Church. The condemned prisoners, half of whom were Brethren, were in the Council House: in front of their window was the scaffold, draped in black cloth, twenty feet high, and twenty-two yards square; from the window they stepped out on to a balcony, and from the balcony to the scaffold ran a short flight of steps. In that Great Square, and on that scaffold, we find the scene of our story.

When early in the morning of Monday, June 21st, the assembled prisoners looked out of the windows of their rooms to take their last view of earth, they saw a splendid, a brilliant, a gorgeous, but to them a terrible scene (1621). They saw God's sun just rising in the east and reddening the sky and shining in each other's faces; they saw the dark black scaffold bathed in light, and the squares of infantry and cavalry ranged around it; they saw the eager, excited throng, surging and swaying in the Square below and crowding on the house-tops to right and left; and they saw on the further side of the square the lovely twin towers of the old Thein Church, where Gregory had knelt and Rockycana had preached in the brave days of old. As the church clocks chimed the hour of five a gun was fired from the castle; the prisoners were informed that their hour had come, and were ordered to prepare for their doom; and Lichtenstein and the magistrates stepped out on to the balcony, an awning above them to screen them from the rising sun. The last act of the tragedy opened.

As there was now a long morning's work to be done, that work was begun at once; and as the heads of the martyrs fell off the block in quick succession the trumpets brayed and the drums beat an accompaniment. Grim and ghastly was the scene in that Great Square in Prague, on that bright June morning well nigh three hundred years ago. There fell the flower of the Bohemian nobility; and there was heard the swan song of the Bohemian Brethren. As the sun rose higher in the eastern sky and shone on the windows of the Council House, the sun of the Brethren's pride and power was setting in a sea of blood; and clear athwart the lingering light stood out, for all mankind to see, the figures of the last defenders of their freedom and their faith. Among the number not one had shown the white feather in prospect of death. Not a cheek was blanched, not a voice faltered as the dread hour drew near. One and all they had fortified themselves to look the waiting angel of death in the face. As they sat in their rooms the evening before—a sabbath evening it was—they had all, in one way or another, drawn nigh to God in prayer. In one room the prisoners had taken the Communion together, in another they joined in singing psalms and hymns; in another they had feasted in a last feast of love. Among these were various shades of faith—Lutherans, Calvinists, Utraquists, Brethren; but now all differences were laid aside, for all was nearly over now. One laid the cloth, and another the plates; a third brought water and a fourth said the simple grace. As the night wore on they lay down on tables and benches to snatch a few hours of that troubled sleep which gives no rest. At two they were all broad awake again, and again the sound of psalms and hymns was heard; and as the first gleams of light appeared each dressed himself as though for a wedding, and carefully turned down the ruffle of his collar so as to give the executioner no extra trouble.

Swiftly, in order, and without much cruelty the gory work was done. The morning's programme had all been carefully arranged. At each corner of the square was a squad of soldiers to hold the people in awe, and to prevent an attempt at rescue. One man, named Mydlar, was the executioner; and, being a Protestant, he performed his duties with as much decency and humanity as possible. He used four different swords, and was paid about -L-100 for his morning's work. With his first sword he beheaded eleven; with his second, five; with his two last, eight. The first of these swords is still to be seen at Prague, and has the names of its eleven victims engraven upon it. Among these names is the name of Wenzel von Budowa. In every instance Mydlar seems to have done his duty at one blow. At his side stood an assistant, and six masked men in black. As soon as Mydlar had severed the neck, the assistant placed the dead man's right hand on the block; the sword fell again; the hand dropped at the wrist; and the men in black, as silent as night, gathered up the bleeding members, wrapped them in clean black cloth, and swiftly bore them away.

The name of Budowa was second on the list. As many of the records of the time were destroyed by fire, we are not able to tell in full what part Budowa had played in the great revolt. He had, however, been a leader on the conquered side. He had fought, as we know, for the Letter of Majesty; he had bearded Rudolph II. in his den; he had openly opposed the election of Ferdinand II.; he had welcomed Frederick, the Protestant Winter King, at the city gates; and, therefore, he was justly regarded by Ferdinand as a champion of the Protestant national faith and an enemy of the Catholic Church and throne. As he was now over seventy years of age it is hardly likely that he had fought on the field of battle. After the battle of the White Mountain he had retired with his family to his country estate. He had then, strange to say, been one of those entrapped into Prague by Lichtenstein, and had been imprisoned in the White Tower. There he was tried and condemned as a rebel, and there, as even Gindely admits, he bore himself like a hero to the last. At first, along with some other nobles, he signed a petition to the Elector of Saxony, imploring him to intercede with the Emperor on their behalf. The petition received no answer. He resigned himself to his fate. He was asked why he had walked into the lion's den. For some reason that I fail to understand Gindely says that what we are told about the conduct of the prisoners has only a literary interest. To my mind the last words of Wenzel of Budowa are of the highest historical importance. They show how the fate of the Brethren's Church was involved in the fate of Bohemia. He had come to Prague as a patriot and as a Brother. He was dying both for his country and for his Church.

"My heart impelled me to come," he said; "to forsake my country and its cause would have been sinning against my conscience. Here am I, my God, do unto Thy servant as seemeth good unto Thee. I would rather die myself than see my country die."

As he sat in his room on the Saturday evening—two days before the execution—he was visited by two Capuchin monks. He was amazed at their boldness. As they did not understand Bohemian, the conversation was conducted in Latin. They informed him that their visit was one of pity.

"Of pity?" asked the white-haired old Baron, "How so?"

"We wish to show your lordship the way to heaven." He assured them that he knew the way and stood on firm ground.

"My Lord only imagines," they rejoined, "that he knows the way of salvation. He is mistaken. Not being a member of the Holy Church, he has no share in the Church's salvation."

But Budowa placed his trust in Christ alone.

"I have this excellent promise," he said, "Whosoever believeth in Him shall not perish but have everlasting life. Therefore, until my last moment, will I abide by our true Church."

Thus did Budowa declare the faith of the Brethren. The Capuchin monks were horrified. They smote their breasts, declared that so hardened a heretic they had never seen, crossed themselves repeatedly, and left him sadly to his fate.

For the last time, on the Monday morning, he was given another chance to deny his faith. Two Jesuits came to see him.

"We have come to save my lord's soul," they said, "and to perform a work of mercy."

"Dear fathers," replied Budowa, "I thank my God that His Holy Spirit has given me the assurance that I will be saved through the blood of the Lamb." He appealed to the words of St. Paul: "I know whom I have believed: henceforth there is laid up for me a crown of righteousness, which the Lord, the righteous judge, shall give me at that day."

"But," said the Jesuits, "Paul there speaks of himself, not of others."

"You lie," said Budowa, "for does he not expressly add: and not to me only, but unto all them also that love his appearing."

And after a little more argumentation, the Jesuits left in disgust.

The last moment in Budowa's life now arrived. The messenger came and told him it was his turn to die. He bade his friends farewell.

"I go," he declared, "in the garment of righteousness; thus arrayed shall I appear before God."

Alone, with firm step he strode to the scaffold, stroking proudly his silver hair and beard.

"Thou old grey head of mine," said he, "thou art highly honoured; thou shalt be adorned with the Martyr-Crown."

As he knelt and prayed he was watched by the pitying eyes of the two kind-hearted Jesuits who had come to see him that morning. He prayed for his country, for his Church, for his enemies, and committed his soul to Christ; the sword flashed brightly in the sun; and one strong blow closed the restless life of Wenzel von Budowa, the "Last of the Bohemians."

And with his death there came the death of the Ancient Church of the Brethren. From the moment when Budowa's hoary head fell from the block the destruction of the Church was only a question of time. As Budowa died, so died the others after him. We have no space to tell here in detail how his bright example was followed; how nearly all departed with the words upon their lips, "Into Thy hands I commend my spirit"; how the drums beat louder each time before the sword fell, that the people might not hear the last words of triumphant confidence in God; how Caspar Kaplir, an old man of eighty-six, staggered up to the scaffold arrayed in a white robe, which he called his wedding garment, but was so weak that he could not hold his head to the block; how Otto von Los looked up and said, "Behold I see the heavens opened"; how Dr. Jessen, the theologian, had his tongue seized with a pair of tongs, cut off at the roots with a knife, and died with the blood gushing from his mouth; how three others were hanged on a gallows in the Square; how the fearful work went steadily on till the last head had fallen, and the black scaffold sweated blood; and how the bodies of the chiefs were flung into unconsecrated ground, and their heads spitted on poles in the city, there to grin for full ten years as a warning to all who held the Protestant faith. In all the story of the Brethren's Church there has been no other day like that. It was the day when the furies seemed to ride triumphant in the air, when the God of their fathers seemed to mock at the trial of the innocent, and when the little Church that had battled so bravely and so long was at last stamped down by the heel of the conqueror, till the life-blood flowed no longer in her veins.

Not, indeed, till the last breath of Church life had gone did the fearful stamping cease. The zeal of Ferdinand knew no bounds. He was determined, not only to crush the Brethren, but to wipe their memory from off the face of the earth. He regarded the Brethren as a noisome pest. Not a stone did he and his servants leave unturned to destroy them. They began with the churches. Instead of razing them to the ground, which would, of course, have been wanton waste, they turned them into Roman Catholic Chapels by the customary methods of purification and rededication. They rubbed out the inscriptions on the walls, and put new ones in their places, lashed the pulpits with whips, beat the altars with sticks, sprinkled holy water to cleanse the buildings of heresy, opened the graves and dishonoured the bones of the dead. Where once was the cup for Communion was now the image of the Virgin. Where once the Brethren had sung their hymns and read their Bibles were now the Confessional and the Mass.

Meanwhile the Brethren had been expelled from Bohemia. It is a striking proof of the influence of the Brethren that Ferdinand turned his attention to them before he troubled about the other Protestants. They had been the first in moral power; they had done the most to spread the knowledge of the Bible; they had produced the greatest literary men of the country; and, therefore, now they must be the first to go. What actually happened to many of the Brethren during the next few years no tongue can tell. But we know enough. We know that Ferdinand cut the Letter of Majesty in two with his scissors. We know that thirty-six thousand families left Bohemia and Moravia, and that the population of Bohemia dwindled from three millions to one. We know that about one-half of the property—lands, houses, castles, churches—passed over into the hands of the King. We know that the University of Prague was handed over to the Jesuits. We know that the scandalous order was issued that all Protestant married ministers who consented to join the Church of Rome might keep their wives by passing them off as cooks. We know that villages were sacked; that Kralitz Bibles, Hymn-books, Confessions, Catechisms, and historical works of priceless value—among others Blahoslaw's "History of the Brethren" —were burned in thousand; and that thus nearly every trace of the Brethren was swept out of the land. We know that some of the Brethren were hacked in pieces, that some were tortured, that some were burned alive, that some swung on gibbets at the city gates and at the country cross-roads among the carrion crows. For six years Bohemia was a field of blood, and Spanish soldiers, drunk and raging, slashed and pillaged on every hand. "Oh, to what torments," says a clergyman of that day, "were the promoters of the Gospel exposed! How they were tortured and massacred! How many virgins were violated to death! How many respectable women abused! How many children torn from their mothers' breasts and cut in pieces in their presence! How many dragged from their beds and thrown naked from the windows! Good God! What cries of woe we were forced to hear from those who lay upon the rack, and what groans and terrible outcries from those who besought the robbers to spare them for God's sake." It was thus that the Brethren, at the point of the sword, were driven from hearth and home: thus that they fled before the blast and took refuge in foreign lands; thus, amid bloodshed, and crime, and cruelty, and nameless torture, that the Ancient Church of the Bohemian Brethren bade a sad farewell to the land of its birth, and disappeared from the eyes of mankind.

Let us review the story of that wonderful Church. What a marvellous change had come upon it! It began in the quiet little valley of Kunwald: it ended in the noisy streets of Prague. It began in peace and brotherly love: it ended amid the tramp of horses, the clank of armour, the swish of swords, the growl of artillery, the whistle of bullets, the blare of trumpets, the roll of drums, and the moans of the wounded and the dying. It began in the teaching of the Sermon on the Mount: it ended amid the ghastly horrors of war. What was it that caused the destruction of that Church? At this point some historians, being short of facts, have thought fit to indulge in philosophical reflections; and, following the stale philosophy of Bildad—that all suffering is the punishment of sin—have informed us that the Brethren were now the victims of internal moral decay. They had lost, we are told, their sense of unity; they had relaxed their discipline; they had become morally weak; and the day of their external prosperity was the day of their internal decline. For this pious and utterly unfounded opinion the evidence usually summoned is the fact that Bishop Amos Comenius, in a sermon entitled "Haggai Redivivus," had some rather severe remarks to make about the sins of his Brethren. But Bishops' sermons are dangerous historical evidence. It is not the business of a preacher to tell the whole truth in one discourse. He is not a witness in the box; he is a prophet aiming at some special moral reform. If a Bishop is lecturing his Brethren for their failings he is sure to indulge, not exactly in exaggeration, but in one-sided statements of the facts. He will talk at length about the sins, and say nothing about the virtues. It is, of course, within the bounds of possibility that when the Brethren became more prosperous they were not so strict in some of their rules as they had been in earlier days; and it is also true that when Wenzel von Budowa summoned his followers to arms, the deed was enough, as one writer remarks, to make Gregory the Patriarch groan in his grave. But of any serious moral decline there is no solid proof. It is absurd to blame the Brethren for mixing in politics, and absurd to say that this mixing was the cause of their ruin. At that time in Bohemia religion and politics were inseparable. If a man took a definite stand in religion he took thereby a definite stand in politics. To be a Protestant was to be a rebel. If Budowa had never lifted a finger, the destruction of the Brethren would have been no less complete. The case of Baron Charles von Zerotin proves the point. He took no part in the rebellion; he sided, in the war, with the House of Hapsburg; he endeavoured, that is, to remain a Protestant and yet at the same time a staunch supporter of Ferdinand; and yet, loyal subject though he was, he was not allowed, except for a few years, to shelter Protestant ministers in his castle, and had finally to sell his estates and to leave the country. At heart, Comenius had a high opinion of his Brethren. For nearly fifty weary years—as we shall see in the next chapter—this genius and scholar longed and strove for the revival of the Brethren's Church, and in many of his books he described the Brethren, not as men who had disgraced their profession, but as heroes holding the faith in purity. He described his Brethren as broad-minded men, who took no part in religious quarrels, but looked towards heaven, and bore themselves affably to all; he said to the exiles in one of his letters, "You have endured to the end"; he described them again, in a touching appeal addressed to the Church of England, as a model of Christian simplicity; and he attributed their downfall in Bohemia, not to any moral weakness, but to their neglect of education. If the Brethren, he argued, had paid more attention to learning, they would have gained the support of powerful friends, who would not have allowed them to perish. I admit, of course, that Comenius was naturally partial, and that when he speaks in praise of the Brethren we must receive his evidence with caution; but, on the other hand, I hold that the theory of a serious moral decline, so popular with certain German historians, is not supported by evidence. If the Brethren had shown much sign of corruption we should expect to find full proof of the fact in the Catholic writers of the day. But such proof is not to hand. Not even the Jesuit historian, Balbin, had anything serious to say against the Brethren. The only Catholic writer, as far as I know, who attacked their character was the famous Papal Nuncio, Carlo Caraffa. He says that the Brethren in Moravia had become a little ambitious and avaricious, "with some degree of luxury in their habits of life"; [53] but he has no remarks of a similar nature to make about the Brethren in Bohemia. The real cause of the fall of the Brethren was utterly different. They fell, not because they were morally weak, but because they were killed by the sword or forcibly robbed of their property. They fell because Bohemia fell; and Bohemia fell for a variety of reasons; partly because her peasants were serfs and had no fight left in them; partly because her nobles blundered in their choice of a Protestant King; and partly because, when all is said, she was only a little country in the grip of a mightier power. In some countries the Catholic reaction was due to genuine religious fervour; in Bohemia it was brought about by brute force; and even with all his money and his men King Ferdinand found the destruction of the Brethren no easy task. He had the whole house of Hapsburg on his side; he had thousands of mercenary soldiers from Spain; he was restrained by no scruples of conscience; and yet it took him six full years to drive the Brethren from the country. And even then he had not completed his work. In spite of his efforts, many thousands of the people still remained Brethren at heart; and as late as 1781, when Joseph II. issued his Edict of Toleration, 100,000 in Bohemia and Moravia declared themselves Brethren. We have here a genuine proof of the Brethren's vigour. It had been handed on from father to son through five generations. For the Brethren there was still no legal recognition in Bohemia and Moravia; the Edict applied to Lutherans and Calvinists only; and if the Brethren had been weak men they might now have called themselves Lutherans or Calvinists. But this, of course, carries us beyond the limits of this chapter. For the present King Ferdinand had triumphed; and word was sent to the Pope at Rome that the Church of the Brethren was no more.

Chapter 16: Comenius and the Hidden Seed (1627-1672)

BUT the cause of the Brethren's Church was not yet lost. As the Brethren fled before the blast, it befell, in the wonderful providence of God, that all their best and noblest qualities—their broadness of view, their care for the young, their patience in suffering, their undaunted faith—shone forth in undying splendour in the life and character of one great man; and that man was the famous John Amos Comenius, the pioneer of modern education and the last Bishop of the Bohemian Brethren. He was born on March 18th, 1592, at Trivnitz, a little market town in Moravia. He was only six years old when he lost his parents through the plague. He was taken in hand by his sister, and was educated at the Brethren's School at Ungarisch-Brod. As he soon resolved to become a minister, he was sent by the Brethren to study theology, first at the Calvinist University of Herborn in Nassau, and then at the Calvinist University of Heidelberg. For two years (1614-1616) he then acted as master in the Brethren's Higher School at Prerau, and then became minister of the congregation at Fulneck. There, too, the Brethren had a school; and there, both as minister and teacher, Comenius, with his young wife and family, was as happy as the livelong day. But his happiness was speedily turned to misery. The Thirty Years' War broke out. What part he took in the Bohemian Revolution we have no means of knowing. He certainly favoured the election of Frederick, and helped his cause in some way. "I contributed a nail or two," he says, [54] "to strengthen the new throne." What sort of nail he means we do not know. The new throne did not stand very long. The troops of Ferdinand appeared at Fulneck. The village was sacked. Comenius reeled with horror. He saw the weapons for stabbing, for chopping, for cutting, for pricking, for hacking, for tearing and for burning. He saw the savage hacking of limbs, the spurting of blood, the flash of fire.

"Almighty God," he wrote in one of his books, "what is happening? Must the whole world perish?"

His house was pillaged and gutted; his books and his manuscripts were burned; and he himself, with his wife and children, had now to flee in hot haste from Fulneck and to take refuge for a while on the estate of Baron Charles von Zerotin at Brandeis-on-the-Adler. To the Brethren Brandeis had long been a sacred spot. There Gregory the Patriarch had breathed his last, and there his bones lay buried; there many an historic Brethren's Synod had been held; and there Comenius took up his abode in a little wood cottage outside the town which tradition said had been built by Gregory himself. He had lost his wife and one of his children on the way from Fulneck; he had lost his post as teacher and minister; and now, for the sake of his suffering Brethren, he wrote his beautiful classical allegory, "The Labyrinth of the World and the Paradise of the Heart." [55] For historical purposes this book is of surpassing value. It is a revelation. It is a picture both of the horrors of the time and of the deep religious life of the Brethren. As Comenius fled from Fulneck to Brandeis he saw sights that harrowed his soul, and now in his cottage at the foot of the hills he described what he had seen. The whole land, said Comenius, was now in a state of disorder. The reign of justice had ended. The reign of pillage had begun. The plot of the book is simple. From scene to scene the pilgrim goes, and everything fills him with disgust. The pilgrim, of course, is Comenius himself; the "Labyrinth" is Bohemia; and the time is the early years of the Thirty Years' War. He had studied the social conditions of Bohemia; he had seen men of all ranks and all occupations; and now, in witty, satirical language, he held the mirror up to nature. What sort of men were employed by Ferdinand to administer justice in Bohemia? Comenius gave them fine sarcastic names. He called the judges Nogod, Lovestrife, Hearsay, Partial, Loveself, Lovegold, Takegift, Ignorant, Knowlittle, Hasty and Slovenly; he called the witnesses Calumny, Lie and Suspicion; and, in obvious allusion to Ferdinand's seizure of property, he named the statute-book "The Rapacious Defraudment of the Land." He saw the lords oppressing the poor, sitting long at table, and discussing lewd and obscene matters. He saw the rich idlers with bloated faces, with bleary eyes, with swollen limbs, with bodies covered with sores. He saw the moral world turned upside down. No longer, said Comenius, did men in Bohemia call things by their right names. They called drunkenness, merriment; greed, economy; usury, interest; lust, love; pride, dignity; cruelty, severity; and laziness, good nature. He saw his Brethren maltreated in the vilest fashion. Some were cast into the fire; some were hanged, beheaded, crucified; [56] some were pierced, chopped, tortured with pincers, and roasted to death on grid-irons. He studied the lives of professing Christians, and found that those who claimed the greatest piety were the sorriest scoundrels in the land. "They drink and vomit," he said, "quarrel and fight, rob and pillage one another by cunning and by violence, neigh and skip from wantonness, shout and whistle, and commit fornication and adultery worse than any of the others." He watched the priests, and found them no better than the people. Some snored, wallowing in feather beds; some feasted till they became speechless; some performed dances and leaps; some passed their time in love-making and wantonness.

For these evils Comenius saw one remedy only, and that remedy was the cultivation of the simple and beautiful religion of the Brethren. The last part of his book, "The Paradise of the Heart," is delightful. Comenius was a marvellous writer. He combined the biting satire of Swift with the devotional tenderness of Thomas `a Kempis. As we linger over the closing sections of his book, we can see that he then regarded the Brethren as almost ideal Christians. Among them he found no priests in gaudy attire, no flaunting wealth, no grinding poverty; and passing their time in peace and quietness, they cherished Christ in their hearts. "All," he says, "were in simple attire, and their ways were gentle and kind. I approached one of their preachers, wishing to speak to him. When, as is our custom, I wished to address him according to his rank, he permitted it not, calling such things worldly fooling." To them ceremonies were matters of little importance. "Thy religion," said the Master to the Pilgrim—i.e., to the Brethren's Church—"shall be to serve me in quiet, and not to bind thyself to any ceremonies, for I do not bind thee by them."

But Comenius did not stay long at Brandeis-on-the-Adler (1628). As Zerotin had sided with the House of Hapsburg, he had been allowed, for a few years, to give shelter to about forty Brethren's ministers; but now commissioners appeared at his Castle, and ordered him to send these ministers away. The last band of exiles now set out for Poland. The leader was Comenius himself. As they bade farewell to their native land they did so in the firm conviction that they themselves should see the day when the Church of the Brethren should stand once more in her ancient home; and as they stood on a spur of the Giant Mountains, and saw the old loved hills and dales, the towns and hamlets, the nestling churches, Comenius raised his eyes to heaven and uttered that historic prayer which was to have so marvellous an answer. He prayed that in the old home God would preserve a "Hidden Seed," which would one day grow to a tree; and then the whole band struck up a hymn and set out for Poland. Pathetic was the marching song they sang:—

Nought have we taken with us,
All to destruction is hurled,
We have only our Kralitz Bibles,
And our Labyrinth of the World.

Comenius led the Brethren to Lissa, in Poland, and Lissa became the metropolis of the exiles.

What happened to many of the exiles no tongue can tell. We know that some Brethren went to Hungary and held together for thirty or forty years; that some were welcomed by the Elector of Saxony and became Lutherans; that some found their way to Holland and became Reformed Protestants; that some settled in Lusatia, Saxony; that a few, such as the Cennicks, crossed the silver streak and found a home in England; and that, finally, a number remained in Bohemia and Moravia, and gathered in the neighbourhood of Landskron, Leitomischl, Kunewalde and Fulneck. What became of these last, the "Hidden Seed," we shall see before very long. For the present they buried their Bibles in their gardens, held midnight meetings in garrets and stables, preserved their records in dovecotes and in the thatched roofs of their cottages, and, feasting on the glorious promises of the Book of Revelation—a book which many of them knew by heart—awaited the time when their troubles should blow by and the call to arise should sound.

Meanwhile Comenius had never abandoned hope. He was sure that the Brethren's Church would revive, and equally sure of the means of her revival. For some years there had flourished in the town of Lissa a famous Grammar School. It was founded by Count Raphael IV. Leszczynski; it had recently become a Higher School, or what Germans call a gymnasium, and now it was entirely in the hands of the Brethren. The patron, Count Raphael V. Leszczynski, was a Brother; [57] the director was John Rybinski, a Brethren's minister; the co-director was another Brethren's minister, Michael Henrici; and Comenius accepted the post of teacher, and entered on the greatest task of his life. He had two objects before him. He designed to revive the Church of the Brethren and to uplift the whole human race; and for each of these purposes he employed the very same method. The method was education. If the Brethren, said Comenius, were to flourish again, they must pay more attention to the training of the young than ever they had done in days gone by. He issued detailed instructions to his Brethren. They must begin, he said, by teaching the children the pure word of God in their homes. They must bring their children up in habits of piety. They must maintain the ancient discipline of the Brethren. They must live in peace with other Christians, and avoid theological bickerings. They must publish good books in the Bohemian language. They must build new schools wherever possible, and endeavour to obtain the assistance of godly nobles. We have here the key to the whole of Comenius's career. It is the fashion now with many scholars to divide his life into two distinct parts. On the one hand, they say, he was a Bishop of the Brethren's Church; on the other hand he was an educational reformer. The distinction is false and artificial. His whole life was of a piece. He never distinguished between his work as a Bishop and his work as an educational reformer. He drew no line between the secular and the sacred. He loved the Brethren's Church to the end of his days; he regarded her teaching as ideal; he laboured and longed for her revival; and he believed with all the sincerity of his noble and beautiful soul that God would surely enable him to revive that Church by means of education and uplift the world by means of that regenerated Church.

And now for thirteen years, in the Grammar School at Lissa, Comenius devoted the powers of his mind to this tremendous task. What was it, he asked, that had caused the downfall of the Brethren in Bohemia and Moravia? It was their cruel and senseless system of education. He had been to a Brethren's School himself, and had come to the conclusion that in point of method the schools of the Brethren were no better than the other schools of Europe. "They are," he declared, "the terror of boys and the slaughter-houses of minds; places where a hatred of literature and books is contracted, where two or more years are spent in learning what might be acquired in one, where what ought to be poured in gently is violently forced and beaten in, and where what ought to be put clearly is presented in a confused and intricate way as if it were a collection of puzzles." The poor boys, he declared, were almost frightened to death. They needed skins of tin; they were beaten with fists, with canes and with birch-rods till the blood streamed forth; they were covered with scars, stripes, spots and weals; and thus they had learned to hate the schools and all that was taught therein.

He had already tried to introduce a reform. He had learned his new ideas about education, not from the Brethren, but at the University of Herborn. He had studied there the theories of Wolfgang Ratich; he had tried to carry out these theories in the Brethren's schools at Prerau and Fulneck; and now at Lissa, where he soon became director, he introduced reforms which spread his fame throughout the civilized world. His scheme was grand and comprehensive. He held that if only right methods were employed all things might be taught to all men. "There is," he said, "nothing in heaven or earth or in the waters, nothing in the abyss under the earth, nothing in the human body, nothing in the soul, nothing in Holy Writ, nothing in the arts, nothing in politics, nothing in the Church, of which the little candidates for wisdom shall be wholly ignorant." His faith in the power of education was enormous. It was the road, he said, to knowledge, to character, to fellowship with God, to eternal life. He divided the educational course into four stages—the "mother school," the popular school, the Latin school and the University; and on each of these stages he had something original to say.

For mothers Comenius wrote a book, entitled the "School of Infancy." In England this book is scarcely known at all: in Bohemia it is a household treasure. Comenius regarded it as a work of first-rate importance. What use, he asked, were schemes of education if a good foundation were not first laid by the mother? For the first six years of his life, said Comenius, the child must be taught by his mother. If she did her work properly she could teach him many marvellous things. He would learn some physics by handling things; some optics by naming colours, light and darkness; some astronomy by studying the twinkling stars; some geography by trudging the neighbouring streets and hills; some chronology by learning the hours, the days and the months; some history by a chat on local events; some geometry by measuring things for himself; some statics by trying to balance his top; some mechanics by building his little toy-house; some dialectics by asking questions; some economics by observing his mother's skill as a housekeeper; and some music and poetry by singing psalms and hymns. As Comenius penned these ideal instructions, he must surely have known that nine mothers out of ten had neither the patience nor the skill to follow his method; and yet he insisted that, in some things, the mother had a clear course before her. His advice was remarkably sound. At what age, ask mothers, should the education of a child begin? It should begin, said Comenius, before the child is born. At that period in her life the expectant mother must be busy and cheerful, be moderate in her food, avoid all worry, and keep in constant touch with God by prayer; and thus the child will come into the world well equipped for the battle of life. She must, of course, nurse the child herself. She must feed him, when weaned, on plain and simple food. She must provide him with picture books; and, above all, she must teach him to be clean in his habits, to obey his superiors, to be truthful and polite, to bend the knee and fold his hands in prayer, and to remember that the God revealed in Christ was ever near at hand.

Again, Comenius has been justly called the "Father of the Elementary School." It was here that his ideas had the greatest practical value. His first fundamental principle was that in all elementary schools the scholars must learn in their native language only. He called these schools "Mother tongue schools." For six or eight years, said Comenius, the scholar must hear no language but his own; and his whole attention must be concentrated, not on learning words like a parrot, but on the direct study of nature. Comenius has been called the great Sense-Realist. He had no belief in learning second-hand. He illustrated his books with pictures. He gave his scholars object lessons. He taught them, not about words, but about things. "The foundation of all learning consists," he said, "in representing clearly to the senses sensible objects." He insisted that no boy or girl should ever have to learn by heart anything which he did not understand. He insisted that nature should be studied, not out of books, but by direct contact with nature herself. "Do we not dwell in the garden of nature," he asked, "as well as the ancients? Why should we not use our eyes, ears and noses as well as they? Why should we not lay open the living book of nature?" He applied these ideas to the teaching of religion and morals. In order to show his scholars the meaning of faith, he wrote a play entitled "Abraham the Patriarch," and then taught them to act it; and, in order to warn them against shallow views of life, he wrote a comedy, "Diogenes the Cynic, Revived." He was no vulgar materialist. His whole object was moral and religious. If Comenius had lived in the twentieth century, he would certainly have been disgusted and shocked by the modern demand for a purely secular education. He would have regarded the suggestion as an insult to human nature. All men, he said, were made in the image of God; all men had in them the roots of eternal wisdom; all men were capable of understanding something of the nature of God; and, therefore, the whole object of education was to develop, not only the physical and intellectual, but also the moral and spiritual powers, and thus fit men and women to be, first, useful citizens in the State, and then saints in the Kingdom of Heaven beyond the tomb. From court to court he would lead the students onward, from the first court dealing with nature to the last court dealing with God. "It is," he said, "our bounden duty to consider the means whereby the whole body of Christian youth may be stirred to vigour of mind and the love of heavenly things." He believed in caring for the body, because the body was the temple of the Holy Ghost; and, in order to keep the body fit, he laid down the rule that four hours of study a day was as much as any boy or girl could stand. For the same reason he objected to corporal punishment; it was a degrading insult to God's fair abode. For the same reason he held that at all severe punishment should be reserved for moral offences only. "The whole object of discipline," he said, "is to form in those committed to our charge a disposition worthy of the children of God." He believed, in a word, in the teaching of religion in day-schools; he believed in opening school with morning prayers, and he held that all scholars should be taught to say passages of Scripture by heart, to sing psalms, to learn a Catechism and to place their trust in the salvation offered through Jesus Christ. And yet Comenius did not insist on the teaching of any definite religious creed. He belonged himself to a Church that had no creed; he took a broader view of religion than either the Lutherans or the Calvinists; he believed that Christianity could be taught without a formal dogmatic statement; and thus, if I understand him aright, he suggested a solution of a difficult problem which baffles our cleverest politicians to-day.

Again Comenius introduced a new way of learning languages. His great work on this subject was entitled "Janua Linguarum Reserata" —i.e., The Gate of Languages Unlocked. Of all his works this was the most popular. It spread his fame all over Europe. It was translated into fifteen different languages. It became, next to the Bible, the most widely known book on the Continent. For one person who read his delightful "Labyrinth," there were thousands who nearly knew the "Janua" by heart. The reason was obvious. The "Labyrinth" was a religious book, and was suppressed as dangerous by Catholic authorities; but the "Janua" was only a harmless grammar, and could be admitted with safety anywhere. It is not the works of richest genius that have the largest sale; it is the books that enable men to get on in life; and the "Janua" was popular because, in truth, "it supplied a long-felt want." It was a Latin grammar of a novel and original kind. For all boys desiring to enter a profession a thorough knowledge of Latin was then an absolute necessity. It was the language in which the learned conversed, the language spoken at all Universities, the language of diplomatists and statesmen, the language of scientific treatises. If a man could make the learning of Latin easier, he was adored as a public benefactor. Comenius's Grammar was hailed with delight, as a boon and a blessing to men. For years all patient students of Latin had writhed in agonies untold. They had learned long lists of Latin words, with their meanings; they had wrestled in their teens with gerunds, supines, ablative absolutes and distracting rules about the subjunctive mood, and they had tried in vain to take an interest in stately authors far above their understanding. Comenius reversed the whole process. What is the use, he asked, of learning lists of words that have no connection with each other? What is the use of teaching a lad grammar before he has a working knowledge of the language? What is the use of expecting a boy to take an interest in the political arguments of Cicero or the dinner table wisdom of Horace? His method was the conversational. For beginners he prepared an elementary Latin Grammar, containing, besides a few necessary rules, a number of sentences dealing with events and scenes of everyday life. It was divided into seven parts. In the first were nouns and adjectives together; in the second nouns and verbs; in the third adverbs, pronouns, numerals and prepositions; in the fourth remarks about things in the school; in the fifth about things in the house; in the sixth about things in the town; in the seventh some moral maxims. And the scholar went through this book ten times before he passed on to the "Janua" proper. The result can be imagined. At the end of a year the boy's knowledge of Latin would be of a peculiar kind. Of grammar he would know but little; of words and phrases he would have a goodly store; and thus he was learning to talk the language before he had even heard of its perplexing rules. One example must suffice to illustrate the method. The beginner did not even learn the names of the cases. In a modern English Latin Grammar, the charming sight that meets our gaze is as follows:—

Nom. Mensa.—A table.
Voc. Mensa.—Oh, table!
Acc. Mensam.—A table.
Gen. Mensae.—Of a table.
Dat. Mensae.—To or for a table.
Abl. Mensa.—By, with or from a table.

The method of Comenius was different. Instead of mentioning the names of the cases, he showed how the cases were actually used, as follows:—

Ecce, tabula nigra.—Look there, a black board.
O tu tabula nigra.—Oh, you black board!
Video tabulam nigram.—I see a black board.
Pars tabulae nigrae.—Part of a black board.
Addo partem tabulae nigrae.—I add a part to a black board.
Vides aliquid in tabula nigra.—I see something on a black board.

With us the method is theory first, practice afterwards; with Comenius the method was practice first, theory afterwards; and the method of Comenius, with modifications, is likely to be the method of the future.

But Comenius's greatest educational work was undoubtedly his "Great Didactic," or the "Art of Teaching All Things to All Men." It was a thorough and comprehensive treatise on the whole science, method, scope and purpose of universal education. As this book has been recently translated into English, I need not here attempt the task of giving an outline of its contents. His ideas were far too grand and noble to put in summary form. For us the point of interest is the fact that while the Thirty Years' War was raging, and warriors like Wallenstein and Gustavus Adolphus were turning Europe into a desert, this scholar, banished from his native land, was devising sublime and broad-minded schemes for the elevation of the whole human race. It is this that makes Comenius great. He played no part in the disgraceful quarrels of the age; he breathed no complaint against his persecutors. "Comenius," said the Jesuit historian Balbin, "wrote many works, but none that were directed against the Catholic Church." As he looked around upon the learned world he saw the great monster Confusion still unslain, and intended to found a Grand Universal College, which would consist of all the learned in Europe, would devote its attention to the pursuit of knowledge in every conceivable branch, and would arrange that knowledge in beautiful order and make the garden of wisdom a trim parterre. He was so sure that his system was right that he compared it to a great clock or mill, which had only to be set going to bring about the desired result. If his scheme could only be carried out, what a change there would be in this dreary earth! What a speedy end to wars and rumours of wars! What a blessed cessation of religious disputes! What a glorious union of all men of all nations about the feet of God!

At last Comenius became so famous that his friend, Samuel Hartlib, invited him to England; and Comenius found upon his arrival that our English Parliament was interested in his scheme (1641). His hopes now rose higher than ever. At last, he thought, he had found a spot where he could actually carry out his grand designs. He had a high opinion of English piety. "The ardour," he wrote, "with which the people crowd to the Churches is incredible. Almost all bring a copy of the Bible with them. Of the youths and men a large number take down the sermons word by word with their pens. Their thirst for the word of God is so great that many of the nobles, citizens also, and matrons study Greek and Hebrew to be able more safely and more sweetly to drink from the very spring of life." Of all countries England seemed to him the best suited for the accomplishment of his designs. He discussed the project with John Dury, with Samuel Hartlib, with John Evelyn, with the Bishop of Lincoln, and probably with John Milton. He wanted to establish an "Academy of Pansophy" at Chelsea; and there all the wisest men in the world would meet, draw up a new universal language, like the framers of Esperanto to-day, and devise a scheme to keep all the nations at peace. His castle in the air collapsed. At the very time when Comenius was resident in London this country was on the eve of a revolution. The Irish Rebellion broke out, the Civil War trod on its heels, and Comenius left England for ever.

From this moment his life was a series of bitter and cruel disappointments. As the Thirty Years' War flickered out to its close, Comenius began to look forward to the day when the Brethren would be allowed to return to Bohemia and Moravia (1648). But the Peace of Westphalia broke his heart. What provision was made in that famous Peace for the poor exiled Brethren? Absolutely none. Comenius was angry and disgusted. He had spent his life in the service of humanity; he had spent six years preparing school books for the Swedish Government; and now he complained—perhaps unjustly—that Oxenstierna, the Swedish Chancellor, had never lifted a finger on behalf of the Brethren.

And yet Comenius continued to hope against hope. The more basely the Brethren were deserted by men, the more certain he was that they would be defended by God. He wrote to Oxenstierna on the subject. "If there is no help from man," he said, "there will be from God, whose aid is wont to commence when that of man ceases."

For eight years the Brethren, undaunted still, held on together as best they could at Lissa; and Comenius, now their chosen leader, made a brave attempt to revive their schools in Hungary. And then came the final, awful crash. The flames of war burst out afresh. When Charles X. became King of Sweden, John Casimir, King of Poland, set up a claim to the Swedish throne. The two monarchs went to war. Charles X. invaded Poland; John Casimir fled from Lissa; Charles X. occupied the town. What part, it may be asked, did the Brethren play in this war? We do not know. As Charles X. was, of course, a Protestant, it is natural to assume that the Brethren sympathised with his cause and hailed him as a deliverer sent by God; but it is one of the strangest features of their history that we never can tell what part they took in these political conflicts. Comenius was now in Lissa. It is said that he openly sided with Charles X., and urged the Brethren to hold out to the bitter end. I doubt it. For a while the Swedish army triumphed. In that army was an old Bohemian general, who swore to avenge the "Day of Blood"; and the churches and convents were plundered, and monks and priests were murdered. For a moment the Day of Blood was avenged, but for a moment only. As the arm of flesh had failed the Brethren in the days of Budowa, so the arm of flesh failed them now.

The Polish army surrounded the walls of Lissa (1656). A panic broke out among the citizens. The Swedish garrison gave way. The Polish soldiers pressed in. Again

Comenius's library was burned, and the grammar school where he had taught was reduced to ashes. The whole town was soon in flames. The fire spread for miles in the surrounding country. As the Brethren fled from their last fond home, with the women and children huddled in waggons, they saw barns and windmills flaring around them, and heard the tramp of the Polish army in hot pursuit. As Pastor John Jacobides and two Acolouths were on their way to Karmin, they were seized, cut down with spades and thrown into a pit to perish. For Samuel Kardus, the last martyr of the fluttering fragment, a more ingenious torture was reserved. He was placed with his head between a door and the door-post, and as the door was gently but firmly closed, his head was slowly crushed to pieces.

And so the hopes of Comenius were blasted. As the aged Bishop drew near to his end, he witnessed the failure of all his schemes. Where now was his beloved Church of the Brethren? It was scattered like autumn leaves before the blast. And yet Comenius hoped on to the bitter end. The news of his sufferings reached the ears of Oliver Cromwell. He offered to find a home for the Brethren in Ireland. If Comenius had only accepted that offer it is certain that Oliver would have been as good as his word. He longed to make Ireland a Protestant country; and the whole modern history of Ireland might have been altered. But Comenius had now become an unpractical dreamer. For all his learning he was very simple-minded; and for all his piety he had a weak side to his character. He had listened in his youth to the prophecies of Christopher Kotter; he had listened also to the ravings of Christina Poniatowski; and now he fell completely under the influence of the vile impostor, Drabik, who pretended to have a revelation from heaven, and predicted that before very long the House of Austria would be destroyed and the Brethren be enabled to return to their native home. Instead, therefore, of accepting Cromwell's offer, Comenius spent his last few years in collecting money for the Brethren; and pleasant it is to record the fact that much of that money came from England. Some was sent by Prince Rupert, and some by officials of the Church of England; and Comenius was able to spend the money in printing helpful, devotional works for the Brethren. His loyalty now to the Brethren was beautiful. It is easy to be faithful to a prosperous Church; Comenius was faithful when the whirl was at the worst. Faster than ever the ship was sinking, but still the brave old white-haired Captain held to his post on the bridge. Few things are more pathetic in history than the way in which Comenius commended the Brethren to the care of the Church of England. "To you, dear friends," he wrote in hope, "we commit our dear mother, the Church herself. Even in her death, which seems approaching, you ought to love her, because in her life she has gone before you for more than two centuries with examples of faith and patience." Of all the links between the old Church of the Brethren and the new, Comenius was the strongest. He handed on the Brethren's Episcopal Orders. He consecrated his son-in-law, Peter Jablonsky; this Peter consecrated his own son, Daniel Ernest; and this Daniel Ernest Jablonsky consecrated David Nitschmann, the first Bishop of the Renewed Church of the Brethren.

He handed on, secondly, the Brethren's system of discipline. He published an edition of the "Ratio Disciplinae," and this it was that fired Zinzendorf's soul with love for the Brethren's Church.

But, thirdly, and most important of all, Comenius kept the old faith burning in the hearts of the "Hidden Seed." For the benefit of those still worshipping in secret in Bohemia and Moravia, he prepared a Catechism, entitled "The Old Catholic Christian Religion in Short Questions and Answers"; and by this Catholic Religion he meant the broad and simple faith of the Bohemian Brethren. "Perish sects," said Comenius; "perish the founders of sects. I have consecrated myself to Christ alone." But the purpose of the Catechism had to be kept a secret. "It is meant," said Comenius, in the preface, "for all the pious and scattered sheep of Christ, especially those at F., G., G., K., K., S., S. and Z." These letters can be easily explained. They stood for the villages of Fulneck, Gersdorf, Gestersdorf, Kunewalde, Klandorf, Stechwalde, Seitendorf and Zauchtenthal; and these are the places from which the first exiles came to renew the Brethren's Church at Herrnhut.

Fifty years before his prayers were answered, Comenius lay silent in the grave (1672). Yet never did bread cast upon the waters more richly return.

SUPPLEMENTARY NOTE.
THE BOHEMIAN BRETHREN AND THE CHURCH OF ENGLAND.

As the relations of the Brethren with England were only of a very occasional nature, it is not easy to weave them into the narrative. But the following particulars will be of special interest; they show the opinion held of the Brethren by officials of the Church of England:—

1. The case of John Bernard.—At some period in the reign of Queen Elizabeth a number of scholarships were founded at Oxford for the benefit of Bohemian students; and in 1583 John Bernard, a Moravian student, took his B.D. degree at Oxford. The record in the University Register is as follows: "Bernardus, John, a Moravian, was allowed to supply B.D. He had studied theology for ten years at German Universities, and was now going to the Universities of Scotland." This proves that the University of Oxford recognised Bernard as a man in holy orders; for none but men in holy orders could take the B.D. degree.

2. The case of Paul Hartmann.—In 1652 (October 15th) Paul Hartmann was ordained a Deacon at a Synod of the Moravian Church at Lissa. In 1657 he came to England, along with his brother, Adam Samuel Hartmann, to raise funds for the exiles. In 1660 he was ordained a Presbyter by Bishop Robert Skinner, of Oxford, in Christ Church; in 1671 he was admitted Chaplain or Petty Canon of Oxford Cathedral; and in 1676 he

became Rector of Shillingford, Berkshire. This proves that Bishop Skinner, of Oxford, recognised Paul Hartmann's status as a Deacon; and that recognition, so far as we know, was never questioned by any Anglican authorities. But that is not the end of the story. At this period a considerable number of Brethren had found a home in England; the Continental Brethren wished to provide for their spiritual needs, and, therefore, in 1675 they wrote a letter to the Anglican Bishops requesting them to consecrate Hartmann a Bishop. Of that letter a copy has been preserved in the Johannis-Kirche at Lissa. "It is no superstition," they wrote, "that fills us with this desire. It is simply our love of order and piety; and the Church of England is the only Protestant Church beside our own that possesses this treasure, and can, therefore, come to our help." For some reason, however, this pathetic request was not carried out. What answer did the Anglican Bishops give? We do not know; no answer has been discovered; and Hartmann remained a Presbyter to the end.

3. The case of Adam Samuel Hartmann.—He was first a minister of the Moravian Church at Lissa (1652-56). In 1657 he came to England to collect money; in 1673 he was consecrated a Moravian Bishop at Lissa; and in 1680 he received the degree of D.D. at Oxford. His diploma refers to him as a Bishop. This suggests, if it does not actually prove, that the University of Oxford recognised him as a valid Bishop.

4. The case of Bishop Amos Comenius.—Of all the Bishops of the Bohemian Brethren Comenius did most to stir up sympathy on their behalf in England. In 1657 he sent the two Hartmanns and Paul Cyrill to the Archbishop of Canterbury with a MS. entitled, "Ultimus in Protestantes Bohemiae confessionis ecclesias Antichristi furor"; in 1660 he dedicated his "Ratio Disciplinae" to the Church of England; and in 1661 he published his "Exhortation of the Churches of Bohemia to the Church of England." In this book Comenius took a remarkable stand. He declared that the Slavonian Churches had been planted by the Apostles; that these Churches had "run up to a head and ripened" in the Unity of the Brethren; and that he himself was now the only surviving Bishop of the remnants of these Churches. In other words, he represented himself as the Bishop of a Church of Apostolic origin. In what way, it may be asked, was this claim received by Anglican authorities? The next case will supply the answer.

5. The case of Archbishop Sancroft.—In 1683 King Charles II. issued a Cabinet Order on behalf of the Brethren; the order was accompanied by an account of their distresses; the account was "recommended under the hands" of William Sancroft, Archbishop of Canterbury, and Henry Compton, Bishop of London; and in that account the statement was deliberately made that the Brethren deserved the assistance of Anglicans, not only because they had "renounced the growing errors of Popery," but also because they had "preserved the Succession of Episcopal Orders." The last words can only bear one meaning; and that meaning obviously is that both the Primate and the Bishop of

London regarded Moravian Episcopal Orders as valid. The next case tells a similar story.

6. The case of Archbishop Wake.—We have now to step over a period of thirty-three years. As soon as James II. came to the throne, the interest of English Churchmen in the Brethren appears to have waned, and neither William III. nor Queen Anne took any steps on their behalf. And yet the connection of the Brethren with England was not entirely broken. The bond of union was Daniel Ernest Jablonsky. He was Amos Comenius's grandson. In 1680 he came to England; he studied three years at Oxford, and finally received the degree of D.D. In 1693 he was appointed Court Preacher at Berlin; in 1699 he was consecrated a Moravian Bishop; and in 1709 he was elected corresponding secretary of the S.P.C.K. Meanwhile, however, fresh disasters had overtaken the Brethren. As the sun was rising on July 29th, 1707, a troop of Russians rode into the town of Lissa, and threw around them balls of burning pitch. The town went up in flames; the last home of the Brethren was destroyed, and the Brethren were in greater distress than ever. At this point Jablonsky nobly came to their aid. He began by publishing an account of their distresses; he tried to raise a fund on their behalf; and finally (1715) he sent his friend, Bishop Sitkovius, to England, to lay their case before Archbishop Wake. Again, as in the case of Archbishop Sancroft, this appeal to the Church of England was successful. The Archbishop brought the case before George I., the King consulted the Privy Council, the Privy Council gave consent; the King issued Letters Patent to all the Archbishops and Bishops of England and Wales, and Wake and John Robinson, Bishop of London, issued a special appeal, which was read in all the London churches. The result was twofold. On the one hand money was collected for the Brethren; on the other, some person or persons unknown denounced them as Hussites, declared that their Bishops could not be distinguished from Presbyters, and contended that, being followers of Wycliffe, they must surely, like Wycliffe, be enemies of all episcopal government. Again Jablonsky came to the Brethren's rescue. He believed, himself, in the Brethren's Episcopal Orders; he prepared a treatise on the subject, entitled, "De Ordine et Successione Episcopali in Unitate Fratrum Bohemorum conservato"; he sent a copy of that treatise to Wake, and Wake, in reply, declared himself perfectly satisfied.

To what conclusion do the foregoing details point? It is needful here to speak with caution and precision. As the claims of the Brethren were never brought before Convocation, we cannot say that the Anglican Church as a body officially recognised the Brethren as a sister Episcopal Church. But, on the other hand, we can also say that the Brethren's orders were never doubted by any Anglican authorities. They were recognised by two Archbishops of Canterbury; they were recognised by Bishop Skinner, of Oxford; they were recognised by the University of Oxford. They were recognised, in a word, by every Anglican authority before whose notice they happened to be brought.

Book 2:

The Revival under Zinzendorf

Chapter 1: The Youth of Count Zinzendorf (1700-1722)

IF the kindly reader will take the trouble to consult a map of Europe he will see that that part of the Kingdom of Saxony known as Upper Lusatia runs down to the Bohemian frontier. About ten miles from the frontier line there stand to-day the mouldering remains of the old castle of Gross-Hennersdorf. The grey old walls are streaked with slime. The wooden floors are rotten, shaky and unsafe. The rafters are worm-eaten. The windows are broken. The damp wall-papers are running to a sickly green. Of roof there is almost none. For the lover of beauty or the landscape painter these ruins have little charm. But to us these tottering walls are of matchless interest, for within these walls Count Zinzendorf, the Renewer of the Brethren's Church, spent the years of his childhood.

He was born at six o'clock in the evening, Wednesday, May 26th, 1700, in the picturesque city of Dresden (1700); the house is pointed out to the visitor; and "Zinzendorf Street" reminds us still of the noble family that has now died out. He was only six weeks old when his father burst a blood-vessel and died; he was only four years when his mother married again; and the young Count—Nicholas Lewis, Count of Zinzendorf and Pottendorf—was handed over to the tender care of his grandmother, Catherine von Gersdorf, who lived at Gross-Hennersdorf Castle. And now, even in childhood's days, little Lutz, as his grandmother loved to call him, began to show signs of his coming greatness. As his father lay on his dying bed, he had taken the child in his feeble arm, and consecrated him to the service of Christ; and now in his grandmother's noble home he sat at the feet of the learned, the pious, and the refined. Never was a child less petted and pampered; never was a child more strictly trained; never was a child made more familiar with the person and teaching of Jesus Christ. Dr. Spener, [58] the famous Pietist leader, watched his growth with fatherly interest. The old lady was a leader in Pietist circles, was a writer of beautiful religious poetry, and guarded him as the apple of her eye. He read the Bible every day. He doted on Luther's Catechism. He had the Gospel story at his finger-ends. His aunt Henrietta, who was rather an oddity, prayed with him morning and night. His tutor, Edeling, was an earnest young Pietist from Franke's school at Halle; and the story of Zinzendorf's early days reads like a mediaeval tale. "Already in my childhood," he says, (1704) "I loved the Saviour, and had abundant communion with Him. In my fourth year I began to seek God earnestly, and determined to become a true servant of Jesus Christ." At the age of six he regarded Christ as his Brother, would talk with Him for hours together as with a familiar friend and was often found rapt in thought (1706), like Socrates in the market-place at Athens. As other children love and trust their parents, so this bright lad with the golden hair loved and trusted Christ. "A thousand times," he said, "I heard Him speak in my heart, and saw Him with the eye of faith."

Already the keynote of his life was struck; already the fire of zeal burned in his bosom. "Of all the qualities of Christ," said He, "the greatest is His nobility; and of all the noble ideas in the world, the noblest is the idea that the Creator should die for His children. If the Lord were forsaken by all the world, I still would cling to Him and love Him." He held prayer-meetings in his private room. He was sure that Christ Himself was present there. He preached sermons to companies of friends. If hearers failed, he arranged the chairs as an audience; and still is shown the little window from which he threw letters addressed to Christ, not doubting that Christ would receive them. As the child was engaged one day in prayer, the rude soldiers of Charles XII. burst into his room. Forthwith the lad began to speak of Christ; and away the soldiers fled in awe and terror. At the age of eight he lay awake at night tormented with atheistic doubts (1708). But the doubts did not last long. However much he doubted with the head he never doubted with the heart; and the charm that drove the doubts away was the figure of the living Christ.

And here we touch the springs of the boy's religion. It is easy to call all this a hot-house process; it is easy to dub the child a precocious prig. But at bottom his religion was healthy and sound. It was not morbid; it was joyful. It was not based on dreamy imagination; it was based on the historic person of Christ. It was not the result of mystic exaltation; it was the result of a study of the Gospels. It was not, above all, self-centred; it led him to seek for fellowship with others. As the boy devoured the Gospel story, he was impressed first by the drama of the Crucifixion; and often pondered on the words of Gerhardt's hymn:—

O Head so full of bruises,
So full of pain and scorn,
Midst other sore abuses,
Mocked with a crown of thorn.

For this his tutor, Edeling, was partly responsible. "He spoke to me," says Zinzendorf, "of Jesus and His wounds."

But the boy did not linger in Holy Week for ever. He began by laying stress on the suffering Christ; he went on to lay stress on the whole life of Christ; and on that life, from the cradle to the grave, his own strong faith was based. "I was," he said, "as certain that the Son of God was my Lord as of the existence of my five fingers." To him the existence of Jesus was a proof of the existence of God; and he felt all his limbs ablaze, to use his own expression, with the desire to preach the eternal Godhead of Christ. "If it were possible," he said, "that there should be another God than Christ I would rather be damned with Christ than happy with another. I have," he exclaimed, "but one passion—tis He, tis only He."

But the next stage in his journey was not so pleasing (1710). At the age of ten he was taken by his mother to Professor Franke's school at Halle; and by mistake he overheard a conversation between her and the pious professor. She described him as a lad of parts, but full of pride, and in need of the curbing rein. He was soon to find how much these words implied. If a boy has been trained by gentle ladies he is hardly well equipped, as a rule, to stand the rough horseplay of a boarding-school; and if, in addition, he boasts blue blood, he is sure to come in for blows. And the Count was a delicate aristocrat, with weak legs and a cough. He was proud of his noble birth; he was rather officious in his manner; he had his meals at Franke's private table; he had private lodgings a few minutes' walk from the school; he had plenty of money in his purse; and, therefore, on the whole, he was as well detested as the son of a lord can be. "With a few exceptions," he sadly says, "my schoolfellows hated me throughout."

But this was not the bitterest part of the pill. If there was any wholesome feeling missing in his heart hitherto, it was what theologians call the sense of sin. He had no sense of sin whatever, and no sense of any need of pardon. His masters soon proceeded to humble his pride. He was introduced as a smug little Pharisee, and they treated him as a viper. Of all systems of school discipline, the most revolting is the system of employing spies; and that was the system used by the staff at Halle. They placed the young Count under boyish police supervision, encouraged the lads to tell tales about him, rebuked him for his misconduct in the measles, lectured him before the whole school on his rank disgusting offences, and treated him as half a rogue and half an idiot. If he pleaded not guilty, they called him a liar, and gave him an extra thrashing. The thrashing was a public school entertainment, and was advertised on the school notice-board. "Next week," ran the notice on one occasion, "the Count is to have the stick." For two years he lived in a moral purgatory. The masters gave him the fire of their wrath, and the boys the cold shoulder of contempt. The masters called him a malicious rebel, and the boys called him a snob. As the little fellow set off for morning school, with his pile of books upon his arm, the others waylaid him, jostled him to and fro, knocked him into the gutter, scattered his books on the street, and then officiously reported him late for school. He was clever, and, therefore, the masters called him idle; and when he did not know his lesson they made him stand in the street, with a pair of ass's ears on his head, and a placard on his back proclaiming to the public that the culprit was a "lazy donkey."

His private tutor, Daniel Crisenius, was a bully, who had made his way into Franke's school by varnishing himself with a shiny coating of piety. If the Count's relations came to see him, Crisenius made him beg for money, and then took the money himself. If his grandmother sent him a ducat Crisenius pocketed a florin. If he wrote a letter home, Crisenius read it. If he drank a cup of coffee, Crisenius would say, "You have me to thank for that, let me hear you sing a song of thanksgiving." If he tried to pour out his soul in prayer, Crisenius mocked him, interrupted him, and introduced disgusting topics of conversation. He even made the lad appear a sneak. "My tutor," says Zinzendorf, "often persuaded me to write letters to my guardian complaining of my hard treatment, and then showed the letters to the inspector."

In vain little Lutz laid his case before his mother. Crisenius thrashed him to such good purpose that he never dared to complain again; and his mother still held that he needed drastic medicine. "I beseech you," she wrote to Franke, "be severe with the lad; if talking will not cure him of lying, then let him feel it."

At last the muddy lane broadened into a highway. One day Crisenius pestered Franke with one of his whining complaints. The headmaster snapped him short.

"I am sick," he said, "of your growlings; you must manage the matter yourself."

As the months rolled on, the Count breathed purer air. He became more manly and bold. He astonished the masters by his progress. He was learning Greek, could speak in French and dash off letters in Latin. He was confirmed, attended the Communion, and wrote a beautiful hymn [59] recording his feelings; and already in his modest way he launched out on that ocean of evangelical toil on which he was to sail all the days of his life.

As the child grew up in Hennersdorf Castle he saw and heard a good deal of those drawing-room meetings [60] which Philip Spener, the Pietist leader, had established in the houses of several noble Lutheran families, and which came in time to be known in Germany as "Churches within the Church." [61] He knew that Spener had been his father's friend. He had met the great leader at the Castle. He sympathised with the purpose of his meetings. He had often longed for fellowship himself, and had chatted freely on religious topics with his Aunt Henrietta. He had always maintained his private habit of personal communion with Christ; and now he wished to share his religion with others. The time was ripe. The moral state of Franke's school was low; the boys were given to vicious habits, and tried to corrupt his soul; and the Count, who was a healthy minded boy, and shrank with disgust from fleshly sins, retorted by forming a number of religious clubs for mutual encouragement and help. "I established little societies," he says, "in which we spoke of the grace of Christ, and encouraged each other in diligence and good works." He became a healthy moral force in the school. He rescued his friend, Count Frederick de Watteville, from the hands of fifty seducers; he persuaded three others to join in the work of rescue; and the five lads established a club which became a "Church within the Church" for boys. They called themselves first "The Slaves of Virtue," next the "Confessors of Christ," and finally the "Honourable Order of the Mustard Seed"; and they took a pledge to be true to Christ, to be upright and moral, and to do good to their fellow-men. Of all the school clubs established by Zinzendorf this "Order of the Mustard Seed" was the most famous and the most enduring. As the boys grew up to man's estate they invited others to join their ranks; the doctrinal basis was broad; and among the members in later years were John Potter, Archbishop of Canterbury, Thomas Wilson, Bishop of Sodor and Man, Cardinal Noailles, the broad-minded Catholic, and General Oglethorpe, Governor of Georgia. For an emblem they had a small shield, with an "Ecce Homo," and the motto, "His wounds our healing"; and each member of the Order wore a gold ring, inscribed with the words, "No man liveth unto himself." The Grand Master of the Order was Zinzendorf himself. He wore a golden cross; the cross had an oval green front; and on that front was painted a mustard tree, with the words beneath, "Quod fuit ante nihil," i.e., what was formerly nothing. [62]

But already the boy had wider conceptions still. As he sat at Franke's dinner table, he listened one day to the conversation of the Danish missionary, Ziegenbalg, who was now home on furlough, and he even saw some dusky converts whom the missionary had brought from Malabar (1715). His missionary zeal was aroused. As his guardian had already settled that Zinzendorf should enter the service of the State, he had, of course, no idea of becoming a missionary himself; [63] but, as that was out of the question, he formed a solemn league and covenant with his young friend Watteville that when God would show them suitable men they would send them out to heathen tribes for whom no one else seemed to care. Nor was this mere playing at religion. As the Count looked back on his Halle days he saw in these early clubs and covenants the germs of his later work; and when he left for the University the delighted Professor Franke said, "This youth will some day become a great light in the world."

As the Count, however, in his uncle's opinion was growing rather too Pietistic, he was now sent to the University at Wittenberg, to study the science of jurisprudence, and prepare for high service in the State (April, 1716). His father had been a Secretary of State, and the son was to follow in his footsteps. His uncle had a contempt for Pietist religion; and sent the lad to Wittenberg "to drive the nonsense out of him." He had certainly chosen the right place. For two hundred years the great University had been regarded as the stronghold of the orthodox Lutheran faith; the bi-centenary Luther Jubilee was fast approaching; the theological professors were models of orthodox belief; and the Count was enjoined to be regular at church, and to listen with due attention and reverence to the sermons of those infallible divines. It was like sending a boy to Oxford to cure him of a taste for dissent. His tutor, Crisenius, went with him, to guard his morals, read his letters, and rob him of money at cards. He had also to master the useful arts of riding, fencing, and dancing. The cards gave him twinges of conscience. If he took a hand, he laid down the condition that any money he might win should be given to the poor. He prayed for skill in his dancing lessons, because he wanted to have more time for more serious studies. He was more devout in his daily life than ever, prayed to Christ with the foil in his hand, studied the Bible in Hebrew and Greek, spent whole nights in prayer, fasted the livelong day on Sundays, and was, in a word, so Methodistic in his habits that he could truly describe himself as a "rigid Pietist." He interfered in many a duel, and rebuked his fellow students for drinking hard; and for this he was not beloved. As he had come to Wittenberg to study law, he was not, of course, allowed to attend the regular theological lectures; but, all the same, he spent his leisure in studying the works of Luther and Spener, and cultivated the personal friendship of many of the theological professors. And here he made a most delightful discovery. As he came to know these professors better, he found that a man could be orthodox without being narrow-minded; and they, for their part, also found that a man could be a rigid Pietist without being a sectarian prig. It was time, he thought, to put an end to the quarrel. He would make peace between Wittenberg and Halle. He would reconcile the Lutherans and Pietists. He consulted with leading professors on both sides; he convinced them of the need for peace; and the rival teachers actually agreed to accept this student of nineteen summers as the agent of the longed-for truce. But here Count Zinzendorf's mother intervened. "You must not meddle," she wrote, "in such weighty matters; they are above your understanding and your powers." And Zinzendorf, being a dutiful son, obeyed. "I think," he said, "a visit to Halle might have been of use, but, of course, I must obey the fourth commandment." [64]

And now, as befitted a nobleman born, he was sent on the grand tour, to give the final polish to his education (1719). He regarded the prospect with horror. He had heard of more than one fine lord whose virtues had been polished away. For him the dazzling sights of Utrecht and Paris had no bewitching charm. He feared the glitter, the glamour, and the glare. The one passion, love to Christ, still ruled his heart. "Ah!" he wrote to a friend, "What a poor, miserable thing is the grandeur of the great ones of the earth! What splendid misery!" As John Milton, on his continental tour, had sought the company of musicians and men of letters, so this young budding Christian poet, with the figure of the Divine Redeemer ever present to his mind, sought out the company of men and women who, whatever their sect or creed, maintained communion with the living Son of God. He went first to Frankfurt-on-the-Main, where Spener had toiled so long, came down the Rhine to Duesseldorf, spent half a year at Utrecht, was introduced to William, Prince of Orange, paid flying calls at Brussels, Antwerp, Amsterdam and Rotterdam, and ended the tour by a six months'stay amid the gaieties of Paris. At Duesseldorf a famous incident occurred. There, in the picture gallery, he saw and admired the beautiful Ecce Homo of Domenico Feti; there, beneath the picture he read the thrilling appeal: "All this I did for thee; what doest thou for Me?"; and there, in response to that appeal, he resolved anew to live for Him who had worn the cruel crown of thorns for all. [65]

At Paris he attended the Court levee, and was presented to the Duke of Orleans, the Regent, and his mother, the Dowager Duchess.

"Sir Count," said the Duchess, "have you been to the opera to-day?"

"Your Highness," he replied, "I have no time for the opera." He would not spend a golden moment except for the golden crown.

"I hear," said the Duchess, "that you know the Bible by heart."

"Ah," said he, "I only wish I did."

At Paris, too, he made the acquaintance of the Catholic Archbishop, Cardinal Noailles. It is marvellous how broad in his views the young man was. As he discussed the nature of true religion with the Cardinal, who tried in vain to win him for the Church of Rome, he came to the conclusion that the true Church of Jesus Christ consisted of many sects and many forms of belief. He held that the Church was still an invisible body; he held that it transcended the bounds of all denominations; he had found good Christians among Protestants and Catholics alike; and he believed, with all his heart and soul, that God had called him to the holy task of enlisting the faithful in all the sects in one grand Christian army, and thus realizing, in visible form, the promise of Christ that all His disciples should be one. He was no bigoted Lutheran. For him the cloak of creed or sect was only of minor moment. He desired to break down all sectarian barriers. He desired to draw men from all the churches into one grand fellowship with Christ. He saw, and lamented, the bigotry of all the sects. "We Protestants," he said, "are very fond of the word liberty; but in practice we often try to throttle the conscience." He was asked if he thought a Catholic could be saved. "Yes," he replied, "and the man who doubts that, cannot have looked far beyond his own small cottage."

"What, then," asked the Duchess of Luynes, "is the real difference between a Lutheran and a Catholic?"

"It is," he replied, "the false idea that the Bible is so hard to understand that only the Church can explain it." He had, in a word, discovered his vocation.

His religion purified his love. As he made his way home, at the close of the tour, he called to see his aunt, the Countess of Castell, and her daughter Theodora (1720); and during his stay he fell ill of a fever, and so remained much longer than he had at first intended. He helped the Countess to put in order the affairs of her estate, took a leading part in the religious services of the castle, and was soon regarded as almost one of the family. At first, according to his usual custom, he would talk about nothing but religion. But gradually his manner changed. He opened out, grew less reserved, and would gossip and chat like a woman. He asked himself the reason of this alteration. He discovered it. He was in love with his young cousin, Theodora. For a while the gentle stream of love ran smooth. His mother and the Countess Castell smiled approval; Theodora, though rather icy in manner, presented him with her portrait; and the Count, who accepted the dainty gift as a pledge of blossoming love, was rejoicing at finding so sweet a wife and so charming a helper in his work, when an unforeseen event turned the current of the stream. Being belated one evening on a journey, he paid a visit to his friend Count Reuss, and during conversation made the disquieting discovery that his friend wished to marry Theodora. A beautiful contest followed. Each of the claimants to the hand of Theodora expressed his desire to retire in favour of the other; and, not being able to settle the dispute, the two young men set out for Castell to see what Theodora herself would say. Young Zinzendorf's mode of reasoning was certainly original. If his own love for Theodora was pure—i.e., if it was a pure desire to do her good, and not a vulgar sensual passion like that with which many love-sick swains were afflicted—he could, he said, fulfil his purpose just as well by handing her over to the care of his Christian friend. "Even if it cost me my life to surrender her," he said, "if it is more acceptable to my Saviour, I ought to sacrifice the dearest object in the world." The two friends arrived at Castell and soon saw which way the wind was blowing; and Zinzendorf found, to his great relief, that what had been a painful struggle to him was as easy as changing a dress to Theodora. The young lady gave Count Reuss her heart and hand. The rejected suitor bore the blow like a stoic. He would conquer, he said, such disturbing earthly emotions; why should they be a thicket in the way of his work for Christ? The betrothal was sealed in a religious ceremony. Young Zinzendorf composed a cantata for the occasion (March 9th, 1721); the cantata was sung, with orchestral accompaniment, in the presence of the whole house of Castell; and at the conclusion of the festive scene the young composer

119

offered up on behalf of the happy couple a prayer so tender that all were moved to tears. His self-denial was well rewarded. If the Count had married Theodora, he would only have had a graceful drawing-room queen. About eighteen months later he married Count Reuss's sister, Erdmuth Dorothea (Sept. 7th, 1722); and in her he found a friend so true that the good folk at Herrnhut called her a princess of God, and the "foster-mother of the Brethren's Church in the eighteenth century." [66]

If the Count could now have had his way he would have entered the service of the State Church; but in those days the clerical calling was considered to be beneath the dignity of a noble, and his grandmother, pious though she was, insisted that he should stick to jurisprudence. He yielded, and took a post as King's Councillor at Dresden, at the Court of Augustus the Strong, King of Saxony. But no man can fly from his shadow, and Zinzendorf could not fly from his hopes of becoming a preacher of the Gospel. If he could not preach in the orthodox pulpit, he would teach in some other way; and, therefore, he invited the public to a weekly meeting in his own rooms on Sunday afternoons from three to seven. He had no desire to found a sect, and no desire to interfere with the regular work of the Church. He was acting, he said, in strict accordance with ecclesiastical law; and he justified his bold conduct by appealing to a clause in Luther's Smalkald Articles. [67] He contended that there provision was made for the kind of meeting that he was conducting; and, therefore, he invited men of all classes to meet him on Sunday afternoons, read a passage of Scripture together, and talk in a free-and-easy fashion on spiritual topics. He became known as rather a curiosity; and Valentine Loescher, the popular Lutheran preacher, mentioned him by name in his sermons, and held him up before the people as an example they would all do well to follow.

But Zinzendorf had not yet reached his goal. He was not content with the work accomplished by Spener, Franke, and other leading Pietists. He was not content with drawing-room meetings for people of rank and money. If fellowship, said he, was good for lords, it must also be good for peasants. He wished to apply the ideas of Spener to folk in humbler life. For this purpose he now bought from his grandmother the little estate of Berthelsdorf, which lay about three miles from Hennersdorf (April, 1722); installed his friend, John Andrew Rothe, as pastor of the village church; and resolved that he and the pastor together would endeavour to convert the village into a pleasant garden of God. "I bought this estate," he said, "because I wanted to spend my life among peasants, and win their souls for Christ."

"Go, Rothe," he said, "to the vineyard of the Lord. You will find in me a brother and helper rather than a patron."

And here let us note precisely the aim this pious Count had in view. He was a loyal and devoted member of the national Lutheran Church; he was well versed in Luther's theology and in Luther's practical schemes; and now at Berthelsdorf he was making an effort to carry into practical effect the fondest dreams of Luther himself. For this, the fellowship of true believers, the great Reformer had sighed in vain; [68] and to this great purpose the Count would now devote his money and his life.

He introduced the new pastor to the people; the induction sermon was preached by Schaefer, the Pietist pastor at Goerlitz; and the preacher used the prophetic words, "God will light a candle on these hills which will illuminate the whole land."

We have now to see how far these words came true. We have now to see how the Lutheran Count applied his ideas to the needs of exiles from a foreign land, and learned to take a vital interest in a Church of which as yet he had never heard.

Chapter 2: Christian David (1690-1722)

IT is recorded in John Wesley's "Journal," [69] that when he paid his memorable visit to Herrnhut he was much impressed by the powerful sermons of a certain godly carpenter, who had preached in his day to the Eskimos in Greenland, and who showed a remarkable knowledge of divinity. It was Christian David, known to his friends as the "Servant of the Lord."

He was born on December 31st, 1690, at Senftleben, in Moravia; he was brought up in that old home of the Brethren; and yet, as far as records tell, he never heard in his youthful days of the Brethren who still held the fort in the old home of their fathers. He came of a Roman Catholic family, and was brought up in the Roman Catholic faith. He sat at the feet of the parish priest, was devout at Mass, invoked his patron saint, St. Anthony, knelt down in awe before every image and picture of the Virgin, regarded Protestants as children of the devil, and grew up to man's estate burning with Romish zeal, as he says, "like a baking oven." He began life as a shepherd; and his religion was tender and deep. As he tended his sheep in the lonesome fields, and rescued one from the jaws of a wolf, he thought how Christ, the Good Shepherd, had given His life for men; and as he sought his wandering sheep in the woods by night he thought how Christ sought sinners till he found them. And yet somehow he was not quite easy in his mind. For all his zeal and all his piety he was not sure that he himself had escaped the snare of the fowler. He turned first for guidance to some quiet Protestants, and was told by them, to his horror, that the Pope was Antichrist, that the worship of saints was a delusion, and that only through faith in Christ could his sins be forgiven. He was puzzled. As these Protestants were ready to suffer for their faith, he felt they must be sincere; and when some of them were cast into prison, he crept to the window of their cell and heard them sing in the gloaming. He read Lutheran books against the Papists, and Papist books against the Lutherans. He was now dissatisfied with both. He could see, he said, that the Papists were wrong, but that did not prove that the Lutherans were right; he could not understand what the Lutherans meant when they said that a man was justified by faith alone; and at last he lost his way so far in this famous theological fog that he hated and loathed the very name of Christ. He turned next for instruction to some Jews; and the Jews, of course, confirmed his doubts, threw scorn upon the whole New Testament, and endeavoured to convince him that they alone were the true Israel of God.

He turned next to the Bible, and the fog lifted a little (1710). He read the Old Testament carefully through, to see if the prophecies there had been fulfilled; and, thereby, he arrived at the firm belief that Jesus was the promised Messiah. He then mastered the New Testament, and came to the equally firm conclusion that the Bible was the Word of God.

And even yet he was not content. As long as he stayed in Catholic Moravia he would have to keep his new convictions a secret; and, longing to renounce the Church of Rome in public, he left Moravia, passed through Hungary and Silesia, and finally became a member of a Lutheran congregation at Berlin.

But the Lutherans seemed to him very stiff and cold. He was seeking for a pearl of great price, and so far he had failed to find it. He had failed to find it in the Church of Rome, failed to find it in the Scriptures, and failed to find it in the orthodox Protestants of Berlin. He had hoped to find himself in a goodly land, where men were godly and true; and he found that even the orthodox Protestants made mock of his pious endeavours. He left Berlin in disgust, and enlisted in the Prussian Army. He did not find much piety there. He served in the war against Charles XII. of Sweden (1715), was present at the siege of Stralsund, thought soldiers no better than civilians, accepted his discharge with joy, and wandered around from town to town, like the old philosopher seeking an honest man. At last, however, he made his way to the town of Goerlitz, in Silesia (1717); and there he came into personal contact with two Pietist clergymen, Schaefer and Schwedler. For the first time in his weary pilgrimage he met a pastor who was also a man. He fell ill of a dangerous disease; he could not stir hand or foot for twenty weeks; he was visited by Schwedler every day; and thus, through the gateway of human sympathy, he entered the kingdom of peace, and felt assured that all his sins were forgiven. He married a member of Schwedler's Church, was admitted to the Church himself, and thus found, in Pietist circles, that very spirit of fellowship and help which Zinzendorf himself regarded as the greatest need of the Church.

But now Christian David must show to others the treasure he had found for himself. For the next five years he made his home at Goerlitz; but, every now and then, at the risk of his life, he would take a trip to Moravia, and there tell his old Protestant friends the story of his new-found joy. He preached in a homely style; he had a great command of Scriptural language; he was addressing men who for many years had conned their Bibles in secret; and thus his preaching was like unto oil on a smouldering fire, and stirred to vigorous life once more what had slumbered for a hundred years since the fatal Day of Blood. He tramped the valleys of Moravia; he was known as the Bush Preacher, and was talked of in every market-place; the shepherds sang old Brethren's hymns on the mountains; a new spirit breathed upon the old dead bones; and thus, through the message of this simple man, there began in Moravia a hot revival of Protestant zeal and hope. It was soon to lead to marvellous results.

For the last three hundred and forty years there had been established in the neighbourhood of Fulneck, in Moravia, a colony of Germans. [70] They still spoke the German language; they lived in places bearing German names and bore German names themselves; they had used a German version of the Bible and a German edition of the Brethren's Hymns; and thus, when David's trumpet sounded, they were able to quit their long-loved homes and settle down in comfort on German soil. At Kunewalde [71] dwelt the Schneiders and Nitschmanns; at Zauchtenthal the Stachs and Zeisbergers; at Sehlen the Jaeschkes and Neissers; and at Senftleben, David's old home, the Grassmanns. For such men there was now no peace in their ancient home. Some were imprisoned; some were loaded with chains; some were yoked to the plough and made to work like horses; and some had to stand in wells of water until nearly frozen to death. And yet the star of hope still shone upon them. As the grand old patriarch, George Jaeschke, saw the angel of death draw near, he gathered his son and grandsons round his bed, and spoke in thrilling, prophetic words of the remnant that should yet be saved.

"It is true," said he, "that our liberties are gone, and that our descendants are giving way to a worldly spirit, so that the Papacy is devouring them. It may seem as though the final end of the Brethren's Church had come. But, my beloved children, you will see a great deliverance. The remnant will be saved. How, I cannot say; but something tells me that an exodus will take place; and that a refuge will be offered in a country and on a spot where you will be able, without fear, to serve the Lord according to His holy Word."

The time of deliverance had come. As Christian David heard of the sufferings which these men had now to endure, his blood boiled with anger. He resolved to go to their rescue. The path lay open. He had made many friends in Saxony. His friend Schaefer introduced him to Rothe; Rothe introduced him to Zinzendorf; and Christian David asked the Count for permission to bring some persecuted Protestants from Moravia to find a refuge in Berthelsdorf. The conversation was momentous. The heart of the Count was touched. If these men, said he, were genuine martyrs, he would do his best to help them; and he promised David that if they came he would find them a place of abode. The joyful carpenter returned to Moravia, and told the news to the Neisser family at Sehlen. "This," said they, "is God's doing; this is a call from the Lord."

And so, at ten o'clock one night, there met at the house of Jacob Neisser, in Sehlen, a small band of emigrants (May 27th, 1722). At the head of the band was Christian David; and the rest of the little group consisted of Augustin and Jacob Neisser, their wives and children, Martha Neisser, and Michael Jaeschke, a cousin of the family. [72] We know but little about these humble folk; and we cannot be sure that they were all descendants of the old Church of the Brethren. Across the mountains they came, by winding and unknown paths. For the sake of their faith they left their goods and chattels behind; long and weary was the march; and at length, worn out and footsore, they arrived, with Christian David at their head, at Zinzendorf's estate at Berthelsdorf (June 8th, 1722).

The streams had met: the new river was formed; and thus the course of Renewed Brethren's History had begun.

Chapter 3: The Founding of Herrnhut (1722-1727)

AS these wanderers from a foreign land had not been able to bring in their pockets certificates of orthodoxy, and might, after all, be dangerous heretics, it occurred to Zinzendorf's canny steward, Heitz, that on the whole it would be more fitting if they settled, not in the village itself, but at a safe and convenient distance. The Count was away; the steward was in charge; and the orthodox parish must not be exposed to infection. As the Neissers, further, were cutlers by trade, there was no need for them in the quiet village. If they wished to earn an honest living they could do it better upon the broad high road.

For these reasons, therefore, he led the exiles to a dismal, swampy stretch of ground about a mile from the village; and told them for the present to rest their bones in an old unfinished farmhouse (June 8th, 1722). The spot itself was dreary and bleak, but the neighbouring woods of pines and beeches relieved the bareness of the scene. It was part of Zinzendorf's estate, and lay at the top of a gentle slope, up which a long avenue now leads. It was a piece of common pasture ground, and was therefore known as the Hutberg, [73] or Watch-Hill. It was on the high road from Loebau to Zittau; it was often used as a camping ground by gypsies and other pedlars; and the road was in such a disgusting state that wagons sometimes sank axle deep in the mud. For the moment the refugees were sick at heart.

"Where," said Mrs. Augustin Neisser, "shall we find bread in this wilderness?"

"If you believe," said Godfrey Marche, tutor to Lady Gersdorf's granddaughters, "you shall see the glory of God."

The steward was quite concerned for the refugees. As he strolled around inspecting the land he noticed one particular spot where a thick mist was rising; and concluding that there a spring was sure to be found, he offered a prayer on their behalf, and registered the solemn vow, "Upon this spot, in Thy name, I will build for them the first house." He laid their needs before Lady Gersdorf, and the good old poetess kindly sent them a cow; he inspected the site with Christian David, and marked the trees he might fell; and thus encouraged, Christian David seized his axe, struck it into a tree, and, as he did so, exclaimed, "Yea, the sparrow hath found a house, and the swallow a nest for herself." [74] (June 17th, 1722)

The first step in the building of Herrnhut had been taken. For some weeks the settlers had still to eat the bread of bitterness and scorn. It was long before they could find a spring of water. The food was poor, the children fell ill; the folk in the neighbourhood laughed; and even when the first house was built they remarked that it would not be standing long.

But already Christian David had wider plans. Already in vivid imagination he saw a goodly city rise, mapped out the courts and streets in his mind, and explained his glowing schemes to the friendly Heitz. The steward himself was carried away with zeal. The very name of the hill was hailed as a promising omen. "May God grant," wrote Heitz to the Count, "that your excellency may be able to build on the hill called the Hutberg a town which may not only itself abide under the Lord's Watch (Herrnhut), but all the inhabitants of which may also continue on the Lord's Watch, so that no silence may be there by day or night." It was thus that Herrnhut received the name which was soon to be famous in the land; and thus that the exiles, cheered anew, resolved to build a glorious City of God.

"We fear," they wrote to the Count himself, "that our settling here may be a burden to you; and therefore we most humbly entreat you to grant us your protection, to continue to help us further still, and to show kindness and love to us poor distressed and simple-minded petitioners."

As the building of the first house proceeded the pious Heitz grew more and more excited. He drove in the first nail; he helped to fix the first pillar; and, finally, when the house was ready, he opened it in solemn religious style, and preached a sort of prophetic sermon about the holy city, the new Jerusalem coming down from God out of heaven. The Count himself soon blessed the undertaking. As he drove along, one winter night, on the road from Strahwalde to Hennersdorf, he saw a strange light shining through the trees (Dec. 2nd). He asked what the light could mean. There, he was told, the Moravian refugees had built the first house on his estate. He stopped the carriage, entered the house, assured the inmates of his hearty goodwill, fell down on his knees, and commended the enterprise to the care of God.

Again the restless David was on the move. As he knelt one day to fix a plank in the new manor-house which Zinzendorf was building in the village, it suddenly flashed on his busy brain that he ought to do something out of the common to show his gratitude to God (1723). His wife had just passed through a dangerous illness; he had vowed to God that if she recovered he would go to Moravia again; and, throwing down his tools on the spot, he darted off in his working clothes, and without a hat on his head, and made his way once more to Sehlen, the old home of the Neissers. He brought a letter from the Neissers in his pocket; he urged the rest of the family to cross the border; and the result was that before many days were gone a band of eighteen more emigrants were on their way to Herrnhut.

His next step had still more momentous results. As he made his way from town to town, and urged his friends to come to "David's City," he had no further aim than to find a home where Protestants could live in peace and comfort. He knew but little, if anything at all, of the old Church of the Brethren; he had never been a member of that Church himself; he had no special interest in her welfare; and the emigrants whom he had brought to Herrnhut were mostly evangelical folk who had been awakened by the preaching of the Pietist pastor, Steinmetz, of Teschen. But now, in the village of Zauchtenthal, he found a band of five young men whose bosoms glowed with zeal for the ancient Church. They were David Nitschmann I., the Martyr; David Nitschmann II., the first Bishop of the Renewed Church; David Nitschmann III., the Syndic; Melchior Zeisberger, the father of the apostle to the Indians; and John Toeltschig, one of the first Moravian preachers in Yorkshire. They were genuine sons of the Brethren; they used the Catechism of Comenius; they sang the Brethren's hymns in their homes; and now they were looking wistfully forward to the time when the Church would renew her strength like the eagle's. For some months they had made their native village the centre of an evangelical revival. At last events in the village came to a crisis; the young men were summoned before the village judge; and the judge, no other than Toeltschig's father, commanded them to close their meetings, and to take their share, like decent fellows, in the drunken jollifications at the public-house. For the brave "Five Churchmen" there was now no way but one. Forthwith they resolved to quit Moravia, and seek for other Brethren at Lissa, in Poland (May 2nd, 1724); and the very next night they set out on their journey, singing the Moravian Emigrants'song:—

Blessed be the day when I must roam,
Far from my country, friends and home,
An exile poor and mean;
My father's God will be my guide,
Will angel guards for me provide,
My soul in dangers screen.
Himself will lead me to a spot
Where, all my cares and griefs forgot,
I shall enjoy sweet rest.
As pants for cooling streams the hart,
I languish for my heavenly part,
For God, my refuge blest.

For them the chosen haven of rest was Lissa. There the great Comenius had taught; and there, they imagined, Brethren lingered still. As they had, however, heard a good deal from David of the "town" being built at Herrnhut, they resolved to pay a passing call on their way. At Lower Wiese they called on Pastor Schwedler. He renewed their zeal for the Church in glowing terms.

"My children," he said, "do you know whose descendants you are? It is a hundred years since the persecutions began against your fathers. You are now to enjoy among us that liberty of conscience for the sake of which they shed their blood. We shall see you blossom and flourish in our midst."

It was a memorable day when they arrived at Herrnhut (May 12th, 1724). The first sight of the holy city did not impress them. The excited David had painted a rosy picture. They expected to find a flourishing town, and all they saw was three small houses, of which only one was finished.

"If three houses make a city," said David Nitschmann, "there are worse places than Herrnhut."

And yet there was something to look at after all. At a little distance from the three small houses, sat Friedrich de Watteville on a log of wood; Christian David was working away at another building; in the afternoon the Count and Countess appeared; and the Count then laid the foundation stone of a college for noblemen's sons. They stayed to see the ceremony. They heard the Count deliver an impressive speech. They heard de Watteville offer a touching prayer. They saw him place his jewels under the stone. They were touched; they stayed; and became the firmest pillars of the rising temple.

And now the stream from Moravia increased in force and volume. Again and again, ten times in all, did the roving David journey to the Moravian dales; and again and again did the loud blast of the trombones in the square announce that yet another band of refugees had arrived. Full many a stirring and thrilling tale had the refugees to tell; how another David Nitschmann, imprisoned in a castle, found a rope at his window and escaped; how David Schneider and another David Nitschmann found their prison doors open; how David Hickel, who had been nearly starved in a dungeon, walked out between his guards in broad daylight, when their backs were turned; how Andrew Beier and David Fritsch had stumbled against their prison door and found that the bolt was loose; how Hans Nitschmann, concealed in a ditch, heard his pursuers, a foot off, say, "This is the place, here he must be," and yet was not discovered after all. No wonder these wanderers felt that angels had screened them on their way. For the sake of their faith they had been imprisoned, beaten, thrust into filthy dungeons. For the sake of their faith they had left behind their goods, their friends, their worldly prospects, had tramped the unknown mountain paths, had slept under hedges, had been attacked by robbers. And now, for the sake of this same faith, these men, though sons of well-to-do people, settled down to lives of manual toil in Herrnhut. And the numbers swelled; the houses rose; and Herrnhut assumed the shape of a hollow square.

At this point, however, a difficulty arose. As the rumour spread in the surrounding country that the Count had offered his estate as an asylum for persecuted Protestants all sorts of religious malcontents came to make Herrnhut their home. Some had a touch of Calvinism, and were fond of discussing free will and predestination; some were disciples of the sixteenth century Anabaptist mystic, Casper Schwenkfeld; some were vague evangelicals from Swabia; some were Lutheran Pietists from near at hand; and some, such as the "Five Churchmen," were descendants of the Brethren's Church, and wished to see her revived on German soil. The result was dissension in the camp. As the settlement grew larger things grew worse. As the settlers learned to know each other better they learned to love each other less. As poverty crept in at the door love flew out of the window. Instead of trying to help each other, men actually tried to cut each other out in business, just like the rest of the world. As the first flush of joy died away, men pointed out each other's motes, and sarcasm pushed charity from her throne; and, worse than all, there now appeared that demon of discord, theological dispute. The chief leader was a religious crank, named Krueger. He was, of course, no descendant of the Brethren's Church. He had quarrelled with a Lutheran minister at Ebersdorf, had been promptly excluded from the Holy Communion, and now came whimpering to Herrnhut, and lifted up his voice against the Lutheran Church. he did not possess the garment of righteousness, he decked himself out with sham excitement and rhetoric; and, as these are cheap ribbons and make a fine show, he soon gained a reputation as a saint. He announced that he had been commissioned by God with the special task of reforming Count Zinzendorf; described Rothe as the "False Prophet" and Zinzendorf as "The Beast"; denounced the whole Lutheran Church as a Babylon, and summoned all in Herrnhut to leave it; and altogether made such a show of piety and holy devotion to God that his freaks and crotchets and fancies and vagaries were welcomed by the best of men, and poisoned the purest blood. His success was marvellous. As the simple settlers listened to his rapt orations they became convinced that the Lutheran Church was no better than a den of thieves; and the greater number now refused to attend the Parish Church, and prepared to form a new sect. Christian David himself was led away. He walked about like a shadow; he was sure that Krueger had a special Divine revelation; he dug a private well for himself, and built himself a new house a few yards from the settlement, so that he might not be smirched by the pitch of Lutheran Christianity. Worse and ever worse waxed the confusion. More "horrible" [75] became the new notions. The eloquent Krueger went out of his mind; and was removed to the lunatic asylum at Berlin. But the evil that he had done lived after him. The whole city on the hill was now a nest of fanatics. It was time for the Count himself to interfere.

For the last five years, while Herrnhut was growing, the Count had almost ignored the refugees; and had quietly devoted his leisure time to his darling scheme of establishing a village "Church within the Church" at Berthelsdorf. He had still his official State duties to perform. He was still a King's Councillor at Dresden. He spent the winter months in the city and the summer at his country-seat; and as long as the settlers behaved themselves as loyal sons of the Lutheran Church he saw no reason to meddle in their affairs. He had, moreover, taken two wise precautions. He had first issued a public notice that no refugee should settle at Herrnhut unless compelled by persecution; and secondly, he had called a meeting of the refugees themselves, and persuaded them to promise that in all their gatherings they would remain loyal to the Augsburg Confession.

Meanwhile, in the village itself, he had pushed his scheme with vigour. He named his house Bethel; his estate was his parish; and his tenants were his congregation. He had never forgotten his boyish vow to do all in his power to extend the Kingdom of Christ; and now he formed another society like the old Order of the Mustard Seed. It was called the "League of the Four Brethren"; it consisted of Zinzendorf, Friedrich de Watteville, and Pastors Rothe and Schaefer; and its object was to proclaim to the world, by means of a league of men devoted to Christ, "that mystery and charm of the Incarnation which was not yet sufficiently recognized in the Church." He had several methods of work. As he wished to reach the young folk of noble rank, he had a school for noblemen's sons built on the Hutberg, and a school for noblemen's daughters down in the village; and the members of the League all signed an agreement to subscribe the needful funds for the undertaking. As he wished, further, to appeal to men in various parts of the country, he established a printing-office at Ebersdorf, and from that office sent books, pamphlets, letters, and cheap editions of the Bible in all directions. As he longed, thirdly, for personal contact with leading men in the Church, he instituted a system of journeys to Halle and other centres of learning and piety. But his best work was done in Berthelsdorf. His steward, Heitz, gave the rustics Bible lessons; Pastor Rothe preached awakening sermons in the parish church, and his preaching was, as the Count declared, "as though it rained flames from heaven"; and he himself, in the summer season, held daily singing meetings and prayer meetings in his own house. Hand in hand did he and Rothe work hard for the flock at Berthelsdorf. On a Sunday morning the pastor would preach a telling sermon in a crowded church; in the afternoon the squire would gather his tenants in his house and expound to them the morning's discourse. The whole village was stirred; the Church was enlarged; and the Count himself was so in earnest that if the slightest hitch occurred in a service he would burst into tears. While things in Herrnhut were growing worse things in Berthelsdorf were growing better; while stormy winds blew on the hill there was peace and fellowship down in the valley. How closely the Count and the pastor were linked may be seen from the following fact. The Count's family pew in the Church was a small gallery or raised box over the vestry; the box had a trap-door in the floor; the pastor, according to Lutheran custom, retired to the vestry at certain points in the service; and the Count, by opening the aforesaid door, could communicate his wishes to the pastor.

He had now to apply his principles to Herrnhut. As long as the settlers had behaved themselves well, and kept their promise to be loyal to the National Church, he had left them alone to follow their own devices; and even if they sang old Brethren's hymns at their meetings, he had no insuperable objection. But now the time had come to take stern measures. He had taken them in out of charity; he had invited them to the meetings in his house; and now they had turned the place into a nest of scheming dissenters. There was war in the camp. On the one hand, Christian David called Rothe a narrow-minded churchman. On the other hand, Rothe thundered from his pulpit against the "mad fanatics" on the hill. As Jew and Samaritan in days of old, so now were Berthelsdorf and Herrnhut.

At this critical point the Count intervened, and changed the duel into a duet (1727). He would have no makers of sects on his estate. With all their faults, he believed that the settlers were at bottom broad-minded people. Only clear away the rubbish and the gold would be found underneath.

"Although our dear Christian David," he said, "was calling me the Beast and Mr. Rothe the False Prophet, we could see his honest heart nevertheless, and knew we could lead him right. It is not a bad maxim," he added, "when honest men are going wrong to put them into office, and they will learn from experience what they will never learn from speculation."

He acted on that maxim now. He would teach the exiles to obey the law of the land, to bow to his authority as lord of the manor, and to live in Christian fellowship with each other. For this purpose, he summoned them all to a mass meeting in the Great House on the Hutberg (May 12th), lectured them for over three hours on the sin of schism, read out the "Manorial Injunctions and Prohibitions," [76] which all inhabitants of Herrnhut must promise to obey, and then submitted a number of "Statutes" as the basis of a voluntary religious society. The effect was sudden and swift. At one bound the settlers changed from a group of quarrelling schismatics to an organized body of orderly Christian tenants; and forthwith the assembled settlers shook hands, and promised to obey the Injunctions and Prohibitions.

As soon as the Count had secured good law and order he obtained leave of absence from Dresden, took up his residence at Herrnhut, and proceeded to organize all who wished into a systematic Church within the Church. For this purpose he prepared another agreement (July 4th), entitled the "Brotherly Union and Compact," signed the agreement first himself, persuaded Christian David, Pastor Schaefer and another neighbouring clergyman to do the same, and then invited all the rest to follow suit. Again, the goodwill was practically universal. As the settlers had promised on May 12th to obey the Manorial Injunctions and Prohibitions, so now, of their own free will, they signed a promise to end their sectarian quarrels, to obey the "Statutes," and to live in fellowship with Christians of all beliefs and denominations. Thus had the Count accomplished a double purpose. As lord of the manor he had crushed the design to form a separate sect; and as Spener's disciple he had persuaded the descendants of the Bohemian Brethren to form another "Church within the Church."

Nor was this all. As the Brethren looked back in later years to those memorable days in Herrnhut, they came to regard the summer months of 1727 as a holy, calm, sabbatic season, when one and all were quickened and stirred by the power of the Spirit Divine. "The whole place," said Zinzendorf himself, "represented a visible tabernacle of God among men." For the next four months the city on the hill was the home of ineffable joy; and the very men who had lately quarrelled with each other now formed little groups for prayer and praise. As the evening shadows lengthened across the square the whole settlement met to pray and praise, and talk with each other, like brothers and sisters of one home. The fancies and vagaries fled. The Count held meetings every day. The Church at Berthelsdorf was crowded out. The good David, now appointed Chief Elder, persuaded all to study the art of love Divine by going through the First Epistle of St. John. The very children were stirred and awakened. The whole movement was calm, strong, deep and abiding. Of vulgar excitement there was none; no noisy meetings, no extravagant babble, no religious tricks to work on the emotions. For mawkish, sentimental religion the Count had an honest contempt. "It is," he said, "as easy to create religious excitement as it is to stir up the sensual passions; and the former often leads to the latter." As the Brethren met in each other's homes, or on the Hutberg when the stars were shining, they listened, with reverence and holy awe, to the still voice of that Good Shepherd who was leading them gently, step by step, to the green pastures of peace.

Amid the fervour the Count made an announcement which caused every cheek to flush with new delight. He had made a strange discovery. At Zittau, not far away, was a reference library; and there, one day, he found a copy of Comenius's Latin version of the old Brethren's "Account of Discipline." (July) His eyes were opened at last. For the first time in his busy life he read authentic information about the old Church of the Brethren; and discovered, to his amazement and joy, that so far from being disturbers of the peace, with a Unitarian taint in their blood, they were pure upholders of the very faith so dear to his own heart.

His soul was stirred to its depths. "I could not," he said, "read the lamentations of old Comenius, addressed to the Church of England, lamentations called forth by the idea that the Church of the Brethren had come to an end, and that he was locking its door—I could not read his mournful prayer, Turn Thou us unto Thee, O Lord, and we shall be turned; renew our days as of old,' without resolving there and then: I, as far as I can, will help to bring about this renewal. And though I have to sacrifice my earthly possessions, my honours and my life, as long as I live I will do my utmost to see to it that this little flock of the Lord shall be preserved for Him until He come."

And even this was not the strangest part of the story. As the Count devoured the ancient treatise, he noticed that the rules laid down therein were almost the same as the rules which he had just drawn up for the refugees at Herrnhut. He returned to Herrnhut, reported his find, and read the good people extracts from the book (Aug. 4th). The sensation was profound. If this was like new milk to the Count it was like old wine to the Brethren; and again the fire of their fathers burned in their veins.

And now the coping stone was set on the temple (Aug. 13th). As the Brethren were learning, step by step, to love each other in true sincerity, Pastor Rothe now invited them all to set the seal to the work by coming in a body to Berthelsdorf Church, and there joining, with one accord, in the celebration of the Holy Communion. The Brethren accepted the invitation with joy. The date fixed was Monday, August 13th. The sense of awe was overpowering. As the Brethren walked down the slope to the church all felt that the supreme occasion had arrived; and all who had quarrelled in the days gone by made a covenant of loyalty and love. At the door of the church the strange sense of awe was thrilling. They entered the building; the service began; the "Confession" was offered by the Count; and then, at one and the same moment, all present, rapt in deep devotion, were stirred by the mystic wondrous touch of a power which none could define or understand. There, in Berthelsdorf Parish Church, they attained at last the firm conviction that they were one in Christ; and there, above all, they believed and felt that on them, as on the twelve disciples on the Day of Pentecost, had rested the purifying fire of the Holy Ghost.

"We learned," said the Brethren, "to love." "From that time onward," said David Nitschmann, "Herrnhut was a living Church of Jesus Christ. We thank the Lord that we ever came to Herrnhut, instead of pressing on, as we intended, to Poland."

And there the humble Brother spoke the truth. As the Brethren returned that evening to Herrnhut, they felt within them a strength and joy they had never known before. They had realised their calling in Christ. They had won the Divine gift of Christian union. They had won that spirit of brotherly love which only the great Good Spirit could give. They had won that sense of fellowship with Christ, and fellowship with one another, which had been the costliest gem in the days of their fathers; and therefore, in future, they honoured the day as the true spiritual birthday of the Renewed Church of the Brethren. It is useless trying to express their feelings in prose. Let us listen to the moving words of the Moravian poet, James Montgomery:—

They walked with God in peace and love,
But failed with one another;
While sternly for the faith they strove,
Brother fell out with brother;
But He in Whom they put their trust,
Who knew their frames, that they were dust,
Pitied and healed their weakness.
He found them in His house of prayer,
With one accord assembled,
And so revealed His presence there,
They wept for joy and trembled;
One cup they drank, one bread they brake,
One baptism shared, one language spake,
Forgiving and forgiven.
Then forth they went, with tongues of flame,
In one blest theme delighting,
The love of Jesus and His Name,
God's children all uniting!
That love, our theme and watchword still;
That law of love may we fulfil,
And love as we are loved.

The next step was to see that the blessing was not lost (Aug. 27th). For this purpose the Brethren, a few days later, arranged a system of Hourly Intercession. As the fire on the altar in the Jewish Temple was never allowed to go out, so the Brethren resolved that in this new temple of the Lord the incense of intercessory prayer should rise continually day and night. Henceforth, Herrnhut in very truth should be the "Watch of the Lord." The whole day was carefully mapped out, and each Brother or Sister took his or her turn. Of all the prayer unions ever organized surely this was one of the most remarkable. It is said to have lasted without interruption for over a hundred years.

Chapter 4: Life at Herrnhut

AS we study the social and religious system which now developed at Herrnhut, it is well to bear in mind the fact that when the Count, as lord of the manor, first issued his "Injunctions and Prohibitions," he was not aware that, in so doing, he was calling back to life once more the discipline of the old Bohemian Brethren. He had not yet read the history of the Brethren, and he had not yet studied Comenius's "Account of Discipline." He knew but little of the Brethren's past, and the little that he knew was wrong; and, having no other plan to guide him, he took as his model the constitution lying ready to hand in the average German village of the day, and adapted that simple constitution to the special needs of the exiles. [77] He had no desire to make Herrnhut independent. It was still to be a part of his estate, and conform to the laws of the land; and still to be the home of a "Church within the Church," as planned by Luther long ago in his famous German Mass.

First, then the Count laid down the rule that all male adults in Herrnhut, no matter to what sect they might belong, should have a voice in the election of twelve Elders; and henceforward these twelve Elders, like those in the neighbouring estates of Silesia, had control over every department of life, and enforced the Injunctions and Prohibitions with an iron hand. They levied the usual rates and taxes to keep the streets and wells in order. They undertook the care of widows and orphans. They watched the relations of single young men and women. They kept a sharp eye on the doings at the inn. They called to order the tellers of evil tales; and they banished from Herrnhut all who disobeyed the laws, or conducted themselves in an unbecoming, frivolous or offensive manner.

The power of the Elders was enormous. If a new refugee desired to settle in Herrnhut, he must first obtain permission from the Elders. If a settler desired to go on a journey, he must first obtain permission from the Elders. If a man desired to build a house; if a trader desired to change his calling; if an apprentice desired to leave his master; if a visitor desired to stay the night, he must first obtain permission from the Elders. If a man fell in love and desired to marry, he must first obtain the approval of the Elders; and until that approval had been obtained, he was not allowed to propose to the choice of his heart. Let us see the reason for this remarkable strictness.

As the Brethren settled down in Herrnhut, they endeavoured, under the Count's direction, to realize the dignity of labour. For rich and poor, for Catholic and Protestant, for all able-bodied men and women, the same stern rule held good. If a man desired to settle at Herrnhut, the one supreme condition was that he earned his bread by honest toil, and lived a godly, righteous and sober life. For industrious Catholics there was a hearty welcome; for vagabonds, tramps and whining beggars there was not a bed to spare. If a man would work he might stay, and worship God according to his conscience; but if he was lazy, he was ordered off the premises. As the Brethren met on Sunday morning for early worship in the public hall, they joined with one accord in the prayer, "Bless the sweat of the brow and faithfulness in business"; and the only business they allowed was business which they could ask the Lord to bless. To them work was a sacred duty, a delight and a means for the common good. If a man is blessed who has found his work, then blessed were the folk at Herrnhut. "We do not work to live," said the Count; "we live to work." The whole aim was the good of each and the good of all. As the grocer stood behind his counter, or the weaver plied his flying shuttle, he was toiling, not for himself alone, but for all his Brethren and Sisters. If a man desired to set up in business, he had first to obtain the permission of the Elders; and the Elders refused to grant the permission unless they thought that the business in question was needed by the rest of the people. "No brother," ran the law at Herrnhut, "shall compete with his brother in trade." No man was allowed to lend money on interest without the consent of the Elders. If two men had any dispute in business, they must come to terms within a week; and if they did not, or went to law, they were expelled. If a man could buy an article in Herrnhut, he was not allowed to buy it anywhere else.

It is easy to see the purpose of these regulations. They were an attempt to solve the social problem, to banish competition, and to put co-operation in its place. For some years the scheme was crowned with glorious success. The settlement grew; the trade flourished; the great firm of Duerninger obtained a world-wide reputation; the women were skilled in weaving and spinning; and the whole system worked so well that in 1747 the Saxon Government besought the Count to establish a similar settlement at Barby. At Herrnhut, in a word, if nowhere else, the social problem was solved. There, at least, the aged and ill could live in peace and comfort; there grim poverty was unknown; there the widow and orphan were free from carking care; and there men and women of humble rank had learned the truth that when men toil for the common good there is a perennial nobleness in work. [78]

For pleasure the Brethren had neither time nor taste. They worked, on the average, sixteen hours a day, allowed only five hours for sleep, and spent the remaining three at meals and meetings. The Count was as Puritanic as Oliver Cromwell himself. For some reason he had come to the conclusion that the less the settlers knew of pleasure the better, and therefore he laid down the law that all strolling popular entertainers should be forbidden to enter the holy city. No public buffoon ever cracked his jokes at Herrnhut. No tight-rope dancer poised on giddy height. No barrel-dancer rolled his empty barrel. No tout for lotteries swindled the simple. No juggler mystified the children. No cheap-jack cheated the innocent maidens. No quack-doctor sold his nasty pills. No melancholy bear made his feeble attempt to dance. For the social joys of private life the laws were stricter still. At Herrnhut, ran one comprehensive clause, there were to be no dances whatever, no wedding breakfasts, no christening bumpers, no drinking parties, no funeral feasts, and no games like those played in the surrounding villages. No bride at Herrnhut ever carried a bouquet. No sponsor ever gave the new arrival a mug or a silver spoon.

For sins of the coarse and vulgar kind there was no mercy. If a man got drunk, or cursed, or stole, or used his fists, or committed adultery or fornication, he was expelled, and not permitted to return till he had given infallible proofs of true repentance. No guilty couple were allowed to "cheat the parson." No man was allowed to strike his wife, and no wife was allowed to henpeck her husband; and any woman found guilty of the latter crime was summoned before the board of Elders and reprimanded in public.

Again, the Count insisted on civil order. He appointed a number of other officials. Some, called servants, had to clean the wells, to sweep the streets, to repair the houses, and to trim the gardens. For the sick there was a board of sick waiters; for the poor a board of almoners; for the wicked a board of monitors; for the ignorant a board of schoolmasters; and each board held a conference every week. Once a week, on Saturday nights, the Elders met in Council; once a week, on Monday mornings, they announced any new decrees; and all inhabitants vowed obedience to them as Elders, to the Count as Warden, and finally to the law of the land. Thus had the Count, as lord of the manor, drawn up a code of civil laws to be binding on all. We have finished the Manorial Injunctions and Prohibitions. We come to the free religious life of the community.

Let us first clear a difficulty out of the way. As the Count was a loyal son of the Lutheran Church, and regarded the Augsburg Confession as inspired, [79] it seems, at first sight, a marvellous fact that here at Herrnhut he allowed the Brethren to take steps which led ere long to the renewal of their Church. He allowed them to sing Brethren's Hymns; he allowed them to revive old Brethren's customs; he allowed them to hold independent meetings; and he even resolved to do his best to revive the old Church himself. His conduct certainly looked very inconsistent. If a man in England were to call himself a loyal member of the Anglican Church, and yet at the same time do his very best to found an independent denomination, he would soon be denounced as a traitor to the Church and a breeder of schism and dissent. But the Count's conduct can be easily explained. It was all due to his ignorance of history. He had no idea that the Bohemian Brethren had ever been an independent Church. He regarded them as a branch of the Reformed persuasion. He regarded them as a "Church within the Church," of the kind for which Luther had longed, and which Spener had already established. He held his delusion down to the end of his days; and, therefore, as Lutheran and Pietist alike, he felt at liberty to help the Brethren in all their religious endeavours.

For this purpose, therefore, he asked the settlers at Herrnhut to sign their names to a voluntary "Brotherly Union"; and the chief condition of the "Union" was that all the members agreed to live in friendship with Christians of other denominations, and also to regard themselves as members of the Lutheran Church. They attended the regular service at the Parish Church. There they took the Holy Communion; there they had their children baptized; and there the young people were confirmed.

Meanwhile the movement at Herrnhut was growing fast. The great point was to guard against religious poison. As the Count had a healthy horror of works of darkness, he insisted that no meetings should be held without a light; and the Brethren set their faces against superstition. They forbade ghost-stories; they condemned the popular old-wives' tales about tokens, omens and death-birds; they insisted that, in case of illness, no meddling busybody should interfere with the doctor; and thus, as homely, practical folk, they aimed at health of body and of mind.

But the chief object of their ambition was health of soul. As the revival deepened, the number of meetings increased. Not a day passed without three meetings for the whole congregation. At five in the morning they met in the hall, and joined in a chorus of praise. At the dinner hour they met again, and then, about nine o'clock, after supper, they sang themselves to rest. At an early period the whole congregation was divided into ninety unions for prayer, and each band met two or three times a week. The night was as sacred as the day. As the night-watchman went his rounds, he sang a verse at the hour, as follows:—

> The clock is eight! to Herrnhut all is told,
> How Noah and his seven were saved of old,
> Hear, Brethren, hear! the hour of nine is come!
> Keep pure each heart, and chasten every home!
> Hear, Brethren, hear! now ten the hour-hand shows;
> They only rest who long for night's repose.
> The clock's eleven, and ye have heard it all,
> How in that hour the mighty God did call.
> It's midnight now, and at that hour you know,
> With lamp to meet the bridegroom we must go.
> The hour is one; through darkness steals the day;
> Shines in your hearts the morning star's first ray?
> The clock is two! who comes to meet the day,
> And to the Lord of days his homage pay?
> The clock is three! the Three in One above
> Let body, soul and spirit truly love.
> The clock is four! where'er on earth are three,
> The Lord has promised He the fourth will be.
> The clock is five! while five away were sent,
> Five other virgins to the marriage went!
> The clock is six, and from the watch I'm free,
> And every one may his own watchman be!

At this task all male inhabitants, over sixteen and under sixty, took their turn. The watchman, in the intervals between the hours, sang other snatches of sacred song; and thus anyone who happened to be lying awake was continually reminded of the presence of God.

On Sunday nearly every hour of the day was occupied by services. At five there was a short meeting, known as the "morning blessing." From six to nine there were meetings for the several "choirs." At ten there was a special service for children. At eleven there was morning worship in the Parish Church. At one the Chief Elder gave a general exhortation. At three, or thereabouts, there was a meeting, called the "strangers' service," for those who had not been able to go to Church; and then the Count or some other layman repeated the morning sermon. At four there was another service at Berthelsdorf; at eight another service at Herrnhut; at nine the young men marched round the settlement singing hymns; and on Monday morning these wonderful folk returned to their labour like giants refreshed with new wine. Their powers of endurance were miraculous. The more meetings they had the more they seemed able to stand. Sometimes the good Pastor Schwedler, of Goerlitz, would give them a sermon three hours long; and sometimes, commencing at six in the morning, he held his congregation enthralled till three in the afternoon.

Again, the Brethren listened day by day to a special message from God. We come now to the origin of the Moravian Text-book. As the Count was a great believer in variety, he very soon started the practice, at the regular evening singing meeting, of giving the people a short address on some Scriptural text or some verse from a hymn. As soon as the singing meeting was over he read out to the company the chosen passage, recommended it as a suitable subject for meditation the following day, and next morning had the text passed round by the Elders to every house in Herrnhut. Next year (1728) the practice was better organized. Instead of waiting for the Count to choose, the Elders selected in advance a number of texts and verses, and put them all together into a box; and then, each evening, one of the Elders put his hand into the box and drew the text for the following day. The idea was that of a special Providence. If Christ, said the Count, took a special interest in every one of His children, He would also take the same kindly interest in every company of believers; and, therefore, He might be safely trusted to guide the hand of the Elder aright and provide the "watchword" needed for the day. Again and again he exhorted the Brethren to regard the text for the day as God's special message to them; and finally, in 1731, he had the texts for the whole year printed, and thus began that Brethren's Text-book which now appears regularly every year, is issued in several tongues, and circulates, in every quarter of the globe, among Christians of all denominations. [80]

In order, next, to keep in touch with their fellow-Christians the Brethren instituted a monthly Saturday meeting, and that Saturday came to be known as "Congregation Day." (Feb. 10th, 1728) At this meeting the Brethren listened to reports of evangelical work in other districts. Sometimes there would be a letter from a travelling Brother; sometimes a visitor from some far-distant strand. The meeting was a genuine sign of moral health. It fostered broadness of mind, and put an end to spiritual pride. Instead of regarding themselves as Pietists, superior to the average professing Christians, the Brethren now rejoiced to hear of the good done by others. They prayed not for their own narrow circle alone, but for all rulers, all churches, and all people that on earth do dwell; and delighted to sing old Brethren's hymns, treating of the Church Universal, such as John Augusta's "Praise God for ever" and "How amiable Thy tabernacles are." At this monthly meeting the Count was in his element. He would keep his audience enthralled for hours together. He would read them first a piece of news in vivid, dramatic style; then he would suddenly strike up a missionary hymn; then he would give them a little more information; and thus he taught them to take an interest in lands beyond the sea.

Another sign of moral health was the "Love-feast." As the Brethren met in each other's houses, they attempted, in quite an unofficial way, to revive the Agape of Apostolic times; and to this end they provided a simple meal of rye-bread and water, wished each other the wish, "Long live the Lord Jesus in our hearts," and talked in a free-and-easy fashion about the Kingdom of God. And here the Brethren were on their guard. In the days of the Apostles there had been scandals. The rich had brought their costly food, and the poor had been left to pine. At Herrnhut this scandal was avoided. For rich and poor the diet was the same, and came from a common fund; in later years it was white bread and tea; and in due time the Love-feast took the form of a meeting for the whole congregation.

Again, the Brethren were wonderfully simple-minded. As we read about their various meetings, it is clear that in their childlike way they were trying to revive the institutions of Apostolic times. For this purpose they even practised the ceremony of foot-washing, as described in the Gospel of St. John. To the Count the clear command of Christ was decisive. "If I then, your Lord and Master," said Jesus, "have washed your feet, ye also ought to wash one another's feet." What words, said the Count, could be more binding than these? "No man," he declared, "can read John xiii. without being convinced that this should be done." He revived the custom, and made it both popular and useful. The ceremony was generally performed by the young, before some special festival. It spread in time to England and Ireland, and was not abandoned till the early years of the nineteenth century [81] (1818).

We come now to the origin of the "choirs." As Zinzendorf studied the Gospel story, he came to the conclusion that in the life of Jesus Christ there was something specially suitable to each estate in life. For the married people there was Christ, the Bridegroom of His Bride, the Church; for the single Brethren, the "man about thirty years of age"; for the single Sisters, the Virgin Mary; for the children, the boy in the temple asking questions. The idea took root. The more rapidly the settlement grew, the more need there was for division and organization. For each class the Master had a special message, and, therefore, each class must have its special meetings and study its special duties. For this purpose a band of single men—led by the ascetic Martin Linner, who slept on bare boards—agreed to live in one house, spent the evenings in united study, and thus laid the basis of the Single Brethren's Choir (Aug. 29th, 1728). For the same purpose the single young women, led by Anna Nitschmann, agreed to live in a "Single Sisters' House," and made a covenant with one another that henceforward they would not make matrimony the highest aim in life, but would rather, like Mary of Bethany, sit at the feet of Christ and learn of Him (May 4th, 1730). For the same purpose the married people met at a love-feast, formed the "married choir," and promised to lead a pure and holy life (Sept. 7th, 1733), "so that their children might be plants of righteousness." For the same purpose the children, in due time, were formed into a "children's choir." The whole aim was efficiency and order. At first the unions were voluntary; in time they became official.

As the years rolled on the whole congregation was systematically divided into ten "choirs," as follows:—The married choir, the widowers, the widows, the Single Brethren, the Single Sisters, the youths, the great girls, the little boys, the little girls, the infants in arms. Each choir had its own president, its own special services, its own festival day, its own love-feasts. Of these choirs the most important were those of the Single Brethren and Single Sisters. As the Brethren at Herrnhut were soon to be busy in evangelistic labours, they found it convenient to have in their ranks a number of men and women who were not bound down by family ties; and though the young people took no celibate vows, they often kept single through life for the sake of the growing cause.

The system invaded the sanctity of family life. As the Count was a family man himself, he very properly took the deepest interest in the training of little children; and, in season and out of season, he insisted that the children of Christian parents should be screened from the seductions of the world, the flesh and the devil. "It is nothing less than a scandal," he said, "that people think so little of the fact that their children are dedicated to the Lord. Children are little kings; their baptism is their anointing; and as kings they ought to be treated from the first." For this purpose he laid down the rule that all infants should be baptized in the hall, in the presence of the whole congregation; and as soon as the children were old enough to learn, he had them taken from their homes, and put the little boys in one school and the little girls in another. And thus the burden of their education fell not on the parents, but on the congregation.

Again, the Count carried out his ideas in the "vasty halls of death." Of all the sacred spots in Herrnhut there were none more sacred and more awe-inspiring than the "God's Acre" which the Brethren laid out on the Hutberg. There, in the bosom of Mother Earth, the same division into choirs was preserved. To the Count the tomb was a holy place. If a visitor ever came to Herrnhut, he was sure to take him to the God's Acre, and tell him the story of those whose bones awaited the resurrection of the just. The God's Acre became the scene of an impressive service (1733). At an early hour on Easter Sunday the Brethren assembled in the sacred presence of the dead, and waited for the sun to rise. As the golden rim appeared on the horizon, the minister spoke the first words of the service. "The Lord is risen," said the minister. "He is risen indeed!" responded the waiting throng. And then, in the beautiful language of Scripture, the Brethren joined in a solemn confession of faith. The trombones that woke the morning echoes led the anthem of praise, and one and all, in simple faith, looked onward to the glorious time when those who lay in the silent tomb should hear the voice of the Son of God, and be caught up in the clouds to meet the Lord in the air. To the Brethren the tomb was no abode of dread. In a tomb the Lord Himself had lain; in a tomb His humble disciples lay "asleep"; and therefore, when a brother departed this life, the mourners never spoke of him as dead. "He is gone home," they said; and so death lost his sting.

Again, the Brethren had a strong belief in direct answers to prayer. It was this that led them to make such use of the "Lot." As soon as the first twelve Elders were elected, the Brethren chose from among the twelve a committee of four by Lot; and in course of time the Lot was used for a great variety of purposes. By the Lot, as we shall see later on, the most serious ecclesiastical problems were settled. By the Lot a sister determined her answer to an offer of marriage. By the Lot a call to service was given, and by the Lot it was accepted or rejected. If once the Lot had been consulted, the decision was absolute and binding. The prayer had been answered, the Lord had spoken, and the servant must now obey. [82]

We have now to mention but one more custom, dating from those great days. It is one peculiar to the Brethren's Church, and is known as the "Cup of Covenant." It was established by the Single Brethren, (1729) and was based on the act of Christ Himself, as recorded in the Gospel of St. Luke. As the Master sat with His twelve disciples in the Upper Room at Jerusalem, we are told that just before the institution of the Lord's Supper, [83] "He took the Cup and gave thanks, and said, Take this and divide it among yourselves'"; and now, in obedience to this command, this ardent band of young disciples made a covenant to be true to Christ, and passed the Cup from hand to hand. Whenever a young brother was called out to the mission field, the whole choir would meet and entrust him to Christ in this simple and scriptural way. It was the pledge at once of united service and united trust. It spread, in course of time, to the other choirs; it is practised still at the annual choir festivals; and its meaning is best expressed in the words of the Brethren's Covenant Hymn:—

Assembling here, a humble band,
Our covenantal pledge to take,
We pass the cup from hand to hand,
From heart to heart, for His dear sake.

It remains to answer two important questions. As we study the life of the Herrnhut Brethren, we cannot possibly fail to notice how closely their institutions resembled the old institutions of the Bohemian Brethren. We have the same care for the poor, the same ascetic ideal of life, the same adherence to the word of Scripture, the same endeavour to revive Apostolic practice, the same semi-socialistic tendency, the same aspiration after brotherly unity, the same title, "Elder," for the leading officials, and the same, or almost the same, method of electing some of these officials by Lot. And, therefore, we naturally ask the question, how far were these Brethren guided by the example of their fathers? The reply is, not at all. At this early stage in their history the Moravian refugees at Herrnhut knew absolutely nothing of the institutions of the Bohemian Brethren. [84] They had no historical records in their possession; they had not preserved any copies of the ancient laws; they brought no books but hymn-books across the border; and they framed their rules and organized their society before they had even heard of the existence of Comenius's "Account of Discipline." The whole movement at Herrnhut was free, spontaneous, original. It was not an imitation of the past. It was not an attempt to revive the Church of the Brethren. It was simply the result of Zinzendorf's attempt to apply the ideals of the Pietist Spener to the needs of the settlers on his estate.

The second question is, what was the ecclesiastical standing of the Brethren at this time? They were not a new church or sect. They had no separate ministry of their own. They were members of the Lutheran Church, regarded Rothe still as their Pastor, attended the Parish Church on Sundays, and took the Communion there once a month; and what distinguished them from the average orthodox Lutheran of the day was, not any peculiarity of doctrine, but rather their vivid perception of a doctrine common to all the Churches. As the Methodists in England a few years later exalted the doctrine of "conversion," so these Brethren at Herrnhut exalted the doctrine of the spiritual presence of Christ. To them the ascended Christ was all in all. He had preserved the "Hidden Seed." He had led them out from Moravia. He had brought them to a watch-tower. He had delivered them from the secret foe. He had banished the devouring demon of discord, had poured out His Holy Spirit upon them at their memorable service in the Parish Church, and had taught them to maintain the unity of the spirit in the bond of peace. He was the "Bridegroom of the Soul," the "Blood Relation of His People," the "King's Son seeking for His Bride, the Church," the "Chief Elder pleading for the Church before God." And this thought of the living and reigning Christ was, therefore, the ruling thought among the Brethren. He had done three marvellous things for the sons of men. He had given His life as a "ransom" for sin, and had thereby reconciled them to God; He had set the perfect example for them to follow; He was present with them now as Head of the Church; and thus, when the Brethren went out to preach, they made His Sacrificial Death, His Holy Life, and His abiding presence the main substance of their Gospel message.

Chapter 5: The Edict of Banishment (1729-1736)

BUT Zinzendorf was not long allowed to tread the primrose path of peace. As the news of his proceedings spread in Germany, many orthodox Lutherans began to regard him as a nuisance, a heretic, and a disturber of the peace; and one critic made the elegant remark: "When Count Zinzendorf flies up into the air, anyone who pulls him down by the legs will do him a great service." He was accused of many crimes, and had many charges to answer. He was accused of founding a new sect, a society for laziness; he was accused of holding strange opinions, opposed to the teaching of the Lutheran Church; he was accused of being a sham Christian, a sort of religious freak; and now he undertook the task of proving that these accusations were false, and of showing all fair-minded men in Germany that the Brethren at Herrnhut were as orthodox as Luther, as respected as the King, and as pious as good old Dr. Spener himself. His methods were bold and straightforward.

He began by issuing a manifesto (Aug. 12th, 1729), entitled the "Notariats-Instrument." As this document was signed by all the Herrnhut Brethren, they must have agreed to its statements; but, on the other hand, it is fairly certain that it was drawn up by Zinzendorf himself. It throws a flood of light on his state of mind. He had begun to think more highly of the Moravian Church. He regarded the Moravians as the kernel of the Herrnhut colony, and now he deliberately informed the public that, so far from being a new sect, these Moravians were descendants of an ancient Church. They were, he declared, true heirs of the Church of the Brethren; and that Church, in days gone by, had been recognized by Luther, Calvin and others as a true Church of Christ. In doctrine that Church was as orthodox as the Lutheran; in discipline it was far superior. As long, therefore, as the Brethren were allowed to do so, they would maintain their old constitution and discipline; and yet, on the other hand, they would not be Dissenters. They were not Hussites; they were not Waldenses; they were not Fraticelli; they honoured the Augsburg Confession; they would still attend the Berthelsdorf Parish Church; and, desirous of cultivating fellowship with all true Christians, they announced their broad position in the sentence: "We acknowledge no public Church of God except where the pure Word of God is preached, and where the members live as holy children of God." Thus Zinzendorf made his policy fairly clear. He wanted to preserve the Moravian Church inside the Lutheran Church! [85]

His next move was still more daring. He was a man of fine missionary zeal. As the woman who found the lost piece of silver invited her friends and neighbours to share in her joy, so Zinzendorf wished all Christians to share in the treasure which he had discovered at Herrnhut. He believed that the Brethren there were called to a world-wide mission. He wanted Herrnhut to be a city set on a hill. "I have no sympathy," he said, "with those comfortable people who sit warming themselves before the fire of the future life." He did not sit long before the fire himself. He visited the University of Jena, founded a society among the students, and so impressed the learned Spangenberg that that great theological scholar soon became a Brother at Herrnhut himself. He visited the University of Halle, and founded another society of students there. He visited Elmsdorf in Vogtland, and founded a society consisting of members of the family of Count Reuss. He visited Berleburg in Westphalia, made the acquaintance of John Conrad Dippel, and tried to lead that straying sheep back to the Lutheran fold. He visited Budingen in Hesse, discoursed on Christian fellowship to the "French Prophets," or "Inspired Ones," and tried to teach their hysterical leader, Rock, a little wisdom, sobriety and charity. He attended the coronation of Christian VI., King of Denmark, at Copenhagen, was warmly welcomed by His Majesty, received the Order of the Danebrog, saw Eskimos from Greenland and a negro from St. Thomas, and thus opened the door, as we shall see later on, for the great work of foreign missions. Meanwhile, he was sending messengers in all directions. He sent two Brethren to Copenhagen, with a short historical account of Herrnhut. He sent two others to London to see the Queen, and to open up negotiations with the Society for Promoting Christian Knowledge. He sent another to Sweden; others to Hungary and Austria; others to Switzerland; others to Moravia; others to the Baltic Provinces, Livonia and Esthonia. And everywhere his object was the same—the formation of societies for Christian fellowship within the National Church.

At this point, however, he acted like a fanatic, and manifested the first symptoms of that weak trait in his character which nearly wrecked his career. As he pondered one day on the state of affairs at Herrnhut, it suddenly flashed upon his mind that the Brethren would do far better without their ancient constitution. He first consulted the Elders and Helpers (Jan. 7th, 1731); he then summoned the whole congregation; and there and then he deliberately proposed that the Brethren should abolish their regulations, abandon their constitution, cease to be Moravians and become pure Lutherans. At that moment Zinzendorf was calmly attempting to destroy the Moravian Church. He did not want to see that Church revive. For some reason of his own, which he never explained in print, he had come to the conclusion that the Brethren would serve Christ far better without any special regulations of their own. But the Brethren were not disposed to meek surrender. The question was keenly debated. At length, however, both sides agreed to appeal to a strange tribunal. For the first time in the history of Herrnhut a critical question of Church policy was submitted to the Lot. [86] The Brethren took two slips of paper and put them into a box. On the first were the words, "To them that are without law, as without law, that I might gain them that are without law," 1 Cor. ix. 21; on the second the words, "Therefore, Brethren, stand fast, and hold the traditions which ye have been taught," 2 Thess. ii. 15. At that moment the fate of the Church hung in the balance; the question at issue was one of life and death; and the Brethren spent a long time in anxious prayer. If the first slip of paper was drawn, the Church would cease to exist; if the second, she might still live by the blessing of God. Young Christel, Zinzendorf's son, now entered the room. He drew the second slip of paper, and the Moravian Church was saved. To Zinzendorf this was an event of momentous importance. As soon as that second slip of paper was drawn, he felt convinced that God had sanctioned the renewal of the Moravian Church.

Next year an event occurred to strengthen his convictions. A body of commissioners from Dresden appeared at Herrnhut (Jan. 19-22, 1732). They attended all the Sunday services, had private interviews with the Brethren, and sent in their report to the Saxon Government. The Count's conduct had excited public alarm. He had welcomed not only Moravians at Herrnhut, but Schwenkfelders at Berthelsdorf; and, therefore, he was now suspected of harbouring dangerous fanatics. For a long time the issue hung doubtful; but finally the Government issued a decree that while the Schwenkfelders must quit the land, the Moravians should be allowed to stay as long as they behaved themselves quietly (April 4th, 1733).

But Zinzendorf was not yet satisfied. He regarded the edict as an insult. The words about "behaving quietly" looked like a threat. As long as the Brethren were merely "tolerated," their peace was in constant danger; and a King who had driven out the Schwenkfelders might soon drive out the Herrnhuters. He was disgusted. At the time when the edict was issued, he himself was returning from a visit to Tuebingen. He had laid the whole case of the Brethren before the Tuebingen Theological Faculty. He had asked these theological experts to say whether the Brethren could keep their discipline and yet be considered good Lutherans; and the experts, in reply, had declared their opinion that the Herrnhut Brethren were as loyal Lutherans as any in the land. Thus the Brethren were standing now on a shaky floor. According to the Tuebingen Theological Faculty they were good members of the National Church; according to the Government they were a "sect" to be tolerated!

Next year he adopted three defensive measures (1734). First, he divided the congregation at Herrnhut into two parts, the Moravian and the purely Lutheran; next, he had himself ordained as a Lutheran clergyman; and third, he despatched a few Moravians to found a colony in Georgia. He was now, he imagined, prepared for the worst. If the King commanded the Moravians to go, the Count had his answer ready. As he himself was a Lutheran clergyman, he would stay at Herrnhut and minister to the Herrnhut Lutherans; and the Moravians could all sail away to Georgia, and live in perfect peace in the land of the free.

Next year he made his position stronger still (1735). As the Moravians in Georgia would require their own ministers, he now had David Nitschmann consecrated a Bishop by Bishop Daniel Ernest Jablonsky (March 13th). The new Bishop was not to exercise his functions in Germany. He was a Bishop for the foreign field only; he sailed with the second batch of colonists for Georgia; and thus Zinzendorf maintained the Moravian Episcopal Succession, not from any sectarian motives, but because he wished to help the Brethren when the storm burst over their heads.

For what really happened, however, Zinzendorf was unprepared (1736). As he made these various arrangements for the Brethren, he entirely overlooked the fact that he himself was in greater danger than they. He was far more widely hated than he imagined. He was condemned by the Pietists because he had never experienced their sudden and spasmodic method of conversion. He offended his own relatives when he became a clergyman; he was accused of having disgraced his rank as a Count; he disgusted a number of other noblemen at Dresden; and the result of this strong feeling was that Augustus III., King of Saxony, issued an edict banishing Zinzendorf from his kingdom. He was accused in this Royal edict of three great crimes. He had introduced religious novelties; he had founded conventicles; and he had taught false doctrine. Thus Zinzendorf was banished from Saxony as a heretic. As soon, however, as the Government had dealt with Zinzendorf, they sent a second Commission to Herrnhut; and the second Commission came to the conclusion that the Brethren were most desirable Lutherans, and might be allowed to stay. Dr. Loescher, one of the commissioners, burst into tears. "Your doctrine," he said, "is as pure as ours, but we do not possess your discipline." At first sight this certainly looks like a contradiction, but the explanation is not far to seek. We find it in the report issued by the Commission. It was a shameless confession of mercenary motives. In that report the commissioners deliberately stated that if good workmen like the Brethren were banished from Herrnhut the Government would lose so much in taxes; and, therefore, the Brethren were allowed to stay because they brought grist to the mill. At the same time, they were forbidden to make any proselytes; and thus it was hoped that the Herrnhut heresy would die a natural death.

When Zinzendorf heard of his banishment, he was not amazed. "What matter!" he said. "Even had I been allowed by law, I could not have remained in Herrnhut at all during the next ten years." He had plans further afield. "We must now," he added, "gather together the Pilgrim Congregation and proclaim the Saviour to the World." It is true that the edict of banishment was repealed (1737); it is true that he was allowed to return to Herrnhut; but a year later a new edict was issued, and the Count was sternly expelled from his native land (1738).

Chapter 6: The Foreign Missions and Their Influence

AS young Leonard Dober lay tossing on his couch, his soul was disquieted within him (1731). He had heard strange news that afternoon, and sleep forsook his eyes. As Count Zinzendorf was on a visit to the court of Christian VI., King of Denmark, he met a West Indian negro slave, by name Antony Ulrich. And Antony was an interesting man. He had been baptized; he had been taught the rudiments of the Christian faith; he had met two other Brethren at the court; his tongue was glib and his imagination lively; and now he poured into Zinzendorf's ears a heartrending tale of the benighted condition of the slaves on the Danish island of St. Thomas. He spoke pathetically of his sister Anna, of his brother Abraham, and of their fervent desire to hear the Gospel.

"If only some missionaries would come," said he, "they would certainly be heartily welcomed. Many an evening have I sat on the shore and sighed my soul toward Christian Europe; and I have a brother and sister in bondage who long to know the living God."

The effect on Zinzendorf was electric. His mind was full of missionary visions. The story of Antony fired his zeal. The door to the heathen world stood open. The golden day had dawned. He returned to the Brethren at Herrnhut, arrived at two o'clock in the morning, and found that the Single Brethren were still on their knees in prayer. Nothing could be more encouraging. At the first opportunity he told the Brethren Antony's touching tale.

Again the effect was electric. As the Brethren met for their monthly service on "Congregation Day" they had often listened to reports of work in various parts of the Continent; already the Count had suggested foreign work; and already a band of Single Brethren (Feb. 11th, 1728) had made a covenant with each other to respond to the first clear sound of the trumpet call. As soon as their daily work was over, these men plunged deep into the study of medicine, geography, and languages. They wished to be ready "when the blessed time should come"; they were on the tiptoe of expectation; and now they were looking forward to the day when they should be summoned to cross the seas to heathen lands. The summons had sounded at last. To Leonard Dober the crisis of his life had come. As he tossed to and fro that summer night he could think about nothing but the poor neglected negroes, and seemed to hear a voice Divine urging him to arise and preach deliverance to the captives. Whence came, he asked, that still, small voice? Was it his own excited fancy, or was it the voice of God? As the morning broke, he was still unsettled in his mind. But already the Count had taught the Brethren to regard the daily Watch-Word as a special message from God. He consulted his text-book. The very answer he sought was there. "It is not a vain thing for you," ran the message, "because it is your life; and through this thing ye shall prolong your days."

And yet Dober was not quite convinced. If God desired him to go abroad He would give a still clearer call. He determined to consult his friend Tobias Leupold, and abide the issue of the colloquy; and in the evening the two young men took their usual stroll together among the brushwood clustering round the settlement. And then Leonard Dober laid bare his heart, and learned to his amazement that all the while Tobias had been in the same perplexing pass. What Dober had been longing to tell him, he had been longing to tell Dober. Each had heard the same still small voice; each had fought the same doubts; each had feared to speak his mind; and now, in the summer gloaming, they knelt down side by side and prayed to be guided aright. Forthwith the answer was ready. As they joined the other Single Brethren, and marched in solemn procession past Zinzendorf's house, they heard the Count remark to a friend, "Sir, among these young men there are missionaries to St. Thomas, Greenland, Lapland, and many other countries."

The words were inspiring. Forthwith the young fellows wrote to the Count and offered to serve in St. Thomas. The Count read the letter to the congregation, but kept their names a secret. The Brethren were critical and cold. As the settlers were mostly simple people, with little knowledge of the world beyond the seas, it was natural that they should shrink from a task which the powerful Protestant Churches of Europe had not yet dared to attempt. Some held the offer reckless; some dubbed it a youthful bid for fame and the pretty imagination of young officious minds. Antony Ulrich came to Herrnhut, addressed the congregation in Dutch, and told them that no one could be a missionary in St. Thomas without first becoming a slave. As the people knew no better they believed him. For a year the issue hung in the scales of doubt. The young men were resolute, confident and undismayed. If they had to be slaves to preach the Gospel, then slaves they would willingly be! [87] At last Dober wrote in person to the congregation and repeated his resolve. The Brethren yielded. The Count still doubted. For the second time a momentous issue was submitted to the decision of the Lot.

"Are you willing," he asked Dober, "to consult the Saviour by means of the Lot?"

"For myself," replied Dober, "I am already sure enough; but I will do so for the sake of the Brethren."

A meeting was held; a box of mottoes was brought in; and Dober drew a slip of paper bearing the words: "Let the lad go, for the Lord is with him." The voice of the Lot was decisive. Of all the meetings held in Herrnhut, this meeting to hear the voice of the Lot was the most momentous in its world-wide importance. The young men were all on fire. If the Lot had only given the word they would now have gone to the foreign field in dozens. For the first time in the history of Protestant Europe a congregation of orthodox Christians had deliberately resolved to undertake the task of preaching the Gospel to the heathen. As the Lot which decided that Dober should go had also decided that his friend Leupold should stay, he now chose as his travelling companion the carpenter, David Nitschmann. The birthday of Moravian Missions now drew near. At three o'clock on the morning of August 21st, 1732, the two men stood waiting in front of Zinzendorf's house. The Count had spent the whole night in prayer. He drove them in his carriage as far as

Bautzen. They alighted outside the little town, knelt down on the quiet roadside, engaged in prayer, received the Count's blessing by imposition of hands, bade him farewell, and set out Westward Ho!

As they trudged on foot on their way to Copenhagen, they had no idea that in so doing they were clearing the way for the great modern missionary movement; and, on the whole, they looked more like pedlars than pioneers of a new campaign. They wore brown coats and quaint three-cornered hats. They carried bundles on their backs. They had only about thirty shillings in their pockets. They had received no clear instructions from the Count, except "to do all in the Spirit of Jesus Christ." They knew but little of the social condition of St. Thomas. They had no example to follow; they had no "Society" to supply their needs; and now they were going to a part of the world where, as yet, a missionary's foot had never trod.

At Copenhagen, where they called at the court, they created quite a sensation. For some years there had existed there a National Missionary College. It was the first Reformed Missionary College in Europe. Founded by King Frederick IV., it was regarded as a regular department of the State. It had already sent Hans Egede to Greenland and Ziegenbalg to Tranquebar, on the Coromandel Coast; and it sent its men as State officials, to undertake the work of evangelisation as a useful part of the national colonial policy. But Dober and Nitschmann were on a different footing. If they had been the paid agents of the State they would have been regarded with favour; but as they were only the heralds of a Church they were laughed at as a brace of fools. For a while they met with violent opposition. Von Plesz, the King's Chamberlain, asked them how they would live.

"We shall work," replied Nitschmann, "as slaves among the slaves."

"But," said Von Plesz, "that is impossible. It will not be allowed. No white man ever works as a slave."

"Very well," replied Nitschmann, "I am a carpenter, and will ply my trade."

"But what will the potter do?"

"He will help me in my work."

"If you go on like that," exclaimed the Chamberlain, "you will stand your ground the wide world over."

The first thing was to stand their ground at Copenhagen. As the directors of the Danish West Indian Company refused to grant them a passage out they had now to wait for any vessel that might be sailing. The whole Court was soon on their side. The Queen expressed her good wishes. The Princess Amalie gave them some money and a Dutch Bible. The Chamberlain slipped some coins into Nitschmann's pocket. The Court Physician gave them a spring lancet, and showed them how to open a vein. The Court Chaplain espoused their cause, and the Royal Cupbearer found them a ship on the point of sailing for St. Thomas.

As the ship cast anchor in St. Thomas Harbour the Brethren realized for the first time the greatness of their task. There lay the quaint little town of Tappus, its scarlet roofs agleam in the noontide sun; there, along the silver beach, they saw the yellowing rocks; and there, beyond, the soft green hills were limned against the azure sky. There, in a word, lay the favoured isle, the "First Love of Moravian Missions." Again the text for the day was prophetic: "The Lord of Hosts," ran the gladdening watchword, "mustereth the host of the battle." As the Brethren stepped ashore next day they opened a new chapter in the history of modern Christianity. They were the founders of Christian work among the slaves. For fifty years the Moravian Brethren laboured in the West Indies without any aid from any other religious denomination. They established churches in St. Thomas, in St. Croix, in St. John's, in Jamaica, in Antigua, in Barbados, and in St. Kitts. They had 13,000 baptized converts before a missionary from any other Church arrived on the scene.

We pass to another field. As the Count was on his visit to the Court in Copenhagen, he saw two little Greenland boys who had been baptized by the Danish missionary, Hans Egede; and as the story of Antony Ulrich fired the zeal of Leonard Dober, so the story of Egede's patient labours aroused the zeal of Matthew Stach and the redoubtable Christian David (1733). In Greenland Egede had failed. In Greenland the Brethren succeeded. As they settled down among the people they resolved at first to be very systematic in their method of preaching the Gospel; and to this end, like Egede before them, they expounded to the simple Eskimo folk the whole scheme of dogmatic theology, from the fall of man to the glorification of the saint. The result was dismal failure. At last the Brethren struck the golden trail. The story is a classic in the history of missions. As John Beck, one balmy evening in June, was discoursing on things Divine to a group of Eskimos, it suddenly flashed upon his mind that, instead of preaching dogmatic theology he would read them an extract from the translation of the Gospels he was now preparing. He seized his manuscript. "And being in an agony," read John Beck, "He prayed more earnestly, and His sweat was as it were great drops of blood falling down to the ground." At this Kajarnak, the brightest in the group, sprang forward to the table and exclaimed, "How was that? Tell me that again, for I, too, would be saved." The first Eskimo was touched. The power was the story of the Cross. From that moment the Brethren altered the whole style of their preaching. Instead of expounding dogmatic theology, they told the vivid human story of the Via Dolorosa, the Crown of Thorns, the Scourging, and the Wounded Side. The result was brilliant success. The more the Brethren spoke of Christ the more eager the Eskimos were to listen.

In this good work the leader was Matthew Stach. He was ordained a Presbyter of the Brethren's Church. He was officially appointed leader of the Greenland Mission. He was recognized by the Danish College of Missions. He was authorized by the King of Denmark to baptize and perform all sacerdotal functions. His work was methodical and thorough. In order to teach the roving Eskimos the virtues of a settled life, he actually took a number of them on a Continental tour, brought them to London, presented them, at Leicester House, to King George II., the Prince of Wales, and the rest of the Royal Family, and thus imbued them with a love of civilisation. At New Herrnhut, in

Greenland, he founded a settlement, as thoroughly organised as Herrnhut in Saxony. He built a church, adorned with pictures depicting the sufferings of Christ. He taught the people to play the violin. He divided the congregation into "choirs." He showed them how to cultivate a garden of cabbages, leeks, lettuces, radishes and turnips. He taught them to care for all widows and orphans. He erected a "Brethren's House" for the "Single Brethren" and a "Sisters'House" for the "Single Sisters." He taught them to join in worship every day. At six o'clock every morning there was a meeting for the baptized; at eight a public service for all the settlers; at nine the children repeated their catechism and then proceeded to morning school; and then, in the evening, when the men had returned with their bag of seals, there was a public preaching service in the church. And at Lichtenfels and Lichtenau the same sort of work was done.

We pass on to other scenes, to Dutch Guinea or Surinam. As the Dutch were still a great colonial power, they had plenty of opportunity to spread the Gospel; and yet, except in India, they had hitherto not lifted a finger in the cause of foreign missions. For the most part the Dutch clergy took not the slightest interest in the subject. They held bigoted views about predestination. They thought that Christ had died for them, but not for Indians and negroes. As the Brethren, however, were good workmen, it was thought that they might prove useful in the Colonies; and so Bishop Spangenberg found it easy to make an arrangement with the Dutch Trading Company, whereby the Brethren were granted a free passage, full liberty in religion, and exemption from the oath and military service (1734). But all this was little more than pious talk. As soon as the Brethren set to work the Dutch pastors opposed them to the teeth. At home and abroad it was just the same. At Amsterdam the clergy met in Synod, and prepared a cutting "Pastoral Letter," condemning the Brethren's theology; and at Paramaribo the Brethren were forbidden to hold any meetings at all. But the Brethren did not stay very long in Paramaribo. Through three hundred miles of jungle and swamp they pressed their way, and came to the homes of the Indian tribes; to the Accawois, who earned their living as professional assassins; to the Warrows, who wallowed in the marshes; to the Arawaks, or "Flour People," who prepared tapioca; to the Caribs, who sought them that had familiar spirits and wizards that peep and mutter. "It seems very dark," they wrote to the Count, "but we will testify of the grace of the Saviour till He lets the light shine in this dark waste." For twenty years they laboured among these Indian tribes; and Salomo Schumann, the leader of the band, prepared an Indian dictionary and grammar. One story flashes light upon their labours. As Christopher Daehne, who had built himself a hut in the forest, was retiring to rest a snake suddenly glided down upon him from the roof, bit him twice or thrice, and coiled itself round his body. At that moment, the gallant herald of the Cross, with death staring him in the face, thought, not of himself, but of the people whom he had come to serve. If he died as he lay the rumour might spread that some of the natives had killed him; and, therefore, he seized a piece of chalk and wrote on the table, "A serpent has killed me." But lo! the text flashed suddenly upon him: "They shall take up serpents; and if they drink any deadly thing it shall not hurt them." He seized the serpent, flung it from him, lay down to sleep in perfect peace, and next morning went about his labours.

We pass now to South Africa, the land of the Boers. For the last hundred years South Africa had been under the rule of the Dutch East India Company; and the result was that the Hottentots and Kaffirs were still as heathen as ever. For their spiritual welfare the Boers cared absolutely nothing. They were strong believers in predestination; they believed that they were elected to grace and the Hottentots elected to damnation; and, therefore, they held it to be their duty to wipe the Hottentots off the face of the earth. "The Hottentots," they said, "have no souls; they belong to the race of baboons." They called them children of the devil; they called them "black wares," "black beasts," and "black cattle"; and over one church door they painted the notice "Dogs and Hottentots not admitted." They ruined them, body and soul, with rum and brandy; they first made them merry with drink, and then cajoled them into unjust bargains; they shot them down in hundreds, and then boasted over their liquor how many Hottentots they had "potted." "With one hundred and fifty men," wrote the Governor, Van Ruibeck, in his journal, "11,000 head of black cattle might be obtained without danger of losing one man; and many savages might be taken without resistance to be sent as slaves to India, as they will always come to us unarmed. If no further trade is to be expected with them, what should it matter much to take six or eight thousand beasts from them." But the most delightful of all Boer customs was the custom of flogging by pipes. If a Hottentot proved a trifle unruly, he was thrashed, while his master, looking on with a gluttonous eye, smoked a fixed number of pipes; and the wreathing smoke and the writhing Hottentot brought balm unto his soul.

And now to this hell of hypocrisy and villainy came the first apostle to the natives. As the famous Halle missionary, Ziegenbalg, was on his way to the Malabar Coast he touched at Cape Town, heard something of the abominations practised, was stirred to pity, and wrote laying the case before two pastors in Holland. The two pastors wrote to Herrnhut; the Herrnhut Brethren chose their man; and in less than a week the man was on his way. George Schmidt was a typical Herrnhut brother. He had come from Kunewalde, in Moravia, had lain six years in prison, had seen his friend, Melchior Nitschmann, die in his arms, and watched his own flesh fall away in flakes from his bones. For twelve months he had now to stay in Amsterdam, first to learn the Dutch language, and secondly to pass an examination in orthodox theology. He passed the examination with flying colours. He received permission from the "Chamber of Seventeen" to sail in one of the Dutch East India Company's ships. He landed at Cape Town. His arrival created a sensation. As he sat in the public room of an inn he listened to the conversation of the assembled farmers (1737).

"I hear," said one, "that a parson has come here to convert the Hottentots."

"What! a parson!" quoth another. "Why, the poor fool must have lost his head."

They argued the case; they mocked; they laughed; they found the subject intensely amusing.

"And what, sir, do you think?" said a waiter to Schmidt, who was sitting quietly in the corner.

"I am the very man," replied Schmidt; and the farmers began to talk about their crops.

For six years George Schmidt laboured all alone among the benighted Hottentots. He began his labours at a military outpost in the Sweet-Milk Valley, about fifty miles east of Cape Town; but finding the company of soldiers dangerous to the morals of his congregation, he moved to a place called Bavian's Kloof, where the town of Genadendal stands to-day. He planted the pear-tree so famous in missionary annals, taught the Hottentots the art of gardening, held public service every evening, had fifty pupils in his day-school, and began to baptize his converts. As he and William, one of his scholars, were returning one day from a visit to Cape Town, they came upon a brook, and Schmidt asked William if he had a mind to be baptized there and then. He answered "Yes." And there, by the stream in a quiet spot, the first fruit of African Missions made his confession of faith in Christ.

"Dost thou believe," asked Schmidt solemnly, "that the Son of God died on the cross for the sins of all mankind? Dost thou believe that thou art by nature a lost and undone creature? Wilt thou renounce the devil and all his works? Art thou willing, in dependence on God's grace, to endure reproach and persecution, to confess Christ before all men, and to remain faithful to him unto death?"

As soon, however, as Schmidt began to baptize his converts the Cape Town clergy denounced him as a heretic, and summoned him to answer for his sins. The great charge against him was that he had not been properly ordained. He had been ordained, not by actual imposition of hands, but by a certificate of ordination, sent out to him by Zinzendorf. To the Dutch clergy this was no ordination at all. What right, said they, had a man to baptize who had been ordained in this irregular manner? He returned to Holland to fight his battle there. And he never set foot on African soil again! The whole argument about the irregular ordination turned out to be a mere excuse. If that argument had been genuine the Dutch clergy could now have had Schimdt ordained in the usual way. But the truth is they had no faith in his mission; they had begun to regard the Brethren as dangerous heretics; and, therefore, for another fifty years they forbade all further mission work in the Dutch Colony of South Africa.

We pass on to other scenes. We go to the Gold Coast in the Dutch Colony of Guinea, where Huckoff, another German Moravian, and Protten, a mulatto theological scholar, attempted to found a school for slaves (1737), and where, again, the work was opposed by the Governor. We pass to another Dutch Colony in Ceylon; and there find David Nitschmann III. and Dr. Eller establishing a society in Colombo, and labouring further inland for the conversion of the Cingalese; and again we find that the Dutch clergy, inflamed by the "Pastoral Letter," were bitterly opposed to the Brethren and compelled them to return to Herrnhut. We take our journey to Constantinople, and find Arvid Gradin, the learned Swede, engaged in an attempt to come to terms with the Greek Church (1740), and thus open the way for the Brethren's Gospel to Asia. We step north to

Wallachia, and find two Brethren consulting about a settlement there with the Haspodar of Bucharest. We arrive at St. Petersburg, and find three Brethren there before us, commissioned to preach the Gospel to the heathen Calmucks. We pass on to Persia and find two doctors, Hocker and Rueffer, stripped naked by robbers on the highway, and then starting a practice at Ispahan (1747). We cross the sandy plains to the city of Bagdad, and find two Brethren in its narrow streets; we find Hocker expounding the Gospel to the Copts in Cairo!

And even this was not the end of the Brethren's missionary labours (1738-42). For some years the Brethren conducted a mission to the Jews. For Jews the Count had special sympathy. He had vowed in his youth to do all he could for their conversion; he had met a good many Jews at Herrnhut and at Frankfurt-on-the-Main; he made a practice of speaking about them in public on the Great Day of Atonement; and in their Sunday morning litany the Brethren uttered the prayer, "Deliver Thy people Israel from their blindness; bring many of them to know Thee, till the fulness of the Gentiles is come and all Israel is saved." The chief seat of this work was Amsterdam, and the chief workers Leonard Dober and Samuel Leiberkuehn. The last man was a model missionary. He had studied theology at Jena and Halle; he was a master of the Hebrew tongue; he was expert in all customs of the Jews; he was offered a professorship at Koenigsberg; and yet, instead of winning his laurels as an Oriental scholar, he preferred to settle down in humble style in the Jewish quarter of Amsterdam, and there talk to his friends the Jews about the Christ he loved so deeply. His method of work was instructive. He never dazed his Jewish friends with dogmatic theology. He never tried to prove that Christ was the Messiah of the prophecies. He simply told them, in a kindly way, how Jesus had risen from the dead, and how much this risen Jesus had done in the world; he shared their hope of a national gathering in Palestine; and, though he could never boast of making converts, he was so beloved by his Jewish friends that they called him "Rabbi Schmuel."

Let us try to estimate the value of all this work. Of all the enterprises undertaken by the Brethren this heroic advance on heathen soil had the greatest influence on other Protestant Churches; and some writers have called the Moravians the pioneers of Protestant Foreign Missions. But this statement is only true in a special sense. They were not the first to preach the Gospel to the heathen. If the reader consults any history of Christian Missions [88] he will see that long before Leonard Dober set out for St. Thomas other men had preached the Gospel in heathen lands.

But in all these efforts there is one feature missing. There is no sign of any united Church action. At the time when Leonard Dober set out from Herrnhut not a single other Protestant Church in the world had attacked the task of foreign missions, or even regarded that task as a Divinely appointed duty. In England the work was undertaken, not by the Church as such, but by two voluntary associations, the S.P.C.K. and the S.P.G.; in Germany, not by the Lutheran Church, but by a few earnest Pietists; in Denmark, not by the Church, but by the State; in Holland, not by the Church, but by one or two pious Colonial Governors; and in Scotland, neither by the Church nor by anyone else. At that time the whole work of foreign missions was regarded as the duty, not of the Churches, but of "Kings, Princes, and States." In England, Anglicans, Independents and Baptists were all more or less indifferent. In Scotland the subject was never mentioned; and even sixty years later a resolution to inquire into the matter was rejected by the General Assembly (1796). In Germany the Lutherans were either indifferent or hostile. In Denmark and Holland the whole subject was treated with contempt. And the only Protestant Church to recognize the duty was this little, struggling Renewed Church of the Brethren. In this sense, therefore, and in this sense only, can we call the Moravians the pioneers of modern missions. They were the first Protestant Church in Christendom to undertake the conversion of the heathen. They sent out their missionaries as authorised agents of the Church. They prayed for the cause of missions in their Sunday Litany. They had several missionary hymns in their Hymn-Book. They had regular meetings to listen to the reading of missionaries' diaries and letters. They discussed missionary problems at their Synods. They appointed a Church Financial Committee to see to ways and means. They sent out officially appointed "visitors" to inspect the work in various countries. They were, in a word, the first Protestant Missionary Church in history; and thus they set an inspiring example to all their stronger sisters.

Again, this work of the Brethren was important because it was thorough and systematic. At first the missionaries were compelled to go out with very vague ideas of their duties. But in 1734 the Brethren published "Instructions for the Colony in Georgia"; in 1737 "Instructions for Missionaries to the East"; in 1738 "Instructions for all Missionaries"; and in 1740 "The Right Way to Convert the Heathen." Thus even during those early years the Moravian missionaries were trained in missionary work. They were told what Gospel to preach and how to preach it. "You are not," said Zinzendorf, in his "Instructions," "to allow yourselves to be blinded by the notion that the heathen must be taught first to believe in God, and then afterwards in Jesus Christ. It is false. They know already that there is a God. You must preach to them about the Son. You must be like Paul, who knew nothing but Jesus and Him crucified. You must speak constantly, in season, and out of season, of Jesus, the Lamb, the Saviour; and you must tell them that the way to salvation is belief in this Jesus, the Eternal Son of God." Instead of discussing doctrinal questions the missionaries laid the whole stress on the person and sacrifice of Christ. They avoided dogmatic language. They used the language, not of the theological world, but of the Gospels. They preached, not a theory of the Atonement, but the story of the Cross. "We must," said Spangenberg, "hold to the fact that the blood and death of Jesus are the diamond in the golden ring of the Gospel."

But alongside this Gospel message the Brethren introduced as far as possible the stern system of moral discipline which already existed at Herrnhut. They lived in daily personal touch with the people. They taught them to be honest, obedient, industrious, and loyal to the Government. They opened schools, taught reading and writing, and instructed the girls in sewing and needlework. They divided their congregations, not only into "Choirs," but also into "Classes." They laid the stress, not on public preaching, but on the individual "cure of souls." For this purpose they practised what was called "The Speaking." At certain fixed seasons, i.e., the missionary, or one of his helpers, had a private interview with each member of the congregation. The old system of the Bohemian Brethren was here revived. [89] At these private interviews there was no possibility of any moral danger. At the head of the men was the missionary, at the head of the women his wife; for the men there were male "Helpers," for the women female "Helpers"; and thus all "speakings" took place between persons of the same sex only. There were three degrees of discipline. For the first offence the punishment was reproof; for the second, suspension from the Communion; for the third, expulsion from the congregation. And thus the Brethren proved up to the hilt that Christian work among the heathen was not mere waste of time.

Again, this work was important because it was public. It was not done in a corner. It was acted on the open stage of history. As these Brethren laboured among the heathen, they were constantly coming into close contact with Governors, with trading companies, and with Boards of Control. In Greenland they were under Danish rule; in Surinam, under Dutch; in North America, under English; in the West Indies, under English, French, Danish, Dutch, Swedish, Spanish, Portuguese; and thus they were teaching a moral lesson to the whole Western European world. At that time the West Indian Islands were the gathering ground for all the powers on the Atlantic seaboard of Europe. There, and there alone in the world, they all had possessions; and there, in the midst of all these nationalities, the Brethren accomplished their most successful work. And the striking fact is that in each of these islands they gained the approval of the Governor. They were the agents of an international Church; they were free from all political complications; they could never be suspected of treachery; they were law-abiding citizens themselves, and taught their converts to be the same; and thus they enjoyed the esteem and support of every great Power in Europe.

And this in turn had another grand result. It prepared the way for Negro Emancipation. We must not, however, give the missionaries too much credit. As Zinzendorf himself was a firm believer in slavery, we need not be surprised to find that the Brethren never came forward as champions of liberty. They never pleaded for emancipation. They never encouraged their converts to expect it. They never talked about the horrors of slavery. They never appealed, like Wilberforce, to Parliament. And yet it was just these modest Brethren who did the most to make emancipation possible. Instead of delivering inflamatory speeches, and stirring up the hot-blooded negroes to rebellion, they taught them rather to be industrious, orderly, and loyal, and thus show that they were fit for liberty. If a slave disobeyed his master they punished him. They acted wisely. If the Brethren had preached emancipation they would simply have made their converts restive; and these converts, by rebelling, would only have cut their own throats. Again and again, in Jamaica and Antigua, the negroes rose in revolt; and again and again the Governors noticed that the Moravian converts took no part in the rebellion.

At last the news of these triumphs arrived in England; and the Privy Council appointed a Committee to inquire into the state of the slave trade in our West Indian possessions (1787). The Committee appealed to the Brethren for information. The reply was drafted by Christian Ignatius La Trobe. As La Trobe was then the English Secretary for the Brethren's missions, he was well qualified to give the required information. He described the Brethren's methods of work, pointed out its results in the conduct of the negroes, and declared that all the Brethren desired was liberty to preach the Gospel. "The Brethren," he said, "never wish to interfere between masters and slaves." The ball was now set fairly rolling. Dr. Porteous, Bishop of London, replied on behalf of the Committee. He was an ardent champion of emancipation. He thanked the Brethren for their information. He informed them how pleased the Committee were with the Brethren's methods of work. At this very time Wilberforce formed his resolution to devote his life to the emancipation of the slaves. He opened his campaign in Parliament two years later. He was a personal friend of La Trobe; he read his report; and he backed up his arguments in Parliament by describing the good results of Moravian work among the slaves. And thus the part played by the Brethren was alike modest and effective. They taught the slaves to be good; they taught them to be genuine lovers of law and order; they made them fit for the great gift of liberty; and thus, by destroying the stale old argument that emancipation was dangerous they removed the greatest obstacle in Wilberforce's way. [90]

Again, this work of the Brethren was important in its influence on several great English missionary pioneers. At missionary gatherings held in England the statement is often made to-day that the first Englishman to go out as a foreign missionary was William Carey, the leader of the immortal "Serampore Three." It is time to explode that fiction. For some years before William Carey was heard of a number of English Moravian Brethren had gone out from these shores as foreign missionaries. In Antigua laboured Samuel Isles, Joseph Newby, and Samuel Watson; in Jamaica, George Caries and John Bowen; in St. Kitts and St. Croix, James Birkby; in Barbados, Benjamin Brookshaw; in Labrador, William Turner, James Rhodes, and Lister; and in Tobago, John Montgomery, the father of James Montgomery, the well-known Moravian hymn-writer and poet. With the single exception of George Caries, who seems to have had some Irish blood in his veins, these early missionaries were as English as Carey himself; and the greater number, as we can see from the names, were natives of Yorkshire. Moreover, William Carey knew of their work. He owed his inspiration partly to them; he referred to their work in his famous pamphlet, "Enquiry into the Obligations of Christians to use Means for the Conversion of the Heathens"; and finally, at the house of Mrs. Beely Wallis, in Kettering, he threw down upon the table some numbers of the first English missionary magazine, [91] "Periodical Accounts relating to the Missions of the Church of the United Brethren," and, addressing his fellow Baptist ministers, exclaimed: "See what the Moravians have done! Can we not follow their example, and in obedience to our heavenly Master go out into the world and preach the Gospel to the heathen." The result was the foundation of the Baptist Missionary Society.

His companion, Marshman, also confessed his obligations to the Brethren (1792).

"Thank you! Moravians," he said, "you have done me good. If I am ever a missionary worth a straw I shall, under our Saviour, owe it to you."

We have next the case of the London Missionary Society. Of that Society one of the founders was Rowland Hill. He was well informed about the labours of the Moravians; he corresponded with Peter Braun, the Moravian missionary in Antigua; and to that correspondence he owed in part his interest in missionary work. But that was not the end of the Brethren's influence. At all meetings addressed by the founders of the proposed Society, the speaker repeatedly enforced his arguments by quotations from the Periodical Accounts; and finally, when the Society was established, the founders submitted to La Trobe, the editor, the following series of questions:—"1. How do you obtain your missionaries? 2. What is the true calling of a missionary? 3. What qualifications do you demand in a missionary? 4. Do you demand scientific and theological learning? 5. Do you consider previous instruction in Divine things an essential? 6. How do you employ your missionaries from the time when they are first called to the time when they set out? 7. Have you found by experience that the cleverest and best educated men make the best missionaries? 8. What do you do when you establish a missionary station? Do you send men with their wives, or single people, or both? 9. What have you found the most effective way of accomplishing the conversion of the heathen? 10. Can you tell us the easiest way of learning a language? 11. How much does your missionary ship [92] cost you?" In reply, La Trobe answered in detail, and gave a full description of the Brethren's methods; and the first heralds of the London Missionary Society went out with Moravian instructions in their pockets and Moravian experience to guide them on their way.

We have next the case of Robert Moffatt, the missionary to Bechuanaland. What was it that first aroused his missionary zeal? It was, he tells us, the stories told him by his mother about the exploits of the Moravians!

In Germany the influence of the Brethren was equally great. At the present time the greatest missionary forces in Germany are the Basel and Leipzig Societies; and the interesting point to notice is that if we only go far enough back in the story we find that each of these societies owed its origin to Moravian influence. [93] From what did the Basel Missionary Society spring? (1819). It sprang from an earlier "Society for Christian Fellowship (1780)," and one object of that earlier society was the support of Moravian Missions. But the influence did not end here. At the meeting when the Basel Missionary Society was formed, three Moravians—Burghardt, Goetze, and Loerschke—were present, the influence of the Brethren was specially mentioned, the work of the Brethren was described, and the text for the day from the Moravian textbook was read. In a similar way the Leipzig Missionary Society sprang from a series of meetings held in Dresden, and in those meetings several Moravians took a prominent part. By whom was the first missionary college in history established? It was established at Berlin by Jaenicke (1800), and Jaenicke had first been a teacher in the Moravian Paedagogium at Niesky. By whom was the first Norwegian Missionary Magazine—the Norsk Missionsblad—edited? By the Moravian minister, Holm. From such facts as these we may draw one broad conclusion; and that broad conclusion is that the Brethren's labours paved the way for some of the greatest missionary institutions of modern times.

Chapter 7: The Pilgrim Band (1736-1743)

AS soon as Zinzendorf was banished from Saxony, he sought another sphere of work. About thirty miles northeast of Frankfurt-on-the-Main there lay a quaint and charming district known as the Wetterau, wherein stood two old ruined castles, called Ronneburg and Marienborn. The owners of the estate, the Counts of Isenberg, had fallen on hard times. They were deep in debt; their estates were running to decay; the Ronneburg walls were crumbling to pieces, and the out-houses, farms and stables were let out to fifty-six dirty families of Jews, tramps, vagabonds and a mongrel throng of scoundrels of the lowest class. As soon as the Counts heard that Zinzendorf had been banished from Saxony, they kindly offered him their estates on lease. They had two objects in view. As the Brethren were pious, they would improve the people's morals; and as they were good workers, they would raise the value of the land. The Count sent Christian David to reconnoitre. Christian David brought back an evil report. It was a filthy place, he said, unfit for respectable people. But Zinzendorf felt that, filthy or not, it was the very spot which God had chosen for his new work. It suited his high ideas. The more squalid the people, the more reason there was for going.

"I will make this nest of vagabonds," he said, "the centre for the universal religion of the Saviour. Christian," he asked, "haven't you been in Greenland?"

"Ah, yes," replied Christian, who had been with the two Stachs, "if it were only as good as it was in Greenland! But at Ronneburg Castle we shall only die."

But the Count would not hear another word, went to see the place for himself, closed with the terms of the Counts of Isenberg, and thus commenced that romantic chapter in the Brethren's History called by some German historians the Wetterau Time.

It was a time of many adventures. As the Count took up his quarters in Ronneburg Castle, he brought with him a body of Brethren and Sisters whom he called the "Pilgrim Band"; and there, on June 17th, 1736, he preached his first sermon in the castle. It was now exactly fourteen years since Christian David had felled the first tree at Herrnhut; and now for another fourteen years these crumbling walls were to be the home of Moravian life. What the members of the Pilgrim Band were we may know from the very name. They were a travelling Church. They were a body of Christians called to the task, in Zinzendorf's own words, "to proclaim the Saviour to the world"; and the Count's noble motto was: "The earth is the Lord's; all souls are His; I am debtor to all." There was a dash of romance in that Pilgrim Band, and more than a dash of heroism. They lived in a wild and eerie district. They slept on straw. They heard the rats and mice hold revels on the worm-eaten staircases, and heard the night wind howl and sough between the broken windows; and from those ruined walls they went out to preach the tidings of the love of Christ in the wigwams of the Indians and the snow-made huts of the Eskimos.

As charity, however, begins at home, the Count and his Brethren began their new labours among the degraded rabble that lived in filth and poverty round the castle. They conducted free schools for the children. They held meetings for men and women in the vaults of the castle. They visited the miserable gipsies in their dirty homes. They invited the dirty little ragamuffins to tea, and the gipsies' children sat down at table with the sons and daughters of the Count. They issued an order forbidding begging, and twice a week, on Tuesdays and Fridays, they distributed food and clothing to the poor. One picture will illustrate this strange campaign. Among the motley medley that lived about the castle was an old grey-haired Jew, named Rabbi Abraham. One bright June evening, Zinzendorf met him, stretched out his hand, and said: "Grey hairs are a crown of glory. I can see from your head and the expression of your eyes that you have had much experience both of heart and life. In the name of the God of Abraham, Isaac and Jacob, let us be friends."

The old man was struck dumb with wonder. Such a greeting from a Christian he had never heard before. He had usually been saluted with the words, "Begone, Jew!" "His lips trembled; his voice failed; and big tears rolled down his wrinkled cheeks upon his flowing beard.

"Enough, father," said the Count; "we understand each other." And from that moment the two were friends. The Count went to see him in his dirty home, and ate black bread at his table. One morning, before dawn, as the two walked out, the old patriarch opened his heart.

"My heart," said he, "is longing for the dawn. I am sick, yet know not what is the matter with me. I am looking for something, yet know not what I seek. I am like one who is chased, yet I see no enemy, except the one within me, my old evil heart."

The Count opened his lips, and preached the Gospel of Christ. He painted Love on the Cross. He described that Love coming down from holiness and heaven. He told the old Jew, in burning words, how Christ had met corrupted mankind, that man might become like God. As the old man wept and wrung his hands, the two ascended a hill, whereon stood a lonely church. And the sun rose, and its rays fell on the golden cross on the church spire, and the cross glittered brightly in the light of heaven.

"See there, Abraham," said Zinzendorf, "a sign from heaven for you. The God of your fathers has placed the cross in your sight, and now the rising sun from on high has tinged it with heavenly splendour. Believe on Him whose blood was shed by your fathers, that God's purpose of mercy might be fulfilled, that you might be free from all sin, and find in Him all your salvation."

"So be it," said the Jew, as a new light flashed on his soul. "Blessed be the Lord who has had mercy upon me."

We have now to notice, step by step, how Zinzendorf, despite his theories, restored the Moravian Church to vigorous life. His first move was dramatic. As he strolled one day on the shore of the Baltic Sea, he bethought him that the time had come to revive the

Brethren's Episcopal Orders in Germany. He wished to give his Brethren a legal standing. In Saxony he had been condemned as a heretic; in Prussia he would be recognized as orthodox; and to this intent he wrote to the King of Prussia, Frederick William I., and asked to be examined in doctrine by qualified Divines of the State Church. The King responded gladly. He had been informed that the Count was a fool, and was, therefore, anxious to see him; and now he sent him a messenger to say that he would be highly pleased if Zinzendorf would come and dine with him at Wusterhausen.

"What did he say?" asked His Majesty of the messenger when that functionary returned.

"Nothing," replied the messenger.

"Then," said the King, "he is no fool."

The Count arrived, and stayed three days. The first day the King was cold; the second he was friendly; the third he was enthusiastic.

"The devil himself," he said to his courtiers, "could not have told me more lies than I have been told about this Count. He is neither a heretic nor a disturber of the peace. His only sin is that he, a well-to-do Count, has devoted himself to the spread of the Gospel. I will not believe another word against him. I will do all I can to help him."

From that time Frederick William I. was Zinzendorf's fast friend. He encouraged him to become a Bishop of the Brethren. The Count was still in doubt. For some months he was terribly puzzled by the question whether he could become a Moravian Bishop, and yet at the same time be loyal to the Lutheran Church; and, in order to come to a right conclusion, he actually came over to England and discussed the whole thorny subject of Moravian Episcopal Orders with John Potter, Archbishop of Canterbury. The Archbishop soon relieved his mind. He informed the Count, first, that in his judgment the Moravian Episcopal Orders were apostolic; and he informed him, secondly, that as the Brethren were true to the teaching of the Augsburg Confession in Germany and the Thirty-nine Articles in England, the Count could honestly become a Bishop without being guilty of founding a new sect. The Count returned to Germany. He was examined in the faith, by the King's command, by two Berlin Divines. He came through the ordeal with flying colours, and finally, on May 20th, he was ordained a Bishop of the Brethren's Church by Bishop Daniel Ernest Jablonsky, Court Preacher at Berlin, and Bishop David Nitschmann (1737).

The situation was now remarkable. As soon as Zinzendorf became a Bishop, he occupied, in theory, a double position. He was a "Lutheran Bishop of the Brethren's Church." On the one hand, like Jablonsky himself, he was still a clergyman of the Lutheran Church; on the other, he was qualified to ordain ministers in the Church of the Brethren. And the Brethren, of course, laid stress on the latter point. They had now episcopal orders of their own; they realized their standing as an independent church; they objected to mere toleration as a sect; they demanded recognition as an orthodox church. "We design," they wrote to the Counts of Isenberg, "to establish a home for thirty or forty families from Herrnhut. We demand full liberty in all our meetings; we demand full

163

liberty to practise our discipline and to have the sacraments, baptism and communion administered by our own ministers, ordained by our own Bohemo-Moravian Bishops." As the Counts agreed to these conditions the Brethren now laid out near the castle a settlement after the Herrnhut model, named it Herrnhaag, and made it a regular training-ground for the future ministers of the Church. At Herrnhut the Brethren were under a Lutheran Pastor; at Herrnhaag they were independent, and ordained their own men for the work. They erected a theological training college, with Spangenberg as head. They had a paedagogium for boys, with Polycarp Mueller as Rector. They had also a flourishing school for girls. For ten years this new settlement at Herrnhaag was the busiest centre of evangelistic zeal in the world. At the theological college there were students from every university in Germany. At the schools there were over 600 children, and the Brethren had to issue a notice that they had no room for more. The whole place was a smithy. There the spiritual weapons were forged for service in the foreign field. "Up, up," Spangenberg would say to the young men at sunrise, "we have no time for dawdling. Why sleep ye still? Arise, young lions!"

And now the Count had a strange adventure, which spurred him to another step forward. As there were certain sarcastic people in Germany who said that Zinzendorf, though willing enough to send out others to die of fever in foreign climes, was content to bask in comfort at home, he determined now to give the charge the lie. He had travelled already on many a Gospel journey. He had preached to crowds in Berlin; he had preached in the Cathedral at Reval, in Livonia, and had made arrangements for the publication of an Esthonian Bible; and now he thought he must go to St. Thomas, where Friedrich Martin, the apostle to the negroes, had built up the strongest congregation in the Mission Field. He consulted the Lot; the Lot said "Yes," and off he set on his journey. The ship flew as though on eagle's wings. As they neared the island, the Count turned to his companion, and said: "What if we find no one there? What if the missionaries are all dead?"

"Then we are there," replied Weber.

"Gens aeterna, these Moravians," exclaimed the Count.

He landed on the island (Jan. 29th, 1739).

"Where are the Brethren?" said he to a negro.

"They are all in prison," was the startling answer.

"How long?" asked the Count.

"Over three months."

"What are the negroes doing in the meantime?"

"They are making good progress, and a great revival is going on. The very imprisonment of the teachers is a sermon."

For three months the Count was busy in St. Thomas. He burst into the Governor's castle "like thunder," and nearly frightened him out of his wits. He had brought with him a document signed by the King of Denmark, in which the Brethren were authorized to preach in the Danish West Indies. He had the prisoners released. He had the whole work in the Danish West Indies placed on a legal basis. He made the acquaintance of six hundred and seventy negroes. He was amazed and charmed by all he saw. "St. Thomas," he wrote, "is a greater marvel than Herrnhut." For the last three years that master missionary, Friedrich Martin, the "Apostle to the Negroes," had been continuing the noble work begun by Leonard Dober; and, in spite of the fierce opposition of the planters and also of the Dutch Reformed Church, had established a number of native congregations. He had opened a school for negro boys, and had thus taken the first step in the education of West Indian slaves. He had taught his people to form societies for Bible study and prayer; and now the Count put the finishing touch to the work. He introduced the Herrnhut system of discipline. He appointed one "Peter" chief Elder of the Brethren, and "Magdalene" chief Elder of the Sisters. He gave some to be helpers, some to be advisers, and some to be distributors of alms; and he even introduced the system of incessant hourly prayer. And then, before he took his leave, he made a notable speech. He had no such conception as "Negro emancipation." He regarded slavery as a Divinely appointed system. "Do your work for your masters," he said, "as though you were working for yourselves. Remember that Christ has given every man his work. The Lord has made kings, masters, servants and slaves. It is the duty of each of us to be content with the station in which God has placed him. God punished the first negroes by making them slaves."

For the work in St. Thomas this visit was important; for the work at home it was still more so. As the Count returned from his visit in St. Thomas, he saw more clearly than ever that if the Brethren were to do their work aright, they must justify their conduct and position in the eyes of the law. His views had broadened; he had grander conceptions of their mission; he began the practice of summoning them to Synods, and thus laid the foundations of modern Moravian Church life.

At the first Synod, held at Ebersdorf (June, 1739), the Count expounded his views at length (1739). He informed the Brethren, in a series of brilliant and rather mystifying speeches, that there were now three "religions" in Germany—the Lutheran, the Reformed and the Moravian; but that their duty and mission in the world was, not to restore the old Church of the Brethren, but rather to gather the children of God into a mystical, visionary, ideal fellowship which he called the "Community of Jesus." For the present, he said, the home of this ideal "Gemeine" would be the Moravian Church. At Herrnhut and other places in Saxony it would be a home for Lutherans; at Herrnhaag it would be a home for Calvinists; and then, when it had done its work and united all the children of God, it could be conveniently exploded. He gave the Moravian Church a rather short life. "For the present," he said, "the Saviour is manifesting His Gemeine to the world in the outward form of the Moravian Church; but in fifty years that Church will be forgotten." It is doubtful how far his Brethren understood him. They listened, admired, wondered, gasped and quietly went their own way.

At the second Synod, held at the Moor Hotel in Gotha, the Count explained his projects still more clearly (1740), and made the most astounding speech that had yet fallen from his lips. "It is," he declared, "the duty of our Bishops to defend the rights of the Protestant Moravian Church, and the duty of all the congregation to be loyal to that Church. It is absolutely necessary, for the sake of Christ's work, that our Church be recognized as a true Church. She is a true Church of God; she is in the world to further the Saviour's cause; and people can belong to her just as much as to any other." If these words meant anything at all, they meant, of course, that Zinzendorf, like the Moravians themselves, insisted on the independent existence of the Moravian Church; and, to prove that he really did mean this, he had Polycarp Mueller consecrated a Bishop. And yet, at the same time, the Count insisted that the Brethren were not to value their Church for her own sake. They were not to try to extend the Church as such; they were not to proselytize from other Churches; they were to regard her rather as a house of call for the "scattered" in all the churches; [94] and, above all, they must ever remember that as soon as they had done their work their Church would cease to exist. If this puzzles the reader he must not be distressed. It was equally puzzling to some of Zinzendorf's followers. Bishop Polycarp Mueller confessed that he could never understand it. At bottom, however, the Count's idea was clear. He still had a healthy horror of sects and splits; he still regarded the Brethren's Church as a "Church within the Church"; he still insisted, with perfect truth, that as they had no distinctive doctrine they could not be condemned as a nonconforming sect; and the goal for which he was straining was that wheresoever the Brethren went they should endeavour not to extend their own borders, but rather to serve as a bond of union evangelical Christians of all denominations.

Next year, at a Synod at Marienborn, the Count explained how this wonderful work was to be done (1740). What was the bond of union to be? It was certainly not a doctrine. Instead of making the bond of union a doctrine, as so many Churches have done, the Brethren made it personal experience. Where creeds had failed experience would succeed. If men, they said, were to he united in one grand evangelical Church, it would be, not by a common creed, but by a common threefold experience—a common experience of their own misery and sin; a common experience of the redeeming grace of Christ; and a common experience of the religious value of the Bible. To them this personal experience was the one essential. They had no rigid doctrine to impose. They did not regard any of the standard creeds as final. They did not demand subscription to a creed as a test. They had no rigid doctrine of the Atonement or of the Divinity of Christ; they had no special process of conversion; and, most striking of all, they had no rigid doctrine of the inspiration of the Bible. They did not believe either in verbal inspiration or in Biblical infallibility. They declared that the famous words, "all Scripture is given by inspiration of God," must be taken in a free and broad way. They held that, though the Bible was inspired, it contained mistakes in detail; that the teaching of St. James was in flat contradiction to the teaching of St. Paul; and that even the Apostles sometimes made a wrong application of the prophecies. To them the value of the Bible consisted, not in its supposed infallibility, but in its appeal to their hearts. "The Bible," they declared, "is a never-failing spring for the heart; and the one thing that authenticates the truth of its message is the fact that what is said in the book is confirmed by the experience of the heart." How modern this sounds.

But how was this universal experience to be attained? The Count had his answer ready. He had studied the philosophical works of Spinoza and Bayle. He was familiar with the trend of the rationalistic movement. He was aware that to thousands, both inside and outside the Church, the God whom Jesus called "Our Father" was no more than a cold philosophical abstraction; and that many pastors in the Lutheran Church, instead of trying to make God a reality, were wasting their time in spinning abstruse speculations, and discussing how many legions of angels could stand on the point of a needle. As this sort of philosophy rather disgusted Zinzendorf, he determined to frame a theology of his own; and thereby he arrived at the conclusion that the only way to teach men to love God was "to preach the Creator of the World under no other shape than that of a wounded and dying Lamb." He held that the Suffering Christ on the Cross was the one perfect expression and revelation of the love of God; he held that the title "Lamb of God" was the favourite name for Christ in the New Testament; he held that the central doctrine of the faith was the "Ransom" paid by Christ in His sufferings and death; and, therefore, he began to preach himself, and taught his Brethren to preach as well, the famous "Blood and Wounds Theology."

And now, at a Synod held in London, the Brethren cleared the decks for action, and took their stand on the stage of history as a free, independent Church of Christ (1741). The situation was alarming. Of all the Protestant Churches in Europe, the Church of the Brethren was the broadest in doctrine and the most independent in action; and yet, during the last few years, the Brethren were actually in danger of bending the knee to a Pope. The Pope in question was Leonard Dober. At the time when Herrnhut was founded, the Brethren had elected a governing board of twelve Elders. Of these twelve Elders, four Over-Elders were set apart for spiritual purposes; and of these four Over-Elders, one was specially chosen as Chief Elder. The first Chief Elder was Augustin Neisser, and the second Martin Linner. As long as the office lay in Linner's hands, there was no danger of the Chief Elder becoming a Pope. He was poor; he was humble; he was weak in health; and he spent his time in praying for the Church and attending to the spiritual needs of the Single Brethren. But gradually the situation altered. For the last six years the office had been held by Leonard Dober. He had been elected by Lot, and was, therefore, supposed to possess Divine authority. He was General Elder of the whole Brethren's Church. He had become the supreme authority in spiritual matters. He had authority over Zinzendorf himself, over all the Bishops, over all the members of the Pilgrim Band, over all Moravian Brethren at Herrnhut, over the pioneers in England and North America, over the missionaries in Greenland, the West Indies, South Africa and Surinam. He had become a spiritual referee. As the work extended, his duties and powers increased. He was Elder, not merely of the Brethren's Church, but of that ideal "Community of Jesus" which ever swam before the vision of the Count. He was becoming a court of appeal in cases of dispute. Already disagreements were rising among the Brethren. At Herrnhut dwelt the old-fashioned, sober, strict Moravians. At Herrnhaag the Brethren, with their freer notions, were already showing dangerous signs of fanaticism. At Pilgerruh, in Holstein, another body were being tempted to break from the Count altogether. And above these disagreeing parties the General Elder sat supreme. His position had become impossible. He was supposed to be above all party disputes; he was the friend of all, the intercessor for all, the broad-minded ideal Brother; and yet, if an actual dispute arose, he would be expected to give a binding decision. For these manifold duties Dober felt unfit; he had no desire to become a Protestant Pope; and, therefore, being a modest man, he wrote to the Conference at Marienborn, and asked for leave to lay down his office. The question was submitted to the Lot. The Lot allowed Dober to resign. The situation was now more dangerous than ever. The Brethren were in a quandary. They could never do without a General Elder. If they did they would cease to be a true "Community of Jesus," and degenerate into a mere party-sect. At last, at a house in Red Lion Street, London, they met to thrash out the question. For the third time a critical question was submitted to the decision of the Lot (Sept. 16th, 1741). "As we began to think about the Eldership," says Zinzendorf himself, in telling the story, "it occurred to us to accept the Saviour as Elder. At the beginning of our deliberations we opened the Textbook. On the one page stood the words, Let us open the door to Christ'; on the other, Thus saith the Lord, etc.; your Master, etc.; show me to my children and to the work of my hands. Away to Jesus! Away! etc.' Forthwith and with one consent we resolved to have no other than Him as our General Elder. He sanctioned it. [95] It was just Congregation Day. We looked at the Watchword for the day. It ran: The glory of the Lord filled the house. We bow before the Lamb's face, etc.' We asked permission. [96] We obtained it. We sang with unequalled emotion: Come, then, for we belong to Thee, and bless us inexpressibly.'" As the story just quoted was written by the poetic Count, it has been supposed that in recording this famous event he added a spiritual flavour of his own. But in this case he was telling the literal truth. At that Conference the Brethren deliberately resolved to ask Christ to undertake the office which had hitherto been held by Leonard Dober; and, to put the matter beyond all doubt, they inscribed on their minutes the resolution: "That the office of General Elder be abolished, and be transferred to the Saviour." [97] At first sight that resolution savours both of blasphemy and of pride; and Ritschl, the great theologian, declares that the Brethren put themselves on a pedestal above all other Churches. For that judgment Moravian writers have largely been to blame. It has been asserted again and again that on that famous "Memorial Day" the Brethren made a "special covenant" with Christ. For that legend Bishop Spangenberg was partly responsible. As that godly writer, some thirty years later, was writing the story of these transactions, he allowed his pious imagination to cast a halo over the facts; and, therefore, he penned the misleading sentence that the chief concern of the Brethren was that Christ "would condescend to enter into a special covenant with His poor Brethren's people, and take us as his peculiar property." For that statement there is not a shadow of evidence. The whole story of the "special covenant" is a myth. In consulting the Lot the Brethren showed their faith; in passing their resolution they showed their wisdom; and the meaning of the resolution was that henceforth the Brethren rejected all human authority in spiritual matters, recognized Christ alone as the Head of the Church, and thereby became the first free Church in Europe. Instead of bowing to any human authority they proceeded now to manage their own affairs; they elected by Lot a Conference of Twelve, and thus laid the foundations of that democratic system of government which exists at the present day. They were thrilled with the joy of their experience; they felt that now, at length, they were free indeed; they resolved that the joyful news should be published in all the congregations on the same day (November 13th); and henceforward that day was held in honour as the day when the Brethren gained their freedom and bowed to the will and law of Christ alone.

And now there was only one more step to take. As soon as the Synod in London was over, Count Zinzendorf set off for America in pursuit of a scheme to be mentioned in its proper place; and as soon as he was safely out of the way, the Brethren at home set about the task of obtaining recognition by the State. They had an easy task before them. For the last ninety-four years—ever since the Peace of Westphalia (1648)—the ruling principle in German had been that each little king and each little prince should settle what the religion should be in his own particular dominions. If the King was a Lutheran, his people must be Lutheran; if the King was Catholic, his people must be Catholic. But now this principle was suddenly thrown overboard. The new King of Prussia, Frederick the Great, was a scoffer. For religion Frederick the Great cared nothing; for the material welfare of his people he cared a good deal. He had recently conquered Silesia; he desired to see his land well tilled, and his people happy and good; and, therefore, he readily granted the Brethren a "Concession," allowing them to settle in Prussia and Silesia (Dec. 25th, 1742). His attitude was that of the practical business man. As long as the Brethren obeyed the law, and fostered trade, they could worship as they pleased. For all he cared, they might have prayed to Beelzebub. He granted them perfect liberty of conscience; he allowed them to ordain their own ministers; he informed them that they would not be subject to the Lutheran consistory; and thus, though not in so many words, he practically recognized the Brethren as a free and independent Church. For the future history of the Brethren's Church, this "Concession" was of vast importance. In one sense it aided their progress; in another it was a fatal barrier. As the Brethren came to be known as good workmen, other magnates speedily followed the king's example; for particular places particular "concessions" were prepared; and thus the Brethren were encouraged to extend their "settlement system." Instead, therefore, of advancing from town to town, the Brethren concentrated their attention on the cultivation of settlement life; and before many years had passed away they had founded settlements at Niesky, Gnadenberg, Gnadenfrei, and Neusalz-on-the-Oder.

Thus, then, had the Brethren sketched the plan of all their future work. They had regained their episcopal orders. They had defined their mission in the world. They had chosen their Gospel message. They had asserted their freedom of thought. They had won the goodwill of the State. They had adopted the "settlement system." They had begun their Diaspora work for the scattered, and their mission work for the heathen; and thus they had revived the old Church of the Brethren, and laid down those fundamental principles which have been maintained down to the present day.

Meanwhile their patriotic instincts had been confirmed. As Christian David had brought Brethren from Moravia, so Jan Gilek brought Brethren from Bohemia; and the story of his romantic adventures aroused fresh zeal for the ancient Church. He had fled from Bohemia to Saxony, and had often returned, like Christian David, to fetch bands of Brethren. He had been captured in a hay-loft by Jesuits. He had been imprisoned for two years at Leitomischl. He had been kept in a dungeon swarming with frogs, mice and other vermin. He had been fed with hot bread that he might suffer from colic. He had been employed as street sweeper in Leitomischl, with his left hand chained to his right foot. At length, however, he made his escape (1735), fled to Gerlachseim, in Silesia, and finally, along with other Bohemian exiles, helped to form a new congregation at Rixdorf, near Berlin. As the Brethren listened to Gilek's story their zeal for the Church of their fathers was greater than ever; and now the critical question was, what would Zinzendorf say to all this when he returned from America?

Chapter 8: The Sifting Time (1743-1750)

AS the Count advanced towards middle age, he grew more domineering in tone, more noble in his dreams, and more foolish in much of his conduct. He was soon to shine in each of these three lights. He returned from America in a fury. For two years he had been busy in Pennsylvania in a brave, but not very successful, attempt to establish a grand "Congregation of God in the Spirit"; and now he heard, to his deep disgust, that his Brethren in Europe had lowered the ideal of the Church, and made vulgar business bargains with worldly powers. What right, he asked, had the Brethren to make terms with an Atheist King? What right had they to obtain these degrading "concessions?" The whole business, he argued, smacked of simony. If the Brethren made terms with kings at all, they should take their stand, not, forsooth, as good workmen who would help to fatten the soil, but rather as loyal adherents of the Augsburg Confession. At Herrnhaag they had turned the Church into a business concern! Instead of paying rent to the Counts of Isenburg, they now had the Counts in their power. They had lent them large sums of money; they held their estates as security; and now, in return for these financial favours, the Counts had kindly recognized the Brethren as "the orthodox Episcopal Moravian Church." The more Zinzendorf heard of these business transactions, the more disgusted he was. He stormed and rated like an absolute monarch, and an absolute monarch he soon became. He forgot that before he went away he had entrusted the management of home affairs to a Board of Twelve. He now promptly dissolved the Board, summoned the Brethren to a Synod at Hirschberg, lectured them angrily for their sins, reduced them to a state of meek submission, and was ere long officially appointed to the office of "Advocate and Steward of all the Brethren's Churches." He had now the reins of government in his hands (1743). "Without your foreknowledge," ran this document, "nothing new respecting the foundation shall come up in our congregations, nor any conclusion of importance to the whole shall be valid; and no further story shall be built upon your fundamental plan of the Protestant doctrine of the Augsburg Confession, and that truthing it in love with all Christians, without consulting you."

He proceeded now to use these kingly powers. He accused the Brethren of two fundamental errors. Instead of trying to gather Christians into one ideal "Community of Jesus," they had aimed at the recognition of the independent Moravian Church; and instead of following the guidance of God, they had followed the dictates of vulgar worldly wisdom. He would cure them of each of these complaints. He would cure them of their narrow sectarian views, and cure them of their reliance on worldly wisdom.

For the first complaint he offered the remedy known as his "Tropus Idea." The whole policy of Zinzendorf lies in those two words. He expounded it fully at a Synod in

Marienborn. The more he studied Church history in general, the more convinced he became that over and above all the Christian Churches there was one ideal universal Christian Church; that that ideal Church represented the original religion of Christ; and that now the true mission of the Brethren was to make that ideal Church a reality on God's fair earth. He did not regard any of the Churches of Christ as Churches in this higher sense of the term. He regarded them rather as religious training grounds. He called them, not Churches, but tropuses. He called the Lutheran Church a tropus; he called the Calvinistic Church a tropus; he called the Moravian Church a tropus; he called the Pilgrim Band a tropus; he called the Memnonites a tropus; and by this word "tropus" he meant a religious school in which Christians were trained for membership in the one true Church of Christ. He would not have one of these tropuses destroyed. He regarded them all as essential. He honoured them all as means to a higher end. He would never try to draw a man from his tropus. And now he set a grand task before the Brethren. As the Brethren had no distinctive creed, and taught the original religion of Christ, they must now, he said, regard it as their Divine mission to find room within their broad bosom for men from all the tropuses. They were not merely to restore the Moravian Church; they were to establish a broader, comprehensive Church, to be known as the "Church of the Brethren"; and that Church would be composed of men from every tropus under heaven. Some would be Lutherans, some Reformed, some Anglicans, some Moravians, some Memnonites, some Pilgrims in the foreign field. For this purpose, and for this purpose only, he now revived the old Brethren's ministerial orders of Presbyter, Deacon and Acoluth; and when these men entered on their duties he informed them that they were the servants, not merely of the Moravian Church, but of the wider "Church of the Brethren." If the Count could now have carried out his scheme, he would have had men from various Churches at the head of each tropus in the Church of the Brethren. For the present he did the best he could, and divided the Brethren into three leading tropuses. At the head of the Moravian tropus was Bishop Polycarp Mueller; at the head of the Lutheran, first he himself, and then, later, Dr. Hermann, Court Preacher at Dresden; and finally, at the head of the Reformed, first his old friend Bishop Friedrich de Watteville, and then, later, Thomas Wilson, Bishop of Sodor and Man. [98] His scheme was now fairly clear. "In future," he said, "we are all to be Brethren, and our Bishops must be Brethren's Bishops; and, therefore, in this Church of the Brethren there will henceforth be, not only Moravians, but also Lutherans and Calvinists, who cannot find peace in their own Churches on account of brutal theologians."

His second remedy was worse than the disease. The great fault in Zinzendorf's character was lack of ballast. For the last few years he had given way to the habit of despising his own common sense; and instead of using his own judgment he now used the Lot. He had probably learned this habit from the Halle Pietists. He carried his Lot apparatus in his pocket; [99] he consulted it on all sorts of topics; he regarded it as the infallible voice of God. "To me," said he, in a letter to Spangenberg, "the Lot and the Will of God are simply one and the same thing. I am not wise enough to seek God's will by my own mental efforts. I would rather trust an innocent piece of paper than my own feelings." He now endeavoured to teach this faith to his Brethren. He founded a society called "The Order of the Little Fools," (June 2nd, 1743) and before very long they were nearly all "little fools." His argument here was astounding. He appealed to the well-known words of Christ Himself. [100] As God, he contended, had revealed His will, not to wise men, but to babes, it followed that the more like babes the Brethren became, the more clearly they would understand the mysteries of grace. They were not to use their own brains; they were to wish that they had no brains; they were to be like children in arms; and thus they would overcome all their doubts and banish all their cares. The result was disastrous. It led to the period known as the "Sifting Time." It is the saddest period in the history of the Brethren's Church. For seven years these Brethren took leave of their senses, and allowed their feelings to lead them on in the paths of insensate folly. They began by taking Zinzendorf at his word. They used diminutives for nearly everything. They addressed the Count as "Papa" and "Little Papa"; they spoke of Christ as "Brother Lambkin"; [101] and they described themselves as little wound-parsons, cross-wood little splinters, a blessed troop of cross-air [102] birds, cross-air little atoms, cross-air little sponges, and cross-air little pigeons.

The chief sinner was the Count himself. Having thrown his common sense overboard, he gave free rein to his fancy, and came out with an exposition of the Holy Trinity which offended the rules of good taste. He compared the Holy Trinity to a family. The father, said he, was God; the mother was the Holy Ghost; their son was Jesus; and the Church of Christ, the Son's fair bride, was born in the Saviour's Side-wound, was betrothed to Christ on the Cross, was married to Christ in the Holy Communion, and was thus the daughter-in-law of the Father and the Holy Ghost. We can all see the dangers of this. As soon as human images of spiritual truths are pressed beyond decent limits, they lead to frivolity and folly; and that was just the effect at Herrnhaag. The more freely the Brethren used these phrases, the more childish they became. They called the Communion the "Embracing of the Man"; and thus they lost their reverence for things Divine.

But the next move of the Count was even worse. For its origin we must go back a few years in his story. As the Count one day was burning a pile of papers he saw one slip flutter down to the ground untouched by the fire (1734). He picked it up, looked at it, and found that it contained the words:—

"Oh, let us in Thy nail-prints see
Our pardon and election free."

At first the effect on Zinzendorf was healthy enough. He regarded the words as a direct message from God. He began to think more of the value of the death of Christ. He altered the style of his preaching; he became more definitely evangelical; and henceforth he taught the doctrine that all happiness and all virtue must centre in the atoning death of Christ. "Since the year 1734," he said, "the atoning sacrifice of Jesus became our only testimony and our one means of salvation." But now he carried this doctrine to excess. Again the cause was his use of the Lot. As long as Zinzendorf used his own mental powers, he was able to make his "Blood and Wounds Theology" a power for good; but as soon as he bade good-bye to his intellect he made his doctrine a laughing-stock and a scandal. Instead of concentrating his attention on the moral and spiritual value of the cross, he now began to lay all the stress on the mere physical details. He composed a "Litany of the Wounds"; and the Brethren could now talk and sing of nothing else (1743). "We stick," they said, "to the Blood and Wounds Theology. We will preach nothing but Jesus the Crucified. We will look for nothing else in the Bible but the Lamb and His Wounds, and again Wounds, and Blood and Blood." Above all they began to worship the Side-wound. "We stick," they declared, "to the Lambkin and His little Side-wound. It is useless to call this folly. We dote upon it. We are in love with it. We shall stay for ever in the little side-hole, where we are so unspeakably blessed."

Still worse, these men now forgot the main moral principle of the Christian religion. Instead of living for others they lived for themselves. Instead of working hard for their living they were now enjoying themselves at the Count's expense; instead of plain living and high thinking they had high living and low thinking; and instead of spending their money on the poor they spent it now on grand illuminations, transparent pictures, and gorgeous musical festivals. No longer was their religion a discipline. It was a luxury, an orgy, a pastime. At Herrnhut the ruling principle was law; at Herrnhaag the ruling principle was liberty. At Herrnhut their religion was legal; at Herrnhaag it was supposed to be evangelical. The walls of their meeting-house were daubed with flaming pictures. In the centre of the ceiling was a picture of the Ascension; in one corner, Mary Magdalene meeting Jesus on the Resurrection morning; in another, our Lord making himself known to the two disciples at Emmaus; in a third Thomas thrusting his hand in the Saviour's side; in a fourth, Peter leaping from a boat to greet the Risen Master on the shores of the Lake of Tiberias. The four walls were equally gorgeous. At one end of the hall was a picture of the Jew's Passover, some Hebrews sprinkling blood on the door-posts, and the destroying angel passing. At the opposite end was a picture of the Last Supper; on another wall Moses lifting up the brazen serpent; on the fourth the Crucifixion. We can easily see the purpose of these pictures. They were all meant to teach the same great lesson. They were appeals through the eye to the heart. They were sermons in paint. If the Brethren had halted here they had done well. But again they rode their horse to death. For them pictures and hymns were not enough. At Marienborn Castle they now held a series of birthday festivals in honour of Zinzendorf, Anna Nitschmann and other Moravian worthies; and these festivals must have cost thousands of pounds. At such times the old castle gleamed with a thousand lights. At night, says a visitor, the building seemed on fire. The walls were hung with festoons. The hall was ornamented with boughs. The pillars were decked with lights, spirally disposed, and the seats were covered with fine linen, set off with sightly ribbons.

But the worst feature of this riotous life is still to be mentioned. If there is any topic requiring delicate treatment, it is surely the question of sexual morality; and now the Count made the great mistake of throwing aside the cloak of modesty and speaking out on sins of the flesh in the plainest possible language. He delivered a series of discourses on moral purity; and in those discourses he used expressions which would hardly be permitted now except in a medical treatise. His purpose was certainly good. He contended that he had the Bible on his side; that the morals of the age were bad; and that the time for plain speaking had come. "At that time," he said, "when the Brethren's congregations appeared afresh on the horizon of the Church, he found, on the one hand, the lust of concupiscence carried to the utmost pitch possible, and the youth almost totally ruined; and on the other hand some few thoughtful persons who proposed a spirituality like the angels." But again the Brethren rode their horse to death. They were not immoral, they were only silly. They talked too freely about these delicate topics; they sang about them in their hymns; they had these hymns published in a volume known as the "Twelfth Appendix" to their Hymn-book; and thus they innocently gave the public the impression that they revelled, for its own sake, in coarse and filthy language.

What judgment are we to pass on all these follies? For the Brethren we may fairly enter the plea that most of them were humble and simple-minded men; that, on the whole, they meant well; and that, in their zeal for the Gospel of Christ, they allowed their feelings to carry them away. And further, let us bear in mind that, despite their foolish style of speech, they were still heroes of the Cross. They had still a burning love for Christ; they were still willing to serve abroad; and they still went out to foreign lands, and laid down their lives for the sake of Him who had laid down His for them. As John Cennick was on his visit to Herrnhaag (1746), he was amazed by the splendid spirit of devotion shown. He found himself at the hub of the missionary world. He saw portraits of missionaries on every hand. He heard a hymn sung in twenty-two different languages. He heard sermons in German, Esthonian, French, Spanish, Swedish, Lettish, Bohemian, Dutch, Hebrew, Danish, and Eskimo. He heard letters read from missionaries in every quarter of the globe.

"Are you ready," said Zinzendorf to John Soerensen, "to serve the Saviour in Greenland?"

"Here am I, send me," said Soerensen. He had never thought of such a thing before.

"But the matter is pressing; we want someone to go at once."

"Well!" replied Soerensen, "that's no difficulty. If you will only get me a new pair of boots I will set off this very day. My old ones are quite worn out, and I have not another pair to call my own."

And the next day the man was off, and served in Greenland forty-six years.

But the grandest case is that of Bishop Cammerhof. He was a fanatic of the fanatics. He revelled in sickly sentimental language. He called himself a "Little Fool" and a "Little Cross-air Bird." He addressed the Count as his "heart's Papa," and Anna Nitschmann as his "Motherkin." He said he would kiss them a thousand times, and vowed he could never fondle them enough! And yet this man had the soul of a hero, and killed himself by overwork among the North American Indians! [103] It is easy to sneer at saints like this as fools; but if fools they were, they were fools for their Master's sake.

But for Zinzendorf it is hard to find any excuse. He had received a splendid education, had moved in refined and cultured circles, and had enjoyed the friendship of learned bishops, of eloquent preachers, of university professors, of philosophers, of men of letters. He had read the history of the Christian Church, knew the dangers of excess, and had spoken against excess in his earlier years. [104] He knew that the Wetterau swarmed with mad fanatics; had read the works of Dippel, of Rock, and of other unhealthy writers; and had, therefore, every reason to be on his guard. He knew the weak points in his own character. "I have," he said, "a genius for extravagance." He had deliberately, of his own free will, accepted the office of "Advocate and Steward" of the Brethren's Church. He was the head of an ancient episcopal Church, with a high reputation to sustain. He had set the Brethren a high and holy task. He was a public and well-known character. As he travelled about from country to country he spread the fame of the Brethren's labours in every great city in Germany, in England, in Switzerland, in North America, and in the West Indies; and by this time he was known personally to the King of Denmark, to Potter, Archbishop of Canterbury, to John and Charles Wesley, to Bengel, the famous commentator, and to many other leaders in the Lutheran Church. And, therefore, by all the laws of honour, he was bound to lead the Brethren upward and keep their record clean. But his conduct now was unworthy of a trusted leader. It is the darkest blot on his saintly character, and the chief reason why his brilliant schemes met with so little favour. At the very time when he placed before the Brethren the noblest and loftiest ideals, he himself had done the most to cause the enemy to blaspheme. No wonder his Tropus idea was laughed to scorn. What sort of home was this, said his critics, that he had prepared for all the Tropuses? What grand ideal "Church of the Brethren" was this, with its childish nonsense, its blasphemous language, its objectionable hymns? As the rumours of the Brethren's excesses spread, all sorts of wild tales were told about them. Some said they were worshippers of the devil; some said they were conspirators against the State; some accused them falsely of immorality, of gluttony, of robbing the poor; and the chief cause of all the trouble was this beautiful poet, this original thinker, this eloquent preacher, this noble descendant of a noble line, this learned Bishop of the Brethren's Church. There is only one explanation of his conduct. He had committed mental suicide, and he paid the penalty. [105]

He had now to retrieve his fallen honour, and to make amends for his guilt. At last he awoke to the stern facts of the case. His position now was terrible. What right had he to lecture the Brethren for sins which he himself had taught them to commit? He shrank from the dreadful task. But the voice of duty was not to be silenced. He had not altogether neglected the Brethren's cause. At the very time when the excesses were at their height he had been endeavouring to obtain for the Brethren full legal recognition in Germany, England, and North America. He won his first victory in Germany. He was allowed (Oct., 1747) to return to Saxony, summoned the Brethren to a Synod at Gross-Krausche in Silesia (1748), and persuaded them to promise fidelity to the Augsburg Confession. He had the Brethren's doctrine and practice examined by a Saxon Royal Commission, and the King of Saxony issued a decree (1749) by which the Brethren were granted religious liberty in his kingdom. Thus the Brethren were now fully recognized by law in Prussia, Silesia, and Saxony. He had obtained these legal privileges just in time, and could now deal with the poor fanatics at Herrnhaag. The situation there had come to a crisis. The old Count of Isenberg died. His successor, Gustavus Friedrich, was a weak-minded man; the agent, Brauer, detested the Brethren; and now Brauer laid down the condition that the settlers at Herrnhaag must either break off their connection with Zinzendorf or else abandon the premises. They chose the latter course. At one blow the gorgeous settlement was shivered to atoms. It had cost many thousands of pounds to build, and now the money was gone for ever. As the Brethren scattered in all directions, the Count saw at last the damage he had done (Feb., 1750). He had led them on in reckless expense, and now he must rush to their rescue. He addressed them all in a solemn circular letter. He visited the various congregations, and urged them to true repentance. He suppressed the disgraceful "Twelfth Appendix," and cut out the offensive passages in his own discourses. He issued treatise after treatise defending the Brethren against the coarse libels of their enemies. And, best of all, and noblest of all, he not only took upon his own shoulders the burden of their financial troubles, but confessed like a man that he himself had steered them on to the rocks. He summoned his Brethren to a Synod. He rose to address the assembly. His eyes were red, his cheeks stained with tears.

"Ah! my beloved Brethren," he said, "I am guilty! I am the cause of all these troubles!"

And thus at length this "Sifting-Time" came to a happy end. The whole episode was like an attack of pneumonia. The attack was sudden; the crisis dangerous; the recovery swift; and the lesson wholesome. For some years after this the Brethren continued to show some signs of weakness; and even in the next edition of their Hymn-book they still made use of some rather crude expressions. But on the whole they had learned some useful lessons. On this subject the historians have mostly been in the wrong. Some have suppressed the facts. This is dishonest. Others have exaggerated, and spoken as if the excesses lasted for two or three generations. This is wicked. [106] The sober truth is exactly as described in these pages. The best judgment was passed by the godly Bishop Spangenberg. "At that time," he said, "the spirit of Christ did not rule in our hearts; and that was the real cause of all our foolery." Full well the Brethren realized their mistake, and honestly they took its lessons to heart. They learned to place more trust in the Bible, and less in their own unbridled feelings. They learned afresh the value of discipline, and of an organised system of government. They became more guarded in their language, more Scriptural in their doctrine, and more practical in their preaching. Nor was this all. Meanwhile the same battle had been fought and won in England and North America.

Chapter 9: Moravians and Methodists

FOR the origin of the Moravian Church in England we turn our eyes to a bookseller's shop in London. It was known as "The Bible and Sun"; it stood a few yards west of Temple Bar; and James Hutton, the man behind the counter, became in time the first English member of the Brethren's Church. But James Hutton was a man of high importance for the whole course of English history. He was the connecting link between Moravians and Methodists; and thus he played a vital part, entirely ignored by our great historians, in the whole Evangelical Revival.

He was born on September 14th, 1715. He was the son of a High-Church clergyman. His father was a non-juror. He had refused, that is, to take the oath of loyalty to the Hanoverian succession, had been compelled to resign his living, and now kept a boarding-house in College Street, Westminster, for boys attending the famous Westminster School. At that school little James himself was educated; and one of his teachers was Samuel Wesley, the elder brother of John and Charles. He had no idea to what this would lead. As the lad grew up in his father's home he had, of course, not the least suspicion that such a body as the Moravian Church existed. He had never heard of Zinzendorf or of Herrnhut. He was brought up a son of the Church of England; he loved her services and doctrine; and all that he desired to see was a revival within her borders of true spiritual life.

The revival was close at hand. For some years a number of pious people—some clergy, and others laymen—had been endeavouring to rouse the Church to new and vigorous life; and to this end they established a number of "Religious Societies." There were thirty or forty of these Societies in London. They consisted of members of the Church of England. They met, once a week, in private houses to pray, to read the Scriptures, and to edify each other. They drew up rules for their spiritual guidance, had special days for fasting and prayer, and attended early Communion once a month. At church they kept a sharp look-out for others "religiously disposed," and invited such to join their Societies. In the morning they would go to their own parish church; in the afternoon they would go where they could hear a "spiritual sermon." Of these Societies one met at the house of Hutton's father. If James, however, is to be believed, the Societies had now lost a good deal of their moral power. He was not content with the one in his own home. He was not pleased with the members of it. They were, he tells us, slumbering or dead souls; they cared for nothing but their own comfort in this world; and all they did when they met on Sunday evenings was to enjoy themselves at small expense, and fancy themselves more holy than other people. He was soon to meet with men of greater zeal.

As James was now apprenticed to a bookseller he thought he could do a good stroke of business by visiting some of his old school-mates at the University of Oxford. He went to Oxford to see them; they introduced him to John and Charles Wesley; and thus he formed an acquaintance that was soon to change the current of his life. What had happened at Oxford is famous in English history. For the last six years both John and Charles had been conducting a noble work. They met, with others, on Sunday evenings, to read the classics and the Greek Testament; they attended Communion at St. Mary's every Sunday. They visited the poor and the prisoners in the gaol. They fasted at regular intervals. For all this they were openly laughed to scorn, and were considered mad fanatics. They were called the Reforming Club, the Holy Club, the Godly Club, the Sacramentarians, the Bible Moths, the Supererogation Men, the Enthusiasts, and, finally, the Methodists.

But Hutton was stirred to the very depths of his soul. He was still living in College Street with his father; next door lived Samuel Wesley, his old schoolmaster; and Hutton, therefore, asked John and Charles to call and see him when next they came up to town. The invitation led to great results. At this time John Wesley received a request from General Oglethorpe, Governor of Georgia, to go out to that colony as a missionary. He accepted the offer with joy; his brother Charles was appointed the Governor's Secretary; and the two young men came up to London and spent a couple of days at Hutton's house. The plot was thickening. Young James was more in love with the Wesleys than ever. If he had not been a bound apprentice he would have sailed with them to Georgia himself (1735). He went down with them to Gravesend; he spent some time with them on board the ship; and there, on that sailing vessel, the Simmonds, he saw, for the first time in his life, a number of Moravian Brethren. They, too, were on their way to Georgia. For the future history of religion in England that meeting on the Simmonds was momentous. Among the passengers were General Oglethorpe, Bishop David Nitschmann, and twenty-three other Brethren, and thus Moravians and Methodists were brought together by their common interest in missionary work.

James Hutton was thrilled. As soon as his apprenticeship was over he set up in business for himself at the "Bible and Sun," founded a new Society in his own back parlour, and made that parlour the centre of the Evangelical Revival (1736). There he conducted weekly meetings; there he established a Poor-box Society, the members paying in a penny a week; there met the men who before long were to turn England upside down; and there he and others were to hear still more of the life and work of the Brethren.

For this he had to thank his friend John Wesley. As John Wesley set out on his voyage to Georgia he began to keep that delightful Journal which has now become an English classic; and before having his Journal printed he sent private copies to Hutton, and Hutton read them out at his weekly meetings. John Wesley had a stirring tale to tell. He admired the Brethren from the first. They were, he wrote, the gentlest, bravest folk he had ever met. They helped without pay in the working of the ship; they could take a blow without losing their tempers; and when the ship was tossed in the storm they were braver than the sailors themselves. One Sunday the gale was terrific. The sea poured in between the decks. The main sail was torn to tatters. The English passengers screamed with terror. The Brethren calmly sang a hymn.

"Was not you afraid?" said Wesley.

"I thank God, no," replied the Brother.

"But were not your women and children afraid?"

"No; our women and children are not afraid to die."

John Wesley was deeply stirred. For all his piety he still lacked something which these Brethren possessed. He lacked their triumphant confidence in God. He was still afraid to die. "How is it thou hast no faith?" he said to himself.

For the present his question remained unanswered; but before he had been very long in Georgia he laid his spiritual troubles before the learned Moravian teacher, Spangenberg. He could hardly have gone to a better spiritual guide. Of all the Brethren this modest Spangenberg was in many ways the best. He was the son of a Lutheran minister. He was Wesley's equal in learning and practical piety. He had been assistant lecturer in theology at Halle University. He was a man of deep spiritual experience; he was only one year younger than Wesley himself; and, therefore, he was thoroughly qualified to help the young English pilgrim over the stile. [107]

"My brother," he said, "I must first ask you one or two questions. Have you the witness within yourself? Does the Spirit of God bear witness with your spirit that you are a child of God?"

John Wesley was so staggered that he could not answer.

"Do you know Jesus Christ?" continued Spangenberg.

"I know he is the Saviour of the world."

"True; but do you know he has saved you?"

"I hope," replied Wesley, "he has died to save me."

"Do you know yourself?"

"I do," said Wesley; but he only half meant what he said.

Again, three weeks later, Wesley was present at a Moravian ordination service. For the moment he forgot the seventeen centuries that had rolled by since the great days of the apostles; and almost thought that Paul the tentmaker or Peter the fisherman was presiding at the ceremony. "God," he said, "has opened me a door into a whole Church."

As James Hutton read these glowing reports to his little Society at the "Bible and Sun" he began to take a still deeper interest in the Brethren. He had made the acquaintance, not only of the Wesleys, but of Benjamin Ingham, of William Delamotte, and of George Whitefield. He was the first to welcome Whitefield to London. He found him openings in the churches. He supplied him with money for the poor. He published his sermons. He founded another Society in Aldersgate Street. He was now to meet with Zinzendorf himself. Once more the connecting link was foreign missionary work. For some years the Count had been making attempts to obtain the goodwill of English Churchmen for the

Brethren's labours in North America. He had first sent three Brethren—Wenzel Neisser, John Toeltschig, and David Nitschmann, the Syndic—to open up negotiations with the Society for Promoting Christian Knowledge; and very disappointed he was when these negotiations came to nothing. He had then sent Spangenberg to London to make arrangements for the first batch of colonists for Georgia. He had then sent the second batch under Bishop David Nitschmann. And now he came to London himself, took rooms at Lindsey House (1737), Chelsea, and stayed about six weeks. He had two purposes to serve. He wished first to talk with Archbishop Potter about Moravian Episcopal Orders. He was just thinking of becoming a Bishop himself. He wanted Potter's opinion on the subject. What position, he asked, would a Moravian Bishop occupy in an English colony? Would it be right for a Moravian Bishop to exercise his functions in Georgia? At the same time, however, he wished to consult with the Board of Trustees for Georgia. He had several talks with the Secretary. The Secretary was Charles Wesley. Charles Wesley was lodging now at old John Hutton's in College Street. He attended a service in Zinzendorf's rooms; he thought himself in a choir of angels; he introduced James Hutton to the Count; and thus another link in the chain was forged.

And now there arrived in England a man who was destined to give a new tone to the rising revival (Jan. 27th, 1738). His name was Peter Boehler; he had just been ordained by Zinzendorf; he was on his way to South Carolina; and he happened to arrive in London five days before John Wesley landed from his visit to America. We have come to a critical point in English history. At the house of Weinantz, a Dutch merchant, John Wesley and Peter Boehler met (Feb. 7th); John Wesley then found Boehler lodgings, and introduced him to Hutton; and ten days later Wesley and Boehler set out together for Oxford (Feb. 17th). The immortal discourse began.

As John Wesley returned to England from his three years' stay in America, he found himself in a sorrowful state of mind. He had gone with all the ardour of youth; he returned a spiritual bankrupt. On this subject the historians have differed. According to High-Church Anglican writers, John Wesley was a Christian saint before he ever set eyes on Boehler's face; [108] according to Methodists he had only a legal religion and was lacking in genuine, saving faith in Christ. His own evidence on the questions seems conflicting. At the time he was sure he was not yet converted; in later years he inclined to think he was. At the time he sadly wrote in his Journal, "I who went to America to convert others was never myself converted to God"; and then, years later, he added the footnote, "I am not sure of this." It is easy, however, to explain this contradiction. The question turns on the meaning of the word "converted." If a man is truly converted to God when his heart throbs with love for his fellows, with a zeal for souls, and with a desire to do God's holy will, then John Wesley, when he returned from America, was just as truly a "converted" man as ever he was in later life. He was devout in prayer; he loved the Scriptures; he longed to be holy; he was pure in thought, in deed, and in speech; he was self-denying; he had fed his soul on the noble teaching of Law's "Serious Call"; and thus, in many ways, he was a beautiful model of what a Christian should be. And yet, after all, he lacked one thing which Peter Boehler possessed. If John Wesley was converted then he did not know it himself. He had no firm, unflinching trust in God. He was not sure that his sins were forgiven. He lacked what Methodists call "assurance," and what St. Paul called "peace with God." He had the faith, to use his own distinction, not of a son, but only of a servant. He was good but he was not happy; he feared God, but he did not dare to love Him; he had not yet attained the conviction that he himself had been redeemed by Christ; and if this conviction is essential to conversion, then John Wesley, before he met Boehler, was not yet a converted man. For practical purposes the matter was of first importance. As long as Wesley was racked by doubts he could never be a persuasive preacher of the Gospel. He was so distracted about himself that he could not yet, with an easy mind, rush out to the rescue of others. He had not "a heart at leisure from itself to soothe and sympathize." The influence of Boehler was enormous. He saw where Wesley's trouble lay, and led him into the calm waters of rest.

"My brother, my brother," he said, "that philosophy of yours must be purged away." [109]

John Wesley did not understand. For three weeks the two men discussed the fateful question; and the more Wesley examined himself the more sure he was he did not possess "the faith whereby we are saved." One day he felt certain of his salvation; the next the doubts besieged his door again.

"If what stands in the Bible is true," he said, "then I am saved"; but that was as far as he could go.

"He knew," said Boehler in a letter to Zinzendorf, "that he did not properly believe in the Saviour."

At last Boehler made a fine practical suggestion (March 5th). He urged Wesley to preach the Gospel to others. John Wesley was thunderstruck. He thought it rather his duty to leave off preaching. What right had he to preach to others a faith he did not yet possess himself? Should he leave off preaching or not?

"By no means," replied Boehler.

"But what can I preach?" asked Wesley.

"Preach faith till you have it," was the classic answer, "and then, because you have it, you will preach faith."

Again he consulted Boehler on the point; and again Boehler, broad-minded man, gave the same wholesome advice.

"No," he insisted, "do not hide in the earth the talent God has given you."

The advice was sound. If John Wesley had left off preaching now, he might never have preached again; and if Boehler had been a narrow-minded bigot, he would certainly have informed his pupil that unless he possessed full assurance of faith he was unfit to remain in holy orders. But Boehler was a scholar and a gentleman, and acted throughout with tact. For some weeks John Wesley continued to be puzzled by Boehler's doctrine of the holiness and happiness which spring from living faith; but at last he came to the firm conclusion that what Boehler said on the subject was precisely what was taught in the

Church of England. He had read already in his own Church homilies that faith "is a sure trust and confidence which a man hath in God that through the merits of Christ his sins are forgiven, and he reconciled to the favour of God"; and yet, clergyman though he was, he had not yet that trust and confidence himself. Instead, therefore, of teaching Wesley new doctrine, Peter Boehler simply informed him that some men, though of course not all, were suddenly converted, that faith might be given in a moment, and that thus a man might pass at once from darkness to light and from sin and misery to righteousness and joy in the Holy Ghost. He had had that very experience himself at Jena; he had known it as a solid fact in the case of others; and, therefore, speaking from his own personal knowledge, he informed Wesley that when a man obtained true faith he acquired forthwith "dominion over sin and constant peace from a sense of forgiveness."

At this Wesley was staggered. He called it a new Gospel. He would not believe that the sense of forgiveness could be given in a moment.

For answer Boehler appealed to the New Testament; and Wesley, looking to see for himself, found that nearly all the cases of conversion mentioned there were instantaneous. He contended, however, that such miracles did not happen in the eighteenth century. Boehler brought four friends to prove that they did. Four examples, said Wesley, were not enough to prove a principle. Boehler promised to bring eight more. For some days Wesley continued to wander in the valley of indecision, and consulted Boehler at every turn of the road. He persuaded Boehler to pray with him; he joined him in singing Richter's hymn, "My soul before Thee prostrate lies"; and finally, he preached a sermon to four thousand hearers in London, enforcing that very faith in Christ which he himself did not yet possess. But Boehler had now to leave for South Carolina. From Southampton he wrote a farewell letter to Wesley. "Beware of the sin of unbelief," he wrote, "and if you have not conquered it yet, see that you conquer it this very day, through the blood of Jesus Christ."

The letter produced its effect. The turning-point in John Wesley's career arrived. He was able to give, not only the day, but the hour, and almost the minute. As he was still under the influence of Boehler's teaching, many writers have here assumed that his conversion took place in a Moravian society. [110] The assumption is false. "In the evening," says Wesley, "I went very unwillingly to a society in Aldersgate Street (May 24th), where one was reading Luther's preface to the Epistle to the Romans." At that time the society in Aldersgate Street had no more connection with the Moravian Church than any other religious society in England. It was founded by James Hutton; it was an ordinary religious society; it consisted entirely of members of the Anglican Church; and there, in an Anglican religious society, Wesley's conversion took place. "About a quarter to nine," he says, "while he was describing the change which God works in the heart through faith in Christ, I felt my heart strangely warmed. I felt I did trust in Christ, Christ alone, for salvation; and an assurance was given me that He had taken away my sins, even mine, and saved me from the law of sin and death."

From that moment, despite some recurring doubts, John Wesley was a changed man. If he had not exactly learned any new doctrine, he had certainly passed through a new experience. He had peace in his heart; he was sure of his salvation; and henceforth, as all readers know, he was able to forget himself, to leave his soul in the hands of God, and to spend his life in the salvation of his fellow-men.

Meanwhile Peter Boehler had done another good work. If his influence over John Wesley was great, his influence over Charles Wesley was almost greater. For some weeks the two men appear to have been in daily communication; Charles Wesley taught Boehler English; and when Wesley was taken ill Boehler on several occasions, both at Oxford and at James Hutton's house in London, sat up with him during the night, prayed for his recovery, and impressed upon him the value of faith and prayer. The faith of Boehler was amazing. As soon as he had prayed for Wesley's recovery, he turned to the sufferer and calmly said, "You will not die now." The patient felt he could not endure the pain much longer.

"Do you hope to be saved?" said Boehler.

"Yes."

"For what reason do you hope it?"

"Because I have used my best endeavours to serve God."

Boehler shook his head, and said no more. As soon as Charles was restored to health, he passed through the same experience as his brother John; and gladly ascribed both recovery and conversion to the faith and prayer of Boehler.

But this was not the end of Boehler's influence. As soon as he was able to speak English intelligibly, he began to give addresses on saving faith to the good folk who met at James Hutton's house; and before long he changed the whole character of the Society. It had been a society of seekers; it became a society of believers. It had been a group of High Churchmen; it became a group of Evangelicals. It had been a free-and-easy gathering; it became a society with definite regulations. For two years the Society was nothing less than the headquarters of the growing evangelical revival; and the rules drawn up by Peter Boehler (May 1st, 1738), just before he left for America, were the means of making it a vital power. In these rules the members were introducing, though they knew it not, a new principle into English Church life. It was the principle of democratic government. The Society was now a self-governing body; and all the members, lay and clerical, stood upon the same footing. They met once a week to confess their faults to each other and to pray for each other; they divided the Society into "bands," with a leader at the head of each; and they laid down the definite rule that "every one, without distinction, submit to the determination of his Brethren." [111] The Society increased; the room at Hutton's house became too small; and Hutton therefore hired first a large room, and then a Baptist Hall, known as the Great Meeting House, in Fetter Lane. [112]

From this time the Society was known as the Fetter Lane Society, and the leading spirits were James Hutton and Charles Wesley. For a while the hall was the home of happiness and peace. As the months rolled on, various Moravians paid passing calls on their way to America; and Hutton, the Wesleys, Delamotte and others became still more impressed with the Brethren's teaching. Charles Wesley was delighted. As he walked across the fields from his house at Islington to the Sunday evening love-feast in Fetter Lane, he would sing for very joy. John Wesley was equally charmed. He had visited the Brethren at Marienborn and Herrnhut (August, 1738). He had listened with delight to the preaching of Christian David. He had had long chats about spiritual matters with Martin Linner, the Chief Elder, with David Nitschmann, with Albin Feder, with Augustin Neisser, with Wenzel Neisser, with Hans Neisser, with David Schneider, and with Arvid Gradin, the historian; he felt he would like to spend his life at Herrnhut; and in his Journal he wrote the words, "Oh, when shall this Christianity cover the earth as the waters cover the sea." At a Watch-Night service in Fetter Lane (Dec. 31st, 1738) the fervour reached its height. At that service both the Wesleys, George Whitefield, Benjamin Ingham, Kinchin and other Oxford Methodists were present, and the meeting lasted till the small hours of the morning. "About three in the morning," says John Wesley, "as we were continuing instant in prayer, the power of God came mightily upon us, insomuch that many cried out for exceeding joy, and many fell to the ground."

And yet all the while there was a worm within the bud. John Wesley soon found serious faults in the Brethren. As he journeyed to Herrnhut, he had called at Marienborn, and there they had given him what seemed to him an unnecessary snub. For some reason which has never been fully explained, they refused to admit him to the Holy Communion; and the only reason they gave him was that he was a "homo perturbatus," i.e., a restless man. [113] For the life of him Wesley could not understand why a "restless man" of good Christian character should not kneel at the Lord's Table with the Brethren; and to make the insult more stinging still, they actually admitted his companion, Benjamin Ingham. But the real trouble lay at Fetter Lane. It is easy to put our finger on the cause. As long as people hold true to the faith and practice of their fathers they find it easy to live at peace with each other; but as soon as they begin to think for themselves they are sure to differ sooner or later. And that was exactly what happened at Fetter Lane. The members came from various stations in life. Some, like the Wesleys, were university men; some, like Hutton, were middle-class tradesmen, of moderate education; some, like Bray, the brazier, were artizans; and all stood on the same footing, and discussed theology with the zeal of novices and the confidence of experts. John Wesley found himself in a strange country. He had been brought up in the realm of authority; he found himself in the realm of free discussion. Some said that saying faith was one thing, and some said that it was another. Some said that a man could receive the forgiveness of his sins without knowing it, and some argued that if a man had any doubts he was not a true Christian at all. As Wesley listened to these discussions he grew impatient and disgusted. The whole tone of the Society was distasteful to his mind. If ever a man was born to rule it was Wesley; and here, at Fetter Lane, instead of being captain, he was merely one of the crew, and could not even undertake a journey without the consent of the Society. The fetters were beginning to gall.

At this point there arrived from Germany a strange young man on his way to America, who soon added fuel to the fire (Oct. 18th, 1739). His name was Philip Henry Molther. He was only twenty-five years old; he had belonged to the Brethren's Church about a year; he had spent some months as tutor in Zinzendorf's family; he had picked up only the weak side of the Brethren's teaching; and now, with all the zeal of youth, he set forth his views in extravagant language, which soon filled Wesley with horror. His power in the Society was immense, and four times a week, in broken English, he preached to growing crowds. At first he was utterly shocked by what he saw. "The first time I entered the meeting," he says, "I was alarmed and almost terror-stricken at hearing their sighing and groaning, their whining and howling, which strange proceeding they call the demonstration of the Spirit and of power." For these follies Molther had a cure of his own. He called it "stillness." As long as men were sinners, he said, they were not to try to obtain saving faith by any efforts of their own. They were not to go to church. They were not to communicate. They were not to fast. They were not to use so much private prayer. They were not to read the Scriptures. They were not to do either temporal or spiritual good. Instead of seeking Christ in these ways, said Molther, the sinner should rather sit still and wait for Christ to give him the Divine revelation. If this doctrine had no other merit it had at least the charm of novelty. The dispute at Fetter Lane grew keener than ever. On the one hand Hutton, James Bell, John Bray, and other simple-minded men regarded Molther as a preacher of the pure Gospel. He had, said Hutton, drawn men away from many a false foundation, and had led them to the only true foundation, Christ. "No soul," said another, "can be washed in the blood of Christ unless it first be brought to one in whom Christ is fully formed. But there are only two such men in London, Bell and Molther." John Bray, the brazier, went further.

"It is impossible," he said, "for anyone to be a true Christian outside the Moravian Church."

As the man was outside that Church himself, and remained outside it all his life, his statement is rather bewildering. [114]

John Wesley was disgusted. He regarded Molther as a teacher of dangerous errors. The two men were poles asunder. The one was a quietist evangelical; the other a staunch High Churchman. According to Molther the correct order was, through Christ to the ordinances of the Church; according to Wesley, through the ordinances to Christ. According to Molther, a man ought to be a believer in Christ before he reads the Bible, or attends Communion, or even does good works; according to Wesley, a man should read his Bible, go to Communion, and do good works in order to become a believer. According to Molther the Sacrament was a privilege, meant for believers only; according to Wesley it was a duty, and a means of grace for all men. According to Molther, the only means of grace was Christ; according to Wesley, there were many means of grace, all leading the soul to Christ. According to Molther there were no degrees in faith; according to Wesley there were. No longer was the Fetter Lane Society a calm abode of peace. Instead of trying to help each other the members would sometimes sit for an hour without speaking a word; and sometimes they only reported themselves without having a proper meeting at all. John Wesley spoke his mind. He declared that Satan was beginning to rule in the Society. He heard that Molther was taken ill, and regarded the illness as a judgment from heaven. At last the wranglings came to an open rupture. At an evening meeting in Fetter Lane (July 16th, 1740), John Wesley, resolved to clear the air, read out from a book supposed to be prized by the Brethren the following astounding doctrine: "The Scriptures are good; prayer is good; communicating is good; relieving our neighbour is good; but to one who is not born of God, none of these is good, but all very evil. For him to read the Scriptures, or to pray, or to communicate, or to do any outward work is deadly poison. First, let him be born of God. Till then, let him not do any of these things. For if he does, he destroys himself."

He read the passage aloud two or three times. "My brethren," he asked, "is this right, or is this wrong?"

"It is right," said Richard Bell, the watchcase maker, "it is all right. It is the truth. To this we must all come, or we never can come to Christ."

"I believe," broke in Bray, the brazier, "our brother Bell did not hear what you read, or did not rightly understand."

"Yes! I heard every word," said Bell, "and I understand it well. I say it is the truth; it is the very truth; it is the inward truth."

"I used the ordinances twenty years," said George Bowers, the Dissenter, of George Yard, Little Britain, "yet I found not Christ. But I left them off for only a few weeks and I found Him then. And I am now as close united to Him as my arm is to my body."

The dispute was coming to a crisis. The discussion lasted till eleven o'clock. Some said that Wesley might preach in Fetter Lane.

"No," said others, "this place is taken for the Germans."

Some argued that Wesley had often put an end to confusions in the Society.

"Confusion!" snapped others, "What do you mean? We never were in any confusion at all."

Next Sunday evening Wesley appeared again (July 20th, 1740). He was resolved what to do.

"I find you," he said, "more and more confirmed in the error of your ways. Nothing now remains but that I should give you up to God. You that are of the same opinion follow me."

As some wicked joker had hidden his hat, he was not able to leave the room with the dignity befitting the occasion; but eighteen supporters answered to his call; and the face of John Wesley was seen in the Fetter Lane Society no more. The breach was final; the wound remained open; and Moravians and Methodists went their several ways. For some years the dispute continued to rage with unabated fury. The causes were various. The damage done by Molther was immense. The more Wesley studied the writings of the Brethren the more convinced he became that in many ways they were dangerous teachers. They thought, he said, too highly of their own Church. They would never acknowledge themselves to be in the wrong. They submitted too much to the authority of Zinzendorf, and actually addressed him as Rabbi. They were dark and secret in their behaviour, and practised guile and dissimulation. They taught the doctrine of universal salvation. Above all, however, John Wesley held that the Brethren, like Molther, laid a one-sided stress on the doctrine of justification by faith alone. They were, he contended, Antinomians; they followed too closely the teaching of Luther; they despised the law, the commandments, good works, and all forms of self-denial.

"You have lost your first joy," said one, "therefore you pray: that is the devil. You read the Bible: that is the devil. You communicate: that is the devil."

In vain Count Zinzendorf, longing for peace, endeavoured to pour oil on the raging waters. The two leaders met in Gray's Inn Gardens and made an attempt to come to a common understanding (Sept. 3rd, 1741). The attempt was useless. The more keenly they argued the question out the further they drifted from each other. For Zinzendorf Wesley had never much respect, and he certainly never managed to understand him. If a poet and a botanist talk about roses they are hardly likely to understand each other; and that was just how the matter stood between Zinzendorf and Wesley. The Count was a poet, and used poetic, language. John Wesley was a level-headed Briton, with a mind as exact as a calculating machine.

"Why have you left the Church of England?" [115] began the Count.

"I was not aware that I had left the Church of England," replied Wesley.

And then the two men began to discuss theology.

"I acknowledge no inherent perfection in this life," said the Count. "This is the error of errors. I pursue it through the world with fire and sword. I trample it under foot. I exterminate it. Christ is our only perfection. Whoever follows after inherent perfection denies Christ."

"But I believe," replied Wesley, "that the Spirit of Christ works perfection in true Christians."

"Not at all," replied Zinzendorf, "All our perfection is in Christ. The whole of Christian perfection is imputed, not inherent. We are perfect in Christ—in ourselves, never."

"What," asked Wesley, in blank amazement, after Zinzendorf had hammered out his point. "Does not a believer, while he increases in love, increase equally in holiness?"

"By no means," said the Count; "the moment he is justified he is sanctified wholly. From that time, even unto death, he is neither more nor less holy. A babe in Christ is as pure in heart as a father in Christ. There is no difference."

At the close of the discussion the Count spoke a sentence which seemed to Wesley as bad as the teaching of Molther.

"We spurn all self-denial," he said, "we trample it under foot. Being believers, we do whatever we will and nothing more. We ridicule all mortification. No purification precedes perfect love."

And thus the Count, by extravagant language, drove Wesley further away from the Brethren than ever.

Meanwhile, at Fetter Lane events were moving fast. As soon as Wesley was out of the way, James Hutton came to the front; a good many Moravians—Bishop Nitschmann, Anna Nitschmann, John Toeltschig, Gussenbauer, and others—began to arrive on the scene; and step by step the Society became more Moravian in character. For this Hutton himself was chiefly responsible. He maintained a correspondence with Zinzendorf, and was the first to introduce Moravian literature to English readers. He published a collection of Moravian hymns, a Moravian Manual of Doctrine, and a volume in English of Zinzendorf's Berlin discourses. He was fond of the Moravian type of teaching, and asked for Moravian teachers. His wish was speedily gratified. The foolish Molther departed. The sober Spangenberg arrived. The whole movement now was raised to a higher level. As soon as Spangenberg had hold of the reins the members, instead of quarrelling with each other, began to apply themselves to the spread of the Gospel; and to this end they now established the "Society for the Furtherance of the Gospel." Its object was the support of foreign missions (1741). At its head was a committee of four, of whom James Hutton was one. For many years the "Society" supported the foreign work of the Brethren in English colonies; and in later years it supplied the funds for the work in Labrador. The next step was to license the Chapel in Fetter Lane. The need was pressing. As long as the members met without a licence they might be accused, at any time, of breaking the Conventicle Act. They wished now to have the law on their side. Already the windows had been broken by a mob. The services now were open to the public. The chapel was becoming an evangelistic hall. The licence was taken (Sept.). The members took upon themselves the name "Moravian Brethren, formerly of the Anglican Communion." But the members at Fetter Lane were not yet satisfied. For all their loyalty to the Church of England, they longed for closer communion with the Church of the Brethren; and William Holland openly asked the question, "Can a man join the Moravian Church and yet remain a member of the Anglican Church?"

"Yes," was the answer, "for they are sister Churches."

For this reason, therefore, and without any desire to become Dissenters, a number of the members of the Fetter Lane Society applied to Spangenberg to establish a congregation of the Moravian Church in England. The cautious Spangenberg paused. For the fourth time a momentous question was put to the decision of the Lot. The Lot sanctioned the move. The London congregation was established (November 10th, 1742). It consisted of seventy-two members of the Fetter Lane Society. Of those members the greater number were Anglicans, and considered themselves Anglicans still. And yet they were Brethren in the fullest sense and at least half of them took office. The congregation was organized on the Herrnhut model. It was divided into "Choirs." At the head of each choir was an Elder; and further there were two Congregation Elders, two Wardens, two Admonitors, two Censors, five Servants, and eight Sick-Waiters. Thus was the first Moravian congregation established in England. For many years this Church in Fetter

Lane was the headquarters of Moravian work in Great Britain. Already a new campaign had been started in Yorkshire; and a few years later Boehler declared that this one congregation alone had sent out two hundred preachers of the Gospel. [116]

Chapter 10: Yorkshire and the Settlement System

AS we follow the strange and eventful story of the renewal of the Brethren's Church, we can hardly fail to be struck by the fact that wherever new congregations were planted the way was first prepared by a man who did not originally belong to that Church himself. At Herrnhut the leader was the Lutheran, Christian David; at Fetter Lane, James Hutton, the Anglican clergyman's son; and in Yorkshire, the clergyman, Benjamin Ingham, who never joined the Moravian Church at all. He had, like the Wesleys and Whitefield, taken part in the Evangelical Revival. He was one of the Oxford Methodists, and had belonged to the Holy Club. He had sailed with John Wesley on his voyage to America, had met the Brethren on board the Simmonds, and had learned to know them more thoroughly in Georgia. He had been with John Wesley to Marienborn, had been admitted to the Communion there, had then travelled on to Herrnhut, and had been "exceedingly strengthened and comforted by the Christian conversation of the Brethren." He had often been at James Hutton's house, had attended services in Fetter Lane, was present at the famous Watch-Night Love-feast, and had thus learned to know the Brethren as thoroughly as Wesley himself. From first to last he held them in high esteem. "They are," he wrote, "more like the Primitive Christians than any other Church now in the world, for they retain both the faith, practice and discipline delivered by the Apostles. They live together in perfect love and peace. They are more ready to serve their neighbours than themselves. In their business they are diligent and industrious, in all their dealings strictly just and conscientious. In everything they behave themselves with great meekness, sweetness and simplicity."

His good opinion stood the test of time. He contradicted Wesley's evidence flatly. "I cannot but observe," he wrote to his friend Jacob Rogers, curate at St. Paul's, Bedford, "what a slur you cast upon the Moravians about stillness. Do you think, my brother, that they don't pray? I wish you prayed as much, and as well. They do not neglect prayers, either in public or in private; but they do not perform them merely as things that must be done; they are inwardly moved to pray by the Spirit. What they have said about stillness has either been strangely misunderstood or strangely misrepresented. They mean by it that we should endeavour to keep our minds calm, composed and collected, free from hurry and dissipation. And is not this right? They are neither despisers nor neglecters of ordinances."

The position of Ingham was peculiar. He was a clergyman without a charge; he resided at Aberford, in Yorkshire; he appears to have been a man of considerable means; and now he devoted all his powers to the moral and spiritual upliftment of the working-classes in the West Riding of Yorkshire. His sphere was the district between Leeds and

Halifax. For ignorance and brutality these Yorkshire people were then supposed to be unmatched in England. The parish churches were few and far between. The people were sunk in heathen darkness. Young Ingham began pure missionary work. He visited the people in their homes; he formed societies for Bible Reading and Prayer; he preached the doctrine of saving faith in Christ; and before long he was able to say that he had fifty societies under his care, two thousand hearers, three hundred inquirers, and a hundred genuine converts. For numbers, however, Ingham cared but little. His object was to bring men into personal touch with Christ. "I had rather," he said, "see ten souls truly converted than ten thousand only stirred up to follow." His work was opposed both by clergy and by laymen. At Colne, in Lancashire, he was attacked by a raging mob. At the head of the mob was the Vicar of Colne himself. The Vicar took Ingham into a house and asked him to sign a paper promising not to preach again. Ingham tore the paper in pieces.

"Bring him out and we'll make him," yelled the mob.

The Vicar went out; the mob pressed in; and clubs were flourished in the air "as thick as a man's leg."

Some wanted to kill him on the spot; others wished to throw him into the river.

"Nay, nay," said others, "we will heave him into the bog, then he will be glad to go into the river and wash and sweeten himself."

A stone "as big as a man's fist," hit him in the hollow of the neck. His coat-tails were bespattered with mud.

"See," said a wit, "he has got wings." At last the Vicar relented, took him into the Vicarage, and thus saved him from an early death.

But Ingham had soon more irons in the fire than he could conveniently manage. If these Yorkshire folk whom he had formed into societies were to make true progress in the spiritual life they must, he held, be placed under the care of evangelical teachers. He could not look after them himself; he was beginning new work further north, in the neighbourhood of Settle; and the best men he knew for his purpose were the Moravians whom he had learned to admire in Georgia, London and Herrnhut. For one Brother, John Toeltschig, Ingham had a special affection, and while he was on his visit to Herrnhut he begged that Toeltschig might be allowed to come with him to England. "B. Ingham," he wrote, "sends greeting, and bids grace and peace to the most Reverend Bishops, Lord Count Zinzendorf and David Nitschmann, and to the other esteemed Brethren in Christ. I shall be greatly pleased if, with your consent, my beloved brother, John Toeltschig, be permitted to stay with me in England as long as our Lord and Saviour shall so approve. I am heartily united with you all in the bonds of love. Farewell. Herrnhut, Sept. 29, 1738." [117] For our purpose this letter is surely of the deepest interest. It proves beyond all reasonable doubt that the Moravians started their evangelistic campaign in England, not from sectarian motives, but because they were invited by English Churchmen who valued the Gospel message they had to deliver. As Hutton had begged for Boehler, so Ingham begged for Toeltschig; and Toeltschig paid a brief visit to Yorkshire (November, 1739), helped Ingham in his work, and so delighted the simple people that they begged that he might come to them again. For a while the request was refused. At last Ingham took resolute action himself, called a mass meeting of Society members, and put to them the critical question: "Will you have the Moravians to work among you?" Loud shouts of approval rang out from every part of the building. As Spangenberg was now in London the request was forwarded to him; he laid it before the Fetter Lane Society; the members organized the "Yorkshire Congregation"; and the "Yorkshire Congregation" set out to commence evangelistic work in earnest (May 26th, 1742). At the head of the band was Spangenberg himself. As soon as he arrived in Yorkshire he had a business interview with Ingham. For Spangenberg shouts of approval were not enough. He wanted everything down in black and white. A document was prepared; the Societies were summoned again; the document was laid before them; and twelve hundred Yorkshire Britons signed their names to a request that the Brethren should work among them. From that moment Moravian work in Yorkshire began. At one stroke—by a written agreement—the Societies founded by Benjamin Ingham were handed over to the care of the Moravian Church. The Brethren entered upon the task with zeal. For some months, with Spangenberg as general manager, they made their head-quarters at Smith House, a farm building near Halifax (July, 1742); and there, on Saturday afternoons, they met for united prayer, and had their meals together in one large room. At first they had a mixed reception. On the one hand a mob smashed the windows of Smith House; on the other, the serious Society members "flocked to Smith House like hungry bees." The whole neighbourhood was soon mapped out, and the workers stationed at their posts. At Pudsey were Gussenbauer and his wife; at Great Horton, near Bradford, Toeltschig and Piesch; at Holbeck, near Leeds, the Browns; and other workers were busy soon at Lightcliffe, Wyke, Halifax, Mirfield, Hightown, Dewsbury, Wakefield, Leeds, Wortley, Farnley, Cleckheaton, Great Gomersal, and Baildon. The Moravian system of discipline was introduced. At the head of the men were John Toeltschig and Richard Viney; at the head of the women Mrs. Pietch and Mrs. Gussenbauer; and Monitors, Servants, and Sick Waiters were appointed just as in Herrnhut. Here was a glorious field of labour; here was a chance of Church extension; and the interesting question was, what use the Brethren would make of it.

At this point Count Zinzendorf arrived in Yorkshire (Feb., 1743), went to see Ingham at Aberford, and soon organized the work in a way of his own which effectually prevented it from spreading. His method was centralization. At that time he held firmly to his pet idea that the Brethren, instead of forming new congregations, should rather be content with "diaspora" work, and at the same time, whenever possible, build a settlement on the Herrnhut or Herrnhaag model, for the cultivation of social religious life. At this time it so happened that the Gussenbauers, stationed at Pudsey, were in trouble; their child was seriously ill; the Count rode over to see them; and while there he noticed the splendid site on which Fulneck stands to-day. If the visitor goes to Fulneck now he can hardly fail to be struck by its beauty. He is sure to admire its long gravel terrace, its neat parterres, its orchards and gardens, and, above all, its long line of plain stately buildings facing the southern sun. But then the slope was wild and unkempt, covered over with briars and brambles. Along the crown were a few small cottages. At one end, called Bankhouse, resided the Gussenbauers. From there the view across the valley was splendid. The estate was known as Falneck. The idea of a settlement rose before Zinzendorf's mind. The spirit of prophecy came upon him, and he named the place "Lamb's Hill." For the next few days the Count and his friends enjoyed the hospitality of Ingham at Aberford; and a few months later Ingham heard that the land and houses at Falneck were on the market. He showed himself a true friend of the Brethren. He bought the estate, gave them part of it for building, let out the cottages to them as tenants, and thus paved the way for the introduction of the Moravian settlement system into England.

For good or for evil that settlement system was soon the leading feature of the English work. The building of Fulneck began. First the Brethren called the place Lamb's Hill, then Gracehall, and then Fulneck, in memory of Fulneck in Moravia. From friends in Germany they received gifts in money, from friends in Norway a load of timber. The Single Brethren were all aglow with zeal; and on one occasion they spent the whole night in saying prayers and singing hymns upon the chosen sites. First rose the Chapel (1746), then the Minister's House and the rooms beneath and just to the east of the Chapel (1748), then the Brethren's and Sisters' Houses (1752), then the Widows' House (1763), then the Shop and Inn (1771), then the Cupola (1779), and then the Boys' Boarding School (1784-5). Thus, step by step, the long line of buildings arose, a sight unlike any other in the United Kingdom.

As the Brethren settled down in that rough Yorkshire country, they had a noble purpose, which was a rebuke to the godless and cynical spirit of the age. "Is a Christian republic possible?" asked the French philosopher, Bayle. According to the world it was not; according to the Brethren it was; and here at Fulneck they bravely resolved to put the matter to the proof. As long as that settlement existed, said they, there would be a kingdom where the law of Christ would reign supreme, where Single Brethren, Single Sisters, and Widows, would be screened from the temptations of the wicked world, where candidates would be trained for the service of the Church and her Master, where missionaries, on their way to British Colonies, could rest awhile, and learn the English language, where children, in an age when schools were scarce, could be brought up in the fear of God, and where trade would be conducted, not for private profit, but for the benefit of all. At Fulneck, in a word, the principles of Christ would be applied to the whole round of Moravian life. There dishonesty would be unknown; cruel oppression would be impossible; doubtful amusements would be forbidden; and thus, like their German Brethren in Herrnhut, these keen and hardy Yorkshire folk were to learn by practical experience that it is more blessed to give than to receive, and more delightful to work for a common cause than for a private balance at the bank.

For this purpose the Brethren established what were then known as diaconies; and a diacony was simply an ordinary business conducted, not by a private individual for his own personal profit, but by some official of the congregation for the benefit of the congregation as a whole. For example, James Charlesworth, a Single Brother, was appointed manager of a cloth-weaving factory, which for some years did a splendid trade with Portugal and Russia, kept the Single Brethren in regular employment, and supplied funds for general Church objects. As the years rolled on, the Brethren established a whole series of congregation-diaconies: a congregation general dealer's shop, a congregation farm, a congregation bakery, a congregation glove factory, and, finally, a congregation boarding-house or inn. At each diacony the manager and his assistants received a fixed salary, and the profits of the business helped to swell the congregation funds. The ideal was as noble as possible. At Fulneck daily labour was sanctified, and men toiled in the sweat of their brows, not because they wanted to line their pockets, but because they wanted to help the cause of Christ. For the sake of the Church the baker kneaded, the weaver plied his shuttle, the Single Sisters did needlework of marvellous beauty and manufactured their famous marble-paper. For many years, too, these Brethren at Fulneck employed a congregation doctor; and the object of this gentleman's existence was not to build up a flourishing practice, but to preserve the good health of his beloved Brethren and Sisters.

We must not, however, regard the Brethren as communists. James Hutton was questioned on this by the Earl of Shelburne.

"Does everything which is earned among you," said the Earl, "belong to the community?"

"No," replied Hutton, "but people contribute occasionally out of what they earn."

And yet this system, so beautiful to look at, was beset by serious dangers. It required more skill than the Brethren possessed, and more supervision than was humanly possible. As long as a business flourished and paid the congregation reaped the benefit; but if, on the other hand, the business failed, the congregation suffered, not only in money, but in reputation. At one time James Charlesworth, in an excess of zeal, mortgaged the manufacturing business, speculated with the money, and lost it; and thus caused others to accuse the Brethren of wholesale robbery and fraud. Again, the system was opposed in a measure to the English spirit of self-help and independence. As long as a man was engaged in a diacony, he was in the service of the Church; he did not receive a sufficient salary to enable him to provide for old age; he looked to the Church to provide his pension and to take care of him when he was ill; and thus he lost that self-reliance which is said to be the backbone of English character. But the most disastrous effect of these diaconies was on the settlement as a whole. They interfered with voluntary giving; they came to be regarded as Church endowments; and the people, instead of opening their purses, relied on the diaconies to supply a large proportion of the funds for the current expenses of congregation life. And here we cannot help but notice the difference between the Moravian diacony system and the well-known system of free-will offerings enforced by John Wesley in his Methodist societies. At first sight, the Moravian system might look more Christian; at bottom, Wesley's system proved the sounder; and thus, while Methodism spread, the Moravian river was choked at the fountain head.

Another feature of settlement life was its tendency to encourage isolation. For many years the rule was enforced at Fulneck that none but Moravians should be allowed to live in that sacred spot; and the laws were so strict that the wonder is that Britons submitted at all. For example, there was actually a rule that no member should spend a night outside the settlement without the consent of the Elders' Conference. If this rule had been confined to young men and maidens, there would not have been very much to say against it; but when it was enforced on business men, who might often want to travel at a moment's notice, it became an absurdity, and occasioned some vehement kicking against the pricks. The Choir-houses, too, were homes of the strictest discipline. At the west end stood the Single Brethren's House, where the young men lived together. They all slept in one large dormitory; they all rose at the same hour, and met for prayers before breakfast; they were all expected to attend certain services, designed for their special benefit; and they had all to turn in at a comparatively early hour. At the east end—two hundred yards away—stood the Single Sisters' House; and there similar rules were in full force. For all Sisters there were dress regulations, which many must have felt as a grievous burden. At Fulneck there was nothing in the ladies' dress to show who was rich and who was poor. They all wore the same kind of material; they had all to submit to black, grey, or brown; they all wore the same kind of three-cornered white shawl; and the only dress distinction was the ribbon in the cap, which showed to which estate in life the wearer belonged. For married women the colour was blue; for widows, white; for young women, pink; and for girls under eighteen, red. At the services in church the audience sat in Choirs, the women and girls on one side, the men and boys on the other. The relations between the sexes were strictly guarded. If a young man desired to marry, he was not even allowed to speak to his choice without the consent of the Elders' Conference; the Conference generally submitted the question to the Lot; and if the Lot gave a stern refusal, he was told that his choice was disapproved by God, and enjoined to fix his affections on someone else. The system had a twofold effect. It led, on the one hand, to purity and peace; on the other, to spiritual pride.

Another feature of this settlement life was the presence of officials. At Fulneck the number of Church officials was enormous. The place of honour was held by the Elders' Conference. It consisted of all the ministers of the Yorkshire District, the Fulneck Single Brethren's Labourer, the Single Sisters' Labouress, and the Widows' Labouress. It met at Fulneck once a month, had the general oversight of the Yorkshire work, and was supposed to watch the personal conduct of every individual member. Next came the Choir Elders' Conference. It consisted of a number of lay assistants, called Choir Helpers, had no independent powers of action, and acted as advisory board to the Elders' Conference. Next came the Congregation Committee. It was elected by the voting members of the congregation, had charge of the premises and finances, and acted as a board of arbitration in cases of legal dispute. Next came the Large Helpers' Conference. It consisted of the Committee, the Elders' Conference, and certain others elected by the congregation. Next came the Congregation Council, a still larger body elected by the

Congregation. At first sight these institutions look democratic enough. In reality, they were not democratic at all. The mode of election was peculiar. As soon as the votes had been collected the names of those at the top of the poll were submitted to the Lot; and only those confirmed by the Lot were held to be duly elected. The real power lay in the hands of the Elders' Conference. They were the supreme court of appeal; they were members, by virtue of their office, of the Committee; and they alone had the final decision as to who should be received as members and who should not. The whole system was German rather than English in conception. It was the system, not of popular control, but of ecclesiastical official authority.

But the most striking feature of the settlement system is still to be mentioned. It was the road, not to Church extension, but to Church extinction. If the chief object which the Brethren set before them was to keep that Church as small as possible, they could hardly have adopted a more successful method. We may express that method in the one word "centralization." For years the centre of the Yorkshire work was Fulneck. At Fulneck met the Elders' Conference. At Fulneck all Choir Festivals were held; at these Festivals the members from the other congregations were expected to be present; and when John de Watteville arrived upon the scene (1754) he laid down the regulation that although in future there were to be "as many congregations as chapels in Yorkshire," yet all were still to be one body, and all members must appear at Fulneck at least once a quarter! At Fulneck alone—in these earlier years—did the Brethren lay out a cemetery; and in that cemetery all funerals were to be conducted. The result was inevitable. As long as the other congregations were tied to the apron strings of Fulneck they could never attain to independent growth. I give one instance to show how the system worked. At Mirfield a young Moravian couple lost a child by death. As the season was winter, and the snow lay two feet deep, they could not possibly convey the coffin to Fulneck; and therefore they had the funeral conducted by the Vicar at Mirfield. For this sin they were both expelled from the Moravian Church. At heart, in fact, these early Brethren had no desire for Moravian Church extension whatever. They never asked anyone to attend their meetings, and never asked anyone to join their ranks. If any person expressed a desire to become a member of the Moravian Church, he was generally told in the first instance "to abide in the Church of England"; and only when he persisted and begged was his application even considered. And even then they threw obstacles in his way. They first submitted his application to the Lot. If the Lot said "No," he was rejected, and informed that the Lord did not wish him to join the Brethren's Church. If the Lot said "Yes," he had still a deep river to cross. The "Yes" did not mean that he was admitted; it only meant that his case would be considered. He was now presented with a document called a "testimonial," informing him that his application was receiving attention. He had then to wait two years; his name was submitted to the Elders' Conference; the Conference inquired into all his motives, and put him through a searching examination; and at the end of the two years he was as likely to be rejected as accepted. For these rules the Brethren had one powerful reason of their own. They had no desire to steal sheep from the Church of England. At

197

the very outset of their campaign they did their best to make their position clear. "We wish for nothing more," they declared, in a public notice in the Daily Advertiser, August 2nd, 1745, "than that some time or other there might be some bishop or parish minister found of the English Church, to whom, with convenience and to the good liking of all sides, we could deliver the care of those persons of the English Church who have given themselves to our care."

Thus did the Brethren, with Fulneck as a centre, commence their work in Yorkshire. At three other villages—Wyke, Gomersal, and Mirfield—they established so-called "country congregations" with chapel and minister's house. The work caused a great sensation. At one time a mob came out from Leeds threatening to burn Fulneck to the ground. At another time a neighbouring landlord sent his men to destroy all the linen hung out to dry. At the first Easter Morning Service in Fulneck four thousand spectators assembled to witness the solemn service. And the result of the Brethren's labours was that while their own numbers were always small they contributed richly to the revival of evangelical piety in the West Riding of Yorkshire.

In the Midlands the system had just the same results. At the village of Ockbrook, five miles from Derby, the Brethren built another beautiful settlement. For some years, with Ockbrook as a centre, they had a clear field for work in the surrounding district; they had preaching places at Eaton, Belper, Codnor, Matlock, Wolverhampton, Sheffield, Dale, and other towns and villages; and yet not a single one of these places ever developed into a congregation.

In Bedfordshire the result was equally fatal. At first the Brethren had a golden chance in Bedford. There, in 1738, there was a terrible epidemic of small-pox; in one week sixty or seventy persons died; nearly all the clergy had fled from the town in terror; and then Jacob Rogers, the curate of St. Paul's, sent for Ingham and Delamotte to come to the rescue. The two clergymen came; some Moravians followed; a Moravian congregation at Bedford was organized; and before long the Brethren had twenty societies round Bunyan's charming home. And yet not one of these societies became a new congregation. As Fulneck was the centre for Yorkshire, so Bedford was the centre for Bedfordshire; and the system that checked expansion in the North strangled it at its birth in the South.

Chapter 11: The Labours of John Cennick (1739-1755)

ONCE more an Anglican paved the way for the Brethren. At the terrible period of the Day of Blood one Brother, named Cennick, fled from Bohemia to England; and now, about a hundred years later, his descendant, John Cennick, was to play a great part in the revival of the Brethren's Church. For all that, John Cennick, in the days of his youth, does not appear to have known very much about his ecclesiastical descent. He was born (1718) and brought up at Reading, and was nursed from first to last in the Anglican fold. He was baptized at St. Lawrence Church; attended service twice a day with his mother; was confirmed and took the Communion; and, finally, at a service in the Church, while the psalms were being read, he passed through that critical experience in life to which we commonly give the name "conversion." For us, therefore, the point to notice is that John Cennick was truly converted to God, and was fully assured of his own salvation before he had met either Moravians or Methodists, and before he even knew, in all probability, that such people as the Moravians existed. We must not ascribe his conversion to Moravian influence. If we seek for human influence at all let us give the honour to his mother; but the real truth appears to be that what John Wesley learned from Boehler, John Cennick learned by direct communion with God. His spiritual experience was as deep and true as Wesley's. He had been, like Wesley, in the castle of Giant Despair, and had sought, like Wesley, to attain salvation by attending the ordinances of the Church. He had knelt in prayer nine times a day; he had watched; he had fasted; he had given money to the poor; he had almost gone mad in his terror of death and of the judgment day; and, finally, without any human aid, in his pew at St. Lawrence Church, he heard, he tells us, the voice of Jesus saying, "I am thy salvation," and there and then his heart danced for joy and his dying soul revived.

At that time, as far as I can discover, he had not even heard of the Oxford Methodists; but a few months later he heard strange news of Wesley's Oxford comrade, Charles Kinchin. The occasion was a private card party at Reading. John Cennick was asked to take a hand, and refused. For this he was regarded as a prig, and a young fellow in the company remarked, "There is just such a stupid religious fellow at Oxford, one Kinchin." Forthwith, at the earliest opportunity, John Cennick set off on foot for Oxford, to seek out the "stupid religious fellow"; found him sallying out of his room to breakfast; was introduced by Kinchin to the Wesleys; ran up to London, called at James Hutton's, and there met George Whitefield; fell on the great preacher's neck and kissed him; and was thus drawn into the stream of the Evangelical Revival at the very period in English history when Wesley and Whitefield first began preaching in the open air. He was soon a Methodist preacher himself (1739). At Kingswood, near Bristol, John Wesley opened a charity school for the children of colliers; and now he gave Cennick the post of head master, and authorized him also to visit the sick and to expound the Scriptures in public. The preacher's mantle soon fell on Cennick's shoulders. At a service held under a sycamore tree, the appointed preacher, Sammy Wather, was late; the crowd asked Cennick to take his place; and Cennick, after consulting the Lot, preached his first sermon in the open air. For the next eighteen months he now acted, like Maxfield and Humphreys, as one of Wesley's first lay assistant preachers; and as long as he was under Wesley's influence he preached in Wesley's sensational style, with strange sensational results. At the services the people conducted themselves like maniacs. Some foamed at the mouth and tore themselves in hellish agonies. Some suffered from swollen tongues and swollen necks. Some sweated enormously, and broke out in blasphemous language. At one service, held in the Kingswood schoolroom, the place became a pandemonium; and Cennick himself confessed with horror that the room was like the habitation of lost spirits. Outside a thunderstorm was raging; inside a storm of yells and roars. One woman declared that her name was Satan; another was Beelzebub; and a third was Legion. And certainly they were all behaving now like folk possessed with demons. From end to end of the room they raced, bawling and roaring at the top of their voices.

"The devil will have me," shrieked one. "I am his servant. I am damned."

"My sins can never be pardoned," said another. "I am gone, gone for ever."

"That fearful thunder," moaned a third, "is raised by the devil; in this storm he will bear me to hell."

A young man, named Sommers, roared like a dragon, and seven strong men could hardly hold him down.

"Ten thousand devils," he roared, "millions, millions of devils are about me."

"Bring Mr. Cennick! Bring Mr. Cennick!" was heard on every side; and when Mr. Cennick was brought they wanted to tear him in pieces.

At this early stage in the great Revival exhibitions of this frantic nature were fairly common in England; and John Wesley, so far from being shocked, regarded the kicks and groans of the people as signs that the Holy Spirit was convicting sinners of their sin. At first Cennick himself had the same opinion; but before very long his common sense came to his rescue. He differed with Wesley on the point; he differed with him also on the doctrine of predestination; he differed with him, thirdly, on the doctrine of Christian perfection; and the upshot of the quarrel that Wesley dismissed John Cennick from his service.

As soon, however, as Cennick was free, he joined forces, first with Howell Harris, and then with Whitefield; and entered on that evangelistic campaign which was soon to bring him into close touch with the Brethren. For five years he was now engaged in preaching in Gloucestershire and Wiltshire (1740-5); and wherever he went he addressed great crowds and was attacked by furious mobs. At Upton-Cheyny the villagers armed themselves with a horn, a drum, and a few brass pans, made the echoes ring with their horrible din, and knocked the preachers on the head with the pans; a genius put a cat in a cage, and brought some dogs to bark at it; and others hit Cennick on the nose and hurled dead dogs at his head. At Swindon—where Cennick and Harris preached in a place called the Grove—some rascals fired muskets over their heads, held the muzzles close up to their faces, and made them as black as tinkers; and others brought the local fire-engine and drenched them with dirty water from the ditches. At Exeter a huge mob stormed the building, stripped some of the women of their clothing, stamped upon them in the open street, and rolled them naked in the gutters. [118] At Stratton, a village not far from Swindon, the mob—an army two miles in length—hacked at the horses' legs, trampled the Cennickers under their feet, and battered Cennick till his shoulders were black and blue. At Langley the farmers ducked him in the village pond. At Foxham, Farmer Lee opposed him; and immediately, so the story ran, a mad dog bit all the farmer's pigs. At Broadstock Abbey an ingenious shepherd dressed up his dog as a preacher, called it Cennick, and speedily sickened and died; and the Squire of Broadstock, who had sworn in his wrath to cut off the legs of all Cennickers who walked through his fields of green peas, fell down and broke his neck. If these vulgar incidents did not teach a lesson they would hardly be worth recording; but the real lesson they teach us is that in those days the people of Wiltshire were in a benighted condition, and that Cennick was the man who led the revival there. As he rode on his mission from village to village, and from town to town, he was acting, not as a wild free-lance, but as the assistant of George Whitefield; and if it is fair to judge of his style by the sermons that have been preserved, he never said a word in those sermons that would not pass muster in most evangelical pulpits to-day. He never attacked the doctrines of the Church of England; he spoke of the Church as "our Church"; and he constantly backed up his arguments by appeals to passages in the Book of Common Prayer. In spite of his lack of University training he was no illiterate ignoramus. The more he knew of the Wiltshire villagers the more convinced he became that what they required was religious education. For their benefit, therefore, he now prepared some simple manuals of instruction: a "Treatise on the Holy Ghost," an "Exhortation to Steadfastness," a "Short Catechism for the Instruction of Youth," a volume of hymns entitled "A New Hymnbook," a second entitled "Sacred Hymns for the Children of God in the Day of their Pilgrimage," and a third entitled "Sacred Hymns for the Use of Religious Societies." What sort of manuals, it may be asked, did Cennick provide? I have read them carefully; and have come to the conclusion that though Cennick was neither a learned theologian nor an original religious thinker, he was fairly well up in his subject. For example, in his "Short Catechism" he shows a ready knowledge of the Bible and a clear understanding of the evangelical position; and in his "Treatise on the Holy Ghost" he quotes at length, not only from the Scriptures and the Prayer-book, but also from Augustine, Athanasius, Tertullian, Chrysostom, Calvin, Luther, Ridley, Hooper, and other Church Fathers and Protestant Divines. He was more than a popular preacher. He was a thorough and competent teacher. He made his head-quarters at the village of Tytherton, near Chippenham (Oct. 25, 1742); there, along with Whitefield, Howell Harris and others, he met his exhorters and stewards in conference;

and meanwhile he established also religious societies at Bath, Brinkworth, Foxham, Malmesbury, and many other villages.

At last, exactly like Ingham in Yorkshire, he found that he had too many irons in the fire, and determined to hand his societies over to the care of the Moravian Church. He had met James Hutton, Zinzendorf, Spangenberg, Boehler, and other Moravians in London, and the more he knew of these men the more profoundly convinced he became that the picture of the Brethren painted by John Wesley in his Journal was no better than a malicious falsehood. At every point in his evidence, which lies before me in his private diary and letters, John Cennick, to put the matter bluntly, gives John Wesley the lie. He denied that the Brethren practised guile; he found them uncommonly open and sincere. He denied that they were Antinomians, who despised good works; he found them excellent characters. He denied that they were narrow-minded bigots, who would never acknowledge themselves to be in the wrong; he found them remarkably tolerant and broad-minded. At this period, in fact, he had so high an opinion of the Brethren that he thought they alone were fitted to reconcile Wesley and Whitefield; and on one occasion he persuaded some Moravians, Wesleyans and Calvinists to join in a united love-feast at Whitefield's Tabernacle, and sing a common confession of faith (Nov. 4th, 1744). [119] John Cennick was a man of the Moravian type. The very qualities in the Brethren that offended Wesley won the love of Cennick. He loved the way they spoke of Christ; he loved their "Blood and Wounds Theology"; and when he read the "Litany of the Wounds of Jesus," he actually, instead of being disgusted, shed tears of joy. For these reasons, therefore, Cennick went to London, consulted the Brethren in Fetter Lane, and besought them to undertake the care of his Wiltshire societies. The result was the same as in Yorkshire. As long as the request came from Cennick alone the Brethren turned a deaf ear. But the need in Wiltshire was increasing. The spirit of disorder was growing rampant. At Bath and Bristol his converts were quarrelling; at Swindon a young woman went into fits and described them as signs of the New Birth; and a young man named Jonathan Wildboar, who had been burned in the hand for stealing linen, paraded the country showing his wound as a proof of his devotion to Christ. For these follies Cennick knew only one cure; and that cure was the "apostolic discipline" of the Brethren. He called his stewards together to a conference at Tytherton; the stewards drew up a petition; the Brethren yielded; some workers came down (Dec. 18th, 1745); and thus, at the request of the people themselves, the Moravians began their work in the West of England.

If the Brethren had now been desirous of Church extension, they would, of course, have turned Cennick's societies into Moravian congregations. But the policy they now pursued in the West was a repetition of their suicidal policy in Yorkshire. Instead of forming a number of independent congregations, they centralized the work at Tytherton, and compelled the other societies to wait in patience. At Bristol, then the second town in the kingdom, the good people had to wait ten years (1755); at Kingswood, twelve years (1757); at Bath, twenty years (1765); at Malmesbury, twenty-five years (1770); at

Devonport, twenty-six years (1771); and the other societies had to wait so long that finally they lost their patience, and died of exhaustion and neglect.

As soon as Cennick, however, had left his societies in the care of the Brethren (1746), he set off on a tour to Germany, spent three months at Herrnhaag, was received as a member, returned a Moravian, and then entered on his great campaign in Ireland. He began in Dublin, and took the city by storm. For a year or so some pious people, led by Benjamin La Trobe, a Baptist student, had been in the habit of meeting for singing and prayer; and now, with these as a nucleus, Cennick began preaching in a Baptist Hall at Skinner's Alley. It was John Cennick, and not John Wesley, who began the Evangelical Revival in Ireland. He was working in Dublin for more than a year before Wesley arrived on the scene. The city was the hunting ground for many sects; the Bradilonians and Muggletonians were in full force; the Unitarians exerted a widespread influence; and the bold way in which Cennick exalted the Divinity of Christ was welcomed like a pulse of fresh air. The first Sunday the people were turned away in hundreds. The hall in Skinner's Alley was crowded out. The majority of his hearers were Catholics. The windows of the hall had to be removed, and the people were in their places day after day three hours before the time. On Sundays the roofs of the surrounding houses were black with the waiting throng; every window and wall became a sitting; and Cennick himself had to climb through a window and crawl on the heads of the people to the pulpit. "If you make any stay in this town," wrote a Carmelite priest, in his Irish zeal, "you will make as many conversions as St. Francis Xavier among the wild Pagans. God preserve you!" At Christmas Cennick forgot his manners, attacked the Church of Rome in offensive language, and aroused the just indignation of the Catholic priests.

"I curse and blaspheme," he said, "all the gods in heaven, but the Babe that lay in Mary's lap, the Babe that lay in swaddling clothes."

The quick-witted Irish jumped with joy at the phrase. From that moment Cennick was known as "Swaddling John"; [120] and his name was introduced into comic songs at the music-halls. As he walked through the streets he had now to be guarded by an escort of friendly soldiers; and the mob, ten or fifteen thousand in number, pelted him with dirt, stones and bricks. At one service, says the local diary, "near 2,000 stones were thrown against Brothers Cennick and La Trobe, of which, however, not one did hit them." Father Duggan denounced him in a pamphlet entitled "The Lady's Letter to Mr. Cennick"; Father Lyons assured his flock that Cennick was the devil in human form; and others passed from hand to hand a pamphlet, written by Gilbert Tennent, denouncing the Moravians as dangerous and immoral teachers.

At this interesting point, when Cennick's name was on every lip, John Wesley paid his first visit to Dublin (August, 1747). For Cennick Wesley entertained a thorough contempt. He called him in his Journal "that weak man, John Cennick"; he accused him of having ruined the society at Kingswood; he was disgusted when he heard that he had become a Moravian; and now he turned him out of Skinner's Alley by the simple process of negotiating privately with the owner of the property, and buying the building over

203

Cennick's head. At one stroke the cause in Skinner's Alley passed over into Methodist hands; and the pulpit in which Cennick had preached to thousands was now occupied by John Wesley and his assistants. From that blow the Brethren's cause in Dublin never fully recovered. For a long time they were unable to find another building, and had to content themselves with meetings in private houses; but at last they hired a smaller building in Big Booter Lane, [121] near St. Patrick's Cathedral; two German Brethren, John Toeltschig and Bryzelius, came over to organize the work; Peter Boehler, two years later, "settled" the congregation; and thus was established, in a modest way, that small community of Moravians whose descendants worship there to the present day.

Meanwhile John Cennick was ploughing another field. For some years he was busily engaged—first as an authorized lay evangelist and then as an ordained Moravian minister—in preaching and founding religious societies in Cos. Antrim, Down, Derry, Armagh, Tyrone, Cavan, Monaghan, and Donegal (1748-55); and his influence in Ulster was just as great as the influence of Whitefield in England. He opened his Ulster campaign at Ballymena. At first he was fiercely opposed. As the rebellion of the young Pretender had been only recently quashed, the people were rather suspicious of new comers. The Pretender himself was supposed to be still at large, and the orthodox Presbyterians denounced Cennick as a Covenanter, a rebel, a spy, a rogue, a Jesuit, a plotter, a supporter of the Pretender, and a paid agent of the Pope. Again and again he was accused of Popery; and one Doffin, "a vagabond and wicked fellow," swore before the Ballymena magistrates that, seven years before, he had seen Cennick in the Isle of Man, and that there the preacher had fled from the arm of the law. As Cennick was pronouncing the benediction at the close of a service in the market-place at Ballymena, he was publicly assaulted by Captain Adair, the Lord of the Manor; and the Captain, whose blood was inflamed with whisky, struck the preacher with his whip, attempted to run him through with his sword, and then instructed his footman to knock him down. At another service, in a field near Ballymena, two captains of militia had provided a band of drummers, and the drummers drummed as only Irishmen can. The young preacher was summoned to take the oath of allegiance and abjuration. But Cennick, like many Moravians, objected to taking an oath. The scene was the bar-parlour of a Ballymena hotel. There sat the justices, Captain Adair and O'Neil of Shane's Castle; and there sat Cennick, the meek Moravian, with a few friends to support him. The more punch the two gentlemen put away the more pious and patriotic they became. For the second time Adair lost his self-control. He called Cennick a rascal, a rogue, and a Jesuit; he drank damnation to all his principles; he asked him why he would not swear and then get absolution from the Pope; and both gentlemen informed our hero that if he refused to take the oath they would clap him in Carrickfergus Gaol that very night. As Cennick, however, still held to his point, they were compelled at last to let him out on bail; and Cennick soon after appealed for protection to Dr. Rider, Bishop of Down and Connor. The good Bishop was a broad-minded man.

"Mr. Cennick," he said, "you shall have fair play in my diocese."

In vain the clergy complained to the Bishop that Cennick was emptying their pulpits. The Bishop had a stinging answer ready.

"Preach what Cennick preaches," he said, "preach Christ crucified, and then the people will not have to go to Cennick to hear the Gospel."

The good Bishop's words are instructive. At that time the Gospel which Cennick preached was still a strange thing in Ulster; and Cennick was welcomed as a true revival preacher. At Ballee and Ballynahone he addressed a crowd of ten thousand. At Moneymore the Presbyterians begged him to be their minister. At Ballynahone the Catholics promised that if he would only pitch his tent there they would never go to Mass again. At Lisnamara, the rector invited him to preach in the parish church. At New Mills the people rushed out from their cabins, barred his way, offered him milk, and besought him, saying, "If you cannot stop to preach, at least come into our houses to pray." At Glenavy the road was lined with a cheering multitude for full two miles. At Castle Dawson, Mr. Justice Downey, the local clergyman, and some other gentry, kissed him in public in the barrack yard. As he galloped along the country roads, the farm labourers in the fields would call out after him, "There goes Swaddling Jack"; he was known all over Ulster as "the preacher"; his fame ran on before him like a herald; Count Zinzendorf called him "Paul Revived"; and his memory lingers down to the present day.

For Cennick, of course, was more than a popular orator. As he was now a minister of the Brethren's Church, he considered it his duty, wherever possible, to build chapels, to organize congregations, and to introduce Moravian books and customs; and in this work he had the assistance of La Trobe, Symms, Caries, Cooke, Wade, Knight, Brampton, Pugh, Brown, Thorne, Hill, Watson, and a host of other Brethren whose names need not be mentioned. I have not mentioned the foregoing list for nothing. It shows that most of Cennick's assistants were not Germans, but Englishmen or Irishmen; and the people could not raise the objection that the Brethren were suspicious foreigners. At this time, in fact, the strength of the Brethren was enormous. At the close of his work, John Cennick himself had built ten chapels, and established two hundred and twenty religious societies. Around Lough Neagh the Brethren lay like locusts; and the work here was divided into four districts. At the north-east corner they had four societies, with chapels at Ballymena, Gloonen, and Grogan, and a growing cause at Doagh; at the north-west corner, a society at Lisnamara, established later as a congregation at Gracefield; at the south-west corner, in Co. Armagh, three chapels were being built; and at the south-east corner, they had several societies, and had built, or were building, chapels at Ballinderry, Glenavy, and Kilwarlin.

At this distance of time the Brethren's work in Ulster has about it a certain glamour of romance. But in reality the conditions were far from attractive. It is hard for us to realize now how poor those Irish people were. They lived in hovels made of loose sods, with no chimneys; they shared their wretched rooms with hens and pigs; and toiling all day in a damp atmosphere, they earned their bread by weaving and spinning. The Brethren themselves were little better off. At Gloonen, a small village near Gracehill, the Brethren of the first Lough Neagh district made their headquarters in a cottage consisting of two rooms and two small "closets"; and this modest abode of one story was known in the neighbourhood as "The Great House at Gloonen." Again, at a Conference held in Gracehill, the Brethren, being pinched for money, solemnly passed a resolution never to drink tea more than once a day.

And yet there is little to show to-day for these heroic labours. If the visitor goes to Ulster now and endeavours to trace the footsteps of Cennick, he will find it almost impossible to realize how great the power of the Brethren was in those palmy days. At Gracehill, near Ballymena, he will find the remains of a settlement. At Ballymena itself, now a growing town, he will find to his surprise that the Brethren's cause has ceased to exist. At Gracefield, Ballinderry, and Kilwarlin—where once Cennick preached to thousands—he will find but feeble, struggling congregations. At Gloonen the people will show him "Cennick's Well"; at Kilwarlin he may stand under "Cennick's Tree"; and at Portmore, near Lough Beg, he will see the ruins of the old church, where Jeremy Taylor wrote his "Holy Living and Holy Dying," and where Cennick slept many a night. At Drumargan (Armagh), he will find a barn that was once a Moravian Chapel, and a small farmhouse that was once a Sisters' House; and at Arva (Co. Cavan), he may stand on a hillock, still called "Mount Waugh," in memory of Joseph Waugh, a Moravian minister. For the rest, however, the work has collapsed; and Cennick's two hundred and twenty societies have left not a rack behind.

For this decline there were three causes. The first was financial. At the very time when the Brethren in Ulster had obtained a firm hold upon the affections of the people the Moravian Church was passing through a financial crisis; and thus, when money would have been most useful, money was not to be had. The second was the bad system of management. Again, as in Yorkshire and Wiltshire, the Brethren pursued the system of centralization; built a settlement at Gracehill, and made the other congregations dependent on Gracehill, just as the Yorkshire congregations were dependent on Fulneck. The third cause was the early death of Cennick himself. At the height of his powers he broke down in body and in mind; and, worn out with many labours, he became the victim of mental depression. For some time the conviction had been stealing upon him that his work in this world was over; and in a letter to John de Watteville, who had twice inspected the Irish work, he said, "I think I have finished with the North of Ireland. If I stay here much longer I fear I shall damage His work." At length, as he rode from Holyhead to London, he was taken seriously ill; and arrived at Fetter Lane in a state of high fever and exhaustion. For a week he lay delirious and rambling, in the room which is now used as the Vestry of the Moravian Chapel; and there, at the early age of thirty-six, he died (July 4th, 1755). If the true success is to labour, Cennick was successful; but if success is measured by visible results, he ended his brief and brilliant career in tragedy, failure and gloom. Of all the great preachers of the eighteenth century, not one was superior to him in beauty of character. By the poor in Ireland he was almost worshipped. He was often attacked and unjustly accused; but he never attacked in return. We search his diary and letters in vain for one single trace of bitter feeling. He was inferior to John Wesley in organizing skill, and inferior to Whitefield in dramatic power; but in devotion, in simplicity, and in command over his audience he was equal to either. At the present time he is chiefly known in this country as the author of the well-known grace before meat, "Be present at our table, Lord"; and some of his hymns, such as "Children of the Heavenly King," and "Ere I sleep, for every favour," are now regarded as classics. His position in the Moravian Church was peculiar. Of all the English Brethren he did the most to extend the cause of the Moravian Church in the United Kingdom, and no fewer than fifteen congregations owed their existence, directly or indirectly, to his efforts; and yet, despite his shining gifts, he was never promoted to any position of special responsibility or honour. He was never placed in sole charge of a congregation; and he was not made superintendent of the work in Ireland. As a soldier in the ranks he began; as a soldier in the ranks he died. He had one blemish in his character. He was far too fond, like most of the Brethren, of overdrawn sentimental language. If a man could read Zinzendorf's "Litany of the Wounds of Jesus," and then shed tears of joy, as Cennick tells us he did himself, there must have been an unhealthy taint in his blood. He was present at Herrnhaag at the Sifting-Time, and does not appear to have been shocked. In time his sentimentalism made him morbid. As he had a wife and two children dependent on him, he had no right to long for an early death; and yet he wrote the words in his pocket-book:—

Now, Lord, at peace with Thee and all below,
Let me depart, and to Thy Kingdom go.

For this blemish, however, he was more to be pitied than blamed. It was partly the result of ill-health and overwork; and, on the whole, it was merely a trifle when set beside that winsome grace, that unselfish zeal, that modest devotion, and that sunny piety, which charmed alike the Wiltshire peasants, the Papist boys of Dublin, and the humble weavers and spinners of the North of Ireland. [122]

Chapter 12: The Appeal to Parliament (1742-1749)

MEANWHILE, however, the Brethren in England had been bitterly opposed. For this there were several reasons. First, the leading Brethren in England were Germans; and that fact alone was quite enough to prejudice the multitude against them (1742-3). For Germans our fathers had then but little liking; they had a German King on the throne, and they did not love him; and the general feeling in the country was that if a man was a foreigner he was almost sure to be a conspirator or a traitor. Who were these mysterious foreigners? asked the patriotic Briton. Who were these "Moravians," these "Herrnhuters," these "Germans," these "Quiet in the Land," these "Antinomians" ? The very names of the Brethren aroused the popular suspicion. If a man could prove that his name was John Smith, the presumption was that John Smith was a loyal citizen; but if he was known as Gussenbauer or Ockershausen, he was probably another Guy Fawkes, and was forming a plot to blow up the House of Commons. At the outset therefore the Brethren were accused of treachery. At Pudsey Gussenbauer was arrested, tried at Wakefield, and imprisoned in York Castle. At Broadoaks, in Essex, the Brethren had opened a school, and were soon accused of being agents of the Young Pretender. They had, it was said, stored up barrels of gunpowder; they had undermined the whole neighbourhood, and intended to set the town of Thaxted on fire. At three o'clock one afternoon a mob surrounded the building, and tried in vain to force their way in. Among them were a sergeant and a corporal. The warden, Metcalfe, admitted the officers, showed them round the house, and finally led them to a room where a Bible and Prayer-book were lying on the table. At this sight the officers collapsed in amazement.

"Aye," said the corporal, "this is proof enough that you are no Papists; if you were, this book would not have lain here."

Another cause of opposition was the Brethren's quiet mode of work. In North America lived a certain Gilbert Tennent; he had met Zinzendorf at New Brunswick; he had read his Berlin discourses; and now, in order to show the public what a dangerous teacher Zinzendorf was, he published a book, entitled, "Some Account of the Principles of the Moravians." (1743) As this book was published at Boston, it did not at first do much harm to the English Brethren; but, after a time, a copy found its way to England; an English edition was published; and the English editor, in a preface, accused the Brethren of many marvellous crimes. They persistently refused, he declared, to reveal their real opinions. They crept into houses and led captive silly women. They claimed that all Moravians were perfect, and taught that the Moravian Church was infallible. They practised an adventurous use of the Lot, had a curious method of discovering and purging out the accursed thing, pledged each other in liquor at their love-feasts, and had an "artful regulation of their convents." Above all, said this writer, the Moravians were tyrannical. As soon as any person joined the Moravian Church, he was compelled to place himself, his family, and his estates entirely at the Church's disposal; he was bound to believe what the Church believed, and to do what the Church commanded; he handed his children over to the Church's care; he could not enter into any civil contract without the Church's consent; and his sons and daughters were given in marriage just as the Church decreed. [123] Gilbert Tennent himself was equally severe. He began by criticizing Zinzendorf's theology; and after remarking that Zinzendorf was a liar, he said that the Brethren kept their disgusting principles secret, that they despised good books, that they slighted learning and reason, that they spoke lightly of Confessions of Faith, that they insinuated themselves into people's affections by smiles and soft discourses about the love of Christ, that they took special care to apply to young persons, females and ignorant people. From all this the conclusion was obvious. At heart the Brethren were Roman Catholics. "The Moravians," said Gilbert, "by this method of proceeding, are propagating another damnable doctrine of the Church of Rome, namely, that Ignorance is the Mother of Devotion." We can imagine the effect of this in Protestant England. At one time Zinzendorf was openly accused in the columns of the Universal Spectator of kidnapping young women for Moravian convents; and the alarming rumour spread on all sides that the Brethren were Papists in disguise.

Another cause of trouble was the Moravian religious language. If the Brethren did not preach novel doctrines they certainly preached old doctrines in a novel way. They called Jesus the Man of Smart; talked a great deal about Blood and Wounds; spoke of themselves as Poor Sinners; and described their own condition as Sinnership and Sinnerlikeness. To the orthodox Churchman this language seemed absurd. He did not know what it meant; he did not find it in the Bible; and, therefore, he concluded that the Brethren's doctrine was unscriptural and unsound.

Another cause of trouble was the Brethren's doctrine of justification by faith alone. Of all the charges brought against them the most serious and the most persistent was the charge that they despised good works. They were denounced as Antinomians. Again and again, by the best of men, this insulting term was thrown at their heads. They taught, it was said, the immoral doctrine that Christ had done everything for the salvation of mankind; that the believer had only to believe; that he need not obey the commandments; and that such things as duties did not exist. At Windsor lived a gentleman named Sir John Thorold. He was one of the earliest friends of the Moravians; he had often attended meetings at Hutton's house; he was an upright, conscientious, intelligent Christian; and yet he accused the Brethren of teaching "that there were no duties in the New Testament." Gilbert Tennent brought the very same accusation. "The Moravian notion about the law," he said, "is a mystery of detestable iniquity; and, indeed, this seems to be the mainspring of their unreasonable, anti-evangelical, and licentious religion." But the severest critic of the Brethren was John Wesley. He attacked them in a "Letter to the Moravian Church," and had that letter printed in his Journal. He attacked them again in his "Short View of the Difference between the Moravian Brethren, lately in England, and the Rev. Mr. John and Charles Wesley." He attacked them again in his "A Dialogue between an Antinomian and his Friend"; and in each of these clever and biting productions his chief charge against them was that they taught Antinomian principles, despised good works, and taught that Christians had nothing to do but believe.

"Do you coolly affirm," he asked, "that this is only imputed to a Believer, and that he has none at all of this holiness in him? Is temperance imputed only to him that is a drunkard still? or chastity to her that goes on in whoredom?"

He accused the Brethren of carrying out their principles; he attacked their personal character; and, boiling with righteous indignation, he denounced them as "licentious spirits and men of careless lives."

As the Brethren, therefore, were now being fiercely attacked, the question arose, what measures, if any, they should take in self-defence. At first they contented themselves with gentle protests. As they had been accused of disloyalty to the throne, James Hutton, Benjamin Ingham, and William Bell, in the name of all the English societies connected with the Brethren's Church, drew up an address to the King, went to see him in person, and assured him that they were loyal subjects and hated Popery and popish pretenders (April 27th, 1744). As they had been accused of attacking the Anglican Church, two Brethren called on Gibson, Bishop of London, and assured him that they had committed no such crime. For the rest, however, the Brethren held their tongues. At a Conference in London they consulted the Lot; and the Lot decided that they should not reply to Gilbert Tennent. For the same reason, probably, they also decided to give no reply to John Wesley.

Meanwhile, however, an event occurred which roused the Brethren to action. At Shekomeko, in Dutchess County, New York, they had established a flourishing Indian congregation; and now, the Assembly of New York, stirred up by some liquor sellers who were losing their business, passed an insulting Act, declaring that "all vagrant preachers, Moravians, and disguised Papists," should not be allowed to preach to the Indians unless they first took the oaths of allegiance and abjuration (1744). James Hutton was boiling with fury. If this Act had applied to all preachers of the Gospel he would not have minded so much; but the other denominations—Presbyterians, Independents, Anabaptists and Quakers—were all specially exempted; and the loyal Moravians were bracketed together with vagrant preachers and Papists in disguise. He regarded the Act as an insult. He wrote to Zinzendorf on the subject. "This," he said, "is the work of Presbyterian firebrands." If an Act like this could be passed in America, who knew what might not happen soon in England? "We ought," he continued, "to utilize this or some other favourable opportunity for bringing our cause publicly before Parliament."

Now was the time, thought the fiery Hutton, to define the position of the Brethren's Church in England. He went to Marienborn to see the Count; a Synod met (1745); his proposal was discussed; and the Synod appointed Abraham von Gersdorf, the official "Delegate to Kings," to appeal to Lord Granville, and the Board of Trade and Plantations, for protection in the Colonies. Lord Granville was gracious. He informed the deputation that though the Act could not be repealed at once the Board of Trade would recommend the repeal as soon as legally possible; and the upshot of the matter was that the Act became a dead letter.

Next year Zinzendorf came to England, and began to do the best he could to destroy the separate Moravian Church in this country (1746). If the Count could only have had his way, he would now have made every Moravian in England return to the Anglican Church. He was full of his "Tropus" idea. He wished to work his idea out in England; he called the English Brethren to a Synod (Sept. 13-16), and persuaded them to pass a scheme whereby the English branch of the Brethren's Church would be taken over entirely by the Church of England. It was one of the most curious schemes he ever devised. At their Sunday services the Brethren henceforward were to use the Book of Common Prayer; their ministers were to be ordained by Anglican and Moravian Bishops conjointly; he himself was to be the head of this Anglican-Moravian Church; and thus the English Moravians would be grafted on to the Church of England. For the second time, therefore, the Count was trying to destroy the Moravian Church. But here, to his surprise, he met an unexpected obstacle. He had forgotten that it takes two to make a marriage. He proposed the union in form to Archbishop Potter; he pleaded the case with all the skill at his command; and the Archbishop promptly rejected the proposal, and the marriage never came off.

As Zinzendorf, therefore, was baffled in this endeavour, he had now to come down from his pedestal and try a more practical plan (1747); and, acting on the sage advice of Thomas Penn, proprietor of Pennsylvania, and General Oglethorpe, Governor of Georgia, he resolved to appeal direct to Parliament for protection in the Colonies. As Oglethorpe himself was a member of the House of Commons, he was able to render the Brethren signal service. He had no objection to fighting himself, and even defended duelling, [124] but he championed the cause of the Brethren. Already, by an Act in 1740, the Quakers had been freed from taking the oath in all our American Colonies; already, further, by another Act (1743), the privilege of affirming had been granted in Pennsylvania, not only to Quakers, but to all foreign Protestants; and now Oglethorpe moved in the House of Commons that the rule existing in Pennsylvania should henceforth apply to all American Colonies. If the Moravians, he argued, were only given a little more encouragement, instead of being worried about oaths and military service, they would settle in larger numbers in America and increase the prosperity of the colonies. He wrote to the Board of Trade and Plantations; his friend, Thomas Penn, endorsed his statements; and the result was that the new clause was passed, and all foreign Protestants in American Colonies— the Moravians being specially mentioned—were free to affirm instead of taking the oath.

But this Act was of no use to the English Brethren. The great question at issue was, what standing were the Brethren to hold in England? On the one hand, as members of a foreign Protestant Church they were entitled to religious liberty; and yet, on the other hand, they were practically treated as Dissenters, and had been compelled to have all their buildings licensed. As they were still accused of holding secret dangerous principles, they now drew up another "Declaration," had it printed, sent it to the offices of the Archbishop of Canterbury, the Lord Chancellor, and the Master of the Rolls, and inserted it in the leading newspapers. At all costs, pleaded the Brethren, let us have a public inquiry. "If any man of undoubted sense and candour," they said, "will take the pains upon himself to fix the accusations against us in their real point of view, hitherto unattainable by the Brethren and perhaps the public too, then we will answer to the expectations of the public, as free and directly as may be expected from honest subjects of the constitution of these realms." The appeal led to nothing; the man of sense and candour never appeared; and still the suffering Brethren groaned under all sorts of vague accusation.

At last, however, Zinzendorf himself came to the rescue of his Brethren, rented Northampton House in Bloomsbury Square, [125] and brought the whole matter to a head. For the second time he took the advice of Oglethorpe and Thomas Penn; and a deputation was now appointed to frame a petition to Parliament that the Brethren in America be exempted, not merely from the oath, but also from military service.

As General Oglethorpe was now in England, he gladly championed the Brethren's cause, presented the petition in the House of Commons, and opened the campaign by giving an account of the past history of the Brethren (Feb. 20th, 1749). For practical purposes this information was important. If the House knew nothing else about the Brethren it knew that they were no sect of mushroom growth. And then Oglethorpe informed the House how the Brethren, already, in bygone days had been kindly treated by England; how Amos Comenius had appealed to the Anglican Church; how Archbishop Sancroft and Bishop Compton had published a pathetic account of their sufferings; and how George I., by the advice of Archbishop Wake, had issued letters patent for their relief. But the most effective part of his speech was the part in which he spoke from personal knowledge. "In the year 1735," he said "they were disquieted in Germany, and about twenty families went over with me to Georgia. They were industrious, patient under the difficulties of a new settlement, laborious beyond what could have been expected. They gave much of their time to prayer, but that hindered not their industry. Prayer was to them a diversion after labour. I mention this because a vulgar notion has prevailed that they neglected labour for prayer." They had spent, he said, -L-100,000 in various industries; they had withdrawn already in large numbers from Georgia because they were compelled to bear arms; and if that colony was to prosper again the Brethren should be granted the privilege they requested, and thus be encouraged to return. For what privilege, after all, did the Brethren ask? For the noble privilege of paying money instead of fighting in battle. The more these Brethren were encouraged, said he, the more the Colonies would prosper; he proposed that the petition be referred to a Committee, and Velters Cornwall, member for Herefordshire, seconded the motion.

As Zinzendorf listened to this speech, some curious feelings must have surged in his bosom. At the Synod of Hirschberg, only six years before, he had lectured the Brethren for making business bargains with Governments; and now he was consenting to such a bargain himself. The debate in the Commons was conducted on business lines; the whole question at issue was, not whether the Moravians were orthodox, but whether it would pay the Government to encourage them; and the British Government took exactly the same attitude towards the Brethren that Frederick the Great had done seven years before. The next speaker made this point clearer than ever. We are not quite sure who it was. It was probably Henry Pelham, the Prime Minister. At any rate, whoever it was, he objected to the petition on practical grounds. He declared that the Moravians were a very dangerous body; that they were really a new sect; that, like the Papists, they had a Pope, and submitted to their Pope in all things; that they made their Church supreme in temporal matters; and that thus they destroyed the power of the civil magistrate. He suspected that the Brethren were Papists in disguise.

"I am at a loss," he said, "whether I shall style the petitioners Jesuits, Papists, or Moravians."

He intended, he declared, to move an amendment that the Moravians be restrained from making converts, and that all who joined their ranks be punished. The fate of England was at stake. If the Moravians converted the whole nation to their superstition, and everyone objected to bearing arms, what then would become of our Army and Navy, and how could we resist invasion? The next speakers, however, soon toned down the alarm. If Pelham's objections applied to the Moravians, they would apply, it was argued, equally to the Quakers; and yet it was a notorious fact that the Colonies where the Quakers settled were the most prosperous places in the Empire. "What place," asked one, "is more flourishing than Pennsylvania?" And if the Moravians objected to bearing arms, what did that matter, so long as they were willing to pay?

For these practical reasons, therefore, the motion was easily carried; a Parliamentary Committee was formed; General Oglethorpe was elected chairman; and the whole history, doctrine and practice of the Brethren were submitted to a thorough investigation. For this purpose Zinzendorf had prepared a number of documents; the documents were laid before the Committee; and, on the evidence of those documents, the Committee based its report. From that evidence three conclusions followed.

In the first place, the Brethren were able to show, by documents of incontestable authenticity, that they really were the true descendants of the old Church of the Brethren. They could prove that Daniel Ernest Jablonsky had been consecrated a Bishop at the Synod of Lissa (March 10th, 1699), that Jablonsky in turn had consecrated Zinzendorf a Bishop, and that thus the Brethren had preserved the old Moravian episcopal succession. They could prove, further, and prove they did, that Archbishops Wake and Potter had both declared that the Moravian episcopacy was genuine; that Potter had described the Moravian Brethren as apostolical and episcopal; and that when Zinzendorf was made a Bishop, Potter himself had written him a letter of congratulation. With such evidence, therefore, as this before them, the Committee were convinced of the genuineness of the Moravian episcopal succession; and when they issued their report they gave due weight to the point.

In the second place, the Brethren were able to show that they had no sectarian motives, and that though they believed in their own episcopacy, they had no desire to compete with the Church of England. "There are," they said, "no more than two episcopal Churches among Protestants: the one known through all the world under the name of Ecclesia Anglicana; the other characterised for at least three ages as the Unitas Fratrum, comprehending generally all other Protestants who choose episcopal constitution. The first is the only one which may justly claim the title of a national church, because she has at her head a Christian King of the same rite, which circumstance is absolutely required to constitute a national church. The other episcopal one, known by the name of Unitas Fratrum, is far from pretending to that title." In that manifesto the Brethren assumed that their episcopal orders were on a par with those of the Church of England; and that assumption was accepted, without the slightest demur, not only by the Parliamentary Committee, but by the bench of Bishops.

In the third place—and this was the crucial point—the Brethren were able to show, by the written evidence of local residents, that wherever they went they made honest, industrious citizens. They had settled down in Pennsylvania; they had done good work at Bethlehem, Nazareth, Gnadenhuetten, Frederick's Town, German Town and Oley; they had won the warm approval of Thomas Penn; and, so far from being traitors, they had done their best to teach the Indians to be loyal to the British throne. They had doubled the value of an estate in Lusatia, and had built two flourishing settlements in Silesia; they had taught the negroes in the West Indies to be sober, industrious and law-abiding; they had tried to uplift the poor Hottentots in South Africa; they had begun a mission in Ceylon, had toiled in plague-stricken Algiers, and had built settlements for the Eskimos in Greenland. If these statements had been made by Moravians, the Committee might have doubted their truth, but in every instance the evidence came, not from Brethren themselves, but from governors, kings and trading officials. The proof was overwhelming. Wherever the Brethren went, they did good work. They promoted trade; they enriched the soul; they taught the people to be both good and loyal; and, therefore, the sooner they were encouraged in America, the better for the British Empire.

As the Committee, therefore, were compelled by the evidence to bring in a good report, the desired leave was granted to bring in a bill "for encouraging the people known by the name of the Unitas Fratrum, or United Brethren, to settle in His Majesty's Colonies in America." Its real purpose, however, was to recognize the Brethren's Church as an ancient Protestant Episcopal Church, not only in the American Colonies, but also in the United Kingdom; and its provisions were to be in force wherever the British flag might fly. The provisions were generous. First, in the preamble, the Brethren were described as "an ancient Protestant Episcopal Church and a sober and quiet industrious people," and, being such, were hereby encouraged to settle in the American Colonies. Next, in response to their own request, they were allowed to affirm instead of taking the oath. The form of affirmation was as follows: "I, A. B., do declare in the presence of Almighty God the witness of the truth of what I say." Next, they were allowed to pay a fixed sum instead of rendering military service, and were also exempted from serving on juries in criminal cases. Next, all members of the Brethren's Church were to prove their claims by producing a certificate, signed by a Moravian Bishop or pastor. Next, the advocate of the Brethren was to supply the Commissioners for Trade and Plantations with a complete list of Moravian bishops and pastors, together with their handwriting and seal; and, finally, anyone who falsely claimed to belong to the Brethren's Church was to be punished as a wilful perjurer.

The first reading was on March 28th, and the passage through the House of Commons was smooth. At the second reading, on April 1st, General Oglethorpe was asked to explain why the privilege of affirming should be extended to Moravians in Great Britain and Ireland. Why not confine it to the American colonies? His answer was convincing. If the privilege, he said, were confined to America, it would be no privilege at all. At that time all cases tried in America could be referred to an English Court of Appeal. If the privilege, therefore, were confined to America, the Brethren would be constantly hampered by vexatious appeals to England; and an English Court might at any moment upset the decision of an American Court. The explanation was accepted; the third reading came on; and the Bill passed the House of Commons unaltered.

In the House of Lords there was a little more opposition. As the Brethren were described as an "Episcopal Church," it was feared that the Bishops might raise an objection; but the Bishops met at Lambeth Palace, and resolved not to oppose. At first Dr. Sherlock, Bishop of London, objected; but even he gave way in the end, and when the Bill came before the Lords not a single Bishop raised his voice against it. The only Bishop who spoke was Maddox, of Worcester, and he spoke in the name of the rest.

"Our Moravian Brethren," he said, "are an ancient Episcopal Church. Of all Protestants, they come the nearest to the Established Church in this kingdom in their doctrine and constitution. And though the enemy has persecuted them from several quarters, the soundness of their faith and the purity of their morals have defended them from any imputation of Popery and immorality."

The one dangerous opponent was Lord Chancellor Hardwicke. He objected to the clause about the certificate. If a man wished to prove himself a Moravian, let him do so by bringing witnesses. What use was a Bishop's certificate? It would not be accepted by any judge in the country.

On the other hand, Lord Granville, in a genial speech, spoke highly of the Brethren. As some members were still afraid that the whole country might become Moravians, and refuse to defend our land against her foes, he dismissed their fears by an anecdote about a Quaker. At one time, he said, in the days of his youth, the late famous admiral, Sir Charles Wager, had been mate on a ship commanded by a Quaker; and on one occasion the ship was attacked by a French privateer. What, then, did the Quaker captain do? Instead of fighting the privateer himself, he gave over the command to Wager, captured the privateer, and made his fortune. But the Brethren, he held, were even broader minded than the Quakers.

"I may compare them," he said, "to a casting-net over all Christendom, to enclose all denominations of Christians. If you like episcopacy, they have it; if you choose the Presbytery of Luther or Calvin, they have that also; and if you are pleased with Quakerism, they have something of that."

With this speech Zinzendorf was delighted. As the little difficulty about the certificate had not yet been cleared away, he suggested that the person bringing the certificate should bring witnesses as well; and with this trifling amendment the Bill at last—on May 12th, the Moravian Memorial Day—was carried without a division.

In one sense this Act was a triumph for the Brethren, and yet it scarcely affected their fortunes in England. Its interest is national rather than Moravian. It was a step in the history of religious toleration, and the great principle it embodied was that a religious body is entitled to freedom on the ground of its usefulness to the State. The principle is one of the deepest importance. It is the fundamental principle to-day of religious liberty in England. But the Brethren themselves reaped very little benefit. With the exception of their freedom from the oath and from military service, they still occupied the same position as before the Act was passed. We come here to one of those contradictions which are the glory of all legal systems. On the one hand, by Act of Parliament, they were declared an Episcopal Church, and could hardly, therefore, be regarded as Dissenters; on the other, they were treated as Dissenters still, and still had their churches licensed as "places of worship for the use of Protestant Dissenters." [126]

Chapter 13: The Battle of the Books (1749-1755)

AS soon as the Act of Parliament was passed, and the settlement at Herrnhaag had been broken up, the Count resolved that the headquarters of the Brethren's Church should henceforward be in London; and to this intent he now leased a block of buildings at Chelsea, known as Lindsey House. The great house, in altered form, is standing still. It is at the corner of Cheyne Walk and Beaufort Street, and is close to the Thames Embankment. It had once belonged to Sir Thomas More, and also to the ducal family of Ancaster. The designs of Zinzendorf were ambitious. He leased the adjoining Beaufort grounds and gardens, spent -L-12,000 on the property, had the house remodelled in grandiose style, erected, close by, the "Clock" chapel and a minister's house, laid out a cemetery, known to this day as "Sharon," and thus made preliminary arrangements for the establishment in Chelsea of a Moravian settlement in full working order. In those days Chelsea was a charming London suburb. From the house to the river side lay a terrace, used as a grand parade; from the bank to the water there ran a short flight of steps; and from there the pleasure-boats, with banners flying, took trippers up and down the shining river. For five years this Paradise was the headquarters of the Brethren's Church. There, in grand style, lived the Count himself, with the members of his Pilgrim Band; there the Brethren met in conference; there the archives of the Church were preserved; and there letters and reports were received from all parts of the rapidly extending mission field.

And now the Count led a new campaign in England. As debates in Parliament were not then published in full, it was always open for an enemy to say that the Brethren had obtained their privileges by means of some underhand trick; and in order to give this charge the lie, the Count now published a folio volume, entitled, "Acta Fratrum Unitatis in Anglia." In this volume he took the bull by the horns. He issued it by the advice of Wilson, Bishop of Sodor and Man. It was a thorough and comprehensive treatise, and contained all about the Moravians that an honest and inquiring Briton would need to know. The first part consisted of the principal vouchers that had been examined by the Parliamentary Committee. The next was an article, "The Whole System of the Twenty-one Doctrinal Articles of the Confession of Augsburg"; and here the Brethren set forth their doctrinal beliefs in detail. The next article was "The Brethren's Method of Preaching the Gospel, according to the Synod of Bern, 1532"; and here they explained why they preached so much about the Person and sufferings of Christ. The next article was a series of extracts from the minutes of German Synods; and here the Brethren showed what they meant by such phrases as "Sinnership" and "Blood and Wounds Theology." But the cream of the volume was Zinzendorf's treatise, "The Rationale of the Brethren's

Liturgies." He explained why the Brethren spoke so freely on certain moral matters, and contended that while they had sometimes used language which prudish people might condemn as indecent, they had done so from the loftiest motives, and had always maintained among themselves a high standard of purity. At the close of the volume was the Brethren's "Church Litany," revised by Sherlock, Bishop of London, a glossary of their religious terms, and a pathetic request that if the reader was not satisfied yet he should ask for further information. The volume was a challenge to the public. It was an honest manifesto of the Brethren's principles, a declaration that they had nothing to conceal, and a challenge to their enemies to do their worst.

The next task of Zinzendorf was to comfort the Brethren's friends. At this period, while Zinzendorf was resident in London, the whole cause of the Brethren in England was growing at an amazing pace; and in Yorkshire, Derbyshire, Bedfordshire, Cheshire, Wiltshire, Gloucestershire, Dublin, and the North of Ireland, the members of the numerous societies and preaching places were clamouring for full admission to the Moravian Church. They assumed a very natural attitude. On the one hand, they wanted to become Moravians; on the other, they objected to the system of discipline enforced so strictly in the settlements, and contended that though it might suit in Germany, it was not fit for independent Britons. But Zinzendorf gave a clear and crushing answer. For the benefit of all good Britons who wished to join the Moravian Church without accepting the Moravian discipline, he issued what he called a "Consolatory Letter"; [127] and the consolation that he gave them was that he could not consider their arguments for a moment. He informed them that the Brethren's rules were so strict that candidates could only be received with caution; that the Brethren had no desire to disturb those whose outward mode of religion was already fixed; that they lived in a mystical communion with Christ which others might not understand; and, finally, that they refused point-blank to rob the other Churches of their members, and preferred to act "as a seasonable assistant in an irreligious age, and as a most faithful servant to the other Protestant Churches." Thus were the society members blackballed; and thus did Zinzendorf prove in England that, with all his faults, he was never a schismatic or a poacher on others' preserves.

Meanwhile, the battle of the books had begun. The first blow was struck by John Wesley. For the last seven years—as his Journal shows—he had seen but little of the Brethren, and was, therefore, not in a position to pass a fair judgment on their conduct; but, on the other hand, he had seen no reason to alter his old opinion, and still regarded them as wicked Antinomians. The Act of Parliament aroused his anger. He obtained a copy of Zinzendorf's Acta Fratrum, and published a pamphlet [128] summarizing its contents, with characteristic comments of his own (1750). He signed himself "A Lover of the Light." His pamphlet was a fierce attack upon the Brethren. The very evidence that had convinced the Parliamentary Committee was a proof to Wesley that the Brethren were heretics and deceivers. He accused them of having deceived the Government and of having obtained their privileges by false pretences. He asserted that they had brought forward documents which gave an erroneous view of their principles and conduct. He hinted that Zinzendorf, in one document, claimed for himself the power, which belonged by right to the King and Parliament only, to transport his Brethren beyond the seas, and that he had deceived the Committee by using the milder word "transfer." He accused the Brethren of hypocritical pretence, threw doubts upon their assumed reluctance to steal sheep from other churches, and hinted that while they rejected the poor they welcomed the rich with open arms. At the close of his pamphlet he declared his conviction that the chief effect of the Brethren's religion was to fill the mind with absurd ideas about the Side-Wound of Christ, and rivers and seas of blood; and, therefore, he earnestly besought all Methodists who had joined the Church of the Brethren to quit their diabolical delusions, to flee from the borders of Sodom, and to leave these Brethren, loved the darkness and rejected the Holy Scriptures.

The next attack was of a milder nature. At Melbourne, in Derbyshire, the Brethren had a small society; and George Baddeley, the local curate, being naturally shocked that so many of his parishioners had ceased to attend the Parish Church, appealed to them in a pamphlet entitled, "A Kind and Friendly Letter to the People called Moravians at Melbourne, in Derbyshire." And kind and friendly the pamphlet certainly was. For the Brethren, as he knew them by personal contact, George Baddeley professed the highest respect; and all that he had to say against them was that they had helped to empty the Parish Church, and had ignorantly taught the people doctrines contrary to Holy Scripture. They made a sing-song, he complained, of the doctrine of the cleansing blood of Christ; they had driven the doctrine of imputation too far, and had spoken of Christ as a personal sinner; they had taught that Christians were as holy as God, and co-equal with Christ, that believers were not to pray, that there were no degrees in faith, and that all who had not full assurance of faith were children of the devil. The pamphlet is instructive. It was not an accurate account of the Brethren's teaching; but it shows what impression their teaching made on the mind of an evangelical country curate.

Another writer, whose name is unknown, denounced the Brethren in his pamphlet "Some Observations." He had read Zinzendorf's Acta Fratrum, was convinced that the Brethren were Papists, and feared that now the Act was passed they would spread their Popish doctrines in the colonies. For this judgment the chief evidence he summoned was a passage in the volume expounding the Brethren's doctrine of the Sacrament; and in his opinion their doctrine was so close to Transubstantiation that ordinary Protestants could not tell the difference between the two.

At Spondon, near Derby, lived Gregory Oldknow; and Gregory published a pamphlet entitled, "Serious Objections to the Pernicious Doctrines of the Moravians and Methodists." (1751) As he did not explain his point very clearly, it is hard to see what objection he had to the Brethren; but as he called them cannibals and German pickpockets, he cannot have had much respect for their personal character. At their love-feasts, he said, their chief object was to squeeze money from the poor. At some of their services they played the bass viol, and at others they did not, which plainly showed that they were unsteady in their minds. And, therefore, they were a danger to Church and State.

At Dublin, John Roche, a Churchman, published his treatise (1751), the "Moravian Heresy." His book was published by private subscription, and among the subscribers were the Archbishop of Armagh, the Bishops of Meath, Raphoe, Waterford, Clogher, Kilmore, Kildare, Derry, and Down and Connor, and several deans, archdeacons and other Irish clergymen. He denounced the Brethren as Antinomians. It is worth while noting what he meant by this term. "The moral acts of a believer," said the Brethren, "are not acts of duty that are necessary to give him a share in the merits of Christ, but acts of love which he is excited to pay the Lamb for the salvation already secured to him, if he will but unfeignedly believe it to be so. Thus every good act of a Moravian is not from a sense of duty, but from a sense of gratitude." Thus Roche denounced as Antinomian the very doctrine now commonly regarded as evangelical. He said, further, that the Moravians suffered from hideous diseases inflicted on them by the devil; but the chief interest of his book is the proof it offers of the strength of the Brethren at that time. He wrote when both Cennick and Wesley had been in Dublin; but Cennick to him seemed the really dangerous man. At first he intended to expose both Moravians and Methodists. "But," he added, "the Moravians being the more dangerous, subtle and powerful sect, and I fear will be the more obstinate, I shall treat of them first."

For the next attack the Brethren were themselves to blame. As the Brethren had sunk some thousands of pounds at Herrnhaag, they should now have endeavoured to husband their resources; and yet, at a Synod held in London, 1749, they resolved to erect choir-houses in England. At Lindsey House they sunk -L-12,000; at Fulneck, in Yorkshire they sunk thousands more; at Bedford they sunk thousands more; and meanwhile they were spending thousands more in the purchase and lease of building land, and in the support of many preachers in the rapidly increasing country congregations. And here they made an amazing business blunder. Instead of cutting their coat according to their cloth, they relied on a fictitious capital supposed to exist on the Continent. At one time John Wesley paid a visit to Fulneck, saw the buildings in course of erection, asked how the cost would be met, and received, he says, the astounding answer that the money "would come from beyond the sea."

At this point, to make matters worse, Mrs. Stonehouse, a wealthy Moravian, died; and one clause in her will was that, when her husband followed her to the grave, her property should then be devoted to the support of the Church Diaconies. Again the English Brethren made a business blunder. Instead of waiting till Mr. Stonehouse died, and the money was actually theirs, they relied upon it as prospective capital, and indulged in speculations beyond their means; and, to cut a long story short, the sad fact has to be recorded that, by the close of 1752, the Moravian Church in England was about -L-30,000 in debt. As soon as Zinzendorf heard the news, he rushed heroically to the rescue, gave security for -L-10,000, dismissed the managers of the Diaconies, and formed a new board of administration.

But the financial disease was too deep-seated to be so easily cured. The managers of the English Diaconies had been extremely foolish. They had invested -L-67,000 with one Gomez Serra, a Portuguese Jew. Gomez Serra suddenly stopped payment, the -L-67,000 was lost, and thus the Brethren's liabilities were now nearly -L-100,000 (1752). Again Zinzendorf, in generous fashion, came to the rescue of his Brethren. He acted in England exactly as he had acted at Herrnhaag. He discovered before long, to his dismay, that many of the English Brethren had invested money in the Diaconies, and that now they ran the serious danger of being imprisoned for debt. He called a meeting of the creditors, pledged himself for the whole sum, and suggested a plan whereby the debt could be paid off in four years. We must not, of course, suppose that Zinzendorf himself proposed to pay the whole -L-100,000 out of his own estates. For the present he made himself responsible, but he confidently relied on the Brethren to repay their debt to him as soon as possible. At all events, the creditors accepted his offer; and all that the Brethren needed now was time to weather the storm.

At this point George Whitefield interfered, and nearly sent the Moravian ship to the bottom (1753). He appealed to the example of Moses and Paul. As Moses, he said, had rebuked the Israelites when they made the golden calf, and as Paul had resisted Peter and Barnabas when carried away with the dissimulation of the Jews, so he, as a champion of the Church of Christ, could hold his peace no longer. He attacked the Count in a fiery pamphlet, entitled, "An Expostulatory Letter to Count Zinzendorf." The pamphlet ran to a second edition, and was circulated in Germany. He began by condemning Moravian customs as unscriptural. "Pray, my lord," he said, "what instances have we of the first Christians walking round the graves of their deceased friends on Easter-Day, attended with haut-boys, trumpets, French horns, violins and other kinds of musical instruments? Or where have we the least mention made of pictures of particular persons being brought into the first Christian assemblies, and of candles being placed behind them, in order to give a transparent view of the figures? Where was it ever known that the picture of the apostle Paul, representing him handing a gentleman and lady up to the side of Jesus Christ, was ever introduced into the primitive love-feasts? Again, my lord, I beg leave to inquire whether we hear anything of eldresses or deaconesses of the apostolical churches seating themselves before a table covered with artificial flowers, against that a little altar surrounded with wax tapers, on which stood a cross, composed either of mock or real diamonds, or other glittering stones?" As the Brethren, therefore, practised customs which had no sanction in the New Testament, George Whitefield concluded that they were encouraging Popery. At this period the Brethren were certainly fond of symbols; and on one occasion, as the London Diary records, Peter Boehler entered Fetter Lane Chapel, arrayed in a white robe to symbolize purity, and a red sash tied at the waist to symbolize the cleansing blood of Christ. But the next point in Whitefield's "letter" was cruel. At the very time when Zinzendorf was giving his money to save his English Brethren from a debtor's prison, Whitefield accused him and his Brethren alike of robbery and fraud. He declared that Zinzendorf was -L-40,000 in debt; that there was little hope that he would ever pay; that his allies were not much better; and that the Brethren had deceived the Parliamentary Committee by representing themselves as men of means. At the very time, said Whitefield, when the Moravian leaders were boasting in Parliament of their great possessions, they were really binding down their English members for thousands more than they could pay. They drew bills on tradesmen without their consent; they compelled simple folk to sell their estates, seized the money, and then sent the penniless owners abroad; and they claimed authority to say to the rich, "Either give us all thou hast, or get thee gone." For these falsehoods Whitefield claimed, no doubt quite honestly, to have good evidence; and to prove his point he quoted the case of a certain Thomas Rhodes. Poor Rhodes, said Whitefield, was one of the Brethren's victims. They had first persuaded him to sell a valuable estate; they had then seized part of his money to pay their debts; and at last they drained his stores so dry that he had to sell them his watch, bureau, horse and saddle, to fly to France, and to leave his old mother to die of starvation in England. For a while this ridiculous story was believed; and the Brethren's creditors, in a state of panic, pressed hard for their money. The little Church of the Brethren was now on the brink of ruin. At one moment Zinzendorf himself expected to be thrown into prison, and was only saved in the nick of time by the arrival of money from Germany. But the English Brethren now showed their manhood. The very men whom Zinzendorf was supposed to have robbed now rose in his defence. Instead of thanking Whitefield for defending them in their supposed distresses, they formed a committee, drew up a statement, [129] dedicated that statement to the Archbishop of York, and declared that there was not a word of truth in Whitefield's charges. They had not, they declared, been robbed by Zinzendorf and the Moravian leaders; on the contrary, they had received substantial benefits from them. Thomas Rhodes himself proved Whitefield in the wrong. He wrote a letter to his own lawyer; James Hutton published extracts from the letter, and in that letter Rhodes declared that he had sold his estate of his own free will, that the Brethren had paid a good price, and that he and his mother were living in perfect comfort. Thus was Whitefield's fiction exploded, and the Brethren's credit restored.

But the next attack was still more deadly. At the time when Whitefield wrote his pamphlet there had already appeared a book entitled "A Candid Narrative of the Rise and Progress of the Herrnhuters"; and Whitefield himself had read the book and had allowed it to poison his mind (1753). The author was Henry Rimius. [130] He had been Aulic Councillor to the King of Prussia, had met Moravians in Germany, and now lived in Oxenden Street, London. For two years this scribbler devoted his energies to an attempt to paint the Brethren in such revolting colours that the Government would expel them from the country. His method was unscrupulous and immoral. He admitted, as he had to admit, that such English Brethren as he knew were excellent people; and yet he gave the impression in his books that the whole Moravian Church was a sink of iniquity. He directed his main attack against Zinzendorf and the old fanatics at Herrnhaag; and thus he made the English Brethren suffer for the past sins of their German cousins. He accused the Brethren of deceiving the House of Commons. He would now show them up in their true colours. "No Government," he said, "that harbours them can be secure whilst their leaders go on at the rate they have done hitherto." He accused them of holding immoral principles dangerous to Church and State. They held, he said, that Christ could make the most villainous act to be virtue, and the most exalted virtue to be vice. They spoke with contempt of the Bible, and condemned Bible reading as dangerous. They denounced the orthodox theology as fit only for dogs and swine, and described the priests of other Churches as professors of the devil. They called themselves the only true Church, the Church of the Lamb, the Church of Blood and Wounds; and claimed that, on the Judgment Day, they would shine forth in all their splendour and be the angels coming in glory. At heart, however, they were not Protestants at all, but Atheists in disguise; and the real object of all their plotting was to set up a godless empire of their own. They claimed to be independent of government. They employed a secret gang of informers. They had their own magistrates, their own courts of justice, and their own secret laws. At their head was Zinzendorf, their Lord Advocate, with the authority of a Pope. As no one could join the Moravian Church without first promising to abandon the use of his reason, and submit in all things to his leaders, those leaders could guide them like little children into the most horrid enterprizes. At Herrnhaag the Brethren had established an independent state, and had robbed the Counts of Buedingen of vast sums of money; and, if they were allowed to do so, they would commit similar crimes in England. They had a fund called the Lamb's Chest, to which all their members were bound to contribute. The power of their Elders was enormous. At any moment they could marry a couple against their will, divorce them when they thought fit, tear children from their parents, and dispatch them to distant corners of the earth. But the great object of the Moravians, said Rimius, was to secure liberty for themselves to practise their sensual abominations. He supported his case by quoting freely, not only from Zinzendorf's sermons, but also from certain German hymn-books which had been published at Herrnhaag during the "Sifting Time"; and as he gave chapter and verse for his statements, he succeeded in covering the Brethren with ridicule. He accused them of blasphemy and indecency. They spoke of Christ as a Tyburn bird, as digging for roots, as vexed by an aunt, and as sitting in the beer-house among the scum of society. They sang hymns to the devil. They revelled in the most hideous and filthy expressions, chanted the praises of lust and sensuality, and practised a number of sensual abominations too loathsome to be described. At one service held in Fetter Lane, Count Zinzendorf, said Rimius, had declared that the seventh commandment was not binding on Christians, and had recommended immorality to his congregation. [131] It is impossible to give the modern reader a true idea of the shocking picture of the Brethren painted by Rimius. For malice, spite, indecency and unfairness, his works would be hard to match even in the vilest literature of the eighteenth century. As his books came out in rapid succession, the picture he drew grew more and more disgusting. He wrote in a racy, sometimes jocular style; and, knowing the dirty taste of the age, he pleased his public by retailing anecdotes as coarse as any in the "Decameron." His chief object was probably to line his own pockets. His first book, "The Candid Narrative," sold well. But his attack was mean and unjust. It is true that he quoted quite correctly from the silly literature of the Sifting-Time; but he carefully omitted to state the fact that that literature had now been condemned by the Brethren themselves, and that only a few absurd stanzas had appeared in English. At the same time, in the approved fashion of all scandal-mongers, he constantly gave a false impression by tearing passages from their original connection. As an attack on the English Brethren, his work was dishonest. He had no solid evidence to bring against them. From first to last he wrote almost entirely of the fanatics at Herrnhaag, and fathered their sins upon the innocent Brethren in England.

Meanwhile, however, a genuine eye-witness was telling a terrible tale. He named his book (1753), "The True and Authentic Account of Andrew Frey." For four years, he said, he lived among the Brethren in Germany, travelled about helping to form societies, and settled down at Marienborn, when the fanaticism there was in full bloom. He was known among the Brethren as Andrew the Great. As he wore a long beard, he was considered rather eccentric. At Marienborn he saw strange sights and heard strange doctrine. At their feasts the Brethren ate like gluttons and drank till they were tipsy. "All godliness, all devotion, all piety," said Rubusch, the general Elder of all the Single Brethren on the Continent, "are no more than so many snares of the devil. Things must be brought to this pass in the community, that nothing shall be spoken of but wounds, wounds, wounds. All other discourse, however Scriptural and pious, must be spued out and trampled under foot." Another, Vieroth, a preacher in high repute among the Brethren, said, in a sermon at Marienborn castle church: "Nothing gives the devil greater joy than to decoy into good works, departing from evil, shalling and willing, trying, watching and examining those souls who have experienced anything of the Saviour's Grace in their hearts." Another, Calic, had defended self-indulgence. "Anyone," he said, "having found lodging, bed and board in the Lamb's wounds cannot but be merry and live according to nature; so that when such a one plays any pranks that the godly ones cry out against them as sins, the Saviour is so far from being displeased therewith that he rejoices the more." In vain Frey endeavoured to correct these cross-air birds; they denounced him as a rogue. He appealed to Zinzendorf, and found to his dismay that the Count was as depraved as the rest. "Do not suffer yourselves to be molested in your merriment," said that trumpet of Satan; and others declared that the Bible was dung, and only fit to be trampled under foot. At last Andrew, disgusted beyond all measure, could restrain his soul no longer; and telling the Brethren they were the wickedest sect that had appeared since the days of the Apostles, and profoundly thankful that their gilded poison had not killed his soul, he turned his back on them for ever. [132]

The next smiter of the Brethren was Lavington, Bishop of Exeter. He called his book "The Moravians Compared and Detected." He had already denounced the Methodists in his "Enthusiasm of Methodists and Papists Compared" (1754); and now he described the Brethren as immoral characters, fitted to enter a herd of swine. In a pompous introduction he explained his purpose, and that purpose was the suppression of the "Brethren's Church in England." "With respect to the settlement of the Moravians in these kingdoms," he said, "it seems to have been surreptitiously obtained, under the pretence of their being a peaceable and innocent sort of people. And peaceable probably they will remain while they are permitted, without control, to ruin families and riot in their debaucheries." Of all the attacks upon the Brethren, this book by Lavington was the most offensive and scurrilous; and the Brethren themselves could hardly believe that it was written by a Bishop. It was unfit for a decent person to read. The good Bishop knew nothing of his subject. As he could not read the German language, he had to rely for his information on the English editions of the works of Rimius and Frey; and all he did was to collect in one volume the nastiest passages in their indictments, compare the Brethren with certain queer sects of the Middle Ages, and thus hold them up before the public as filthy dreamers and debauchees of the vilest order.

And now, to give a finishing touch to the picture, John Wesley arose once more (1755). He, too, had swallowed the poison of Rimius and Frey, and a good deal of other poison as well. At Bedford a scandal-monger informed him that the Brethren were the worst paymasters in the town; and at Holbeck another avowed that the Brethren whom he had met in Yorkshire were quite as bad as Rimius had stated. As Wesley printed these statements in his journal they were soon read in every county in England. But Wesley himself did not assert that these statements were true. He wished, he said, to be quite fair to the Brethren; he wished to give them a chance of clearing themselves; and, therefore, he now published his pamphlet entitled "Queries to Count Zinzendorf." It contained the whole case in a nutshell. For the sum of sixpence the ordinary reader had now the case against the Brethren in a popular and handy form.

Thus the Brethren, attacked from so many sides, were bound to bestir themselves in self-defence. The burden of reply fell on Zinzendorf. His life and conversation were described as scandalous; his hymns were denounced as filthy abominations, and his discourses as pleas for immorality; and the Brethren for whose sake he had sacrificed his fortune were held up before the British public as political conspirators, atheists, robbers of the poor, kidnappers of children, ruiners of families, and lascivious lovers of pleasure. But the Count was a busy man. James Hutton says that he worked on the average eighteen hours a day. He was constantly preaching, writing, relieving the distressed, paying other people's debts, and providing the necessaries of life for a hundred ministers of the Gospel. He had dealt with similar accusations in Germany, had published a volume containing a thousand answers to a thousand questions, and was loth to go over the whole ground again. For some time he clung to the hope that the verdict of Parliament and the common sense of Englishmen would be sufficient protection against abuse; and he gallantly defended the character of Rimius, and spoke with generous enthusiasm of Whitefield. The best friends of the Brethren, such as Lord Granville and the Bishops of London and Worcester, advised them to treat Rimius with contemptuous silence. But a reply became a necessity. As long as the Brethren remained silent, their enemies asserted that this very silence was a confession of guilt; and some mischievous scoundrel, in the name, but without the consent, of the Brethren, inserted a notice in the General Advertiser that they intended to reply to Rimius in detail. For these reasons, therefore, Zinzendorf, James Hutton, Frederick Neisser, and others who preferred to write anonymously, now issued a series of defensive pamphlets. [133] The Count offered to lay before the public a full statement of his financial affairs; and James Hutton, in a notice in several newspapers, promised to answer any reasonable questions. It is needless to give the Brethren's defence in detail. The plain facts of the case were beyond all dispute. In two ways the accusations of Rimius and Frey were out of court. First they accused the whole Church of the Brethren of sins which had only been committed by a few fanatics at Marienborn and Herrnhaag; and, secondly, that fanaticism had practically ceased before the Act of Parliament was passed. The Count here stood upon firm ground. He pointed out that the accusers of the Brethren had nearly always taken care to go to the Wetterau for their material; and he contended that it was a shame to blame innocent Englishmen for the past sins, long ago abandoned, of a few foreign fanatics. He appealed confidently to the public. "We are so well known to our neighbours," he said, "that all our clearing ourselves of accusations appears to them quite needless." In reply to the charge of using indecent language, he contended that his purpose was good, and justified by the results; and that, as soon as he found himself misunderstood, he had cut out all doubtful phrases from his discourses.

James Hutton explained their use of childish language. At this period the Brethren, in some of their hymns, used a number of endearing epithets which would strike the modern reader as absurd. For example, they spoke of the little Lamb, the little Jesus, the little Cross-air Bird. But even here they were not so childish as their critics imagined. The truth was, these phrases were Bohemian in origin. In the Bohemian language diminutives abound. In Bohemia a servant girl is addressed as "demercko" —i.e., little, little maid; and the literal translation of "mug mily Bozicko" —a phrase often used in public worship—is "my dear, little, little God."

But the Brethren had a better defence than writing pamphlets. Instead of taking too much notice of their enemies, they began to set their English house in order. For the first time they now published an authorized collection of English Moravian hymns (1754); and in the preface they clearly declared their purpose. The purpose was twofold: first, the proclamation of the Gospel; second, the cultivation of personal holiness. If we judge this book by modern standards, we shall certainly find it faulty; but, on the other hand, it must be remembered that it rendered a very noble service to the Christianity of the eighteenth century. The chief burden of the hymns was Ecce Homo. If the Brethren had never done anything else, they had at least placed the sufferings of Christ in the forefront of their message. With rapturous enthusiasm the Brethren depicted every detail of the Passion History; and thus they reminded their hearers of events which ordinary Christians had almost forgotten. At times the language they used was gruesome; and, lost in mystic adoration, the Brethren, in imagination, trod the Via Dolorosa. They nestled in the nail-prints; they kissed the spear; they gazed with rapt and holy awe on the golden head, the raven locks, the pallid cheeks, the foaming lips, the melting eyes, the green wreath of thorns, the torn sinews, the great blue wounds, and the pierced palms, like rings of gold, beset with rubies red. In one stanza they abhorred themselves as worms; in the next they rejoiced as alabaster doves; and, glorying in the constant presence of the Well-Beloved, they feared not the King of Terrors, and calmly sang of death as "the last magnetic kiss, to consummate their bliss." But, despite its crude and extravagant language, this hymn-book was of historic importance. At that time the number of hymn-books in England was small; the Anglicans had no hymn-book at all, and never sang anything but Psalms; and thus the Brethren were among the first to make the adoration of Christ in song an essential part of public worship. It was here that the Brethren excelled, and here that they helped to free English Christianity from the chilling influence of Deism. The whole point was quaintly expressed by Bishop John Gambold:—

The Doctrine of the Unitas
By Providence was meant,
In Christendom's degenerate days,
That cold lump to ferment,
From Scripture Pearls to wipe the dust,
Give blood-bought grace its compass just,
In praxis, truth from shew to part,
God's Power from Ethic Art.

But the last line must not be misunderstood. It did not mean that the Brethren despised ethics. Of all the charges brought against them, the charge that they were Antinomians was the most malicious and absurd. At the very time when their enemies were accusing them of teaching that good works were of no importance, they inserted in their Litany for Sunday morning worship a number of petitions which were alone enough to give that charge the lie. The petitions were as follows:—

O! that we might never see a necessitous person go unrelieved!
O! that we might see none suffer for want of clothing!
O! that we might be eyes to the blind and feet to the lame!
O! that we could refresh the heart of the Fatherless!
O! that we could mitigate the burden of the labouring man, and be ourselves not ministered unto but minister!
Feed its with that princely repast of solacing others!
O! that the blessing of him who was ready to perish might come upon us!
Yea! may our hearts rejoice to see it go well with our enemies.

Again, therefore, as in their hymns, the Brethren laid stress on the humane element in Christianity. [134]

But their next retort to their enemies was the grandest of all. At a Synod held in Lindsey House, they resolved that a Book of Statutes was needed, and requested Zinzendorf to prepare one (1754). The Count was in a quandary. He could see that a Book of Statutes was required, but he could not decide what form it should take. If he framed the laws in his own language, his critics would accuse him of departing from the Scriptures; and if he used the language of Scripture, the same critics would accuse him of hedging and of having some private interpretation of the Bible. At length he decided to use the language of Scripture. He was so afraid of causing offence that, Greek scholar though he was, he felt bound to adhere to the Authorised Version. If Zinzendorf had used his own translation his enemies would have accused him of tampering with the Word of God. The book appeared. It was entitled, Statutes: or the General Principles of Practical Christianity, extracted out of the New Testament. It was designed for the use of all English Moravians, and was sanctioned and adopted by the Synod on May 12th, 1755. It was thorough and systematic. For fathers and mothers, for sons and daughters, for masters and servants, for governors and governed, for business men, for bishops and pastors, the appropriate commandments were selected from the New Testament. In a printed notice on the title page, the Brethren explained their own interpretation of those commandments. "Lest it should be thought," they said, "that they seek, perhaps, some subterfuge in the pretended indeterminate nature of Scripture-style, they know very well that it becomes them to understand every precept and obligation in the same manner as the generality of serious Christians understand the same (and this is a thing, God be praised, pretty well fixed), or, if at all differently, then always stricter." The purpose of the book was clear. It was a handy guide to daily conduct. It was meant to be learned by heart, and was issued in such size and form that it could be carried about in the pocket. It was "a faithful monitor to souls who, having been first washed through the blood of Jesus, do now live in the Spirit, to walk also in the Spirit." To the Brethren this little Christian guide was a treasure. As long as they ordered their daily conduct by these "convenient rules for the house of their pilgrimage," they could smile at the sneers of Rimius and his supporters. The Moravian influence in England was now at high tide. At the very time when their enemies were denouncing them as immoral Antinomians, they established their strongest congregations at Fulneck, Gomersal, Wyke, Mirfield, Dukinfield, Bristol, and Gracehill (1755); and in all their congregations the "Statutes" were enforced with an iron hand.

Thus did the Brethren repel the attacks of their assailants. From this chapter one certain conclusion follows. The very fact that the Brethren were so fiercely attacked is a proof how strong they were. As the reader wanders over England, he may see, if he knows where to look, memorials of their bygone labours. In Northampton is an auction room that was once a Moravian chapel. In Bullock Smithy is a row of cottages named "Chapel Houses," where now the Brethren are forgotten. In a private house at Bolton, Lancashire, will be found a cupboard that was once a Moravian Pulpit. In Wiltshire stands the "two o'clock chapel," where Cennick used to preach. We may learn much from such memorials as these. We may learn that the Brethren played a far greater part in the Evangelical Revival than most historians have recognised; that they worked more like the unseen leaven than like the spreading mustard tree; that they hankered not after earthly pomp, and despised what the world calls success; and that, reviled, insulted, and misrepresented, they pursued their quiet way, content with the reward which man cannot give.

Chapter 14: The American Experiments (1734-1762)

IN order to have a clear view of the events recorded in this chapter, we must bear in mind that the Brethren worked according to a definite Plan; they generally formed their "Plan" by means of the Lot; and this "Plan," speaking broadly, was of a threefold nature. The Brethren had three ideals: First, they were not sectarians. Instead of trying to extend the Moravian Church at the expense of other denominations, they consistently endeavoured, wherever they went, to preach a broad and comprehensive Gospel, to avoid theological disputes, to make peace between the sects, and to unite Christians of all shades of belief in common devotion to a common Lord. Secondly, by establishing settlements, they endeavoured to unite the secular and the sacred. At these settlements they deliberately adopted, for purely religious purposes, a form of voluntary religious socialism. They were not, however, socialists or communists by conviction; they had no desire to alter the laws of property; and they established their communistic organization, not from any political motives, but because they felt that, for the time at least, it would be the most economical, would foster Christian fellowship, would sanctify daily labour, and would enable them, poor men though they were, to find ways and means for the spread of the Gospel. And thirdly, the Brethren would preach that Gospel to all men, civilized or savage, who had not heard it before. With these three ideals before us, we trace their footsteps in North America.

The first impulse sprang from the kindness of Zinzendorf's heart. At Goerlitz, a town a few miles from Herrnhut, there dwelt a small body of Schwenkfelders; and the King of Saxony issued an edict banishing them from his dominions (1733). As soon as Zinzendorf heard of their troubles he longed to find them a home. He opened negotiations with the trustees of the Colony of Georgia. The negotiations were successful. The Governor of Georgia, General Oglethorpe, was glad to welcome good workmen; a parcel of land was offered, and the poor Schwenkfelders, accompanied by Boehnisch, a Moravian Brother, set off for their American home. For some reason, however, they changed their minds on the way, and, instead of settling down in Georgia, went on to Pennsylvania. The land in Georgia was now crying out for settlers. At Herrnhut trouble was brewing. If the spirit of persecution continued raging, the Brethren themselves might soon be in need of a home. The Count took time by the forelock. As soon as the storm burst over Herrnhut, the Brethren might have to fly; and, therefore, he now sent Spangenberg to arrange terms with General Oglethorpe. Again the negotiations were successful; the General offered the Brethren a hundred acres; and a few weeks later, led by Spangenberg, the first batch of Moravian colonists arrived in Georgia (1734). The next batch was the famous company on the Simmonds. The new settlement was on the banks of the Savannah River. For some years, with Spangenberg as general manager, the Brethren tried to found a flourishing farm colony. The learned Spangenberg was a practical man. In spite of the fact that he had been a University lecturer, he now put his hand to the plough like a labourer to the manner born. He was the business agent; he was the cashier; he was the spiritual leader; he was the architect; and he was the medical adviser. As the climate of Georgia was utterly different from the climate of Saxony, he perceived at once that the Brethren would have to be careful in matters of diet, and rather astonished the Sisters by giving them detailed instructions about the cooking of rice and beef. The difference between him and Zinzendorf was enormous. At St. Croix, a couple of years before, a band of Moravian Missionaries had died of fever; and while Zinzendorf immortalized their exploits in a hymn, the practical Spangenberg calmly considered how such heroic tragedies could be prevented in the future. In political matters he was equally far-seeing. As the Brethren were now in an English colony, it was, he said, their plain duty to be naturalized as Englishmen as soon as possible; and, therefore, in a letter to Zinzendorf, he implored him to become a British subject himself, to secure for the Brethren the rights of English citizens, and, above all, if possible to obtain letters patent relieving the Brethren from the obligation to render military service. But on Zinzendorf all this wisdom was thrown away. Already the ruin of the colony was in sight. At the very time when the Brethren's labours should have been crowned with success, Captain Jenkins, at the bar of the House of Commons, was telling how his ear had been cut off by Spaniards (1738). The great war between England and Spain broke out. The chief aim of Spain was to destroy our colonial supremacy in America. Spanish soldiers threatened Georgia. The Brethren were summoned to take to arms and help to defend the colony against the foe. But the Brethren objected to taking arms at all. The farm colony was abandoned; and the scene shifts to Pennsylvania.

Meanwhile, the good Spangenberg had been busy in Pennsylvania, looking after the interests of the Schwenkfelders. He attended their meetings, wore their clothing—a green coat, without buttons or pockets—studied the works of Schwenkfeld, and organized them into what he called an "Economy." In other words, he taught them to help each other by joining in common work on a communist basis. At the same time, he tried to teach them to be a little more broad-minded, and not to quarrel so much with other Christians. But the more he talked of brotherly love the more bigoted the poor Schwenkfelders became. At this time the colony had become a nest of fanatics. For some years, in response to the generous offers of Thomas Penn, all sorts of persecuted refugees had fled to Pennsylvania; and now the land was infested by a motley group of Episcopalians, Quakers, Baptists, Separatists, Sabbatarians, Unitarians, Lutherans, Calvinists, Memnonites, Presbyterians, Independents, Inspired Prophets, Hermits, Newborn Ones, Dunckers, and Protestant Monks and Nuns. Thus the land was filled with "religions" and almost empty of religion. Instead of attending to the spiritual needs of the people, each Church or sect was trying to prove itself in the right and all the others in the wrong; and the only principle on which they agreed was the principle of disagreeing with each other.

The result was heathendom and babel. Most of the people attended neither church nor chapel; most of the parents were unbaptized, and brought up their children in ignorance; and, according to a popular proverb of the day, to say that a man professed the Pennsylvania religion was a polite way of calling him an infidel.

As soon, therefore, as Zinzendorf heard from Spangenberg of these disgraceful quarrels a glorious vision rose before his mind; and the conviction flashed upon him that Pennsylvania was the spot where the Brethren's broad evangel was needed most. There, in the midst of the quarrelling sects he would plant the lily of peace; there, where the cause of unity seemed hopeless, he would realize the prayer of Christ, "that they all may be one." For two reason, America seemed to him the true home of the ideal Church of the Brethren. First, there was no State Church; and, therefore, whatever line he took, he could not be accused of causing a schism. Secondly, there was religious liberty; and, therefore, he could work out his ideas without fear of being checked by edicts. For these reasons he first sent out another batch of colonists, led by Bishop Nitschmann; and then, in due time, he arrived on the scene himself. The first move had the promise of good. At the spot the Lehigh and the Monocany meet the Brethren had purchased a plot of ground (1741}; they all lived together in one log-house; they proposed to build a settlement like Herrnhut; and there, one immortal Christmas Eve, Count Zinzendorf conducted a consecration service. Above them shone the keen, cold stars, God's messengers of peace; around them ranged the babel of strife; and the Count, remembering how the Prince of Peace had been born in a humble wayside lodging, named the future settlement Bethlehem. The name had a twofold meaning. It was a token of the Brethren's mission of peace; and it reminded them that the future settlement was to be a "House of Bread" for their evangelists.

The Count was now in his element. For two years he did his best to teach the quarrelling sects in Pennsylvania to help and esteem each other; and the bond of union he set before them was a common experience of the redeeming grace of Christ. He had come to America, not as a Moravian Bishop, but as a Lutheran clergyman; and he was so afraid of being suspected of sectarian motives that, before he set out from London, he had purposely laid his episcopal office aside. For some months, therefore, he now acted as Lutheran clergyman to a Lutheran congregation in Philadelphia; and meanwhile he issued a circular, inviting German Christians of all denominations to meet in Conference. His purpose, to use his own phrase, was to establish a grand "Congregation of God in the Spirit." At first the outlook was hopeful. From all sects deputies came, and a series of "Pennsylvanian Synods" was held. Again, however, the Count was misled by his own ignorance of history. At this time he held the erroneous view that the Union of Sendomir in Poland (1570) was a beautiful union of churches brought about by the efforts of the Brethren; he imagined also that the Bohemian Confession (1575) had been drawn up by the Brethren; and, therefore, he very naturally concluded that what the Brethren had accomplished in Poland and Bohemia they could accomplish again in Pennsylvania. But the stern facts of the case were all against him. At the very time when he was endeavouring to establish a "Congregation of God in the Spirit" in Pennsylvania, he heard that his own Brethren in Germany were departing from his ideals; and, therefore, he had to return to Germany, and hand on his American work to Spangenberg (1743).

For that task the broad-minded Spangenberg was admirably fitted, and now he held a number of titles supposed to define his mission. First, he was officially appointed "General Elder" in America; second, he was consecrated a Bishop, and was thus head of the American Moravian Church; and third, he was "Vicarius generalis episcoporum"; i.e., General Vicar of the Bishops. For the next four years the Pennsylvania Synods, with the broad-minded Spangenberg as President, continued to meet with more or less regularity. In 1744 they met twice; in 1745 three times; in 1746 four times; in 1747 three times; and in 1748 twice. But gradually the Synods altered in character. At first representatives attended from a dozen different bodies; then only Lutherans, Calvinists and Moravians; then only Moravians; and at length, when John de Watteville arrived upon the scene, he found that for all intents and purposes the Pennsylvanian Synod had become a Synod of the Moravian Church. He recognized the facts of the case, abolished the "Congregation of the Spirit," and laid the constitutional foundations of the Brethren's Church in North America (1748). Thus Zinzendorf's scheme of union collapsed, and the first American experiment was a failure.

Meanwhile, Bishop Spangenberg had been busy with the second. If this man was inferior to Zinzendorf in genius he was far above him as a practical politician. He now accomplished his "Masterpiece." [135] The task before him was twofold. He had to find both men and money; and from the first he bravely resolved to do without one penny of assistance from Germany. He called his plan the "Economy," and an economical plan it certainly was. His great principle was subdivision of labour. As the work in America was mostly among poor people—some immigrants, others Red Indians—he perceived that special measures must be taken to cover expenses; and, therefore, he divided his army into two main bodies. The one was the commissariat department; the other was the fighting line. The one was engaged in manual labour; the other was preaching the gospel. The one was stationed chiefly at Bethlehem; the other was scattered in different parts of North America. About ten miles north-west of Bethlehem the Brethren purchased a tract of land from George Whitefield, gave it the name of Nazareth, and proposed to build another settlement there. At first the two settlements were practically worked as one. For eighteen years they bore between them almost the whole financial burden of the Brethren's work in North America. There, at the joint settlement of Bethlehem-Nazareth, the "Economy" was established. There lay the general "camp"; there stood the home of "the Pilgrim Band"; there was built the "School of the Prophets"; there, to use Spangenberg's vivid phrase, was the "Saviour's Armoury." The great purpose which the Brethren set before them was to preach the Gospel in America without making the American people pay. Instead of having their preachers supported by contributions from their congregations, they would support these preachers themselves. For this task the only capital that Spangenberg possessed was two uncultivated tracts of land, three roomy dwelling-houses, two or three outhouses and barns, his own fertile genius, and a body of

Brethren and Sisters willing to work. His method of work was remarkable. In order, first, to cut down the expenses of living, he asked his workers then and there to surrender the comforts of family life. At Bethlehem stood two large houses. In one lived all the Single Brethren; in the other the families, all the husbands in one part, all the wives in another, all the children (under guardians) in the third. At Nazareth there was only one house; and there lived all the Single Sisters. As the Sisters set off through the forest to their home in Nazareth, they carried their spinning-wheels on their shoulders; and two hours after their arrival in the house they were driving their wheels with zeal. At Bethlehem the energy of all was amazing. Bishop Spangenberg was commonly known as Brother Joseph; and Brother Joseph, in a letter to Zinzendorf, explained the purpose of his scheme. "As Paul," he said, "worked with his own hands, so as to be able to preach the Gospel without pay, so we, according to our ability, will do the same; and thus even a child of four will be able, by plucking wool, to serve the Gospel."

For patient devotion and heroic self-sacrifice these humble toilers at the Bethlehem-Nazareth "Economy" are unsurpassed in the history of the Brethren's Church. They built their own houses; they made their own clothes and boots; they tilled the soil and provided their own meat, vegetables, bread, milk, and eggs; they sawed their own wood, spun their own yarn, and wove their own cloth; and then, selling at the regular market price what was not required for their personal use, they spent the profits in the support of preachers, teachers, and missionaries in various parts of North America. For a motto they took the words: "In commune oramus, in commune laboramus, in commune patimur, in commune gaudeamus"; i.e., together we pray, together we labour, together we suffer, together we rejoice. The motive, however, was not social, but religious. "It is nothing," said Spangenberg himself, "but love to the Lamb and His Church." For this cause the ploughman tilled the soil, the women sewed, the joiner sawed, the blacksmith plied his hammer; for this cause the fond mothers, with tears in their eyes, handed over their children to the care of guardians, so that they themselves might be free to toil for the Master. Thus every trade was sanctified; and thus did all, both old and young, spend all their powers for the Gospel's sake. If there is any distinction between secular and sacred, that distinction was unknown at Bethlehem and Nazareth. At Bethlehem the Brethren accounted it an honour to chop wood for the Master's sake; and the fireman, said Spangenberg, felt his post as important "as if he were guarding the Ark of the Covenant." For the members of each trade or calling a special series of services was arranged; and thus every toiler was constantly reminded that he was working not for himself but for God. The number of lovefeasts was enormous. At the opening of the harvest season the farm labourers held an early morning lovefeast; the discourse was partly on spiritual topics and partly on rules of diet; then the sickles were handed out; and the whole band, with hymns of praise on their lips, set off for the harvest field. For days at a time the Single Brethren would be in the forest felling trees; but before they set off they had a lovefeast, and when they returned they had another. As soon as the joiners had the oil-mill ready they celebrated the event in a lovefeast. The spinners had a lovefeast once a week. The joiners, the weavers, the cartwrights, the smiths, the hewers of wood, the milkers of cows, the knitters, the sewers, the cooks, the washerwomen—all had their special lovefeasts. At one time the joyful discovery was made that a Brother had served a year in the kitchen, and was ready to serve another; and thereupon the whole settlement held a general lovefeast in his honour. For the mothers a special meeting was held, at which an expert gave instructions on the art of bringing up children; and at this meeting, while the lecturer discoursed or occasional hymns were sung, the women were busy with their hands. One made shoes, another tailored, another ground powder for the chemist's shop, another copied invoices and letters, another sliced turnips, another knitted socks. For each calling special hymns were composed and sung. If these hymns had been published in a volume we should have had a Working-man's Hymnbook. Thus every man and woman at Bethlehem-Nazareth had enlisted in the missionary army. Never, surely, in the history of Protestant Christianity were the secular and the sacred more happily wedded. "In our Economy," said Spangenberg, "the spiritual and physical are as closely united as a man's body and soul; and each has a marked effect upon the other." If a man lost his touch with Christ it was noticed that he was careless in his work; but as long as his heart was right with God his eye was clear and his hand steady and firm. At the head of the whole concern stood Spangenberg, a business man to the finger tips. If genius is a capacity for taking pains, then Spangenberg was a genius of the finest order. He drew up regulations dealing with every detail of the business, and at his office he kept a strict account of every penny expended, every yard of linen woven, every pound of butter made, and every egg consumed. As long as Spangenberg was on the spot the business arrangements were perfect; he was assisted by a Board of Directors, known as the Aufseher Collegium; and so great was the enterprise shown that before the close of his first period of administration the Brethren had several farms and thirty-two industries in full working order. It was this which impressed our House of Commons, and enabled them, in the Act of 1749, to recognize the Brethren "as a sober and industrious people." For that Act the credit must be given, not to the airy dreams of Zinzendorf, but to the solid labours of Spangenberg. At the time when the Bill was under discussion the chief stress was laid, in both Houses, on the results of Spangenberg's labours; and so deeply was Earl Granville impressed that he offered the Brethren a hundred thousand acres in North Carolina. At length, accompanied by five other Brethren, Spangenberg himself set off to view the land, selected a site, organized another "Economy," established two congregations, named Bethabara and Bethany, and thus became the founder of the Southern Province of the Brethren's Church in America.

But his greatest success was in the Northern Province. For many years the Brethren at Bethlehem-Nazareth maintained nearly all the preachers in North America. In Pennsylvania they had preachers at Germantown, Philadelphia, Lancaster, York, Donegal, Heidelberg, Lebanon, Lititz, Oley, Allemaengel, Emmaus, Salisbury, Falkner's Swamp, the Trappe, Mahanatawny, Neshaminy, and Dansbury. In Maryland they had a station at Graceham. In Jersey they had stations at Maurice River, Racoon, Penn's Neck,

Oldman's Creek, Pawlin's Hill, Walpack, and Brunswick; in Rhode Island, at Newport; in Maine, at Broadbay; in New York, at Canajoharie; and other stations at Staten Island and Long Island. They opened fifteen schools for poor children; they paid the travelling expenses of missionaries to Surinam and the West Indies; they maintained a number of missionaries to the Red Indians. Thus did Spangenberg, by means of his "Economy," establish the Moravian Church in North America. We must not misunderstand his motives. He never made his system compulsory, and he never intended it to last. If any Brother objected to working for the "Economy," and preferred to trade on his own account, he was free to do so; and as soon as the "Economy" had served its purpose it was abolished by Spangenberg himself (1762). It is easy to object that his system interfered with family life. It is easy to say that this Moravian Bishop had no right to split families into sections, to herd the husbands in one abode and the wives in another, to tear children from their mothers' arms and place them under guardians. But Brother Joseph had his answer to this objection. At Bethlehem, he declared, the members of the "Economy" were as happy as birds in the sunshine; and, rejoicing in their voluntary sacrifice, they vowed that they would rather die than resign this chance of service. The whole arrangement was voluntary. Not a man or woman was pressed into the service. If a man joins the volunteers he is generally prepared, for the time being, to forego the comforts of family life, and these gallant toilers of the "Economy" were volunteers for God.

Another feature of Spangenberg's work was his loyalty as a British citizen. As long as he was resident in a British Colony he considered it his duty, German though he was, to stand by the British flag; and while that famous war was raging which ended in the brilliant capture of Quebec, and the conquest of Canada, Brother Joseph and the Moravian Brethren upheld the British cause from first to last. The Red Indians were nearly all on the side of France. As the Brethren, therefore, preached to the Indians, they were at first suspected of treachery, and were even accused of inciting the Indians to rebellion; but Spangenberg proved their loyalty to the hilt. At Gnadenhuetten, on the Mahony River, the Brethren had established a Mission Station (1755); and there, one night, as they sat at supper, they heard the farm dogs set up a warning barking.

"It occurs to me," said Brother Senseman, "that the Congregation House is still open; I will go and lock it; there may be stragglers from the militia in the neighbourhood." And out he went.

At that moment, while Senseman was about his duty, the sound of footsteps was heard; the Brethren opened the door; and there stood a band of painted Indians, with rifles in their hands. The war-whoop was raised. The first volley was fired. John Nitschmann fell dead on the spot. As the firing continued, the Brethren and Sisters endeavoured to take refuge in the attic; but before they could all clamber up the stairs five others had fallen dead. The Indians set fire to the building. The fate of the missionaries was sealed. As the flames arose, one Brother managed to escape by a back door, another let himself down from the window, another was captured, scalped alive, and left to die; and the rest, huddled in the blazing garret, were roasted to death.

"Dear Saviour, it is well," said Mrs. Senseman, as the cruel flames lapped round her; "it is well! It is what I expected."

No longer could the Brethren's loyalty be doubted; and Spangenberg acted, on behalf of the British, with the skill of a military expert. As he went about in his regimentals his critics remarked that he looked far more like an army officer than an apostle of the Lord. For him the problem to solve was, how to keep the Indians at bay; and he actually advised the British authorities to construct a line of forts, pointed out the strategic importance of Gnadenhuetten, and offered the land for military purposes. At Bethlehem and the other Brethren's settlements he had sentinels appointed and barricades constructed; at all specially vulnerable points he had blockhouses erected; and the result was that the Brethren's settlements were among the safest places in the country. At Bethlehem the Brethren sheltered six hundred fugitives. The plans of Spangenberg were successful. Not a single settlement was attacked. In spite of the war and the general unsettlement, the business of the "Economy" went on as usual; the Brethren labouring in the harvest field were protected by loyal Indians; and amid the panic the Brethren founded another settlement at Lititz. Thus did Spangenberg, in a difficult situation, act with consummate wisdom; and thus did he set an example of loyalty for Moravian missionaries to follow in days to come.

And yet, despite his wisdom and zeal, the Moravian Church at this period did not spread rapidly in America. For this, Zinzendorf was largely to blame. If the Count had been a good business man, and if he had realized the importance of the American work, he would have left the management of that work entirely in Spangenberg's hands. But his treatment of Spangenberg was peculiar. At first he almost ignored his existence, and broke his heart by not answering his letters (1744-48); and then, when he found himself in trouble, and affairs at Herrnhaag were coming to a crisis, he sent John de Watteville in hot haste to Bethlehem, summoned Spangenberg home, and kept him busy writing ponderous apologies. As soon as Spangenberg had completed his task, and done his best to clear Zinzendorf's character, he set off for Bethlehem again, and established the Brethren's cause in North Carolina; but before he had been two years at work the Count was in financial difficulties, and summoned him home once more (1753). His last stay in America was his longest (1754-1762). He was still there when Zinzendorf died. As soon as Zinzendorf was laid in his grave the Brethren in Germany formed a Board of Management; but, before long, they discovered that they could not do without Spangenberg. He left America for ever. And thus Brother Joseph was lost to America because he was indispensable in Germany.

The second cause of failure was the system of management. For the most part the men who took Spangenberg's place in America—such as John de Watteville and John Nitschmann—were obsessed with Zinzendorf's ideas about settlements; and, instead of turning the numerous preaching places into independent congregations they centralized the work round the four chief settlements of Bethlehem, Nazareth, Lititz and Salem. We have seen how the settlement system worked in England. It had precisely the same result in America.

The third cause of failure was financial complications. As long as Spangenberg was on the spot he kept the American finances independent; but when he left for the last time the American Province was placed under the direct control of the General Directing Board in Germany, the American and German finances were mixed, the accounts became hopelessly confused, and American affairs were mismanaged. It is obvious, on the face of it, that a Directing Board with its seat in Germany was incapable of managing efficiently a difficult work four thousand miles away; and yet that was the system pursued for nearly a hundred years (1762-1857).

We come now to the brightest part of our American story—the work among the Red Indians. At this period almost the whole of North America was the home of numerous Indian tribes. Along the upper valley of the Tennessee River, and among the grand hills of Georgia, Alabama, and Western Alabama were the Cherokees. In Mississippi were the Natchez; near the town of Augusta the Uchies; between the Tennessee and the Ohio, the Mobilians; in Central Carolina, the Catawbas; to the west of the Mississippi the Dahcotas; in New England, New Jersey, Maryland, Virginia, and the region stretching to the great lakes, the Delawares; and finally, in New York, Pennsylvania, and the region enclosed by Lakes Huron, Erie, and Ontario, the Iroquois. Thus, the Brethren in America were surrounded by Indian tribes; and to those Indian tribes they undertook to preach the Gospel.

The first step was taken by Christian Henry Rauch. As soon as he arrived in Pennsylvania he offered himself for the Indian Mission, went to the Indian town of Shekomeko (1740), and began to preach the Gospel in a manner which became famous in Moravian history. First, at a Conference in Bethlehem, the story was told by Tschoop, one of his earliest converts; and then it was officially quoted by Spangenberg, as a typical example of the Brethren's method of preaching. "Brethren," said Tschoop, "I have been a heathen, and grown old among the heathen; therefore I know how the heathen think. Once a preacher came and began to explain that there was a God. We answered, Dost thou think us so ignorant as not to know that? Go to the place whence thou camest!' Then, again, another preacher came, and began to teach us, and to say, You must not steal, nor lie, nor get drunk, and so forth.' We answered, Thou fool, dost thou think that we do not know that? Learn first thyself, and then teach the people to whom thou belongest to leave off these things. For who steal, or lie, or who are more drunken than thine own people?' And then we dismissed him."

But Rauch came with a very different message.

He told us of a Mighty One, the Lord of earth and sky,
Who left His glory in the Heavens, for men to bleed and die;
Who loved poor Indian sinners still, and longed to gain their love,

And be their Saviour here and in His Father's house above.
And when his tale was ended—"My friends," he gently said,
"I am weary with my journey, and would fain lay down my head;
So beside our spears and arrows he laid him down to rest,
And slept as sweetly as the babe upon its mother's breast.
Then we looked upon each other, and I whispered, "This is new;
Yes, we have heard glad tidings, and that sleeper knows them true;
He knows he has a Friend above, or would he slumber here,
With men of war around him, and the war-whoop in his ear.?"
So we told him on the morrow that he need not journey on,
But stay and tell us further of that loving, dying One;
And thus we heard of Jesus first, and felt the wondrous power,
Which makes His people willing, in His own accepted hour.

"Thus," added Tschoop, "through the grace of God an awakening took place among us. I say, therefore, Brethren, preach Christ our Saviour, and His sufferings and death, if you will have your words to gain entrance among the heathen."

As soon, therefore, as Rauch had struck this note, the Brethren boldly undertook the task of preaching to all the Red Indians in North America. The Count himself set off to spy the land, and undertook three dangerous missionary journeys. First, accompanied by his daughter Benigna, and an escort of fourteen, he visited the Long Valley beyond the Blue Mountains, met a delegation of the League of the Iroquois, and received from them, in solemn style, a fathom made of one hundred and sixty-eight strings of wampum (1742). The fathom was a sign of goodwill. If a missionary could only show the fathom he was sure of a kindly welcome. In his second journey Zinzendorf went to Shekomeko, organised the first Indian Mission Church, and baptized three converts as Abraham, Isaac and Jacob. In his third journey he visited the Wyoming Valley, and interviewed the chiefs of the Shawanese and Mohicans. He was here in deadly peril. As he sat one afternoon in his tent two hissing adders darted across his body; and a few days later some suspicious Indians plotted to take his life. But a government agent arrived on the scene, and Zinzendorf's scalp was saved.

And now the Brethren began the campaign in earnest. At Bethlehem Spangenberg had a Mission Conference and a Mission College. The great hero of the work was David Zeisberger. He was, like most of these early missionaries, a German. He was born at Zauchtenthal, in Moravia; had come with his parents to Herrnhut; had followed them later to Georgia; and was now a student at Spangenberg's College at Bethlehem. For sixty-three years he lived among the Indians, and his life was one continual series of thrilling adventures and escapes. He became almost an Indian. He was admitted a member of the Six Nations, received an Indian name, and became a member of an Indian family. He was an Iroquois to the Iroquois, a Delaware to the Delawares. He understood the hidden science of belts and strings of wampum; he could unriddle their mysterious messages and make speeches in their bombastic style; and he spoke in their speech and thought in their thoughts, and lived their life in their wigwams. He loved their majestic prairies, stretching beyond the Blue Mountains. He loved their mighty rivers and their deep clear lakes. Above all, he loved the red-brown Indians themselves. Full well he knew what trials awaited him. If the reader has formed his conception of the Indians from Fenimore Cooper's novels, he will probably think that Zeisberger spent his life among a race of gallant heroes. The reality was rather different. For the most part the Indians of North America were the reverse of heroic. They were bloodthirsty, drunken, lewd and treacherous. They spent their time in hunting buffaloes, smoking pipes, lolling in the sun, and scalping each other's heads. They wasted their nights in tipsy revels and dances by the light of the moon. They cowered in terror of evil spirits and vicious and angry gods. But Zeisberger never feared and never despaired. As long as he had such a grand Gospel to preach, he felt sure that he could make these savages sober, pure, wise, kind and brave, and that God would ever shield him with His wing. He has been called "The Apostle to the Indians." As the missionaries of the early Christian Church came to our rude fathers in England, and made us a Christian people, so Zeisberger desired to be an Augustine to the Indians, and found a Christian Indian kingdom stretching from Lake Michigan to the Ohio.

He began his work with the League of the Iroquois, commonly called the Six Nations (1745). At Onondaga, their headquarters, where he and Bishop Cammerhof had arranged to meet the Great Council, the meeting had to be postponed till the members had recovered from a state of intoxication. But Cammerhof addressed the chiefs, brought out the soothing pipe of tobacco, watched it pass from mouth to mouth, and received permission for two missionaries to come and settle down. From there, still accompanied by Cammerhof, Zeisberger went on to the Senecas. He was welcomed to a Pandemonium of revelry. The whole village was drunk. As he lay in his tent he could hear fiendish yells rend the air; he went out with a kettle, to get some water for Cammerhof, and the savages knocked the kettle out of his hand; and later, when the shades of evening fell, he had to defend himself with his fists against a bevy of lascivious women, whose long hair streamed in the night wind, and whose lips swelled with passion. For Cammerhof the journey was too much; in the bloom of youth he died (1751).

But Zeisberger had a frame of steel. Passing on from tribe to tribe, he strode through darkling woods, through tangled thickets, through miry sloughs, through swarms of mosquitoes; and anon, plying his swift canoe, he sped through primeval forests, by flowers of the tulip tree, through roaring rapids, round beetling bluffs, past groups of mottled rattlesnakes that lay basking in the sun. At the present time, in many Moravian manses, may be seen an engraving of a picture by Schuessele, of Philadelphia, representing Zeisberger preaching to the Indians. The incident occurred at Goschgoschuenk, on the Alleghany River (1767). In the picture the service is represented as being held in the open air; in reality it was held in the Council House. In the centre of the house was the watch-fire. Around it squatted the Indians—the men on one side, the women on the other; and among those men were murderers who had played their part, twelve years before, in the massacre on the Mahony River. As soon as Zeisberger rose to speak, every eye was fixed upon him; and while he delivered his Gospel message, he knew that at any moment a tomahawk might cleave his skull, and his scalp hang bleeding at the murderer's girdle. "Never yet," he wrote, "did I see so clearly painted on the faces of the Indians both the darkness of hell and the world-subduing power of the Gospel."

As the years rolled on, this dauntless hero won completely the confidence of these suspicious savages. He was known as "Friend of the Indians," and was allowed to move among them at his ease. In vain the sorcerers plotted against him. "Beware," they said to the simple people, "of the man in the black coat." At times, in order to bring down the vengeance of the spirits on Zeisberger's head, they sat up through the night and gorged themselves with swine's flesh; and, when this mode of enchantment failed, they baked themselves in hot ovens till they became unconscious. Zeisberger still went boldly on. Wherever the Indians were most debauched, there was he in the midst of them. Both the Six Nations and the Delawares passed laws that he was to be uninterrupted in his work. Before him the haughtiest chieftains bowed in awe. At Lavunakhannek, on the Alleghany River, he met the great Delaware orator, Glikkikan, who had baffled Jesuits and statesmen, and had prepared a complicated speech with which he meant to crush Zeisberger for ever; but when the two men came face to face, the orator fell an easy victim, forgot his carefully prepared oration, murmured meekly: "I have nothing to say; I believe your words," submitted to Zeisberger like a child, and became one of his warmest friends and supporters. In like manner Zeisberger won over White Eyes, the famous Delaware captain; and, hand in hand, Zeisberger and White Eyes worked for the same great cause. "I want my people," said White Eyes, "now that peace is established in the country, to turn their attention to peace in their hearts. I want them to embrace that religion which is taught by the white teachers. We shall never be happy until we are Christians."

It seemed as though that time were drawing nigh (1765-81). Zeisberger was a splendid organizer. As soon as the "Indian War" was over, he founded a number of Christian settlements, and taught the Indians the arts of industry and peace. For the Iroquois he founded the settlements of Friedenshuetten (Tents of Peace), on the Susquehanna, Goschgoschuenk, on the Alleghany, and Lavunakhannek and Friedenstadt (Town of Peace), on the Beaver River; and for the Delawares he founded the settlements of Schoenbrunn (Beautiful Spring), Gnadenhuetten (Tents of Grace), Lichtenau (Meadow of Light), on the Tuscawaras, and Salem, on the Muskinghum. His settlements were like diamonds flashing in the darkness. Instead of the wildness of the desert were nut trees, plums, cherries, mulberries and all manner of fruits; instead of scattered wigwams, orderly streets of huts; instead of filth, neatness and cleanliness; instead of drunken brawls and orgies, the voice of children at the village school, and the voice of morning and evening prayer.

No longer were the Indians in these settlements wild hunters. They were now steady business men. They conducted farms, cultivated gardens, grew corn and sugar, made butter, and learned to manage their local affairs as well as an English Urban District Council. At the head of each settlement was a Governing Board, consisting of the Missionaries and the native "helpers"; and all affairs of special importance were referred to a general meeting of the inhabitants. The system filled the minds of visitors with wonder. "The Indians in Zeisberger's settlements," said Colonel Morgan, "are an example to civilized whites."

No longer, further, were the Indians ignorant savages. Zeisberger was a great linguist. He mastered the Delaware and Iroquois languages. For the benefit of the converts in his setlements, and with the assistance of Indian sachems, he prepared and had printed a number of useful books: first (1776), "A Delaware Indian and English Spelling-book," with an appendix containing the Lord's Prayer, the Ten Commandments, some Scripture passages and a Litany; next (1803), in the Delaware language, "A Collection of Hymns for the use of the Christian Indians," translated from the English and German Moravian Hymn-books, and including the Easter, Baptismal and Burial Litanies; next, a volume of "Sermons to Children," translated from the German; next, a translation of Spangenberg's "Bodily Care of Children"; next, "A Harmony of the Four Gospels," translated from the Harmony prepared by Samuel Leiberkuehn; and last, a grammatical treatise on the Delaware conjugations. Of his services to philology, I need not speak in detail. He prepared a lexicon, in seven volumes, of the German and Onondaga languages, an Onondaga Grammar, a Delaware Grammar, a German-Delaware Dictionary, and other works of a similar nature. As these contributions to science were never published, they may not seem of much importance; but his manuscripts have been carefully preserved, some in the library of the Philosophical Society at Philadelphia, others at Harvard University.

Thus did Zeisberger, explorer and scholar, devote his powers to the physical, moral and spiritual improvement of the Indians. For some years his success was brilliant; and when, on Easter Sunday morning, his converts gathered for the early service, they presented a scene unlike any other in the world. As the sun rose red beyond the great Blue Mountains, as the morning mists broke gently away, as the gemmed trees whispered with the breath of spring, the Indians repeated in their lonely cemetery the same solemn Easter Litany that the Brethren repeated at Herrnhut, Zeisberger read the Confession of Faith, a trained choir led the responses, the Easter hymn swelled out, and the final "Amen" rang over the plateau and aroused the hosts of the woodland.

Away in the forest, how fair to the sight
Was the clear, placid lake as it sparkled in light,
And kissed with low murmur the green shady shore,
Whence a tribe had departed, whose traces it bore.
Where the lone Indian hastened, and wondering hushed

His awe as he trod o'er the mouldering dust!
How bright were the waters—how cheerful the song,
Which the wood-bird was chirping all the day long,
And how welcome the refuge those solitudes gave
To the pilgrims who toiled over mountain and wave;
Here they rested—here gushed forth, salvation to bring,
The fount of the Cross, by the "Beautiful Spring."

And yet the name of this wonderful man is almost unknown in England. We are just coming to the reason. At the very time when his influence was at its height the American War of Independence broke out, and Zeisberger and his converts, as an Indian orator put it, were between two exceeding mighty and wrathful gods, who stood opposed with extended jaws. Each party wished the Indians to take up arms on its side. But Zeisberger urged them to be neutral. When the English sent the hatchet of war to the Delawares, the Delawares politely sent it back. When a letter came to Zeisberger, requesting him to arouse his converts, to put himself at their head, and to bring the scalps of all the rebels he could slaughter, he threw the sheet into the flames. For this policy he was suspected by both sides. At one time he was accused before an English court of being in league with the Americans. At another time he was accused by the Americans of being in league with the English. At length the thunderbolt fell. As the Christian Indians of Gnadenhuetten were engaged one day in tilling the soil, the American troops of Colonel Williamson appeared upon the scene, asked for quarters, were comfortably, lodged, and then, disarming the innocent victims, accused them of having sided with the British. For that accusation the only ground was that the Indians had shown hospitality to all who demanded it; but this defence was not accepted, and Colonel Williamson decided to put the whole congregation to death (March 28th, 1782). The log huts were turned into shambles; the settlers were allowed a few minutes for prayer; then, in couples, they were summoned to their doom; and in cold blood the soldiers, with tomahawks, mallets, clubs, spears and scalping knives, began the work of butchery. At the end of the performance ninety corpses lay dabbled with blood on the ground. Among the victims were six National Assistants, a lady who could speak English and German, twenty-four other women, eleven boys and eleven girls. The Blood-Bath of Gnadenhuetten was a hideous crime. It shattered the Indian Mission. The grand plans of Zeisberger collapsed in ruin. As the war raged on, and white men encroached more and more on Indian soil, he found himself and his converts driven by brute force from one settlement after another. Already, before the war broke out, this brutal process had commenced; and altogether it continued for twenty years. In 1769 he had to abandon Goschgoschuenk; in 1770, Lavunakhannek; in 1772, Friedenshuetten; in 1773, Friedenstadt; in 1780, Lichtenau; in 1781, Gnadenhuetten, Salem and Schoenbrunn; in 1782, Sandusky; in 1786, New Gnadenhuetten; in 1787, Pilgerruh; in 1791, New Salem. As the old man drew near his end, he endeavoured to stem the torrent of destruction by founding two new settlements—Fairfield, in Canada, and Goshen, on the Tuscawaras; but even these had to be abandoned a few years after his death. Amid the Indians he had lived; amid the Indians, at Goshen, he lay on his death-bed (1808). As the news of his approaching dissolution spread, the chapel bell was tolled: his converts, knowing the signal, entered the room; and then, uniting their voices in song, they sang him home in triumphant hymns which he himself had translated from the hymns of the Ancient Brethren's Church.

Chapter 15: The Last Days of Zinzendorf (1755-1760)

AS Zinzendorf drew near to his end, he saw that his efforts in the cause of Christ had not ended as he had hoped. His design was the union of Christendom, his achievement the revival of the Church of the Brethren. He had given the "Hidden Seed" a home at Herrnhut. He had discovered the ancient laws of the Bohemian Brethren. He had maintained, first, for the sake of the Missions, and, secondly, for the sake of his Brethren, the Brethren's Episcopal Succession. He had founded the Pilgrim Band at Marienborn, had begun the Diaspora work in the Baltic Provinces, had gained for the Brethren legal recognition in Germany, England and North America, and had given the stimulus to the work of foreign missions. At the same time, he had continually impressed his own religious ideas upon his followers; and thus the Renewed Church of the Brethren was a Church of a twofold nature. The past and the present were dove-tailed. From the Bohemian Brethren came the strict discipline, the ministerial succession, and the martyr-spirit; from Zinzendorf the idea of "Church within the Church," the stress laid on the great doctrine of reconciliation through the blood of Christ, and the fiery missionary enthusiasm. Without Zinzendorf the Bohemian Brethren would probably have never returned to life; and without the fibre of the Bohemian Brethren, German Pietism would have died a natural death.

We must, however, keep clear of one misconception. Whatever else the Renewed Church of the Brethren was, it did not spring from a union of races. It was not a fusion of German and Czech elements. As the first settlers at Herrnhut came from Moravia, it is natural to regard them as Moravian Czechs; but the truth is that they were Germans in blood, and spoke the German language. It was, therefore, the German element of the old Brethren's Church that formed the backbone of the Renewed Church. It was Germans, not Czechs, who began the foreign missionary work; Germans who came to England, and Germans who renewed the Brethren's Church in America. In due time pure Czechs from Bohemia came and settled at Rixdorf and Niesky; but, speaking broadly, the Renewed Church of the Brethren was revived by German men with German ideas.

As the Church, therefore, was now established in the three provinces of Germany, Great Britain and North America, one problem only still awaited solution. The problem was the welding of the provinces. That welding was brought about in a simple way. If the reader is of a thoughtful turn of mind, he must have wondered more than once where the Brethren found the money to carry on their enterprises. They had relied chiefly on two sources of income: first, Zinzendorf's estates; second, a number of business concerns known as Diaconies. As long as these Diaconies prospered, the Brethren were able to keep their heads above water; but the truth is, they had been mismanaged. The Church was now on the verge of bankruptcy; and, therefore, the Brethren held at Taubenheim the so-called "Economical Conference." (1755)

In the time of need came the deliverer, Frederick Koeber. His five measures proved the salvation of the Church. First, he separated the property of Zinzendorf from the general property of the Church. Secondly, he put this general property under the care of a "College of Directors." Thirdly, he made an arrangement whereby this "College" should pay off all debts in fixed yearly sums. Fourthly, he proposed that all members of the Church should pay a fixed annual sum to general Church funds. And fifthly, on the sound principle that those who pay are entitled to a vote, he suggested that in future all members of the Church should have the right to send representatives to the General Directing Board or Conference. In this way he drew the outlines of the Moravian Church Constitution.

Meanwhile, Count Zinzendorf's end was drawing near. The evening of his life he spent at Herrnhut, for where more fitly could he die?

"It will be better," he said, "when I go home; the Conferences will last for ever."

He employed his last days in revising the Text-book, which was to be daily food for the Pilgrim Church (1760); and when he wrote down the final words, "And the King turned His face about, and blessed all the congregation of Israel," his last message to the Brethren was delivered. As his illness—a violent catarrhal fever—gained the mastery over him, he was cheered by the sight of the numerous friends who gathered round him. His band of workers watched by his couch in turn. On the last night about a hundred Brethren and Sisters assembled in the death chamber. John de Watteville sat by the bedside.

"Now, my dear friend," said the dying Count, "I am going to the Saviour. I am ready. I bow to His will. He is satisfied with me. If He does not want me here any more, I am ready to go to Him. There is nothing to hinder me now."

He looked around upon his friends. "I cannot say," he said, "how much I love you all. Who would have believed that the prayer of Christ, That they may be one,'could have been so strikingly fulfilled among us. I only asked for first-fruits among the heathen, and thousands have been given me...Are we not as in Heaven? Do we not live together like the angels? The Lord and His servants understand one another...I am ready."

As the night wore on towards morning, the scene, says one who was present, was noble, charming, liturgical. At ten o'clock, his breathing grew feebler (May 9th, 1760); and John de Watteville pronounced the Old Testament Benediction, "The Lord bless thee and keep thee. The Lord make His face shine upon thee and be gracious unto thee. The Lord lift up His countenance upon thee and give thee peace." As de Watteville spoke the last words of the blessing, the Count lay back on his pillow and closed his eyes; and a few seconds later he breathed no more.

At Herrnhut it is still the custom to announce the death of any member of the congregation by a chorale played on trombones; and when the trombones sounded that morning all knew that Zinzendorf's earthly career had closed. The air was thick with mist.

"It seemed," said John Nitschmann, then minister at Herrnhut, "as though nature herself were weeping." As the Count's body lay next day in the coffin, arrayed in the robe he had worn so often when conducting the Holy Communion, the whole congregation, choir by choir, came to gaze for the last time upon his face. For a week after this the coffin remained closed; but on the funeral day it was opened again, and hundreds from the neighbouring towns and villages came crowding into the chamber. At the funeral all the Sisters were dressed in white; and the number of mourners was over four thousand. At this time there were present in Herrnhut Moravian ministers from Holland, England, Ireland, North America and Greenland; and these, along with the German ministers, took turns as pall-bearers. The trombones sounded. John Nitschmann, as precentor, started the hymn; the procession to the Hutberg began. As the coffin was lowered into the grave some verses were sung, and then John Nitschmann spoke the words: "With tears we sow this seed in the earth; but He, in his own good time, will bring it to life, and will gather in His harvest with thanks and praise! Let all who wish for this say, Amen.'"

"Amen," responded the vast, weeping throng. The inscription on the grave-stone is as follows: "Here lie the remains of that immortal man of God, Nicholas Lewis, Count and Lord of Zinzendorf and Pottendorf; who, through the grace of God and his own unwearied service, became the honoured Ordinary of the Brethren's Church, renewed in this eighteenth century. He was born at Dresden on May 26th, 1700, and entered into the joy of his Lord at Herrnhut on May 9th, 1760. He was appointed to bring forth fruit, and that his fruit should remain."

Thus, in a halo of tearful glory, the Count-Bishop was laid to rest. For many years the Brethren cherished his memory, not only with affection, but with veneration; and even the sober Spangenberg described him as "the great treasure of our times, a lovely diamond in the ring on the hand of our Lord, a servant of the Lord without an equal, a pillar in the house of the Lord, God's message to His people." But history hardly justifies this generous eulogy; and Spangenberg afterwards admitted himself that Zinzendorf had two sides to his character. "It may seem a paradox," he wrote, "but it really does seem a fact that a man cannot have great virtues without also having great faults." The case of Zinzendorf is a case in point. At a Synod held a few years later (1764), the Brethren commissioned Spangenberg to write a "Life of Zinzendorf." As the Count, however, had been far from perfect, they had to face the serious question whether Spangenberg should be allowed to expose his faults to public gaze. They consulted the Lot: the Lot said "No"; and, therefore, they solemnly warned Spangenberg that, in order to avoid creating a false impression, he was "to leave out everything which would not edify the public." The loyal Spangenberg obeyed. His "Life of Zinzendorf" appeared in eight large volumes. He desired, of course, to be honest; he was convinced, to use his own words, that "an historian is responsible to God and men for the truth"; and yet, though he told the truth, he did not tell the whole truth. The result was lamentable. Instead of a life-like picture of Zinzendorf, the reader had only a shaded portrait, in which both the beauties and the defects were carefully toned down. The English abridged edition was still more colourless. [136] For a hundred years the character of Zinzendorf lay hidden beneath a pile of pious phrases, and only the recent researches of scholars have enabled us to see him as he was. He was no mere commonplace Pietist. He was no mere pious German nobleman, converted by looking at a picture. His faults and his virtues stood out in glaring relief. His very appearance told the dual tale. As he strolled the streets of Berlin or London, the wayfarers instinctively moved to let him pass, and all men admired his noble bearing, his lofty brow, his fiery dark blue eye, and his firm set lips; and yet, on the other hand, they could not fail to notice that he was untidy in his dress, that he strode on, gazing at the stars, and that often, in his absent-mindedness, he stumbled and staggered in his gait. In his portraits we can read the same double story. In some the prevailing tone is dignity; in others there is the faint suggestion of a smirk. His faults were those often found in men of genius. He was nearly always in a hurry, and was never in time for dinner. He was unsystematic in his habits, and incompetent in money matters. He was rather imperious in disposition, and sometimes overbearing in his conduct. He was impatient at any opposition, and disposed to treat with contempt the advice of others. For example, when the financial crisis arose at Herrnhaag, Spangenberg advised him to raise funds by weekly collections; but Zinzendorf brushed the advice aside, and retorted, "It is my affair." He was rather short-tempered, and would stamp his foot like an angry child if a bench in the church was not placed exactly as he desired. He was superstitious in his use of the Lot, and damaged the cause of the Brethren immensely by teaching them to trust implicitly to its guidance. He was reckless in his use of extravagant language; and he forgot that public men should consider, not only what they mean themselves, but also what impression their words are likely to make upon others. He was not always strictly truthful; and in one of his pamphlets he actually asserted that he himself was in no way responsible for the scandals at Herrnhaag. For these reasons the Count made many enemies. He was criticized severely, and sometimes justly, by men of such exalted character as Bengel, the famous German commentator, and honest John Wesley in England; he was reviled by vulgar scribblers like Rimius; and thus, like his great contemporary, Whitefield, he

> Stood pilloried on Infamy's high stage,
> And bore the pelting scorn of half an age;
> The very butt of slander and the blot
> For every dart that malice ever shot.

But serious though his failings were, they were far outshone by his virtues. Of all the religious leaders of the eighteenth century, he was the most original in genius and the most varied in talent; and, therefore, he was the most misunderstood, the most fiercely hated, the most foully libelled, the most shamefully attacked, and the most fondly adored. In his love for Christ he was like St. Bernard, in his mystic devotion like Madame Guyon; and Herder, the German poet, described him as "a conqueror in the spiritual world." It was those who knew him best who admired him most. By the world at large he was despised, by orthodox critics abused, by the Brethren honoured, by his intimate friends almost worshipped. According to many orthodox Lutherans he was an atheist; but the Brethren commonly called him "the Lord's disciple." He was abstemious in diet, cared little for wine, and drank chiefly tea and lemonade. He was broad and Catholic in his views, refused to speak of the Pope as Antichrist, and referred to members of the Church of Rome as "Brethren"; and, while he remained a Lutheran to the end, he had friends in every branch of the Church of Christ. He had not a drop of malice in his blood. He never learned the art of bearing a grudge, and when he was reviled, he never reviled again. He was free with his money, and could never refuse a beggar. He was a thoughtful and suggestive theological writer, and holds a high place in the history of dogma; and no thinker expounded more beautifully than he the grand doctrine that the innermost nature of God is revealed in all its glory to man in the Person of the suffering Man Christ Jesus. He was a beautiful Christian poet; his hymns are found to-day in every collection; his "Jesus, Thy blood and righteousness" was translated into English by John Wesley; and his noble "Jesus, still lead on!" is as popular in the cottage homes of Germany as Newman's "Lead, kindly light" in England. Of the three great qualities required in a poet, Zinzendorf, however, possessed only two. He had the sensibility; he had the imagination; but he rarely had the patience to take pains; and, therefore, nearly all his poetry is lacking in finish and artistic beauty. He was an earnest social reformer; he endeavoured, by means of his settlement system, to solve the social problem; and his efforts to uplift the working classes were praised by the famous German critic, Lessing. The historian and theologian, Albrecht Ritschl, has accused him of sectarian motives and of wilfully creating a split in the Lutheran Church. The accusation is absolutely false. There is nothing more attractive in the character of Zinzendorf than his unselfish devotion to one grand ideal. On one occasion, after preaching at Berlin, he met a young lieutenant. The lieutenant was in spiritual trouble.

"Let me ask you," said Zinzendorf, "one question: Are you alone in your religious troubles, or do you share them with others?"

The lieutenant replied that some friends and he were accustomed to pray together.

"That is right," said Zinzendorf. "I acknowledge no Christianity without fellowship."

In those words he pointed to the loadstar of his life. For that holy cause of Christian fellowship he spent every breath in his body and every ducat in his possession. For that cause he laboured among the peasants of Berthelsdorf, in the streets of Berlin, in the smiling Wetterau, in the Baltic Provinces, on the shores of Lake Geneva, in the wilds of Yorkshire, by the silver Thames, on West Indian plantations, and in the wigwams of the Iroquois and the Delaware. It is not always fair to judge of men by their conduct. We must try, when possible, to find the ruling motive; and in motive Zinzendorf was always unselfish. Sometimes he was guilty of reckless driving; but his wagon was hitched to a star. No man did more to revive the Moravian Church, and no man did more, by his very ideals, to retard her later expansion. It is here that we can see most clearly the contrast between Zinzendorf and John Wesley. In genius Zinzendorf easily bore the palm; in practical wisdom the Englishman far excelled him. The one was a poet, a dreamer, a thinker, a mystic; the other a practical statesman, who added nothing to religious thought, and yet uplifted millions of his fellow men. At a Synod of the Brethren held at Herrnhut (1818), John Albertini, the eloquent preacher, described the key-note of Zinzendorf's life. "It was love to Christ," said Albertini, "that glowed in the heart of the child; the same love that burned in the young man; the same love that thrilled his middle-age; the same love that inspired his every endeavour." In action faulty, in motive pure; in judgment erring, in ideals divine; in policy wayward, in purpose unselfish and true; such was Zinzendorf, the Renewer of the Church of the Brethren. [137]

Book 3:

The Rule of the Germans

Chapter 1: The Church and Her Mission (1760-1775)

AS we enter on the closing stages of our journey, the character of the landscape changes; and, leaving behind the wild land of romance and adventure, we come out on the broad, high road of slow but steady progress. The death of Zinzendorf was no crushing blow. At first some enemies of the Brethren rejoiced, and one prophet triumphantly remarked: "We shall now see an end of these Moravians." But that time the prophet spoke without his mantle. Already the Brethren were sufficiently strong to realize their calling in the world. In Saxony they had established powerful congregations at Herrnhut and Kleinwelke; in Silesia, at Niesky, Gnadenberg, Gnadenfrei and Neusalz; in Central Germany, at Ebersdorf, Neudietendorf and Barby; in North Germany, at Rixdorf and Berlin; in West Germany, at Neuwied-on-the-Rhine; in Holland, at Zeist, near Utrecht. At first sight this list does not look very impressive; but we must, of course, bear in mind that most of these congregations were powerful settlements, that each settlement was engaged in Diaspora work, and that the branches of that work had extended to Denmark, Switzerland and Norway. In Great Britain a similar principle held good. In England the Brethren had flourishing causes at Fulneck, Gomersal, Mirfield, Wyke, Ockbrook, Bedford, Fetter Lane, Tytherton, Dukinfield, Leominster; in Ireland, at Dublin, Gracehill, Gracefield, Ballinderry and Kilwarlin; and around each of these congregations were numerous societies and preaching places. In North America they had congregations at Bethlehem, Emmaus, Graceham, Lancaster, Lititz, Nazareth, New Dorp, New York, Philadelphia, Schoeneck and York (York Co.); and in addition, a number of preaching places. In Greenland they had built the settlements of New Herrnhut and Lichtenau. In the West Indies they had established congregations in St. Thomas, St. Croix, St. Jan, Jamaica and Antigua. In Berbice and Surinam they had three main centres of work. Among the Red Indians Zeisberger was busily engaged. As accurate statistics are not available, I am not able to state exactly how many Moravians there were then in the world; but we know that in the mission-field alone they had over a thousand communicant members and seven thousand adherents under their special care.

As soon, then, as the leading Brethren in Herrnhut—such as John de Watteville, Leonard Dober, David Nitschmann, the Syndic, Frederick Koeber, and others—had recovered from the shock occasioned by Zinzendorf's death, they set about the difficult task of organizing the work of the whole Moravian Church. First, they formed a provisional Board of Directors, known as the Inner Council; next, they despatched two messengers to America, to summon the practical Spangenberg home to take his place on the board; and then, at the earliest convenient opportunity, they summoned their colleagues to Marienborn for the first General Representative Synod of the Renewed

Church of the Brethren. As the Count had left the affairs of the Church in confusion, the task before the Brethren was enormous (1764). They had their Church constitution to frame; they had their finances to straighten out; they had their mission in the world to define; they had, in a word, to bring order out of chaos; and so difficult did they find the task that eleven years passed away before it was accomplished to any satisfaction. For thirty years they had been half blinded by the dazzling brilliance of Zinzendorf; but now they began to see a little more clearly. As long as Zinzendorf was in their midst, an orderly system of government was impossible. It was now an absolute necessity. The reign of one man was over; the period of constitutional government began. At all costs, said the sensible Frederick Koeber, the Count must have no successor. For the first time the Synod was attended by duly elected congregation deputies: those deputies came not only from Germany, but from Great Britain, America and the mission-field; and thus the voice of the Synod was the voice, not of one commanding genius, but of the whole Moravian Church.

The first question to settle was the Church's Mission. For what purpose did the Moravian Church exist? To that question the Brethren gave a threefold answer. First, they said, they must labour in the whole world; second, their fundamental doctrine must be the doctrine of reconciliation through the merits of the life and sufferings of Christ as set forth in the Holy Scriptures and in the Augsburg Confession; and, third, in their settlements they would continue to enforce that strict discipline—including the separation of the sexes—without which the Gospel message would be a mockery. Thus the world was their parish, the cross their message, the system of discipline their method.

Secondly, the Brethren framed their constitution. Of all the laws ever passed by the Brethren, those passed at the first General Synod had, for nearly a hundred years (1764-1857), the greatest influence on the progress of the Moravian Church. The keyword is "centralization." If the Church was to be a united body, that Church, held the Brethren, must have a central court of appeal, a central administrative board, and a central legislative authority. At this first Constitutional Synod, therefore, the Brethren laid down the following principles of government: That all power to make rules and regulations touching the faith and practice of the Church should be vested in the General Synod; that this General Synod should consist of all bishops and ministers of the Church and of duly elected congregation deputies; that no deputy should be considered duly elected unless his election had been confirmed by the Lot; and that during an inter-synodal period the supreme management of Church affairs should be in the hands of three directing boards, which should all be elected by the Synod, and be responsible to the next Synod. The first board was the Supreme Board of Management. It was called the Directory, and consisted of nine Brethren. The second was the Brethren's ministry of foreign affairs. It was called the Board of Syndics, and managed the Church's relations with governments. The third was the Brethren's treasury. It was called the Unity's Warden's Board, and managed the Church finances. For us English readers, however, the chief point to notice is that, although these boards were elected by the General Synod, and although, in theory, they were international in character, in actual fact they consisted entirely of Germans; and, therefore, we have the astounding situation that during the next ninety-three years the whole work of the Moravian Church—in Germany, in Holland, in Denmark, in Great Britain, in North America, and in the rapidly extending mission-field—was managed by a board or boards consisting of Germans and resident in Germany. There all General Synods were held; there lay all supreme administrative and legislative power.

Of local self-government there was practically none. It is true that so-called "Provincial Synods" were held; but these Synods had no power to make laws. At this period the Moravian Church was divided, roughly, into the six Provinces of Upper Lusatia, Silesia, Holland, England, Ireland, and America; and in each of these Provinces Synods might be held. But a Provincial Synod was a Synod only in name. "A Provincial Synod," ran the law, "is an assembly of the ministers and deputies of the congregations of a whole province or land who lay to heart the weal or woe of their congregations, and lay the results of their conferences before the General Synod or the Directory, which is constituted from one General Synod to another. In other places and districts, indeed, that name does not suit; but yet in every congregation and district a solemn conference of that sort may every year be holden, and report be made out of it to the Directory and General Synod."

In individual congregations the same principle applied. There, too, self-government was almost unknown. At the head of each congregation was a board known as the Elders' Conference; and that Elders' Conference consisted, not of Brethren elected by the Church members, but of the minister, the minister's wife, and the choir-labourers, all appointed by the supreme Directing Board. It is true that the members of the congregation had power to elect a committee, but the powers of that committee were strictly limited. It dealt with business matters only, and all members of the Elders' Conference were ex officio members of the Committee. We can see, then, what this curious system meant. It meant that a body of Moravian members in London, Dublin or Philadelphia were under the authority of a Conference appointed by a Directing Board of Germans resident in Germany.

The next question to settle was finance; and here again the word "centralization" must be our guide through the jungle. At that time the finances had sunk so low that at this first General Synod most of the ministers and deputies had to sleep on straw, and now the great problem to settle was, how to deal with Zinzendorf's property. As long as Zinzendorf was in the flesh he had generously used the income from his estates for all sorts of Church purposes. But now the situation was rather delicate. On the one hand, Zinzendorf's landed property belonged by law to his heirs, i.e., his three daughters, and his wife's nephew, Count Reuss; on the other hand, he had verbally pledged it to the Brethren to help them out of their financial troubles. The problem was solved by purchase. In exchange for Zinzendorf's estates at Berthelsdorf and Gross-Hennersdorf, the Brethren offered the heirs the sum of -L-25,000. The heirs accepted the offer; the deeds of sale were prepared; and thus Zinzendorf's landed property became the property of the Moravian Church. We must not call this a smart business transaction. When the Brethren purchased Zinzendorf's estates, they purchased his debts as well; and those debts amounted now to over -L-150,000. The one thing the Brethren gained was independence. They were no longer under an obligation to the Zinzendorf family.

At the next General Synod, held again at Marienborn (1769), the centralizing principle was still more emphatically enforced. As the three separate boards of management had not worked very smoothly together, the Brethren now abolished them, and resolved that henceforth all supreme administrative authority should be vested in one grand comprehensive board, to be known as the Unity's Elders' Conference. [138] The Conference was divided into three departments—the College of Overseers, the College of Helpers, and the College of Servants. It is hard for English readers to realize what absolute powers this board possessed. The secret lies in the Brethren's use of the Lot. Hitherto the use of the Lot had been haphazard; henceforth it was a recognized principle of Church government. At this Synod the Brethren laid down the law that all elections, [139] appointments and important decisions should be ratified by the Lot. It was used, not only to confirm elections, but often, though not always, to settle questions of Church policy. It was often appealed to at Synods. If a difficult question came up for discussion, the Brethren frequently consulted the Lot. The method was to place three papers in a box, and then appoint someone to draw one out. If the paper was positive, the resolution was carried; if the paper was negative, the resolution was lost; if the paper was blank, the resolution was laid on the table. The weightiest matters were settled in this way. At one Synod the Lot decided that George Waiblinger should be entrusted with the task of preparing an "Exposition of Christian Doctrine"; and yet when Waiblinger fulfilled his duty, the Brethren were not satisfied with his work. At another Synod the Lot decided that Spangenberg should not be entrusted with that task, and yet the Brethren were quite convinced that Spangenberg was the best man for the purpose. But perhaps the greatest effect of the Lot was the power and dignity which it conferred on officials. No man could be a member of the U.E.C. unless his election had been confirmed by the Lot; and when that confirmation had been obtained, he felt that he had been appointed, not only by his Brethren, but also by God. Thus the U.E.C., appointed by the Lot, employed the Lot to settle the most delicate questions. For example, no Moravian minister might marry without the consent of the U.E.C. The U.E.C. submitted his choice to the Lot; and if the Lot decided in the negative, he accepted the decision as the voice of God. In the congregations the same practice prevailed. All applications for church membership and all proposals of marriage were submitted to the Local Elders' Conference; and in each case the Conference arrived at its decision by consulting the Lot. To some critics this practice appeared a symptom of lunacy. It was not so regarded by the Brethren. It was their way of seeking the guidance of God; and when they were challenged to justify their conduct, they appealed to the example of the eleven Apostles as recorded in Acts i. 26, and also to the promise of Christ, "Whatsoever ye shall ask in My name, I will do it."

At this Synod the financial problem came up afresh. The Brethren tried a bold experiment. As the Church's debts could not be extinguished in any other way, they determined to appeal to the generosity of the members; and to this end they now resolved that the property of the Church should be divided into as many sections as there were congregations, that each congregation should have its own property and bear its own burden, and that each congregation-committee should supply the needs of its own minister. Of course, money for general Church purposes would still be required: but the Brethren trusted that this would come readily from the pockets of loving members.

But love, though a beautiful silken bond, is sometimes apt to snap. The new arrangement was violently opposed. What right, asked grumblers, had the Synod to saddle individual congregations with the debts of the whole Church? The local managers of diaconies proved incompetent. At Neuwied one Brother lost -L-6,000 of Church money in a lottery. The financial pressure became harder than ever. James Skinner, a member of the London congregation, suggested that the needful money should be raised by weekly subscriptions. In England this proposal might have found favour; in Germany it was rejected with contempt. The relief came from an unexpected quarter. At Herrnhut the members were celebrating the congregation Jubilee (1772); and twenty poor Single Sisters there, inspired with patriotic zeal, concocted the following letter to the U.E.C.: "After maturely weighing how we might be able, in proportion to our slender means, to contribute something to lessen the debt on the Unity—i.e., our own debt—we have cheerfully agreed to sacrifice and dispose of all unnecessary articles, such as gold and silver plate, watches, snuff-boxes, rings, trinkets and jewellery of every kind for the purpose of establishing a Sinking Fund, on condition that not only the congregation at Herrnhut, but all the members of the Church everywhere, rich and poor, old and young, agree to this proposal. But this agreement is not to be binding on those who can contribute in other ways." The brave letter caused an immense sensation. The spirit of generosity swept over the Church like a freshening breeze. For very shame the other members felt compelled to dive into their pockets; and the young men, not being possessed of trinkets, offered free labour in their leisure hours. The good folk at Herrnhut vied with each other in giving; and the Brethren at Philadelphia vied with the Brethren at Herrnhut. The Sinking Fund was established. In less than twelve months the Single Sisters at Herrnhut raised -L-1,300; the total contributions at Herrnhut amounted to -L-3,500; and in three years the Sinking Fund had a capital of -L-25,000. Thus did twenty Single Sisters earn a high place on the Moravian roll of honour. At the same time, the U.E.C. were able to sell the three estates of Marienborn, Herrnhaag and Lindsey House; and in these ways the debt on the Church was gradually wiped off.

The third constitutional Synod was held at Barby, on the Elbe, near Magdeburg (1775). At this Synod the power of the U.E.C. was strengthened. In order to prevent financial crises in future, the Brethren now laid down the law that each congregation, though having its own property, should contribute a fixed annual quota to the general fund; that all managers of local diaconies should be directly responsible to the U.E.C.;

and that each congregation should send in to the U.E.C. an annual financial statement. In this way, therefore, all Church property was, directly or indirectly, under the control of the U.E.C. The weakness of this arrangement is manifest. As long as the U.E.C. was resident in Germany, and as long as it consisted almost exclusively of Germans, it could not be expected to understand financial questions arising in England and America, or to fathom the mysteries of English and American law; and yet this was the system in force for the next eighty-two years. It is true that the Brethren devised a method to overcome this difficulty. The method was the method of official visitations. At certain periods a member of the U.E.C. would pay official visitations to the chief congregations in Germany, England, America and the Mission Field. For example, Bishop John Frederick Reichel visited North America (1778-1781) and the East Indies; Bishop John de Watteville (1778-1779) visited in England, Ireland, Scotland and Wales; and John Henry Quandt (1798) visited Neuwied-on-the-Rhine. In some ways the method was good, in others bad. it was good because it fostered the unity of the Church, and emphasized its broad international character. It was bad because it was cumbrous and expensive, because it exalted too highly the official element, and because it checked local independent growth.

Finally, at this third constitutional Synod, the Brethren struck a clear note on doctrinal questions. The main doctrines of the Church were defined as follows: (1) The doctrine of the universal depravity of man; that there is no health in man, and that since the fall he has no power whatever left to help himself. (2) The doctrine of the Divinity of Christ; that God, the Creator of all things, was manifest in the flesh, and reconciled us unto Himself; that He is before all things, and that by Him all things consist. (3) The doctrine of the atonement and the satisfaction made for us by Jesus Christ; that He was delivered for our offences, and raised again for our justification; and that by His merits alone we receive freely the forgiveness of sin and sanctification in soul and body. (4) The doctrine of the Holy Spirit and the operations of His grace; that it is He who worketh in us conviction of sin, faith in Jesus, and pureness of heart. (5) The doctrine of the fruits of faith; that faith must evidence itself by willing obedience to the commandments of God, from love and gratitude to Him. In those doctrines there was nothing striking or peculiar. They were the orthodox Protestant doctrines of the day; they were the doctrines of the Lutheran Church, of the Church of England, and the Church of Scotland; and they were, and are, all to be found in the Augsburg Confession, in the Thirty-nine Articles, and in the Westminster Confession.

Such, then, were the methods and doctrines laid down by the three constitutional Synods. In methods the Brethren were distinctive; in doctrine they were "orthodox evangelical." We may now sum up the results of this chapter. We have a semi-democratic Church constitution. We have a governing board, consisting mostly of Germans, and resident in Germany. We have the systematic use of the Lot. We have a broad evangelical doctrinal standpoint. We are now to see how these principles and methods worked out in Germany, Great Britain and America.

Chapter 2: The Fight for the Gospel (1775-1800)

IF a man stands up for the old theology when new theology is in the air, he is sure to be praised by some for his loyalty, and condemned by others for his stupidity; and that was the fate of the Brethren in Germany during the closing years of the eighteenth century. The situation in Germany was swiftly changing. The whole country was in a theological upheaval. As soon as the Brethren had framed their constitution, they were summoned to the open field of battle. For fifty years they had held their ground against a cold and lifeless orthodoxy, and had, therefore, been regarded as heretics; and now, as though by a sudden miracle, they became the boldest champions in Germany of the orthodox Lutheran faith. Already a powerful enemy had entered the field. The name of the enemy was Rationalism. As we enter the last quarter of the eighteenth century, we hear the sound of tramping armies and the first mutterings of a mighty storm. The spirit of free inquiry spread like wildfire. In America it led to the War of Independence; in England it led to Deism; in France it led to open atheism and all the horrors of the French Revolution. In Germany, however, its effect was rather different. If the reader knows anything of Germany history, he will probably be aware of the fact that Germany is a land of many famous universities, and that these universities have always played a leading part in the national life. It is so to-day; it was so in the eighteenth century. In England a Professor may easily become a fossil; in Germany he often guides the thought of the age. For some years that scoffing writer, Voltaire, had been openly petted at the court of Frederick the Great; his sceptical spirit was rapidly becoming fashionable; and now the professors at the Lutheran Universities, and many of the leading Lutheran preachers, were expounding certain radical views, not only on such vexed questions as Biblical inspiration and the credibility of the Gospel narratives, but even on some of the orthodox doctrines set forth in the Augsburg Confession. At Halle University, John Semler propounded new views about the origin of the Bible; at Jena, Griesbach expounded textual criticism; at Goettingen, Eichhorn was lecturing on Higher Criticism; and the more the views of these scholars spread, the more the average Church members feared that the old foundations were giving way.

Amid the alarm, the Brethren came to the rescue. It is needful to state their position with some exactness. We must not regard them as blind supporters of tradition, or as bigoted enemies of science and research. In spite of their love of the Holy Scriptures, they never entered into any controversy on mere questions of Biblical criticism. They had no special theory of Biblical inspiration. At this time the official Church theologian was Spangenberg. He was appointed to the position by the U.E.C.; he was commissioned to prepare an Exposition of Doctrine; and, therefore, the attitude adopted by Spangenberg may be taken as the attitude of the Brethren. But Spangenberg himself did not believe that the whole Bible was inspired by God. "I cannot assert," he wrote in one passage, "that every word in the Holy Scriptures has been inspired by the Holy Ghost and given thus to the writers. For example, the speeches at the end of the book of Job, ascribed there to God, are of such a nature that they cannot possibly have proceeded from the Holy Ghost." He believed, of course, in the public reading of Scripture; but when the Brethren were planning a lectionary, he urged them to make a distinction between the Old and New Testaments. "Otherwise," he declared, "the reading of the Old Testament may do more harm than good." He objected to the public reading of Job and the Song of Songs.

But advanced views about the Bible were not the main feature of the rationalistic movement. A large number of the German theologians were teaching what we should call "New Theology." Instead of adhering to the Augsburg Confession, a great many of the Lutheran professors and preachers were attacking some of its leading doctrines. First, they denied the doctrine of the Fall, whittled away the total depravity of man, and asserted that God had created men, not with a natural bias to sin, but perfectly free to choose between good and evil. Secondly, they rejected the doctrine of reconciliation through the meritorious sufferings of Christ. Thirdly, they suggested that the doctrine of the Holy Trinity was an offence to reason. Around these three doctrines the great battle was fought. To the Brethren those doctrines were all fundamental, all essential to salvation, and all precious parts of Christian experience; and, therefore, they defended them against the Rationalists, not on intellectual, but on moral and spiritual grounds. The whole question at issue, in their judgment, was a question of Christian experience. The case of Spangenberg will make this clear. To understand Spangenberg is to understand his Brethren. He defended the doctrine of total depravity, not merely because he found it in the Scriptures, but because he was as certain as a man can be that he had once been totally depraved himself; and he defended the doctrine of reconciliation because, as he wrote to that drinking old sinner, Professor Basedow, he had found all grace and freedom from sin in the atoning sacrifice of Jesus. He often spoke of himself in contemptuous language; he called himself a mass of sins, a disgusting creature, an offence to his own nostrils; and he recorded his own experience when he said: "It has pleased Him to make out of me—a revolting creature—a child of God, a temple of the Holy Ghost, a member of the body of Christ, all heir of eternal life." There we have Spangenberg's theology in a sentence; there shines the Brethren's experimental religion. The doctrine of the Trinity stood upon the same basis. In God the Father they had a protector; in God the Son an ever present friend; in God the Holy Ghost a spiritual guide; and, therefore, they defended the doctrine of the Trinity, not because it was in the Augsburg Confession, but because, in their judgment, it fitted their personal experience.

And yet the Brethren were not controversialists. Instead of arguing with the rationalist preachers, they employed more pleasing methods of their own.

The first method was the publication of useful literature. The most striking book, and the most influential, was Spangenberg's Idea Fidei Fratrum; i.e., Exposition of the

Brethren's Doctrine (1778). For many years this treatise was prized by the Brethren as a body of sound divinity; and although it can no longer be regarded as a text-book for theological students, it is still used and highly valued at some of the Moravian Mission stations. [140] From the first the book sold well, and its influence in Germany was great. It was translated into English, Danish, French, Swedish, Dutch, Bohemian and Polish. Its strength was its loyalty to Holy Scripture; its weakness its lack of original thought. If every difficult theological question is to be solved by simply appealing to passages of Scripture, it is obvious that little room is left for profound and original reflection; and that, speaking broadly, was the method adopted by Spangenberg in this volume. His object was twofold. On the one hand, he wished to be true to the Augsburg Confession; on the other hand, he would admit no doctrine that was not clearly supported by Scripture. The book was almost entirely in Scriptural language. The conventional phrases of theology were purposely omitted. In spite of his adherence to the orthodox faith, the writer never used such phrases as Trinity, Original Sin, Person, or Sacrament. He deliberately abandoned the language of the creeds for the freer language of Scripture. It was this that helped to make the book so popular. The more fiercely the theological controversy raged, the more ready was the average working pastor to flee from the dust and din of battle by appealing to the testimony of the Bible.

"How evangelical! How purely Biblical!" wrote Spangenberg's friend, Court Councillor Frederick Falke (June 10th, 1787). Christian David Lenz, the Lutheran Superintendent at Riga, was charmed. "Nothing," he wrote, "has so convinced me of the purity of the Brethren's evangelical teaching as your Idea Fidei Fratrum. It appeared just when it was needed. In the midst of the universal corruption, the Brethren are a pillar of the truth." The Danish Minister of Religion, Adam Struensee, who had been a fellow-student with Spangenberg at Jena, was eloquent in his praises. "A great philosopher at our University," he wrote to Spangenberg, "complained to me about our modern theologians; and then added: I am just reading Spangenberg's Idea. It is certain that our successors will have to recover their Christian theology from the Moravian Brethren.'" But the keenest criticism was passed by Caspar Lavater. His mixture of praise and blame was highly instructive. He contrasted Spangenberg with Zinzendorf. In reading Zinzendorf, we constantly need the lead pencil. One sentence we wish to cross out; the next we wish to underline. In reading Spangenberg we do neither. "In these recent works of the Brethren," said Lavater, "I find much less to strike out as unscriptural, but also much less to underline as deep, than in the soaring writings of Zinzendorf."

And thus the Brethren, under Spangenberg's guidance, entered on a new phase. In originality they had lost; in sobriety they had gained; and now they were honoured by the orthodox party in Germany as trusted champions of the faith delivered once for all unto the saints.

The same lesson was taught by the new edition of the Hymn-book (1778). It was prepared by Christian Gregor. The first Hymn-book, issued by the Renewed Church of the Brethren, appeared in 1735. It consisted chiefly of Brethren's hymns, written mostly by Zinzendorf; and during the next fifteen years it was steadily enlarged by the addition of twelve appendices. But in two ways these appendices were faulty. They were far too bulky, and they contained some objectionable hymns. As soon, however, as the Brethren had recovered from the errors of the Sifting-Time, Count Zinzendorf published a revised Hymn-book in London (1753-4); and then, a little later, an extract, entitled "Hymns of Sharon." But even these editions were unsatisfactory. They contained too many hymns by Brethren, too many relics of the Sifting-Time, and too few hymns by writers of other Churches. But the edition published by Gregor was a masterpiece. It contained the finest hymns of Christendom from nearly every source. It was absolutely free from extravagant language; and, therefore, it has not only been used by the Brethren from that day to this, but is highly valued by Christians of other Churches. In 1784 Christian Gregor brought out a volume of "Chorales," where noble thoughts and stately music were wedded.

The next class of literature issued was historical. The more fiercely the orthodox Gospel was attacked, the more zealously the Brethren brought out books to show the effect of that Gospel on the lives of men. In 1765, David Cranz, the historian, published his "History of Greenland." He had been for fourteen months in Greenland himself. He had studied his subject at first hand; he was a careful, accurate, conscientious writer; his book soon appeared in a second edition (1770), and was translated into English, Dutch, Swedish and Danish; and whatever objections philosophers might raise against the Gospel of reconciliation, David Cranz was able to show that by the preaching of that Gospel the Brethren in Greenland had taught the natives to be sober, industrious and pure. In 1777 the Brethren published G. A. Oldendorp's elaborate "History of the Mission in the Danish West Indies," and, in 1789, G. H. Loskiel's "History of the Mission Among the North American Indians." In each case the author had been on the spot himself; and in each case the book was welcomed as a proof of the power of the Gospel.

The second method was correspondence and visitation. In spite of their opposition to rationalistic doctrine the Brethren kept in friendly touch with the leading rationalist preachers. Above all, they kept in touch with the Universities. The leader of this good work was Spangenberg. Where Zinzendorf had failed, Spangenberg succeeded. It is a curious feature of Zinzendorf's life that while he won the favour of kings and governments, he could rarely win the favour of learned Churchmen. As long as Zinzendorf reigned supreme, the Brethren were rather despised at the Universities; but now they were treated with marked respect. At one time the U.E.C. suggested that regular annual visits should be paid to the Universities of Halle, Wittenberg and Leipzig; and in one year Bishop Layritz, a member of the U.E.C., visited the Lutheran Universities of Halle, Erlangen, Tuebingen, Strasburg, Erfurt and Leipzig, and the Calvinist Universities of Bern, Geneva and Basle. In response to a request from Walch of Goettingen, Spangenberg wrote his "Brief Historical Account of the Brethren" and his "Account of the Brethren's Work Among the Heathen"; and, in response to a request from Koester of Gieszen, he wrote a series of theological articles for that scholar's "Encyclopaedia." Meanwhile, he was in constant correspondence with Schneider at Eisenach, Lenz at Riga,

Reinhard at Dresden, Roos at Anhausen, Tittman at Dresden, and other well-known Lutheran preachers. For thirteen years (1771-1784) the seat of the U.E.C. was Barby; and there they often received visits from leading German scholars. At one time the notorious Professor Basedow begged, almost with tears in his eyes, to be admitted to the Moravian Church; but the Brethren could not admit a man, however learned he might be, who sought consolation in drink and gambling. On other occasions the Brethren were visited by Campe, the Minister of Education; by Salzmann, the founder of Schnepfenthal; and by Becker, the future editor of the German Times. But the most distinguished visitor at Barby was Semler, the famous rationalist Professor at Halle. "He spent many hours with us," said Spangenberg (1773). "He expounded his views, and we heard him to the end. In reply we told him our convictions, and then we parted in peace from each other." When Semler published his "Abstract of Church History," he sent a copy to Spangenberg; and Spangenberg returned the compliment by sending him the latest volume of his "Life of Zinzendorf." At these friendly meetings with learned men the Brethren never argued. Their method was different. It was the method of personal testimony. "It is, I imagine, no small thing," said Spangenberg, in a letter to Dr. J. G. Rosenmueller, "that a people exists among us who can testify both by word and life that in the sacrifice of Jesus they have found all grace and deliverance from sin." And thus the Brethren replied to the Rationalists by appealing to personal experience.

The third method was the education of the young. For its origin we turn to the case of Susannah Kuehnel. At the time of the great revival in Herrnhut (1727), the children had not been neglected; Susannah Kuehnel, a girl of eleven, became the leader of a revival. "We had then for our master," said Jacob Liebich, "an upright and serious man, who had the good of his pupils much at heart." The name of the master was Krumpe. "He never failed," continued Liebich, "at the close of the school to pray with us, and to commend us to the Lord Jesus and His Spirit during the time of our amusements. At that time Susannah Kuehnel was awakened, and frequently withdrew into her father's garden, especially in the evenings, to ask the grace of the Lord and to seek the salvation of her soul with strong crying and tears. As this was next door to the house where we lived (there was only a boarded partition between us), we could hear her prayers as we were going to rest and as we lay upon our beds. We were so much impressed that we could not fall asleep as carelessly as formerly, and asked our teachers to go with us to pray. Instead of going to sleep as usual, we went to the boundaries which separated the fields, or among the bushes, to throw ourselves before the Lord and beg Him to turn us to Himself. Our teachers often went with us, and when we had done praying, and had to return, we went again, one to this place and another to that, or in pairs, to cast ourselves upon our knees and pray in secret." Amid the fervour occurred the events of August 13th. The children at Herrnhut were stirred. For three days Susannah Kuehnel was so absorbed in thought and prayer that she forgot to take her food; and then, on August 17th, having passed through a severe spiritual struggle, she was able to say to her father: "Now I am become a child of God; now I know how my mother felt and feels." We are not to pass this story over as a mere pious anecdote. It illustrates an important Moravian principle. For the next forty-two years the Brethren practised the system of training the children of Church members in separate institutions; the children, therefore, were boarded and educated by the Church and at the Church's expense; [141] and the principle underlying the system was that children from their earliest years should receive systematic religious training. If the child, they held, was properly trained and taught to love and obey Jesus Christ, he would not need afterwards to be converted. He would be brought up as a member of the Kingdom of God. As long as the Brethren could find the money, they maintained this "Children's Economy." The date of Susannah's conversion was remembered, and became the date of the annual Children's Festival; and in every settlement and congregation special meetings for children were regularly held. But the system was found too expensive. At the Synod of 1769 it was abandoned. No longer could the Brethren maintain and educate the children of all their members; thencefoward they could maintain and educate only the children of those in church service.

For the sons of ministers they established a Paedagogium; for the daughters of ministers a Girls' School at Kleinwelke, in Saxony; and for candidates for ministerial service a Theological Seminary, situated first at Barby, then at Niesky, and finally at Gnadenfeld, in Silesia. At the same time, the Brethren laid down the rule that each congregation should have its own elementary day school. At first these schools were meant for Moravians only; but before long they were thrown open to the public. The principle of serving the public steadily grew. It began in the elementary schools; it led to the establishment of boarding-schools. The first step was taken in Denmark. At Christiansfeld, in Schleswig-Holstein, the Brethren had established a congregation by the special request of the Danish Government; and there, in 1774, they opened two boarding-schools for boys and girls. From that time the Brethren became more practical in their methods. Instead of attempting the hopeless task of providing free education, they now built a number of boarding-schools; and at the Synod of 1782 they officially recognized education as a definite part of their Church work. The chief schools were those at Neuwied-on-the-Rhine; Gnadenfrei, in Silesia; Ebersdorf, in Vogt-land; and Montmirail, in Switzerland. The style of architecture adopted was the Mansard. As the standard of education was high, the schools soon became famous; and as the religion taught was broad, the pupils came from all Protestant denominations. On this subject the well-known historian, Kurtz, has almost told the truth. He informs us that during the dreary period of Rationalism, the schools established by the Brethren were a "sanctuary for the old Gospel, with its blessed promises and glorious hopes." It would be better, however, to speak of these schools as barracks. If we think of the Brethren as retiring hermits, we shall entirely misunderstand their character. They fought the Rationalists with their own weapons; they gave a splendid classical, literary and scientific education; they enforced their discipline on the sons of barons and nobles; they staffed their schools with men of learning and piety; and these men, by taking a personal interest in the religious life of their pupils, trained up a band of fearless warriors for the holy cause of the Gospel. It was this force of personal influence and example that made the schools so famous; this that won the confidence of the public; and this that caused the Brethren to be so widely trusted as defenders of the faith and life of the Lutheran Church.

The fourth method employed by the Brethren was the Diaspora. Here again, as in the public schools, the Brethren never attempted to make proselytes. At the Synod of 1782, and again at a Conference of Diaspora-workers, held at Herrnhut (1785), the Brethren emphatically laid down the rule that no worker in the Diaspora should ever attempt to win converts for the Moravian Church. The Diaspora work was now at the height of its glory. In Lusatia the Brethren had centres of work at Herrnhut, Niesky and Kleinwelke; in Silesia, at Gnadenfrei, Gnadenberg, Gnadenfeld and Neusalz; in Pomerania, at Ruegen and Mecklenburg; in East Prussia, at Danzig, Koenigsberg and Elbing; in Thuringia, at Neudietendorf; in the Palatinate and the Wetterau; at Neuwied; in Brandenburg, at Berlin and Potsdam; in Denmark, at Christiansfeld, Schleswig, Fuehnen, and Copenhagen; in Norway, at Christiana, Drammen and Bergen; in Sweden, at Stockholm and Gothenburg; in Switzerland, at Basel, Bern, Zuerich and Montmirail; and finally, in Livonia and Esthonia, they employed about a hundred preachers and ministered to about six thousand souls. At this rate it would appear that the Moravians in Germany were increasing by leaps and bounds; but in reality they were doing nothing of the kind. At this time the Moravian influence was felt in every part of Germany; and yet during this very period they founded only the three congregations of Gnadenfeld, Gnadau, and Koenigsfeld.

But the greatest proof of the Brethren's power was their influence over Schleiermacher. Of all the religious leaders in Germany Schleiermacher was the greatest since Luther; and Schleiermacher learned his religion, both directly and indirectly, from the Brethren. It is sometimes stated in lives of Schleiermacher that he received his earliest religious impressions from his parents; but, on the other hand, it should be remembered that both his parents, in their turn, had come under Moravian influence. His father was a Calvinistic army chaplain, who had made the acquaintance of Brethren at Gnadenfrei (1778). He there adopted the Brethren's conception of religion; he became a Moravian in everything but the name; his wife passed through the same spiritual experience; he then settled down as Calvinist pastor in the colony of Anhalt; and finally, for the sake of his children, he visited the Brethren again at Gnadenfrei (1783). His famous son was now a lad of fifteen; and here, among the Brethren at Gnadenfrei, the young seeker first saw the heavenly vision. "It was here," he said, "that I first became aware of man's connection with a higher world. It was here that I developed that mystic faculty which I regard as essential, and which has often upheld and saved me amid the storms of doubt."

But Schleiermacher's father was not content. He had visited the Brethren both at Herrnhut and Niesky; he admired the Moravian type of teaching; and now he requested the U.E.C. to admit both his sons as pupils to the Paedagogium at Niesky. But the U.E.C. objected. The Paedagogium, they said, was meant for Moravian students only. As the old man, however, would take no refusal, the question was put to the Lot; the Lot gave consent; and to Niesky Schleiermacher and his brother came. For two years, therefore,

Schleiermacher studied at the Brethren's Paedagogium at Niesky; and here he learned some valuable lessons (1783-5). He learned the value of hard work; he formed a friendship with Albertini, and plunged with him into a passionate study of Greek and Latin literature; and he learned by personal contact with bright young souls that religion, when based on personal experience, is a thing of beauty and joy. Above all, he learned from the Brethren the value of the historical Christ. The great object of Schleiermacher's life was to reconcile science and religion. He attempted for the Germans of the eighteenth century what many theologians are attempting for us to-day. He endeavoured to make a "lasting treaty between living Christian faith and the spirit of free inquiry." He found that treaty existing already at Niesky. As the solemn time of confirmation drew near, the young lad was carried away by his feelings, and expected his spiritual instructor to fan the flame. "But no!" says Schleiermacher, "he led me back to the field of history. He urged me to inquire into the facts and quietly think out conclusions for myself." Thus Schleiermacher acquired at Niesky that scientific frame of mind, and also that passionate devotion to Christ, which are seen in every line he wrote.

From Niesksy he passed to the Theological Seminary at Barby (1785-87). But here the influence was of a different kind. Of the three theological professors at Barby— Baumeister, Bossart, and Thomas Moore—not one was intellectually fitted to deal with the religious difficulties of young men. Instead of talking frankly with the students about the burning problems of the day, they simply lectured on the old orthodox lines, asserted that certain doctrines were true, informed the young seekers that doubting was sinful, and closed every door and window of the college against the entrance of modern ideas. But modern ideas streamed in through the chinks. Young Schleiermacher was now like a golden eagle in a cage. At Niesky he had learned to think for himself; at Barby he was told that thinking for himself was wrong. He called the doctrines taught by the professors "stupid orthodoxy." He rejected, on intellectual grounds, their doctrine of the eternal Godhead of Christ; and he rejected on moral and spiritual grounds their doctrines of the total depravity of man, of eternal punishment, and of the substitutionary sufferings of Christ. He wrote a pathetic letter to his father. "I cannot accept these doctrines," he said. He begged his father to allow him to leave the college; the old man reluctantly granted the request; and Schleiermacher, therefore, left the Brethren and pursued his independent career.

And yet, though he differed from the Brethren in theology, he felt himself at one with them in religion. In one sense, he remained a Moravian to the end. He called himself a "Moravian of the higher order"; and by that phrase he probably meant that he had the Brethren's faith in Christ, but rejected their orthodox theology. He read their monthly magazine, "Nachrichten." He maintained his friendship with Bishop Albertini, and studied his sermons and poems. He kept in touch with the Brethren at Berlin, where his sister, Charlotte, lived in one of their establishments. He frequently stayed at Gnadenfrei, Barby, and Ebersdorf. He chatted with Albertini at Berthelsdorf. He described the Brethren's singing meetings as models. "They make a deep religious impression," he said, "which is often of greater value than many sermons." He loved their celebration of Passion Week, their triumphant Easter Morning service, and their beautiful Holy Communion. "There is no Communion to compare with theirs," he said; and many a non-Moravian has said the same. He admired the Moravian Church because she was free; and in one of his later writings he declared that if that Church could only be reformed according to the spirit of the age, she would be one of the grandest Churches in the world. "In fundamentals," he said, "the Brethren are right; it is only their Christology and theology that are bad, and these are only externals. What a pity they cannot separate the surface from the solid rock beneath." To him the fundamental truth of theology was the revelation of God in Jesus Christ; and that also was the fundamental element in the teaching of Zinzendorf. [142]

Meanwhile the great leader of the Brethren had passed away from earth. At the advanced age of eighty-eight, Bishop Spangenberg died at Berthelsdorf (1792). In history Spangenberg has not received his deserts. We have allowed him to be overshadowed by Zinzendorf. In genius, he was Zinzendorf's inferior; in energy, his equal; in practical wisdom, his superior. He had organized the first Moravian congregation in England, i.e., the one at Fetter Lane; he superintended the first campaign in Yorkshire; he led the vanguard in North America; he defended the Brethren in many a pamphlet just after the Sifting-Time; he gave their broad theology literary form; and for thirty years, by his wisdom, his skill, and his patience, he guided them through many a dangerous financial crisis. Amid all his labours he was modest, urbane and cheerful. In appearance his admirers called him apostolic. "He looked," said one, "as Peter must have looked when he stood before Ananias, or John, when he said, Little children, love each other."

"See there, Lavater," said another enthusiast, "that is what a Christian looks like."

But the noblest testimony was given by Becker, the editor of the German Times. In an article in that paper, Becker related how once he had an interview with Spangenberg, and how Spangenberg recounted some of his experiences during the War in North America. The face of the Bishop was aglow. The great editor was struck with amazement. At length he stepped nearer to the white-haired veteran, and said:—

"Happy man! reveal to me your secret! What is it that makes you so strong and calm? What light is this that illumines your soul? What power is this that makes you so content? Tell me, and make me happy for ever."

"For this," replied the simple Spangenberg, his eyes shining with joy, "for this I must thank my Saviour."

There lay the secret of Spangenberg's power; and there the secret of the services rendered by the Brethren when pious evangelicals in Germany trembled at the onslaught of the new theologians. For these services the Brethren have been both blamed and praised. According to that eminent historian, Ritschl, such men as Spangenberg were the bane of the Lutheran Church. According to Dorner, the evangelical theologian, the Brethren helped to save the Protestant faith from ruin. "When other Churches," says Dorner, "were sunk in sleep, when darkness was almost everywhere, it was she, the humble priestess of the sanctuary, who fed the sacred flame." Between two such doctors of divinity who shall judge? But perhaps the philosopher, Kant, will be able to help us. He was in the thick of the rationalist movement; and he lived in the town of Koenigsberg, where the Brethren had a Society. One day a student complained to Kant that his philosophy did not bring peace to the heart.

"Peace!" replied the great philosopher, "peace of heart you will never find in my lecture room. If you want peace, you must go to that little Moravian Church over the way. That is the place to find peace." [143]

Chapter 3: A Fall and a Recovery (1800-1857)

AS the Rationalist movement spread in Germany, it had two distinct effects upon the Brethren. The first was wholesome; the second was morbid. At first it aroused them to a sense of their duty, and made them gallant soldiers of the Cross; and then, towards the close of the eighteenth century, it filled them with a horror of all changes and reforms and of all independence in thought and action. The chief cause of this sad change was the French Revolution. At first sight it may seem that the French Revolution has little to do with our story; and Carlyle does not discuss this part of his subject. But no nation lives to itself; and Robespierre, Mirabeau and Marat shook the civilized world. In England the French Revolution caused a general panic. At first, of course, it produced a few revolutionaries, of the stamp of Tom Paine; but, on the whole, its general effect was to make our politicians afraid of changes, to strengthen the forces of conservatism, and thus to block the path of the social and political reformer. Its effect on the Brethren was similar. As the news of its horrors spread through Europe, good Christian people could not help feeling that all free thought led straight to atheism, and all change to revolution and murder; and, therefore, the leading Brethren in Germany opposed liberty because they were afraid of license, and reform because they were afraid of revolution.

For the long period, therefore of eighteen years, the Moravian Church in Germany remained at a standstill (1800-18). At Herrnhut the Brethren met in a General Synod, and there the Conservatives won a signal victory. Already the first shots in the battle had been fired, and already the U.E.C. had taken stern measures. Instead of facing the situation frankly, they first shut their own eyes and then tried to make others as blind as themselves. At this Synod the deputy for Herrnhut was a lawyer named Riegelmann; and, being desirous to do his duty efficiently, he had asked for a copy of the "Synodal Results" of 1764 and 1769. His request was moderate and sensible. No deputy could possibly do his duty unless he knew the existing laws of the Church. But his request was sternly refused. He was informed that no private individual was entitled to a copy of the "Results." Thus, at the opening of the nineteenth century, a false note was struck; and the Synod deliberately prevented honest inquiry. Of the members, all but two were church officials. For all practical purposes the laymen were unrepresented. At the head of the conservative party was Godfrey Cunow. In vain some English ministers requested that the use of the Lot should no longer be enforced in marriages. The arguments of Cunow prevailed. "Our entire constitution demands," he said, "that in our settlements no marriage shall be contracted without the Lot." But the Brethren laid down a still more depressing principle. For some years the older leaders had noticed, with feelings of mingled pain and horror, that revolutionary ideas had found a home even in quiet

Moravian settlements; and in order to keep such ideas in check, the Synod now adopted the principle that the true kernel of the Moravian Church consisted, not of all the communicant members, but only of a "Faithful Few." We can hardly call this encouraging. It tempted the "Faithful Few" to be Pharisees, and banned the rest as black sheep. And the Pastoral Letter, drawn up by the Synod, and addressed to all the congregations, was still more disheartening. "It will be better," ran one fatal sentence, "for us to decrease in numbers and increase in piety than to be a large multitude, like a body without a spirit." We call easily see what such a sentence means. It means that the Brethren were afraid of new ideas, and resolved to stifle them in their birth.

The new policy produced strange results. At the Theological Seminary in Niesky the professors found themselves in a strange position. If they taught the old theology of Spangenberg, they would be untrue to their convictions; if they taught their convictions, they would be untrue to the Church; and, therefore, they solved the problem by teaching no theology at all. Instead of lecturing on the Bible, they lectured now on philosophy; instead of expounding the teaching of Christ and His Apostles, they expounded the teaching of Kant, Fichte and Jacobi; and when the students became ministers, they had little but philosophy to offer the people. For ordinary people philosophy is as tasteless as the white of an egg. As the preachers spoke far above the heads of the people, they soon lost touch with their flocks; the hungry sheep looked up, and were not fed; the sermons were tinkling brass and clanging cymbal; and the ministers, instead of attending to their pastoral duties, were hidden away in their studies in clouds of philosophical and theological smoke, and employed their time composing discourses, which neither they nor the people could understand. Thus the shepherds lived in one world, and the wandering sheep in another; and thus the bond of sympathy between pastor and people was broken. For this reason the Moravian Church in Germany began now to show signs of decay in moral and spiritual power; and the only encouraging signs of progress were the establishment of the new settlement of Koenigsfeld in the Black Forest, the Diaspora work in the Baltic Provinces, officially recognized by the Czar, the growth of the boarding-schools, and the extension of foreign missions. In the boarding-schools the Brethren were at their best. At most of them the pupils were prepared for confirmation, and the children of Catholics were admitted. But the life in the congregations was at a low ebb. No longer were the Brethren's Houses homes of Christian fellowship; they were now little better than lodging-houses, and the young men had become sleepy, frivolous, and even in some cases licentious. For a short time the U.E.C. tried to remedy this evil by enforcing stricter rules; and when this vain proceeding failed, they thought of abolishing Brethren's Houses altogether. At the services in Church the Bible was little read, and the people were content to feed their souls on the Hymn-book and the Catechism. The Diacony managers were slothful in business, and the Diaconies ceased to pay. The subscriptions to central funds dwindled. The fine property at Barby was abandoned. The Diaspora work was curtailed.

Another cause of decay was the growing use of the Lot. For that growth the obvious reason was that, when the Brethren saw men adrift on every side, they felt that they themselves must have an anchor that would hold. It was even used in the boarding-schools. No pupil could be admitted to a school unless his application had been confirmed by the Lot. [144] No man could be a member of a Conference, no election was valid, no law was carried, no important business step was taken, without the consent of the Lot. For example, it was by the decision of the Lot that the Brethren abandoned their cause at Barby; and thus, afraid of intellectual progress, they submitted affairs of importance to an external artificial authority. Again and again the U.E.C. desired to summon a Synod; and again and again the Lot rejected the proposal.

Meanwhile another destructive force was working. Napoleon Buonaparte was scouring Europe, and the German settlements were constantly invaded by soldiers. At Barby, Generals Murat and Bernadotte were lodged in the castle, and entertained by the Warden. At Gnadau the French made the chapel their headquarters, killed and ate the live stock, ransacked the kitchens and cellars, cleared out the stores, and made barricades of the casks, wheelbarrows and carts. At Neudietendorf the Prussians lay like locusts. At Ebersdorf, Napoleon lodged in the Brethren's House, and quartered twenty or thirty of his men in every private dwelling. At Kleinwelke, where Napoleon settled with the whole staff of the Grand Army, the Single Sisters had to nurse two thousand wounded warriors; and the pupils in the boarding-school had to be removed to Uhyst. At Gnadenberg the settlement was almost ruined. The furniture was smashed, the beds were cut up, the tools of the tradesmen were spoiled, and the soldiers took possession of the Sisters'House. But Napoleon afterwards visited the settlement, declared that he knew the Brethren to be a quiet and peaceable people, and promised to protect them in future. He did not, however, offer them any compensation; his promise of protection was not fulfilled; and a few months later his own soldiers gutted the place again. At Herrnhut, on one occasion, when the French were there, the chapel was illuminated, and a service was held to celebrate Napoleon's birthday; and then a little later Bluecher arrived on the scene, and summoned the people to give thanks to God for a victory over the French. At Niesky the whole settlement became a general infirmary. Amid scenes such as this Church progress was impossible. The cost in money was enormous. At Herrnhut alone the levies amounted to - L-3,000; to this must be added the destruction of property and the feeding of thousands of troops of both sides; and thus the Brethren's expenses were increased by many thousands of pounds.

At length, however, at Waterloo Napoleon met his conqueror; the great criminal was captured and sent to St. Helena; and then, while he was playing chess and grumbling at the weather, the Brethren met again at Herrnhut in another General Synod (1818). At this Synod some curious regulations were made. For the purpose of cultivating personal holiness, Bishop Cunow proposed that henceforward the members of the Moravian Church should be divided into two classes. In the first class he placed the ordinary members—i.e., those who had been confirmed or who had been received from other

270

Churches; and all belonging to this class were allowed to attend Communion once a quarter. His second class was a sacred "Inner Circle." It consisted of those, and only those, who made a special religious profession. No one could be admitted to this "Inner Circle" without the sanction of the Lot; and none but those belonging to the "Circle" could be members of the Congregation Council or Committee. All members belonging to this class attended the Communion once a month. For a wonder this strange resolution was carried, and remained in force for seven years; and at bottom its ruling principle was that only those elected by the Lot had any real share in Church government. But the question of the Lot was still causing trouble. Again there came a request from abroad—this time from America—that it should no longer be enforced in marriages. For seven years the question was keenly debated, and the radicals had to fight very hard for victory. First the Synod passed a resolution that the Lot need not be used for marriages except in the regular settlements; then the members in the settlements grumbled, and were granted the same privilege (1819), and only ministers and missionaries were compelled to marry by Lot; then the ministers begged for liberty, and received the same privilege as the laymen (1825); and, finally, the missionaries found release (1836), and thus the enforced use of the Lot in marriages passed out of Moravian history.

But the Brethren had better work on hand than to tinker with their constitution. At the root of their troubles had been the neglect of the Bible. In order, therefore, to restore the Bible to its proper position in Church esteem, the Brethren now established the Theological College at Gnadenfeld (1818). There John Plitt took the training of the students in hand; there systematic lectures were given on Exegesis, Dogmatics, Old Testament Introduction, Church History, and Brethren's History; there, in a word, John Plitt succeeded in training a band of ministers who combined a love for the Bible with love for the Brethren's Church. At the same time, the Synod appointed an "Educational Department" in the U.E.C.; the boarding-schools were now more efficiently managed; and the number of pupils ran up to thirteen hundred.

Amid this new life the sun rose on the morning of the 17th of June, 1722, a hundred years after Christian David had felled the first tree at Herrnhut. The Brethren glanced at the past. The blood of the martyrs seemed dancing in their veins. At Herrnhut the archives of the Church had been stored; Frederick Koelbing had ransacked the records; and only a few months before he had produced his book, "Memorial Days of the Renewed Brethren's Church." From hand to hand the volume passed, and was read with eager delight. The spirit of patriotic zeal was revived. Never surely was there such a gathering in Herrnhut as on that Centenary Day. From all the congregations in Germany, from Denmark, from Sweden, from Holland, from Switzerland, from England, the Brethren streamed to thank the Great Shepherd for His never-failing kindnesses. There were Brethren and friends of the Brethren, clergymen and laymen, poor peasants in simple garb from the old homeland in Moravia, and high officials from the Court of Saxony in purple and scarlet and gold. As the vast assembly pressed into the Church, the trombones sounded forth, and the choir sang the words of the Psalmist, so rich in historic associations: "Here the sparrow hath found a home, and the swallow a nest for her young, even thine altars, oh, Lord of Hosts!" It was a day of high jubilation and a day of penitent mourning; a day of festive robes and a day of sack-cloth and ashes. As the great throng, some thousands in number, and arranged in choirs, four and four, stood round the spot on the roadside where Christian David had raised his axe, and where a new memorial-stone now stood, they rejoiced because during those hundred years the seed had become a great tree, and they mourned because the branches had begun to wither and the leaves begun to fall. The chief speaker was John Baptist Albertini, the old friend of Schleiermacher. Stern and clear was the message he gave; deep and full was the note it sounded. "We have lost the old love," he said; "let us repent. Let us take a warning from the past; let us return unto the Lord." With faces abashed, with heads bowed, with hearts renewed, with tears of sorrow and of joy in their eyes, the Brethren went thoughtfully homewards.

At the next General Synod (1825), however, they made an alarming discovery. In spite of the revival of Church enthusiasm, they found that during the last seven years they had lost no fewer than one thousand two hundred members; and, searching about to find the cause, they found it in Bishop Cunow's "Inner Circle." It was time to abolish that "Circle"; and abolished it therefore was.

At the next General Synod (1836), the Brethren took another step forward. In order to encourage the general study of the Bible, they arranged that in every congregation regular Bible readings should be held; and, in order to deepen the interest in evangelistic work, they decreed that a prayer meeting should be held the first Monday of every month. At this meeting the topic of intercession was to be, not the mere prosperity of the Brethren, but the cultivation of good relations with other Churches and the extension of the Kingdom of God throughout the world.

The next sign of progress was the wonderful revival in the Paedagogium at Niesky (1841). For nine years that important institution, where ministerial candidates were trained before they entered the Theological Seminary, had been under the management of Frederick Immanuel Kleinschmidt; and yet, despite his sternness and piety, the boys had shown but a meagre spirit of religion. If Kleinschmidt rebuked them, they hated him; if he tried to admonish them privately, they told him fibs. There, at the very heart of the young Church life, religion was openly despised; and the Paedagogium had now become little better than an ordinary private school. If a boy, for example, wished to read his Bible, he had to do so in French, pretend that his purpose was simply to learn a new language, and thus escape the mockery of his schoolmates. The case was alarming. If piety was despised in the school of the prophets, what pastors was Israel likely to have in the future?

The revival began very quietly. One boy, Prince Reuss, was summoned home to be present at his father's death-bed; and when he returned to the school a few days later found himself met by an amount of sympathy which boys are not accustomed to show. A change of some kind had taken place during his absence. The nightwatchman, Hager, had been heard praying in his attic for the boys. A boy, in great trouble with a trigonometrical problem which would not come right, had solved the difficulty by linking work with prayer. The boys in the "First Room" —i.e., the elder boys—made an agreement to speak with one another openly before the Holy Communion.

At length, on November 13th, when the Brethren in the other congregations were celebrating the centenary of the Headship of Christ, there occurred, at the evening Communion at Niesky, "something new, something unusual, something mightily surprising." With shake of hand and without a word those elder boys made a solemn covenant to serve Christ. Among them were two who, fifty years later, were still famous Moravian preachers; and when they recalled the events of that evening they could give no explanation to each other. "It was," they said, in fond recollection, "something unusual, but something great and holy, that overcame us and moved us. It must have been the Spirit of Christ." For those boys that wonderful Communion service had ever sacred associations; and Bishop Wunderling, in telling the story, declared his own convictions. "The Lord took possession of the house," he said, "bound all to one another and to Himself, and over all was poured the spirit of love and forgiveness, and a power from above was distributed from the enjoyment of the Communion."

"What wonder was it," wrote one boy home, "that when we brothers united to praise the Lord, He did not put to shame our longings and our faith, but kindled others from our fire."

In this work the chief leaders were Kleinschmidt the headmaster, Gustave Tietzen, Ferdinand Geller, and Ernest Reichel. At first, of course, there was some danger that the boys would lose their balance; but the masters, in true Moravian style, checked all signs of fanaticism. It is hardly correct to call the movement a revival. It is better to call it an awakening. It was fanned by historic memories, was very similar to the first awakening at Herrnhut, and soon led to very similar results. No groans, or tears, or morbid fancies marred the scene. In the playground the games continued as usual. On every hand were radiant faces, and groups in earnest chat. No one ever asked, "Is so-and-so converted?" For those lads the burning question was, "In what way can I be like Christ?" As the boys retired to rest at night, they would ask the masters to remember them in prayer, and the masters asked the same in return of the boys. The rule of force was over. Before, old Kleinschmidt, like our English Dr. Temple, had been feared as a "just beast." Now he was the lovable father. At revivals in schools it has sometimes happened that while the boys have looked more pious, they have not always been more diligent and truthful; but at Niesky the boys now became fine models of industry, honesty and good manners. They confessed their faults to one another, gave each other friendly warnings, formed unions for prayer, applied the Bible to daily life, were conscientious in the class-room and in the playground; and then, when these golden days were over, went out with tongues of flame to spread the news through the Church. The real test of a revival is its lasting effect on character. If it leads to selfish dreaming, it is clay; if it leads to life-long sacrifice, it is gold; and well the awakening at Niesky stood the test.

At the next General Synod all present could see that the Moravian Church was now restored to full life, and the American deputies, who had come to see her decently interrred, were amazed at her hopefulness and vigour. At that Synod the signs of vigorous life were many (1848). For the first time the Brethren opened their meetings to the public, allowed reporters to be present, and had the results of their proceedings printed and sold. For the first time they now resolved that, instead of shutting themselves up in settlements, they would try, where possible, to establish town and country congregations. For the first time they now agreed that, in the English and American congregations, new members might be received without the sanction of the Lot. Meanwhile, the boys awakened at Niesky were already in harness. Some had continued their studies at Gnadenfeld, and were now powerful preachers. Some had become teachers at Koenigsfeld, Kleinwelke, and Neuwied. Some were preaching the Gospel in foreign lands. Along the Rhine, in South and West Germany, in Metz and the Wartebruch, and in Russian Poland, the Brethren opened new fields of Diaspora work; and away in the broadening mission field the energy was greater than ever. In Greenland a new station was founded at Friedrichstal; in Labrador, at Hebron; in Surinam, at Bambey; in South Africa, at Siloh and Goshen; on the Moskito Coast, at Bluefields; in Australia, at Ebenezer; and in British India, near Tibet, at Kyelang.

And thus our narrative brings us down to 1857. We may pause to sum up results. If a church is described as making progress, most readers generally wish to know how many new congregations she has founded, and how many members she has gained. But progress of that kind was not what the Brethren desired; and during the period covered by this chapter they founded only one new congregation. They had still only seventeen congregations in Germany, in the proper sense of that word; but, on the other hand, they had fifty-nine Diaspora centres, and about one hundred and fifty Diaspora workers. At the heart, therefore, of all their endeavours we see the design, not to extend the Moravian Church, but to hold true to the old ideals of Zinzendorf. In that sense, at least, they had made good progress. They showed to the world a spirit of brotherly union; they were on good terms with other Churches; they made their schools and their Diaspora centres homes of Christian influence; and, above all, like a diamond set in gold, there flashed still with its ancient lustre the missionary spirit of the fathers.

Chapter 4: The British Collapse (1760-1801)

OF all the problems raised by the history of the Brethren, the most difficult to solve is the one we have now to face. In the days of John Wesley, the Moravians in England were famous; in the days of Robertson, of Brighton, they were almost unknown. For a hundred years the Moravians in England played so obscure and modest a part in our national life that our great historians, such as Green and Lecky, do not even notice their existence, and the problem now before us is, what caused this swift and mysterious decline?

As the companions of Zinzendorf—Boehler, Cennick, Rogers and Okeley—passed one by one from the scenes of their labours, there towered above the other English Brethren a figure of no small grandeur. It was Benjamin La Trobe, once a famous preacher in England. He sprang from a Huguenot family, and had first come forward in Dublin. He had been among the first there to give a welcome to John Cennick, had held to Cennick when others left him, had helped to form a number of his hearers into the Dublin congregation, and had been with Cennick on his romantic journey's among the bogs and cockpits of Ulster. As the years rolled on, he came more and more to the front. At Dublin he had met a teacher of music named Worthington, and a few years later La Trobe and Worthington were famous men at Fulneck. When Fulneck chapel was being built, La Trobe stood upon the roof of a house to preach. When the chapel was finished, La Trobe became Brethren's labourer, and his friend Worthington played the organ. In those days Fulneck Chapel was not large enough to hold the crowds that came, and La Trobe had actually to stand upon the roof to harangue the vast waiting throng. As Cennick had been before in Ireland, so La Trobe was now in England. He was far above most preachers of his day. "He enraptured his audience," says an old account, "by his resistless eloquence. His language flowed like rippling streams, and his ideas sparkled like diamonds. His taste was perfect, and his illustrations were dazzling; and when he painted the blackness of the human heart, when he depicted the matchless grace of Christ, when he described the beauty of holiness, he spoke with an energy, with a passion, with a dignified sweep of majestic power which probed the heart, and pricked the conscience, and charmed the troubled breast." It was he of whom it is so quaintly recorded in a congregation diary: "Br. La Trobe spoke much on many things."

For twenty-one years this brilliant preacher was the chief manager of the Brethren's work in England; and yet, though he was not a German himself, his influence was entirely German in character (1765-86). He was manager of the Brethren's English finances; he was appointed to his office by the German U.E.C.; and thus, along with James Hutton as Secretary, he acted as official representative of the Directing Board in England.

In many ways his influence was all for good. He helped to restore to vigorous life the "Society for the Furtherance of the Gospel" (1768) remained its President till his death, and did much to further its work in Labrador. He was a diligent writer and translator. He wrote a "Succinct View of the Missions" of the Brethren (1771), and thus brought the subject of foreign missions before the Christian public; and in order to let inquirers know what sort of people the Moravians really were, he translated and published Spangenberg's "Idea of Faith," Spangenberg's "Concise Account of the Present Constitution of the Unitas Fratrum," and David Cranz's "History of the Brethren." The result was good. The more people read these works by La Trobe, the more they respected the Brethren. "In a variety of publications," said the London Chronicle, "he removed every aspersion against the Brethren, and firmly established their reputation." He was well known in higher circles, was the friend of Dr. Johnson, and worked in union with such well-known Evangelical leaders as Rowland Hill, William Romaine, John Newton, Charles Wesley, Hannah More, Howell Harris, and Bishop Porteous, the famous advocate of negro emancipation. Above all, he cleansed the Brethren's reputation from the last stains of the mud thrown by such men as Rimius and Frey. He was a friend of the Bishop of Chester; he was a popular preacher in Dissenting and Wesleyan Chapels; he addressed Howell Harris's students at Trevecca; he explained the Brethren's doctrines and customs to Lord Hillsborough, the First Commissioner of the Board of Trade and Plantations; and thus by his pen, by his wisdom and by his eloquence, he caused the Brethren to be honoured both by Anglicans and by Dissenters. At this period James Hutton—now a deaf old man—was a favourite at the Court of George III. No longer were the Brethren denounced as immoral fanatics; no longer did John Wesley feel it his duty to expose their errors. As John Wesley grew older and wiser, he began to think more kindly of the Brethren. He renewed his friendship with James Hutton, whom he had not seen for twenty-five years (Dec. 21, 1771); he visited Bishop John Gambold in London, and recorded the event in his Journal with the characteristic remark, "Who but Count Zinzendorf could have separated such friends as we are?" He called, along with his brother Charles, on John de Watteville at Lindsey House; and, above all, when Lord Lyttleton, in his book "Dialogues of the Dead," attacked the character of the Brethren, John Wesley himself spoke out nobly in their defence. "Could his lordship," he wrote in his Journal (August 30th, 1770), "show me in England many more sensible men than Mr. Gambold and Mr. Okeley? And yet both of these were called Moravians...What sensible Moravian, Methodist or Hutchinsonian did he ever calmly converse with? What does he know of them but from the caricatures drawn by Bishop Lavington or Bishop Warburton? And did he ever give himself the trouble of reading the answers to these warm, lively men? Why should a good-natured and a thinking man thus condemn whole bodies by the lump?" But the pleasantest proof of Wesley's good feeling was still to come. At the age of eighty he went over to Holland, visited the Brethren's beautiful settlement at Zeist, met there his old friend, Bishop Anthony Seifferth, and asked to hear some Moravian music and singing. The day was Wesley's birthday. As it happened, however, to be "Children's Prayer-Day" as well, the minister, being busy with many meetings, was not able to ask Wesley to dinner; and, therefore, he invited him instead to come to the children's love-feast. John Wesley went to the chapel, took part in the love-feast, and heard the little children sing a "Birth-Day Ode" in his honour (June 28th, 1783). The old feud between Moravians and Methodists was over. It ended in the children's song. [145]

One instance will show La Trobe's reputation in England (1777). At that time there lived in London a famous preacher, Dr. Dodd; and now, to the horror of all pious people, Dr. Dodd was accused and convicted of embezzlement, and condemned to death. Never was London more excited. A petition with twenty-three thousand signatures was sent up in Dodd's behalf. Frantic plots were made to rescue the criminal from prison. But Dodd, in his trouble, was in need of spiritual aid; and the two men for whom he sent were John Wesley and La Trobe. By Wesley he was visited thrice; by La Trobe, at his own request, repeatedly; and La Trobe was the one who brought comfort to his soul, stayed with him till the end, and afterwards wrote an official account of his death.

And yet, on the other hand, the policy now pursued by La Trobe was the very worst policy possible for the Moravians in England. For that policy, however, we must lay the blame, not on the man, but on the system under which he worked. As long as the Brethren's Church in England was under the control of the U.E.C., it followed, as a matter of course, that German ideas would be enforced on British soil; and already, at the second General Synod, the Brethren had resolved that the British work must be conducted on German lines. Never did the Brethren make a greater blunder in tactics. In Germany the system had a measure of success, and has flourished till the present day; in England it was doomed to failure at the outset. La Trobe gave the system a beautiful name. He called it the system of "United Flocks." On paper it was lovely to behold; in practice it was the direct road to consumption. In name it was English enough; in nature it was Zinzendorf's Diaspora. At no period had the Brethren a grander opportunity of extending their borders in England than during the last quarter of the eighteenth century. In Yorkshire, with Fulneck as a centre, they had four flourishing congregations, societies in Bradford and Leeds, and preaching places as far away as Doncaster and Kirby Lonsdale, in Westmoreland. In Lancashire, with Fairfield as a centre, they were opening work in Manchester and Chowbent. In Cheshire, with Dukinfield as a centre, they had a number of societies on the "Cheshire Plan," including a rising cause at Bullock-Smithy, near Stockport. In the Midlands, with Ockbrook as a centre, they had preaching places in a dozen surrounding villages. In Bedfordshire, with Bedford as a centre, they had societies at Riseley, Northampton, Eydon, Culworth and other places. In Wales, with Haverfordwest as a centre, they had societies at Laughharne, Fishguard, Carmarthen and Carnarvon. In Scotland, with Ayre [146] as a centre, they had societies at Irvine and Tarbolton, and preaching-places at Annan, Blackhall, Dumfries, Edinburgh, Glasgow, Kilsyth, Kilmarnock, Ladyburn, Prestwick, Westtown, and twenty smaller places. In the West of England, with Bristol and Tytherton as centres, they had preaching-places at Apperley, in Gloucestershire; Fome and Bideford, in Somerset; Plymouth and Exeter, in

Devon; and many villages in Wiitshire. In the North of Ireland, with Gracehill as a centre, they had preaching-places at Drumargan, Billies, Arva (Cavan), and many other places.

For the Brethren, therefore, the critical question was, what to do with the societies and preaching-places? There lay the secret of success or failure; and there they committed their great strategic blunder. They had two alternatives before them. The one was to treat each society or preaching-place as the nucleus of a future congregation; the other was to keep it as a mere society. And the Brethren, in obedience to orders from Germany, chose the latter course. At the Moravian congregations proper the strictest rules were enforced; in most congregations there were Brethren's and Sisters' Houses; and all full members of the Moravian Church had to sign a document known as the "Brotherly Agreement." (1771) In that document the Brethren gave some remarkable pledges. They swore fidelity to the Augsburg Confession. They promised to do all in their power to help the Anglican Church, and to encourage all her members to be loyal to her. They declared that they would never proselytize from any other denomination. They promised that no marriage should take place without the consent of the Elders; that all children must be educated in one of the Brethren's schools; that they would help to support the widows, old people and orphans; that no member should set up in business without the consent of the Elders; that they would never read any books of a harmful nature. At each congregation these rules— and others too many to mention here—were read in public once a year; each member had a printed copy, and any member who broke the "Agreement" was liable to be expelled. Thus the English Brethren signed their names to an "Agreement" made in Germany, and expressing German ideals of religious life. If it never became very popular, we need not wonder. But this "Agreement" was not binding on the societies and preaching-places. As the Brethren in Germany founded societies without turning them into settlements, so the Brethren in England conducted preaching-places without turning them into congregations and without asking their hearers to become members of the Moravian Church; and a strict rule was laid down that only such hearers as had a "distinct call to the Brethren's Church" should be allowed to join it. The distinct call came through the Lot. At nearly all the societies and preaching-places, therefore, the bulk of the members were flatly refused admission to the Moravian Church; they remained, for the most part, members of the Church of England; and once a quarter, with a Moravian minister at their head, they marched in procession to the Communion in the parish church. For unselfishness this policy was unmatched; but it nearly ruined the Moravian Church in England. At three places—Woodford, [147] Baildon and Devonport—the Brethren turned societies into congregations; but most of the others were sooner or later abandoned. In Yorkshire the Brethren closed their chapel at Pudsey, and abandoned their societies at Holbeck, Halifax, Wibsey and Doncaster. At Manchester they gave up their chapel in Fetter Lane. In Cheshire they retreated from Bullock Smithy; in the Midlands from Northampton; in London from Chelsea; in Somerset from Bideford and Frome; in Devon from Exeter and Plymouth; in Gloucestershire from Apperley; in Scotland from Irvine, Glasgow, Edinburgh, Dumfries and thirty or forty other places; [148] in Wales from Fishguard,

Laugharn, Carmarthen and Carnarvon; in Ireland from Arva, Billies, Drumargan, Ballymena, Gloonen, Antrim, Dromore, Crosshill, Artrea, Armagh, and so on. And the net result of this policy was that when Bishop Holmes, the Brethren's Historian, published his "History of the Brethren" (1825), he had to record the distressing fact that in England the Moravians had only twenty congregations, in Ireland only six, and that the total number of members was only four thousand eight hundred and sixty-seven. The question is sometimes asked to-day: How is it that the Moravian Church is so small? For that smallness more reasons than one may be given; but one reason was certainly the singular policy expounded in the present chapter. [149]

Chapter 5: The British Advance (1801-1856)

BUT our problem is not yet solved. As soon as the nineteenth century opened, the Brethren began to look forward with hope to the future; and their leading preachers still believed in the divine and holy calling of the Moravian Church. Of those preachers the most famous was Christian Frederick Ramftler. He was a typical Moravian minister. He was a type in his character, in his doctrine, and in his fortunes. He came of an old Moravian family, and had martyr's blood in his veins. He was born at the Moravian settlement at Barby (1780). At the age of six he attended a Good Friday service, and was deeply impressed by the words, "He bowed his head and gave up the ghost"; and although he could never name the date of his conversion, he was able to say that his religion was based on the love of Christ and on the obligation to love Christ in return. At the age of seven he was sent to the Moravian school at Kleinwelke; he then entered the Paedagogium at Barby, and completed his education by studying theology at Niesky. At that place he was so anxious to preach the Gospel that, as he had no opportunity of preaching in the congregation, he determined to preach to the neighbouring Wends; and, as he knew not a word of their language, he borrowed one of their minister's sermons, learned it by heart, ascended the pulpit, and delivered the discourse with such telling energy that the delighted people exclaimed: "Oh, that this young man might always preach to us instead of our sleepy parson." For that freak he was gravely rebuked by the U.E.C., and he behaved with more discretion in the future. For two years he served the Church as a schoolmaster, first at Neusalz-on-the-Oder, and then at Uhyst; and then, to his surprise, he received a call to England. For the moment he was staggered. He consulted the Lot; the Lot gave consent; and, therefore, to England he came. For six years he now served as master in the Brethren's boarding-school at Fairfield; and then, in due course, he was called as minister to the Brethren's congregation at Bedford. As soon, however, as he accepted the call, he was informed that he would have to marry; his wife was found for him by the Church; the marriage turned out a happy one; and thus, with her as an official helpmate, he commenced his ministerial career (1810). At Bedford he joined with other ministers—such as Legh Richmond and S. Hillyard—in founding Bible associations. At Fulneck—where he was stationed twelve years—he was so beloved by his congregation that one member actually said: "During seven years your name has not once been omitted in our family prayers." At Bristol he was noted for his missionary zeal, took an interest in the conversion of the Jews, and often spoke at public meetings on behalf of the Church Missionary Society; and in one year he travelled a thousand miles on behalf of the "London Association in aid of Moravian Missions." In manner he was rough and abrupt; at heart he was gentle as a woman. He was a strict disciplinarian, a keen questioner, and an unflinching demander of a Christian walk. Not one jot or tittle would he allow his people to yield to the loose ways of the world. In his sermons he dealt hard blows at cant; and in his private conversation he generally managed to put his finger upon the sore spot. One day a collier came to see him, and complained, in a rather whining tone, that the path of his life was dark.

"H'm," growled Ramftler, who hated sniffling, "is it darker than it was in the coal-pit?"

The words proved the collier's salvation.

In all his habits Ramftler was strictly methodical. He always rose before six; he always finished his writing by eleven; and he kept a list of the texts from which he preached. As that list has been preserved, we are able to form some notion of his style; and the chief point to notice is that his preaching was almost entirely from the New Testament. At times, of course, he gave his people systematic lectures on the Patriarchs, the Prophets and the Psalms; but, speaking, broadly, his favourite topic was the Passion History. Above all, like most Moravian ministers, he was an adept in dealing with children. At the close of the Sunday morning service, he came down from the pulpit, took his seat at the Communion table, put the children through their catechism, and then asked all who wished to be Christians to come and take his hand.

At length, towards the close of his life, he was able to take some part in pioneer work. Among his numerous friends at Bristol was a certain Louis West.

"Have you never thought," said Ramftler, "of becoming a preacher of the Gospel?"

"I believe," replied West, "I shall die a Moravian minister yet."

"Die as a minister!" snapped Ramftler. "You ought to live as one!"

The words soon came true. In response to an invitation from some pious people, Ramftler paid a visit to Brockweir, a little village on the Wye, a few miles above Tintern. The village was a hell on earth. It was without a church, and possessed seven public-houses. There was a field of labour for the Brethren. As soon as Ramftler could collect the money, he had a small church erected, laid the corner-stone himself, and had the pleasure of seeing West the first minister of the new congregation.

And like Ramftler was many another of kindred blood. At Wyke, John Steinhauer (1773-76), the children's friend, had a printing press, wherewith he printed hymns and passages of Scripture in days when children's books were almost unknown. At Fulneck the famous teacher, Job Bradley, served for forty-five years (1765-1810), devoted his life to the spiritual good of boys, and summed up the passion of his life in the words he was often heard to sing:—

Saviour, Saviour, love the children;
Children, children, love the Saviour.

At Kimbolton, Bishop John King Martyn founded a new congregation. At Kilwarlin, Basil Patras Zula revived a flagging cause. If the Moravian Church was small in England, it was not because her ministers were idle, or because they were lacking in moral and spiritual power.

And yet, fine characters though they were, these men could do little for Church extension. They were still tied down by the "Brotherly Agreement." They aimed at quality rather than quantity. As long as the Brethren's work in England remained under German management, that "Brotherly Agreement" remained their charter of faith and practice. For power and place they had not the slightest desire. At their public service on Sunday mornings they systematically joined in the prayer, "From the unhappy desire of becoming great, preserve us, gracious Lord and God." As long as they were true to the Agreement and the Bible, they do not appear to have cared very much whether they increased in numbers or not. For them the only thing that mattered was the cultivation of personal holiness. As the preaching-places fell away they devoted their attention more and more to the care of the individual. They had a deep reverence for the authority of Scripture. No man could be a member of the Moravian Church unless he promised to read his Bible and hold regular family worship. "The Bible," ran one clause of the Agreement, "shall be our constant study; we will read it daily in our families, with prayer for the influence of the Holy Spirit of God." If that duty was broken, the member was liable to expulsion. And the same held good with the other clauses of the "Agreement." We often read in the congregation diaries of members being struck off the rolls for various sins. For cursing, for lying, for slandering, for evil-speaking, for fraud, for deceit, for drunkenness, for sabbath breaking, for gambling or any other immorality—for all these offences the member, if he persisted in his sin, was summarily expelled. In some of their ideals the Brethren were like the Puritans; in others like the Quakers. They were modest in dress, never played cards, and condemned theatres and dancing as worldly follies. As they still entertained a horror of war, they preferred not to serve as soldiers; and any Moravian could obtain a certificate from the magistrates exempting him from personal military service. [150] At the same time, they were loyal to Church and State, had a great love for the Church of England, regarded that Church as the bulwark of Protestantism, detested Popery, and sometimes spoke of the Pope as the Man of Sin. And yet, sturdy Protestants though they were, they had a horror of religious strife. "We will abstain from religious controversy," was another clause in the Agreement; and, therefore, they never took any part in the religious squabbles of the age. For example, the Brethren took no part in the fight for Catholic emancipation. As they did not regard themselves as Dissenters, they declined to join the rising movement for the separation of Church and State; and yet, on the other hand, they lived on good terms with all Evangelical Christians, and willingly exchanged pulpits with Methodists and Dissenters. At this period their chief doctrine was redemption through the blood of Christ. I have noticed, in reading the memoirs of the time, that although the authors differed in character, they were all alike in their spiritual experiences. They all spoke of themselves as "poor sinners"; they all condemned their own self-righteousness; and they all traced what virtues they possessed to the meritorious sufferings of the Redeemer. Thus the Brethren stood for a

Puritan standard, a Bible religion and a broad Evangelical Faith. "Yon man," said Robert Burns's father in Ayr, "prays to Christ as though he were God." But the best illustration of the Brethren's attitude is the story of the poet himself. As Robert and his brother Gilbert were on their way one Sunday morning to the parish church at Tarbolton, they fell in with an old Moravian named William Kirkland; and before long the poet and Kirkland began discussing theology. Burns defended the New Lights, the Moravian the Old Lights. At length Burns, finding his arguments of no avail, exclaimed: "Oh, I suppose I've met with the Apostle Paul this morning."

"No," retorted the Moravian Evangelical, "you have not met the Apostle Paul; but I think I have met one of those wild beasts which he says he fought with at Ephesus."

Meanwhile, the Brethren showed other signs of vigour. The first, and one of the most influential, was their system of public school education. At the General Synod in 1782 a resolution had been passed that education should be a recognized branch of Church work; and, therefore, following the example set in Germany, the English Brethren now opened a number of public boarding-schools. In 1782-1785 they began to admit non-Moravians to the two schools already established at Fulneck. In 1792 they opened girls' schools at Dukinfield and Gomersal; in 1794 a girls' school at Wyke; in 1796 a girls' school at Fairfield; in 1798 a girls' school at Gracehill; in 1799 a girls' school at Ockbrook; in 1801 a boys' school at Fairfield, and a girls' school at Bedford; in 1805 a boys' school at Gracehill; and, in 1813, a boys' school at Ockbrook. At these schools the chief object of the Brethren was the formation of Christian character. They were all established at settlements or at flourishing congregations, and the pupils lived in the midst of Moravian life. For some years the religion taught was unhealthy and mawkish, and both boys and girls were far too strictly treated. They were not allowed to play competitive games; they were under the constant supervision of teachers; they had scarcely any exercise but walks; and they were often rather encouraged in the notion that it was desirable to die young. At one time the girls at Fulneck complained that not one of their number had died for six months; and one of the Fulneck records runs: "By occasion of the smallpox our Saviour held a rich harvest among the children, many of whom departed in a very blessed manner." As long as such morbid ideas as these were taught, both boys and girls became rather maudlin characters. The case of the boys at Fulneck illustrates the point. They attended services every night in the week; they heard a great deal of the physical sufferings of Christ; they were encouraged to talk about their spiritual experiences; and yet they were often found guilty of lying, of stealing, and of other more serious offences. At first, too, a good many of the masters were unlearned and ignorant men. They were drafted in from the Brethren's Houses; they taught only the elementary subjects; they had narrow ideas of life; and, instead of teaching the boys to be manly and fight their own battles, they endeavoured rather to shield them from the world. But as time went on this coddling system was modified. The standard of education was raised; the masters were often learned men preparing for the ministry; the laws against competitive games were repealed; and the religious instruction became more sensible and practical. If the parents desired it, their children, at a suitable age, were prepared for confirmation, confirmed by the local Moravian minister, and admitted to the Moravian Communion service. The pupils came from all denominations. Sometimes even Catholics sent their children, and allowed them to receive religious instruction. [151] But no attempt was ever made to make proselytes. For many years these schools enjoyed a high reputation as centres of high-class education and of strict moral discipline. At all these schools the Brethren made much of music; and the music was all of a solemn devotional character.

"The music taught," said Christian Ignatuis La Trobe, "is both vocal and instrumental; the former is, however, confined to sacred compositions, congregational, choral, and orchestral, the great object being to turn this divine art to the best account for the service and edification of the Church." At that time (about 1768) the dormitory of Fulneck Boys' School was over the chapel; and La Trobe tells us how he would keep himself awake at night to hear the congregation sing one of the Liturgies to the Father, Son and Spirit. [152] Thus the Brethren, true to their old ideal, endeavoured to teach the Christian religion without adding to the numbers of the Moravian Church. It is hardly possible to over-estimate the influence of these schools. In Ireland the schools at Gracehill were famous. The pupils came from the highest ranks of society. At one time it used to be said that the mere fact that a boy or girl had been educated at Gracehill was a passport to the best society. In Yorkshire the Brethren were educational pioneers. The most famous pupil of the Brethren was Richard Oastler. At the age of eight (1797) that great reformer—the Factory King—was sent by his parents to Fulneck School; and years later, in an address to the boys, he reminded them how great their privileges were. "Ah, boys," he said, "let me exhort you to value your privileges. I know that the privileges of a Fulneck schoolboy are rare."

But the greatest influence exercised by the Brethren was in the cause of foreign missions. For that blessing we may partly thank Napoleon Buonaparte. As that eminent philanthropist scoured the continent of Europe, he had no intention of aiding the missionary cause; but one result of his exploits was that when Christian people in England heard how grievously the German Brethren had suffered at his hands their hearts were filled with sympathy and the desire to help. At Edinburgh a number of gentlemen founded the "Edinburgh Association in Aid of Moravian Missions"; at Glasgow others founded the "Glasgow Auxiliary Society"; at Bristol and London some ladies formed the "Ladies' Association" (1813); in Yorkshire the Brethren themselves formed the "Yorkshire Society for the Spread of the Gospel among the Heathen" (1827); at Sheffield James Montgomery, the Moravian poet, appealed to the public through his paper, the Iris; and the result was that in one year subscriptions to Moravian Missions came in from the Church Missionary Society, and from other missionary and Bible societies. In Scotland money was collected annually at Edinburgh, Elgin, Dumfries, Horndean, Haddington, Kincardine, Perth, Falkirk, Jedwater, Calton, Bridgetown, Denny, Greenock, Stirling, Paisley, Anstruther, Inverkeithing, Aberdeen, Lochwinnoch, Leith, Tranent, St. Ninian's, Brechin, Montrose; in England at Bath, Bristol, Birmingham, Henley, Berwick, St. Neots,

Bedford, Northampton, Colchester, York, Cambridge; in Ireland at Ballymena, Belfast, Carrickfergus, Lurgan, Cookstown, Dublin. As the interest of Englishmen in Foreign Missions was still in its infancy, a long list like this is remarkable. But the greatest proof of the rising interest in missions was the foundation of the "London Association in Aid of Moravian Missions" (1817). It was not a Moravian Society. The founders were mostly Churchmen; but the basis was undenominational, and membership was open to all who were willing to subscribe. At first the amount raised by the Association was a little over - L-1,000 a year; but as time went on the annual income increased, and in recent years it has sometimes amounted to -L-17,000. It is hard to mention a nobler instance of broad-minded charity. For some years the secretary of this Association has generally been an Anglican clergyman; he pleads for Moravian Missions in parish churches; the annual sermon is preached in St. Paul's Cathedral; and thus the Brethren are indebted to Anglican friends for many thousands of pounds. Another proof of interest in Moravian Missions was the publication of books on the subject by non-Moravian writers. At Edinburgh an anonymous writer published "The Moravians in Greenland" (1830) and "The Moravians in Labrador" (1833). Thus the Brethren had quickened missionary enthusiasm in every part of the United Kingdom.

At home, meanwhile, the Brethren moved more slowly. As they did not wish to interfere with the Church of England, they purposely confined their forward movement almost entirely to villages and neglected country districts. In 1806 they built a chapel in the little village of Priors Marston, near Woodford; in 1808 they founded the congregation at Baildon, Yorkshire; in 1818 they began holding services at Stow, near Bedford; in 1823 they founded the congregation at Kimbolton; in 1827 they founded the congregation at Pertenhall; in 1833 at Brockweir-on-the-Wye; in 1834 they started a cause at Stratford-on-Avon, but abandoned it in 1839; in 1836 at Salem, Oldham. In 1829 they founded the Society for Propagating the Gospel in Ireland; in 1839 they began holding services at Tillbrook, near Bedford; and in 1839 they endeavoured, though in vain, to establish a new congregation at Horton, Bradford. In comparison with the number of societies abandoned, the number of new congregations was infinitesimal. The same tale is told by their statistical returns. In 1824 they had 2,596 communicant members; in 1834, 2,698; in 1850, 2,838; and, in 1857, 2,978; and thus we have the startling fact that, in spite of their efforts at church extension, they had not gained four hundred members in thirty-three years. For this slowness, however, the reasons were purely mechanical; and all the obstacles sprang from the Brethren's connection with Germany.

First, we have the persistent use of the Lot. For some years the English Brethren adhered to the custom of enforcing its use in marriages; and even when it was abolished in marriages they still used it in applications for membership. No man could be a member of the Moravian Church without the consent of the Lot; and this rule was still enforced at the Provincial Synod held at Fairfield in 1847. Sometimes this rule worked out in a curious way. A man and his wife applied for admission to the Church; the case of each was put separately to the Lot; the one was accepted, the other was rejected; and both were disgusted and pained.

Another barrier to progress was the system of ministerial education. For a few years (1809-27) there existed at Fulneck a high-class Theological Seminary; but it speedily sickened and died; and henceforward all candidates for the ministry who desired a good education were compelled to go to Germany. Thus the Brethren now had two classes of ministers. If the candidate was not able to go to Germany, he received but a poor education; and if, on the other hand, he went to Germany, he stayed there so long—first as a student, and then as a master—that when he returned to England, he was full of German ideas of authority, and often spoke with a German accent. And thus Englishmen naturally obtained the impression that the Church was not only German in origin, but meant chiefly for Germans.

Another cruel barrier was the poverty of the ministers. They were overworked and underpaid. They had generally five or six services to hold every Sunday; they had several meetings during the week; they were expected to interview every member at least once in two months; they were entirely without lay assistants; their wives held official positions, and were expected to share in the work; and yet, despite his manifold duties, there was scarcely a minister in the Province whose salary was enough to enable him to make ends meet. At one time the salary of the minister in London was only -L-50 a year; at Fulneck it was only 8s. a week; in other places it was about the same. There was no proper sustentation fund; and the result was that nearly all the ministers had to add to their incomes in other ways. In most cases they kept little schools for the sons and daughters of gentry in the country districts; but as they were teaching five days a week, they could not possibly pay proper attention to their ministerial duties. If the minister had been a single man, he might easily have risen above his troubles; but as he was compelled by church law to marry, his case was often a hard one; and at the Provincial Synod held at Fulneck, the Brethren openly confessed the fact that one of the chief hindrances to progress was lack of time on the part of the ministers (1835).

Another barrier was the absolute power of officials and the limited power of the laity. No Church can expect to make much progress unless its institutions are in tune with the institutions of the country. For good or for evil, England was growing democratic; and, therefore, the Moravian Church should have been democratic too. But in those days the Moravian Church was the reverse of democratic. In theory each congregation had the power to elect its own committee; in fact, no election was valid unless ratified by the Lot. In theory each congregation had the power to send a deputy to the Provincial Synod; in fact, only a few ever used the privilege. At the first Provincial Synod of the nineteenth century (1824), only four deputies were present; at the second (1835), only seven; at the third (1847), only nine; at the fourth (1853), only twelve; at the fifth (1856), only sixteen; and thus, when the deputies did appear, they could always be easily outvoted by the ministers.

Another hindrance was the Brethren's peculiar conception of their duty to their fellow-men in this country. In spite of their enthusiasm for Foreign Missions, they had little enthusiasm for Home Missions; and clinging still to the old Pietist notion of a "Church within the Church," they had not yet opened their eyes to the fact that godless Englishmen were quite as plentiful as godless Red Indians or Hottentots. For proof let us turn to the "Pastoral Letter" drawn up by commission of the Synod at Fulneck (1835). At that Synod, the Brethren prepared a revised edition of the "Brotherly Agreement"; and then, to enforce the principles of the "Agreement," they commissioned the P.E.C. [153] to address the whole Church in a "Pastoral Letter." But neither in the Agreement nor in the Letter did the Brethren recommend Home Mission work. They urged their flocks to hold prayer meetings, to distribute tracts, to visit the sick, to invite outsiders to the House of God; they warned them against the corruption of business life; and they even besought them not to meddle in politics or to wear party colours. In Ireland they were not to join Orange Lodges; and in England they were not to join trade unions. Thus the Brethren distinctly recommended their people not to take too prominent a part in the social and political life of the nation.

Again, twelve years later, at the next Synod, held at Fairfield (1847), the Brethren issued another "Pastoral Letter." In this letter the members of the P.E.C. complained that some were denying the doctrine of eternal punishment, that the parents were neglecting the religious education of their children, that the Bible was not systematically read, that the "speaking" before the Holy Communion was neglected, that the old custom of shaking hands at the close of the Sacrament was dying out, that the members' contributions were not regularly paid, and that private prayer meetings were not held as of old; and, therefore, the Brethren pleaded earnestly for the revival of all these good customs. And yet, even at this late stage, there was no definite reference in the "Letter" to Home Mission Work.

Another cause of paralysis was the lack of periodical literature. We come here to an astounding fact. For one hundred and eight years (1742-1850), the Moravians struggled on in England without either an official or an unofficial Church magazine; and the only periodical literature they possessed was the quarterly missionary report, "Periodical Accounts." Thus the Church members had no means of airing their opinions. If a member conceived some scheme of reform, and wished to expound it in public, he had to wait till the next Provincial Synod; and as only five Synods were held in fifty years, his opportunity did not come very often. Further, the Brethren were bound by a rule that no member should publish a book or pamphlet dealing with Church affairs without the consent of the U.E.C. or of a Synod.

At length, however, this muzzling order was repealed; and the first Briton to speak his mind in print was an Irishman, John Carey. For some time this man, after first reviving a dying cause at Cootehill, in Co. Cavan, had been making vain endeavours to arouse the Irish Moravians to a sense of their duty (1850); but all he had received in return was official rebukes. He had tried to start a new cause in Belfast; he had gathered together a hundred and fifty hearers; he had rented a hall for worship in King Street; and then the Irish Elders' Conference, in solemn assembly at Gracehill, strangled the movement at its birth. Instead of encouraging and helping Carey, they informed him that his work was irregular, forbade him to form a Society, and even issued a notice in the Guardian disowning his meetings. But Carey was not to be disheartened; and now, at his own risk, he issued his monthly magazine, The Fraternal Messenger. The magazine was a racy production. As John Carey held no official position, he was able to aim his bullets wherever he pleased; and, glowing with patriotic zeal, he first gave a concise epitome of the "History of the Brethren," and then dealt with burning problems of the day. If the magazine did nothing else, it at least caused men to think. Among the contributors was Bishop Alexander Hasse. He had visited certain places in Ireland—Arva, Billies, and Drumargan—where once the Brethren had been strong; he gave an account of these visits; and thus those who read the magazine could not fail to see what glorious opportunities had been thrown away in the past.

At the next Synod, held in Fulneck, all present could see that a new influence was at work (1853). For the first time the Brethren deliberately resolved that, in their efforts for the Kingdom of God, they should "aim at the enlargement of the Brethren's Church." They sanctioned the employment of lay preachers; they established the Moravian Magazine, edited by John England; and they even encouraged a modest attempt to rekindle the dying embers at such places as Arva and Drumargan.

At the next Synod, held again at Fulneck, the Brethren showed a still clearer conception of their duties (1856). The Synodal sermon was preached by William Edwards. He was a member of the Directing Board, and must have spoken with a sense of responsibility; and in that sermon he deliberately declared that, instead of following the German plan of concentrating their energy on settlements, the Brethren ought to pay more attention to town and country congregations. "It is here," he said, "that we lie most open to the charge of omitting opportunities of usefulness." And the members of the Synod were equally emphatic. They made arrangements for a Training Institution; they rejected the principle, which had ruled so long, of a "Church within the Church"; and, thirdly,—most important point of all—they resolved that a society be formed, called the Moravian Home Mission, and that the object of that society should be, not only to evangelize in dark and neglected districts, but also to establish, wherever possible, Moravian congregations. The chief leader in this new movement was Charles E. Sutcliffe. He had pleaded the cause of Home Missions for years; and now he was made the general secretary of the new Home Mission society.

In one way, however, the conduct of the Brethren was surprising. As we have now arrived at that point in our story when the Moravian Church, no longer under the rule of the U.E.C., was to be divided into three independent provinces, it is natural to ask what part the British Moravians played in this Home Rule movement; what part they played, i.e., in the agitation that each Province should have its own property, hold its own Provincial Synods, and manage its own local affairs. They played a very modest part, indeed! At this Synod they passed three resolutions: first, that the British P.E.C. should be empowered to summon a Provincial Synod with the consent of the U.E.C.; second, that the Synod should be empowered to elect its own P.E.C.; and third, that "any measure affecting our own province, carried by a satisfactory majority, shall at once pass into law for the province, with the sanction of the Unity's Elders' Conference, without waiting for a General Synod." But in other respects the British Moravians were in favour of the old constitution. They were not the true leaders of the Home Rule movement. They made no demand for a separation of property; they were still willing to bow to the authority of the German Directing Board; they still declared their belief in the use of the Lot in appointments to office; and the agitation in favour of Home Rule came, not from Great Britain, but from North America. To North America, therefore, we must now turn our attention.

Chapter 6: The Struggle in America (1762-1857)

FOR nearly a century the Moravians in America had felt as uncomfortable as David in Saul's armour; and the armour in this particular instance was made of certain iron rules forged at the General Synods held in Germany. As soon as Spangenberg had left his American friends, the work was placed, for the time being, under the able management of Bishop Seidal, Bishop Hehl, and Frederick William von Marschall; and then, in due course, the American Brethren were informed that a General Synod had been held at Marienborn (1764), that certain Church principles had there been laid down, and that henceforward their duty, as loyal Moravians, was to obey the laws enacted at the General Synods, and also to submit, without asking questions, to the ruling of the German Directing Board. The Americans meekly obeyed. The system of Government adopted was peculiar. At all costs, said the Brethren in Germany, the unity of the Moravian Church must be maintained; and, therefore, in order to maintain that unity the Directing Board, from time to time, sent high officials across the Atlantic on visitations to America. In 1765 they sent old David Nitschmann; in 1770 they sent Christian Gregor, John Lorentz, and Alexander von Schweinitz; in 1779 they sent Bishop John Frederick Reichel; in 1783 they sent Bishop John de Watteville; in 1806 they sent John Verbeck and John Charles Forester; and thus they respectfully reminded the American Brethren that although they lived some thousands of miles away, they were still under the fatherly eye of the German Directing Board. For this policy the German Brethren had a noble reason. As the resolutions passed at the General Synods were nearly always confirmed by the Lot, they could not help feeling that those resolutions had some Divine authority; and, therefore, what God called good in Germany must be equally good in America. For this reason they enforced the settlement system in America just as strictly as in Germany. Instead of aiming at church extension they centralized the work round the four settlements of Bethlehem, Nazareth, Salem and Lititz. There, in the settlements, they enforced the Brotherly Agreement; there they insisted on the use of the Lot; there they fostered diaconies, choirs, Brethren's Houses and Sisters' Houses, and all the features of settlement life; and there alone they endeavoured to cultivate the Moravian Quietist type of gentle piety. Thus the Brethren in America were soon in a queer position. As there was no State Church in America, and as, therefore, no one could accuse them of being schismatics, they had just as much right to push their cause as any other denomination; and yet they were just as much restricted as if they had been dangerous heretics. Around them lay an open country, with a fair field and no favour; within their bosoms glowed a fine missionary zeal; and behind them, far away at Herrnhut, sat the Directing Board, with their hands upon the curbing rein.

If this system of government favoured unity, it also prevented growth. It was opposed to American principles, and out of place on American soil. What those American principles were we all know. At that famous period in American history, when the War of Independence broke out, and the Declaration of Independence was framed, nearly all the people were resolute champions of democratic government. They had revolted against the rule of King George III.; they stood for the principle, "no taxation without representation"; they erected democratic institutions in every State and County; they believed in the rights of free speech and free assembly; and, therefore, being democratic in politics, they naturally wished to be democratic in religion. But the Moravians were on the horns of a dilemma. As they were not supposed to meddle with politics, they did not at first take definite sides in the war. They objected to bearing arms; they objected to taking oaths; and, therefore, of course, they objected also to swearing allegiance to the Test Act (1777). But this attitude could not last for ever. As the war continued, the American Moravians became genuine patriotic American citizens. For some months the General Hospital of the American Army was stationed at Bethlehem; at another time it was stationed at Lititz; and some of the young Brethren joined the American Army, and fought under General Washington's banner for the cause of Independence. For this natural conduct they were, of course, rebuked; and in some cases they were even expelled from the Church.

At this point, when national excitement was at its height, Bishop Reichel arrived upon the scene from Germany, and soon instructed the American Brethren how to manage their affairs (1779). He acted in opposition to American ideals. Instead of summoning a Conference of ministers and deputies, he summoned a Conference consisting of ministers only; the American laymen had no chance of expressing their opinions; and, therefore, acting under Reichel's influence, the Conference passed the astounding resolution that "in no sense shall the societies of awakened, affiliated as the fruit of the former extensive itinerations, be regarded as preparatory to the organisation of congregations, and that membership in these societies does not at all carry with it communicant membership or preparation for it." There lay the cause of the Brethren's failure in America. In spite of its rather stilted language, we can easily see in that sentence the form of an old familiar friend. It is really our German friend the Diaspora, and our English friend the system of United Flocks. For the next sixty-four years that one sentence in italics was as great a barrier to progress in America as the system of United Flocks in England. As long as that resolution remained in force, the American Moravians had no fair chance of extending; and all the congregations except the four settlements were treated, not as hopeful centres of work, but as mere societies and preaching-places. Thus again, precisely as in Great Britain, did the Brethren clip their own wings; thus again did they sternly refuse admission to hundreds of applicants for Church membership. A few figures will make this clear. At Graceham the Brethren had 90 adherents, but only 60 members (1790); at Lancaster 258 adherents, but only 72 members; at Philadelphia 138 adherents, but only 38 members; at Oldmanscreek 131 adherents, but only 37 members; at Staten Island 100 adherents, but only 20 members; at Gnadenhuetten 41 adherents, but only 31 members; at Emmaus 93 adherents, but only 51 members; at Schoeneck 78 adherents, but only 66 members; at Hebron 72 adherents, but only 24 members; at York 117 adherents, but only 38 members; and at Bethel 87 adherents, but only 23 members. If these figures are dry, they are at least instructive; and the grand point they prove is that the American Moravians, still dazzled by Zinzendorf's "Church within the Church" idea, compelled hundreds who longed to join their ranks as members to remain outside the Church. In Germany this policy succeeded; in England, where a State Church existed, it may have been excusable; but in America, where a State Church was unknown, it was senseless and suicidal.

And yet the American Moravians did not live entirely in vain. Amid the fury of American politics, they cultivated the three Moravian fruits of piety, education and missionary zeal. At Bethlehem they opened a Girls' School; and so popular did that school become that one of the directors, Jacob Van Vleck, had to issue a circular, stating that during the next eighteen months no more applications from parents could be received. It was one of the finest institutions in North America; and among the thousands of scholars we find relatives of such famous American leaders as Washington, Addison, Sumpter, Bayard, Livingstone and Roosevelt. At Nazareth the Brethren had a school for boys, known as "Nazareth Hall." If this school never served any other purpose, it certainly taught some rising Americans the value of order and discipline. At meals the boys had to sit in perfect silence; and when they wished to indicate their wants, they did so, not by using their tongues, but by holding up the hand or so many fingers. The school was divided into "rooms"; each "room" contained only fifteen or eighteen pupils; these pupils were under the constant supervision of a master; and this master, who was generally a theological scholar, was the companion and spiritual adviser of his charges. He joined in all their games, heard them sing their hymns, and was with them when they swam in the "Deep Hole" in the Bushkill River on Wednesday and Saturday afternoons, when they gathered nuts in the forests, and when they sledged in winter in the surrounding country.

For foreign missions these American Brethren were equally enthusiastic. They established a missionary society known as the "Society for Propagating the Gospel Among the Brethren" (1787); they had that society enrolled as a corporate body; they were granted by Congress a tract of 4,000 acres in the Tuscawaras Valley; and they conducted a splendid mission to the Indians in Georgia, New York, Connecticut, Massachusetts, Pennsylvania, Ohio, Michigan, Canada, Kansas and Arkansas.

But work of this kind was not enough to satisfy the American Brethren. As the population increased around them they could not help feeling that they ought to do more in their native land; and the yoke of German authority galled them more and more. In their case there was some excuse for rebellious feelings. If there is anything a genuine American detests, it is being compelled to obey laws which he himself has not helped to make; and that was the very position of the American Brethren. In theory they were able to attend the General Synods; in fact, very few could undertake so long a journey. At one Synod (1782) not a single American Brother was present; and yet the decisions of the Synod were of full force in America.

At length the Americans took the first step in the direction of Home Rule. For forty-eight years their Provincial Synods had been attended by ministers only; but now by special permission of the U.E.C., they summoned a Provincial Synod at Lititz consisting of ministers and deputies (1817). At this Synod they framed a number of petitions to be laid before the next General Synod in Germany. They requested that the monthly "speaking" should be abolished; that Brethren should be allowed to serve in the army; that the American Provincial Helpers' Conference should be allowed to make appointments without consulting the German U.E.C.; that the congregations should be allowed to elect their own committees without using the Lot; that all adult communicant members should be entitled to a vote; that the use of the Lot should be abolished in marriages, in applications for membership, and in the election of deputies to the General Synod; and, finally, that at least one member of the U.E.C. should know something about American affairs. Thus did the Americans clear the way for Church reform. In Germany they were regarded as dangerous radicals. They were accused of an unwholesome desire for change. They designed, it was said, to pull down everything old and set up something new. At the General Synod (1818) most of their requests were refused; and the only point they gained was that the Lot need not be used in marriages in town and country congregations. At the very time when the Americans were growing more radical, the Germans, as we have seen already, were growing more conservative. [154]

But the American Brethren were not disheartened. In addition to being leaders in the cause of reform, they now became the leaders in the Home Mission movement; and here they were twenty years before their British Brethren. In 1835, in North Carolina, they founded a "Home Missionary Society"; in 1844 they abolished the settlement system; in 1849 they founded a general "Home Missionary Society"; in 1850 they founded a monthly magazine, the Moravian Church Miscellany; in 1855 they founded their weekly paper the Moravian, and placed all their Home Mission work under a general Home Mission Board. Meanwhile, they had established new congregations at Colored Church, in North Carolina (1822; Hope, in Indiana (1830); Hopedale, in Pennsylvania (1837); Canal Dover, in Ohio (1840); West Salem, in Illinois 1844; Enon, in Indiana (1846); West Salem for Germans, in Edwards County (1848); Green Bay, in Wisconsin (1850); Mount Bethell, in Caroll County (1851); New York (1851); Ebenezer, in Wisconsin (1853); Brooklyn (1854); Utica, in Oneida County (1854); Watertown, in Wisconsin (1854); and Lake Mills, in Wisconsin (1856). At the very time when the British Moravians were forming their first Home Mission Society, the Americans had founded fourteen new congregations; and thus they had become the pioneers in every Moravian onward movement.

But their greatest contribution to progress is still to be mentioned. Of all the Provincial Synods held in America, the most important was that which met at Bethlehem on May

2nd, 1855. As their Home Mission work had extended so rapidly they now felt more keenly than ever how absurd it was the American work should still be managed by a Directing Board in Germany; and, therefore, they now laid down the proposal that American affairs should be managed by an American Board, elected by an American Provincial Synod (1855). In other words, the Americans demanded independence in all American affairs. They wished, in future, to manage their own concerns; they wished to make their own regulations at their own Provincial Synods; they established an independent "Sustentation Fund," and desired to have their own property; and therefore they requested the U.E.C. to summon a General Synod at the first convenient opportunity to consider their resolutions. Thus, step by step, the American Moravians prepared the way for great changes. If these changes are to be regarded as reforms, the American Moravians must have the chief praise and glory. They were the pioneers in the Home Mission movement; they were the staunchest advocates of democratic government; they had long been the stoutest opponents of the Lot; and now they led the way in the movement which ended in the separation of the Provinces. In England their demand for Home Rule awakened a partial response; in Germany it excited anger and alarm; and now Moravians all over the world were waiting with some anxiety to see what verdict would be passed by the next General Synod. [155]

Chapter 7: The Seperation of the Provinces (1857-1899)

AS soon as the American demands became known in Germany, the German Brethren were much disturbed in their minds; they feared that if these demands were granted the unity of the Moravian Church would be destroyed; and next year they met in a German Provincial Synod, condemned the American proposals as unsound, and pathetically requested the American Brethren to reconsider their position (1856). And now, to make the excitement still keener, an anonymous writer, who called himself "Forscher" (Inquirer), issued a pamphlet hotly attacking some of the time-honoured institutions of the Church. He called his pamphlet, "Die Bruederkirche: Was ist Wahrheit?" i.e., The Truth about the Brethren's Church, and in his endeavour to tell the truth he penned some stinging words. He asserted that far too much stress had been laid on the "Chief Eldership of Christ"; he denounced the abuse of the Lot; he declared that the Brethren's settlements were too exclusive; he criticized Zinzendorf's "Church within the Church" idea; he condemned the old "Diacony" system as an unholy alliance of the secular and the sacred; and thus he described as sources of evil the very customs which many Germans regarded as precious treasures. As this man was really John Henry Buchner, he was, of course, a German in blood; but Buchner was then a missionary in Jamaica, and thus his attack, like the American demands, came from across the Atlantic. No wonder the German Brethren were excited. No wonder they felt that a crisis in the Church had arrived. For all loyal Moravians the question now was whether the Moravian Church could stand the strain; and, in order to preserve the true spirit of unity, some Brethren at Gnadenfeld prepared and issued an "Appeal for United Prayer." "At this very time," they declared, "when the Church is favoured with an unusual degree of outward prosperity, the enemy of souls is striving to deal a blow at our spiritual union by sowing among us the seeds of discord and confusion"; and therefore they besought their Brethren—German, English and American alike—to banish all feelings of irritation, and to join in prayer every Wednesday evening for the unity and prosperity of the Brethren's Church.

At length, June 8th, 1857, the General Synod met at Herrnhut (1857). In his opening sermon Bishop John Nitschmann struck the right note. He reminded his Brethren of the rock from which they were hewn; he appealed to the testimony of history; and he asserted that the testimony of history was that the Moravian Church had been created, not by man, but by God. "A word," he said, "never uttered before at a Brethren's Synod has lately been heard among us—the word separation.' Separation among Brethren! The very sound sends a pang to the heart of every true Brother!" With that appeal ringing in their ears, the Brethren addressed themselves to their difficult task; a committee was formed to examine the American proposals; the spirit of love triumphed over the spirit of discord; and finally, after much discussion, the new constitution was framed.

If the unity of the Church was to be maintained, there must, of course, still be one supreme authority; and, therefore the Brethren now decided that henceforward the General Synod should be the supreme legislative, and the U.E.C. the supreme administrative, body. But the constitution of the General Synod was changed. It was partly an official and partly an elected body. On the one hand, there were still a number of ex-officio members; on the other a large majority of elected deputies. Thus the General Synod was now composed of: (1) Ex-officio members: i.e., the twelve members of the U.E.C.; all Bishops of the Church; one member of the English and one of the American P.E.C.; the Secretarius Unitatis Fratrum in Anglia; the administrators of the Church's estates in Pennsylvania and North Carolina; the Director of the Warden's Department; the Director of the Missions Department; the Unity's Librarian. (2) Elected members: i.e., nine deputies from each of the three Provinces, elected by the Synods of these Provinces. As these twenty-seven deputies could be either ministers or laymen, it is clear that the democratic principle was now given some encouragement; but, on the other hand, the number of officials was still nearly as great as the number of deputies. The functions of the General Synod were defined as follows: (a) To determine the doctrines of the Church, i.e., to decide all questions which may arise upon this subject. (b) To decide as to all essential points of Liturgy. (c) To prescribe the fundamental rules of order and discipline. (d) To determine what is required for membership in the Church. (e) To nominate and appoint Bishops. (f) To manage the Church's Foreign Missions and Educational Work. (g) To inspect the Church's general finances. (h) To elect the U.E.C. (i) To form and constitute General Synods, to fix the time and place of their meetings, and establish the basis of their representation. (j) To settle everything concerning the interests of the Moravian Church as a whole.

As the U.E.C. were elected by the General Synod, it was natural that they should still possess a large share of administrative power; and therefore they were now authorized to manage all concerns of a general nature, to represent the Church in her dealings with the State, and with other religious bodies, and to see that the principles and regulations established by the General Synod were carried out in every department of Church work. For the sake of efficiency the U.E.C. were divided into three boards, the Educational, Financial, and Missionary; they managed, in this way, the schools in Germany, the general finances, and the whole of the foreign missions; and meanwhile, for legal reasons, they also acted as P.E.C. for the German Province of the Church. Thus the first part of the problem was solved, and the unity of the Moravian Church was maintained.

The next task was to satisfy the American demand for Home Rule. For this purpose the Brethren now resolved that each Province of the Church should have its own property; that each Province should hold its own Provincial Synod; and that each of the three Provincial Synods should have power to make laws, provided these laws did not conflict with the laws laid down by a General Synod. As the U.E.C. superintended the work in Germany, there was no further need for a new arrangement there; but in Great Britain and North America the Provincial Synod in each case was empowered to elect its own P.E.C., and the P.E.C., when duly elected, managed the affairs of the Province. They had the control of all provincial property. They appointed ministers to their several posts; they summoned Provincial Synods when they thought needful; and thus each Province possessed Home Rule in all local affairs.

For the next twenty-two years this constitution—so skilfully drawn—remained unimpaired. At best, however, it was only a compromise; and in 1879 an alteration was made (1879). As Mission work was the only work in which the whole Church took part as such, it was decided that only the Mission Department of the U.E.C. should be elected by the General Synod; the two other departments, the Educational and Financial, were to be nominated by the German Provincial Synod; and in order that the British and American Provinces should have a court of appeal, a new board, called the Unity Department, was created. It consisted of six members, i.e., the four members of the Missions Department, one from the Educational Department, and one from the Finance Department. At the same time the U.E.C., divided still into its three departments, remained the supreme Board of Management.

But this arrangement was obviously doomed to failure (1890). In the first place it was so complex that few could understand it, and only a person of subtle intellect could define the difference between the functions of the U.E.C. and the functions of the Unity Department; and, in the second place, it was quite unfair to the German Brethren. In Germany the U.E.C. still acted as German P.E.C.; of its twelve members four were elected, not by a German Provincial Synod, but by the General Synod; and, therefore, the Germans were ruled by a board of whom only eight members were elected by the Germans themselves. At the next General Synod, therefore (1889), the U.E.C. was divided into two departments: first, the Foreign Mission Department, consisting of four members, elected by the General Synod; second, the German P.E.C., consisting of eight members, elected by the German Provincial Synod. Thus, at last, thirty-two years after the British and American Provinces, did the German Province attain Provincial independence.

But even this arrangement proved unsatisfactory. As we thread our way through these constitutional changes, we can easily see where the trouble lay. At each General Synod the problem was, how to reconcile the unity of the Church with the rights of its respective Provinces; and so far the problem had not been solved. The flaw in the last arrangement is fairly obvious. If the U.E.C. was still the supreme managing board, it was unfair to the Americans and Britons that eight of its twelve members should be really the German P.E.C., elected by the German Provincial Synod.

The last change in the constitution was of British origin (1898). At a Provincial Synod held in Mirfield, the British Moravians sketched a plan whereby the U.E.C. and the Unity Department would both cease to exist; and when the next General Synod met at Herrnhut, this plan was practically carried into effect. At present, therefore, the Moravian Church is constituted as follows (1899): First, the supreme legislative body is still the General Synod; second, the Church is divided into four Provinces, the German, the British, the American North, and the American South; third, each of these four Provinces holds its own Provincial Synods, makes its own laws, and elects its own P.E.C.; fourth, the foreign mission work is managed by a Mission Board, elected by the General Synod; and last, the supreme U.E.C., no longer a body seated in Germany and capable of holding frequent meetings, is now composed of the Mission Board and the four governing boards of the four independent Provinces. In one sense, the old U.E.C. is abolished; in another, it still exists. It is abolished as a constantly active Directing Board; it exists as the manager of certain Church property, [156] as the Church's representative in the eyes of the law, and as the supreme court of appeal during the period between General Synods. As some of the members of this composite board live thousands of miles from each other, they are never able to meet all together. And yet the Board is no mere fiction. In theory, its seat is still at Berthelsdorf; and, in fact, it is still the supreme administrative authority, and as such is empowered to see that the principles laid down at a General Synod are carried out in every branch of the Moravian Church. [157]

And yet, though the Moravian Church is still one united ecclesiastical body, each Province is independent in the management of its own affairs. For example, let us take the case of the British Province. The legislative body is the Provincial Synod. It is composed of, first, all ordained ministers of the Church in active congregation service; second, the Advocatus Fratrum in Anglia and the Secretarius Fratrum in Anglia; third, lay deputies elected by the congregations. At a recent British Provincial Synod (1907) the rule was laid down that every congregation possessing more than one hundred and fifty members shall be entitled to send two deputies to the Synod; and thus there is a tendency in the British Province for the lay element to increase in power. In all local British matters the power of the Provincial Synod is supreme. It has power to settle the time and place of its own meetings, to supervise the administration of finances, to establish new congregations, to superintend all official Church publications, to nominate Bishops, and to elect the Provincial Elders' Conference. As the U.E.C. act in the name and by the authority of a General Synod, so the P.E.C. act in the name and by the authority of a Provincial Synod. They see to the execution of the laws of the Church, appoint and superintend all ministers, pay official visits once in three years to inspect the state of the congregations, examine candidates for the ministry, administer the finances of the Province, and act as a Court of Appeal in cases of dispute.

The same principles apply in individual congregations.

As each Province manages its own affairs subject to the general laws of the Church, so each congregation manages its own affairs subject to the general laws of the Province. As far as its own affairs are concerned, each congregation is self-ruling. All members over eighteen years who have paid their dues are entitled to a vote. They are empowered to elect a deputy for the Provincial Synod; they elect also, once in three years, the congregation committee; and the committee, in co-operation with the minister, is expected to maintain good conduct, honesty and propriety among the members of the congregation, to administer due discipline and reproof, to consider applications for membership, to keep in order the church, Sunday-school, minister's house, and other congregation property, and to be responsible for all temporal and financial concerns.

Thus the constitution of the Moravian Church may be described as democratic. It is ruled by committees, conferences and synods; and these committees, conferences and synods all consist, to a large extent, of elected deputies. As the Moravians have Bishops, the question may be asked, what special part the Bishops play in the government of the Church? The reply may be given in the words of the Moravians themselves. At the last General Synod the old principle was reasserted, that "the office of a Bishop imparts in and by itself no manner of claim to the control of the whole Church or of any part of it; the administration of particular dioceses does therefore not belong to the Bishops." Thus Moravian Bishops are far from being prelates. They are authorized to ordain the presbyters and deacons; they examine the spiritual condition of the ordinands; and, above all, they are called to act as "intercessors in the Church of God." But they have no more ruling power as such than any other minister of the Church.

Finally, a word must be said about the use of the Lot. As long as the Lot was used at all, it interfered to some extent with the democratic principle; but during the last twenty or thirty years it had gradually fallen into disuse, and in 1889 all reference to the Lot was struck out of the Church regulations; and while the Brethren still acknowledge the living Christ as the only Lord and Elder of the Church, they seek His guidance, not in any mechanical way, but through prayer, and reliance on the illumination of the Holy Spirit.

Book 4:

The Modern Moravians

Chapter 1: The Modern Moravians (1857-1907)

WHEN the Brethren made their maiden speech in the Valley of Kunwald four hundred and fifty years ago, they little thought that they were founding a Church that would spread into every quarter of the civilized globe. If this narrative, however, has been written to any purpose, it has surely taught a lesson of great moral value; and that lesson is that the smallest bodies sometimes accomplish the greatest results. At no period have the Brethren been very strong in numbers; and yet, at every stage of their story, we find them in the forefront of the battle. Of all the Protestant Churches in England, the Moravian Church is the oldest; and wherever the Brethren have raised their standard, they have acted as pioneers. They were Reformers sixty years before Martin Luther. They were the first to adopt the principle that the Bible is the only standard of faith and practice. They were among the first to issue a translation of the Bible from the original Hebrew and Greek into the language of the people. They led the way, in the Protestant movement, in the catechetical instruction of children. They published the first Hymn Book known to history. They produced in Comenius the great pioneer of modern education. They saved the Pietist movement in Germany from an early grave; they prepared the way for the English Evangelical Revival; and, above all, by example rather than by precept, they aroused in the Protestant Churches of Christendom that zeal for the cause of foreign missions which some writers have described as the crowning glory of the nineteenth century. And now we have only one further land to explore. As the Moravians are still among the least of the tribes of Israel, it is natural to ask why, despite their smallness, they maintain their separate existence, what part they are playing in the world, what share they are taking in the fight against the Canaanite, for what principles they stand, what methods they employ, what attitude they adopt towards other Churches, and what solution they offer of the social and religious problems that confront us at the opening of the twentieth century.

Section I.—MORAVIAN PRINCIPLES—If the Moravians have any distinguishing principle at all, that principle is one which goes back to the beginnings of their history. For some years they have been accustomed to use as a motto the famous words of Rupertus Meldenius: "In necessariis unitas; in non-necessariis libertas; in utrisque caritas" —in essentials unity; in non-essentials liberty; in both, charity. But the distinction between essentials and non-essentials goes far behind Rupertus Meldenius. If he was the first to pen the saying, he was certainly not the first to lay down the principle. For four hundred and fifty years this distinction between essentials and non-essentials has been a fundamental principle of the Brethren. From whom, if from any one, they learned it we do not know. It is found in no mediaeval writer, and was taught neither by Wycliffe nor by Hus. But the Brethren held it at the outset, and hold it still. It is found in the works of Peter of Chelcic; [158] it was fully expounded by Gregory the Patriarch; it was taught by the Bohemian Brethren in their catechisms; it is implied in all Moravian teaching to-day. To Moravians this word "essentials" has a definite meaning. At every stage in their history we find that in their judgment the essentials on which all Christians should agree to unite are certain spiritual truths. It was so with the Bohemian Brethren; it is so with the modern Moravians. In the early writings of Gregory the Patriarch, and in the catechisms of the Bohemian Brethren, the "essentials" are such things, and such things only, as faith, hope, love and the doctrines taught in the Apostles'Creed; and the "non-essentials," on the other hand, are such visible and concrete things as the church on earth, the ministry, the sacraments, and the other means of grace. In essentials they could allow no compromise; in non-essentials they gladly agreed to differ. For essentials they often shed their blood; but non-essentials they described as merely "useful" or "accidental."

The modern Moravians hold very similar views. For them the only "essentials" in religion are the fundamental truths of the Gospel as revealed in Holy Scripture. In these days the question is sometimes asked, What is the Moravian creed? The answer is, that they have no creed, apart from Holy Scripture. For the creeds of other churches they have the deepest respect. Thy have declared their adherence to the Apostles'Creed. They confess that in the Augsburg Confession the chief doctrines of Scripture are plainly and simply set forth; they have never attacked the Westminster Confession or the Articles of the Church of England; and yet they have never had a creed of their own, and have always declined to bind the consciences of their ministers and members by any creed whatever. Instead of binding men by a creed, they are content with the broader language of Holy Scripture. At the General Synod of 1857 they laid down the principle that the "Holy Scriptures of the Old and New Testament are, and shall remain, the only rule of our faith and practice"; and that principle has been repeatedly reaffirmed. They revere the Holy Scriptures as the Word of God; they acknowledge no other canon or rule of doctrine; they regard every human system of doctrine as imperfect; and, therefore, they stand to-day for the position that Christians should agree to unite on a broad Scriptural basis. Thus the Moravians claim to be an Union Church. At the Synod of 1744 they declared that they had room within their borders for three leading tropuses, the Moravian, the Lutheran and the Reformed; and now, within their own ranks, they allow great difference of opinion on doctrinal questions.

Meanwhile, of course, they agree on certain points. If the reader consults their own official statements—e.g., those laid down in the "Moravian Church Book" —he will notice two features of importance. First, he will observe that (speaking broadly) the Moravians are Evangelicals; second, he will notice that they state their doctrines in very general terms. In that volume it is stated that the Brethren hold the doctrines of the Fall and the total depravity of human nature, of the love of God the Father, of the real Godhead and the real Humanity of Jesus Christ, of justification by faith, of the Holy

Ghost and the operations of His grace, of good works as the fruit of faith, of the fellowship of all believers with Christ and with each other, and, finally, of the second coming of Christ and the resurrection of the dead to condemnation or to life. But none of these doctrines are defined in dogmatic language, and none of them are imposed as creeds. As long as a man holds true to the broad principles of the Christian faith, he may, whether he is a minister or a layman, think much as he pleases on many other vexed questions. He may be either a Calvinist or an Arminian, either a Higher Critic or a defender of plenary inspiration, and either High Church or Methodistic in his tastes. He may have his own theory of the Atonement, his own conception of the meaning of the Sacraments, his own views on Apostolical Succession, and his own belief about the infallibility of the Gospel records. In their judgment, the main essential in a minister is not his orthodox adherence to a creed, but his personal relationship to Jesus Christ. For this reason they are not afraid to allow their candidates for the ministry to sit at the feet of professors belonging to other denominations. At their German Theological College in Gnadenfeld, the professors systematically instruct the students in the most advanced results of critical research; sometimes the students are sent to German Universities; and the German quarterly magazine—Religion und Geisteskultur—a periodical similar to our English "Hibbert Journal," is edited by a Moravian theological professor. At one time an alarming rumour arose that the Gnadenfeld professors were leading the students astray; the case was tried at a German Provincial Synod, and the professors proved their innocence by showing that, although they held advanced views on critical questions, they still taught the Moravian central doctrine of redemption through Jesus Christ. In England a similar spirit of liberty prevails. For some years the British Moravians have had their own Theological College; it is situated at Fairfield, near Manchester; and although the students attend lectures delivered by a Moravian teacher, they receive the greater part of their education, first at Manchester University, and then either at the Manchester University Divinity School, or at the Free Church College in Glasgow or Edinburgh, or at any other suitable home of learning. Thus do the Moravians of the twentieth century tread in the footsteps of the later Bohemian Brethren; and thus do they uphold the principle that when the heart is right with Christ, the reasoning powers may be allowed free play.

In all other "non-essentials" they are equally broad. As they have never quarrelled with the Church of England, they rather resent being called Dissenters; as they happen to possess Episcopal Orders, they regard themselves as a true Episcopal Church; and yet, at the same time, they live on good terms with all Evangelical Dissenters, exchange pulpits with Nonconformist ministers, and admit to their Communion service members of all Evangelical denominations. They celebrate the Holy Communion once a month; they sing hymns describing the bread and wine as the Body and Blood of Christ; and yet they have no definite doctrine of the presence of Christ in the Eucharist. They practise Infant Baptism; but they do not hold any rigid view about Baptismal Regeneration. They practise Confirmation; [159] and yet they do not insist on confirmation as an absolute condition, in all cases, of church membership. If the candidate, for example, is advanced in years, and shrinks from the ordeal of confirmation, he may be admitted to the Moravian Church by reception; and members coming from other churches are admitted in the same way. They practise episcopal ordination, but do not condemn all other ordinations as invalid; and a minister of another Protestant Church may be accepted as a Moravian minister without being episcopally ordained. At the Sacraments, at weddings and at ordinations, the Moravian minister generally wears a surplice; and yet there is no reference to vestments in the regulations of the Church. In some congregations they use the wafer at the Sacrament, in others ordinary bread; and this fact alone is enough to show that they have no ruling on the subject. Again, the Moravians observe what is called the Church year. They observe, that is, the seasons of Advent, Lent, Easter, Whitsuntide, and Trinity; and yet they do not condemn as heretics those who differ from them on this point. If there is any season specially sacred to Moravians, it is Holy Week. To them it is generally known as Passion Week. On Palm Sunday they sing a "Hosannah" composed by Christian Gregor; at other services during the week they read the Passion History together, from a Harmony of the Four Gospels; on the Wednesday evening there is generally a "Confirmation"; on Maundy Thursday they celebrate the Holy Communion; on Good Friday, where possible, they have a series of special services; and on Easter Sunday they celebrate the Resurrection by an early morning service, held in England about six o'clock, but on the Continent at sunrise. Thus the Brethren are like High Churchmen in some of their observances, and very unlike them in their ecclesiastical principles. As the customs they practise are hallowed by tradition, and have often been found helpful to the spiritual life, they do not lightly toss them overboard; but, on the other hand, they do not regard those customs as "essential." In spiritual "essentials" they are one united body; in "non-essentials," such as ceremony and orders, they gladly agree to differ; and, small though they are in numbers, they believe that here they stand for a noble principle, and that some day that principle will be adopted by every branch of the militant Church of Christ. According to Romanists the true bond of union among Christians is obedience to the Pope as Head of the Church; according to some Anglicans, the "Historic Episcopate"; according to Moravians, a common loyalty to Scripture and a common faith in Christ; and only the future can show which, if any, of these bases of union will be accepted by the whole visible Church of Christ. Meanwhile, the Brethren are spreading their principles in a variety of ways.

Section II.—THE MORAVIANS IN GERMANY.—In Germany, and on the Continent generally, they still adhere in the main to the ideal set up by Zinzendorf. We may divide their work into five departments.

First, there is the ordinary pastoral work in the settlements and congregations. In Germany the settlement system still flourishes. Of the twenty-six Moravian congregations on the Continent, no fewer than twelve are settlements. In most cases these settlements are quiet little Moravian towns, inhabited almost exclusively by Moravians; the Brethren's Houses and Sisters' Houses are still in full working order; the very hotel is under direct church control; and the settlements, therefore, are models of order, sobriety, industry and piety. There the visitor will still find neither poverty nor wealth; there, far from the madding crowd, the angel of peace reigns supreme. We all know how Carlyle once visited Herrnhut, and how deeply impressed he was. At all the settlements and congregations the chief object of the Brethren is the cultivation of personal piety and Christian fellowship. We can see this from the number of services held. At the settlements there are more services in a week than many a pious Briton would attend in a month. In addition to the public worship on Sunday, there is a meeting of some kind every week-night. One evening there will be a Bible exposition; the next, reports of church work; the next, a prayer meeting; the next a liturgy meeting; the next, another Bible exposition; the next, an extract from the autobiography of some famous Moravian; the next, a singing meeting. At these meetings the chief thing that strikes an English visitor is the fact that no one but the minister takes any prominent part. The minister gives the Bible exposition; the minister reads the report or the autobiography; the minister offers the prayer; and the only way in which the people take part is by singing the liturgies and hymns. Thus the German Moravians have nothing corresponding to the "prayer meetings" held in England in Nonconformist churches. In some congregations there are "prayer unions," in which laymen take part; but these are of a private and unofficial character.

Meanwhile, a good many of the old stern rules are still strictly enforced, and the Brethren are still cautious in welcoming new recruits. If a person not born in a Moravian family desires to join the Moravian Church, he has generally to exercise a considerable amount of patience. He must first have lived some time in the congregation; he must have a good knowledge of Moravian doctrines and customs; he must then submit to an examination on the part of the congregation-committee; he must then, if he passes, wait about six months; his name is announced to the congregation, and all the members know that he is on probation; and, therefore, when he is finally admitted, he is a Moravian in the fullest sense of the term. He becomes not only a member of the congregation, but a member of his particular "choir." The choir system is still in force; for each choir there are special services and special labourers; and though the Single Brethren and Single Sisters are now allowed to live in their own homes, the choir houses are still occupied, and still serve a useful purpose.

Second, there is the "Inner Mission." In this way each congregation cares for the poor and neglected living near at hand. There are Bible and tract distributors, free day schools, Sunday schools, work schools, technical schools, rescue homes, reformatories, orphanages and young men's and young women's Christian associations. In spite of the exclusiveness of settlement life, it is utterly untrue to say that the members of the settlements live for themselves alone. They form evangelistic societies; they take a special interest in navvies, road menders, pedlars, railwaymen and others cut off from regular church connection; they open lodging-houses and temperance restaurants; and thus they endeavour to rescue the fallen, to fight the drink evil, and to care for the bodies and souls of beggars and tramps, of unemployed workmen, and of starving and ragged children.

Third, there is the work of Christian education. In every Moravian congregation there are two kinds of day schools. For those children who are not yet old enough to attend the elementary schools, the Brethren provide an "Infant School"; and here, having a free hand, they are able to instil the first principles of Christianity; and, secondly, for the older children, they have what we should call Voluntary Schools, manned by Moravian teachers, but under Government inspection and control. At these schools the Brethren give Bible teaching three hours a week; special services for the scholars are held; and as the schools are open to the public, the scholars are instructed to be loyal to whatever Church they happen to belong. In England such broadness would be regarded as a miracle; to the German Moravians it is second nature. In their boarding-schools they pursue the same broad principle. At present they have nine girls' schools and five boys' boarding-schools; the headmaster is always a Moravian minister; the teachers in the boys' schools are generally candidates for the ministry; and, although in consequence of Government requirements the Brethren have now to devote most of their energy to purely secular subjects, they are still permitted and still endeavour to keep the religious influence to the fore. For more advanced students they have a Paedagogium at Niesky; and the classical education there corresponds to that imparted at our Universities. At Gnadenfeld they have a Theological Seminary, open to students from other churches.

Fourth, there is the Brethren's medical work, conducted by a Diakonissen-Verband, or Nurses' Union. It was begun in 1866 by Dr. Hermann Plitt. At Gnadenfeld the Brethren have a small hospital, known as the Heinrichstift; at Emmaus, near Niesky, are the headquarters of the Union; the work is managed by a special committee, and is supported by Church funds; and on the average about fifty nurses are employed in ministering to the poor in twenty-five different places. Some act as managers of small sick-houses; others are engaged in teaching poor children; and others have gone to tend the lepers in Jerusalem and Surinam.

Fifth, there is the Brethren's Diaspora work, which now extends all over Germany. There is nothing to be compared to this work in England. It is not only peculiar to the Moravians, but peculiar to the Moravians on the Continent; and the whole principle on which it is based is one which the average clear-headed Briton finds it hard to understand. If the Moravians in England held services in parish churches—supposing such an arrangement possible—formed their hearers into little societies, visited them in their homes, and then urged them to become good members of the Anglican Church, their conduct would probably arouse considerable amazement. And yet that is exactly the kind of work done by the Moravians in Germany to-day. In this work the Brethren in Germany make no attempt to extend their own borders. The Moravians supply the men; the Moravians supply the money; and the National Lutheran Church reaps the benefit. Sometimes the Brethren preach in Lutheran Churches; sometimes, by permission of the Lutheran authorities, they even administer the Communion; and wherever they go they urge their hearers to be true to the National Church. In England Zinzendorf's "Church within the Church" idea has never found much favour; in Germany it is valued both by Moravians and by Lutherans. At present the Brethren have Diaspora centres in Austrian Silesia, in Wartebruch, in Neumark, in Moravia, in Pomerania, in the Bavarian Palatinate, in Wuertemburg, along the Rhine from Karlsruhe to Duesseldorf, in Switzerland, in Norway and Sweden, in Russian Poland, and in the Baltic Provinces. We are not, of course, to imagine for a moment that all ecclesiastical authorities on the Continent regard this Diaspora work with favour. In spite of its unselfish purpose, the Brethren have occasionally been suspected of sectarian motives. At one time the Russian General Consistory forbade the Brethren's Diaspora work in Livonia (1859); at another time the Russian Government forbade the Brethren's work in Volhynia; and the result of this intolerance was that some of the Brethren fled to South America, and founded the colony of Bruederthal in Brazil (1885), while others made their way to Canada, appealed for aid to the American P.E.C., and thus founded in Alberta the congregations of Bruederfeld and Bruederheim. Thus, even in recent years, persecution has favoured the extension of the Moravian Church; but, generally speaking, the Brethren pursue their Diaspora work in peace and quietness. They have now about sixty or seventy stations; they employ about 120 Diaspora workers, and minister thus to about 70,000 souls; and yet, during the last fifty years, they have founded only six new congregations—Goldberg (1858), Hansdorf (1873), Breslau (1892), and Locle and Montmirail in Switzerland (1873). Thus do the German Moravians uphold the Pietist ideals of Zinzendorf.

Section III.—THE MORAVIANS IN GREAT BRITAIN.—For the last fifty years the most striking feature about the British Moravians is the fact that they have steadily become more British in all their ways, and more practical and enthusiastic in their work in this country. We can see it in every department of their work.

They began with the training of their ministers. As soon as the British Moravians became independent, they opened their own Theological Training Institution; and then step by step they allowed their students to come more and more under English influences. At first the home of the Training College was Fulneck; and, as long as the students lived in that placid abode, they saw but little of the outside world. But in 1874 the College was removed to Fairfield; then the junior students began to attend lectures at the Owens College; then (1886) they began to study for a degree in the Victoria University; then (1890) the theological students were allowed to study at Edinburgh or Glasgow; and the final result of this broadening process is that the average modern Moravian minister is as typical an Englishman as any one would care to meet. He has English blood in his veins; he bears an English name; he has been trained at an English University; he has learned his theology from English or Scotch Professors; he has English practical ideas of Christianity; and even when he has spent a few years in Germany—as still happens in exceptional cases—he has no more foreign flavour about him than the Lord Mayor of London.

Again, the influence of English ideas has affected their public worship. At the Provincial Synods of 1878 and 1883, the Brethren appointed Committees to revise their Hymn-book; and the result was that when the next edition of the Hymn-book appeared (1886), it was found to contain a large number of hymns by popular English writers. And this, of course, involved another change. As these popular English hymns were wedded to popular English tunes, those tunes had perforce to be admitted into the next edition of the Tune-book (1887); and thus the Moravians, like other Englishmen, began now to sing hymns by Toplady, Charles Wesley, George Rawson and Henry Francis Lyte to such well-known melodies as Sir Arthur Sullivan's "Coena Domini," Sebastian Wesley's "Aurelia," and Hopkins's "Ellers." But the change in this respect was only partial. In music the Moravians have always maintained a high standard. With them the popular type of tune was the chorale; and here they refused to give way to popular clamour. At this period the objection was raised by some that the old chorales were too difficult for Englishmen to sing; but to this objection Peter La Trobe had given a crushing answer. [160] At St. Thomas, he said, Zinzendorf had heard the negroes sing Luther's fine "Gelobet seiest"; at Gnadenthal, in South Africa, Ignatius La Trobe had heard the Hottentots sing Grummer's "Jesu, der du meine Seele"; in Antigua the negroes could sing Hassler's "O Head so full of bruises"; and therefore, he said, he naturally concluded that chorales which were not above the level of Negroes and Hottentots could easily be sung, if they only tried, by Englishmen, Scotchmen and Irishmen of the nineteenth century. And yet, despite this official attitude, certain standard chorales fell into disuse, and were replaced by flimsier English airs.

Another proof of the influence of English ideas is found in the decline of peculiar Moravian customs. At present the British congregations may be roughly divided into two classes. In some, such as Fulneck, Fairfield, Ockbrook, Bristol, and other older congregations, the old customs are retained; in others they are quite unknown. In some we still find such things as Love-feasts, the division into choirs, the regular choir festivals, the observance of Moravian Memorial Days; in others, especially in those only recently established, these things are absent; and the consequence is that in the new congregations the visitor of to-day will find but little of a specific Moravian stamp. At the morning service he will hear the Moravian Litany; in the Hymn-book he will find some hymns not found in other collections; but in other respects he would see nothing specially distinctive.

Meanwhile, the Brethren have adopted new institutions. As the old methods of church-work fell into disuse, new methods gradually took their place; and here the Brethren followed the example of their Anglican and Nonconformist friends. Instead of the special meetings for Single Brethren and Single Sisters, we now find the Christian Endeavour, and Men's and Women's Guilds; instead of the Boys' Economy, the Boys' Brigade; instead of the Brethren's House, the Men's Institute; instead of the Diacony, the weekly offering, the sale of work, and the bazaar; and instead of the old Memorial Days, the Harvest Festival and the Church and Sunday-school Anniversary.

But the most important change of all is the altered conception of the Church's mission. At the Provincial Synod held in Bedford the Brethren devoted much of their time to the Home Mission problem (1863); and John England, who had been commissioned to write a paper on "Our Aim and Calling," defined the Church's mission in the words: "Such, then, I take to be our peculiar calling. As a Church to preach Christ and Him crucified, every minister and every member. As a Church to evangelize, every minister and every member." From that moment those words were accepted as a kind of motto; and soon a great change was seen in the character of the Home Mission Work. In the first half of the nineteenth century nearly all the new causes begun were in quiet country villages; in the second half, with two exceptions, they were all in growing towns and populous districts. In 1859 new work was commenced at Baltonsborough, in Somerset, and Crook, in Durham; in 1862 at Priors Marston, Northamptonshire; in 1867 at Horton, Bradford; in 1869 at Westwood, in Oldham; in 1871 at University Road, Belfast; in 1874 at Heckmondwike, Yorkshire; in 1888 at Wellfield, near Shipley; in 1890 at Perth Street, Belfast; in 1896 at Queen's Park, Bedford; in 1899 at Openshaw, near Manchester, and at Swindon, the home of the Great Western Railway Works; in 1907 at Twerton, a growing suburb of Bath; and in 1908 in Hornsey, London. Of the places in this list, all except Baltonsborough and Priors Marston are in thickly populated districts; and thus during the last fifty years the Moravians have been brought more into touch with the British working man.

Meanwhile there has been a growing freedom of speech. The new movement began in the College at Fairfield. For the first time in the history of the British Province a number of radical Moravians combined to express their opinions in print; and, led and inspired by Maurice O'Connor, they now (1890) issued a breezy pamphlet, entitled Defects of Modern Moravianism. In this pamphlet they were both critical and constructive. Among other reforms, they suggested: (a) That the Theological Students should be allowed to study at some other Theological College; (b) that a Moravian Educational Profession be created; (c) that all British Moravian Boarding Schools be systematically inspected; (d) that the monthly magazine, The Messenger, be improved, enlarged, and changed into a weekly paper; (e) that in the future the energies of the Church be concentrated on work in large towns and cities; (f) and that all defects in the work of the Church be openly stated and discussed.

The success of the pamphlet was both immediate and lasting. Of all the Provincial Synods held in England the most important in many ways was that which met at Ockbrook a few months after the publication of this pamphlet. It marks the beginning of a new and brighter era in the history of the Moravian Church in England. For thirty years the Brethren had been content to hold Provincial Synods every four or five years (1890); but now, in accordance with a fine suggestion brought forward at Bedford two years before, and ardently supported by John Taylor, the Advocatus Fratrum in Anglia, they began the practice of holding Annual Synods. In the second place, the Brethren altered the character of their official church magazine. For twenty-seven years it had been a monthly of very modest dimensions. It was known as The Messenger; it was founded at the Bedford Synod (1863); and for some years it was well edited by Bishop Sutcliffe. But now this magazine became a fortnightly, known as The Moravian Messenger. As soon as the magazine changed its form it increased both in influence and in circulation. It was less official, and more democratic, in tone; it became the recognised vehicle for the expression of public opinion; and its columns have often been filled with articles of the most outspoken nature. And thirdly, the Brethren now resolved that henceforth their Theological Students should be allowed to study at some other Theological College.

But the influence of the pamphlet did not end here. At the Horton Synod (1904) arrangements were made for the establishment of a teaching profession, and at Baildon (1906) for the inspection of the Boarding Schools; and thus nearly all the suggestions of the pamphlet have now been carried out.

Finally, the various changes mentioned have all contributed, more or less, to alter the tone of the Moravian pulpit. As long as the work was mostly in country villages the preaching was naturally of the Pietistic type. But the Moravian preachers of the present day are more in touch with the problems of city life. They belong to a democratic Church; they are brought into constant contact with the working classes; they are interested in modern social problems; they believe that at bottom all social problems are religious; and, therefore, they not only foster such institutions as touch the daily life of the masses, but also in their sermons speak out more freely on the great questions of the day. In other words, the Moravian Church in Great Britain is now as British as Britain herself.

Section IV.—THE MORAVIANS IN AMERICA.—In America the progress was of a similar kind. As soon as the American Brethren had gained Home Rule, they organized their forces in a masterly manner; arranged that their Provincial Synod should meet once in three years; set apart -L-5,000 for their Theological College at Bethlehem; and, casting aside the Diaspora ideas of Zinzendorf, devoted their powers to the systematic extension of their Home Mission work. It is well to note the exact nature of their policy. With them Home Mission work meant systematic Church extension. At each new Home Mission station they generally placed a fully ordained minister; that minister was granted the same privileges as the minister of any other congregation; the new cause was encouraged to strive for self support; and, as soon as possible, it was allowed to send a deputy to the Synod. At Synod after Synod Church extension was the main topic of discussion; and the discussion nearly always ended in some practical proposal. For example, at the Synod of 1876 the Brethren formed a Church Extension Board; and that Board was entrusted with the task of raising -L-10,000 in the next three years. Again, in 1885, they resolved to build a new Theological College, elected a Building Committee to collect the money, and raised the sum required so rapidly that in 1892 they were able to open Comenius Hall at Bethlehem, free of debt. Meanwhile the number of new congregations was increasing with some rapidity. At the end of fifty years of Home Rule the Moravians in North

America had one hundred and two congregations; and of these no fewer than sixty-four were established since the separation of the Provinces. The moral is obvious. As soon as the Americans obtained Home Rule they more than doubled their speed; and in fifty years they founded more congregations than they had founded during the previous century. In 1857 they began new work at Fry's Valley, in Ohio; in 1859 at Egg Harbour City; in 1862 at South Bethlehem; in 1863 at Palmyra; in 1865 at Riverside; in 1866 at Elizabeth, Freedom, Gracehill, and Bethany; in 1867 at Hebron and Kernersville; in 1869 at Northfield, Philadelphia and Harmony; in 1870 at Mamre and Unionville; in 1871 at Philadelphia; in 1872 at Sturgeon Bay; in 1873 at Zoar and Gerah; in 1874 at Berea; in 1877 at Philadelphia and East Salem; in 1880 at Providence; in 1881 at Canaan and Goshen; in 1882 at Port Washington, Oakland, and Elim; in 1886 at Hector and Windsor; in 1887 at Macedonia, Centre Ville, and Oakgrove; in 1888 at Grand Rapids and London; in 1889 at Stapleton and Calvary; in 1890 at Spring Grove and Clemmons; in 1891 at Bethel, Eden and Bethesda; in 1893 at Fulp and Wachovia Harbour; in 1894 at Moravia and Alpha; in 1895 at Bruederfeld and Bruederheim; in 1896 at Heimthal, Mayodon and Christ Church; in 1898 at Willow Hill; in 1901 at New York; in 1902 at York; in 1904 at New Sarepta; and in 1905 at Strathcona. For Moravians this was an exhilarating speed; and the list, though forbidding in appearance, is highly instructive. In Germany Church extension is almost unknown; in England it is still in its infancy; in America it is practically an annual event; and thus there are now more Moravians in America than in England and Germany combined. In Germany the number of Moravians is about 8,000; in Great Britain about 6,000; in North America about 20,000.

From this fact a curious conclusion has been drawn. As the American Moravians have spread so rapidly, the suspicion has arisen in certain quarters that they are not so loyal as the Germans and British to the best ideals of the Moravian Church; and one German Moravian writer has asserted, in a standard work, that the American congregations are lacking in cohesion, in brotherly character, and in sympathy with true Moravian principles. [161] But to this criticism several answers may be given. In the first place, it is well to note what we mean by Moravian ideals. If Moravian ideals are Zinzendorf's ideals, the criticism is true. In Germany, the Brethren still pursue Zinzendorf's policy; in England and America that policy has been rejected. In Germany the Moravians still act as a "Church within the Church"; in England and America such work has been found impossible. But Zinzendorf's "Church within the Church" idea is no Moravian "essential." It was never one of the ideals of the Bohemian Brethren; it sprang, not from the Moravian Church, but from German Pietism; and, therefore, if the American Brethren reject it they cannot justly be accused of disloyalty to original Moravian principles.

For those principles they are as zealous as any other Moravians. They have a deep reverence for the past. At their Theological Seminary in Bethlehem systematic instruction in Moravian history is given; and the American Brethren have their own Historical Society. For twenty years Bishop Edmund de Schweinitz lectured to the students on Moravian history; and, finally, in his "History of the Unitas Fratrum," he gave to the public the fullest account of the Bohemian Brethren in the English language; and in recent years Dr. Hamilton, his succesor, has narrated in detail the history of the Renewed Church of the Brethren. Second, the Americans, when put to the test, showed practical sympathy with German Brethren in distress. As soon as the German refugees arrived from Volhynia, the American Moravians took up their cause with enthusiasm, provided them with ministers, helped them with money, and thus founded the new Moravian congregations in Alberta. And third, the Americans have their share of Missionary zeal. They have their own "Society for Propagating the Gospel"; they have their own Missionary magazines; and during the last quarter of a century they have borne nearly the whole burden, both in money and in men, of the new mission in Alaska. And thus the three branches of the Moravian Church, though differing from each other in methods, are all united in their loyalty to the great essentials.

Section V.—BONDS OF UNION.—But these essentials are not the only bonds of union. At present Moravians all over the world are united in three great tasks.

First, they are united in their noble work among the lepers at Jerusalem. It is one of the scandals of modern Christianity that leprosy is still the curse of Palestine; and the only Christians who are trying to remove that curse are the Moravians. At the request of a kind-hearted German lady, Baroness von Keffenbrink-Ascheraden, the first Moravian Missionary went out to Palestine forty years ago (1867). There, outside the walls of Jerusalem, the first hospital for lepers, named Jesus Hilfe, was built; there, for some years, Mr. and Mrs. Tappe laboured almost alone; and then, when the old hospital became too small, the new hospital, which is standing still, was built, at a cost of -L-4,000, on the Jaffa Road. In this work, the Moravians have a twofold object. First, they desire to exterminate leprosy in Palestine; second, as opportunity offers, they speak of Christ to the patients. But the hospital, of course, is managed on the broadest lines. It is open to men of all creeds; there is no religious test of any kind; and if the patient objects to the Gospel it is not forced upon him. At present the hospital has accommodation for about fifty patients; the annual expense is about -L-4,000; the Managing Committee has its headquarters in Berthelsdorf; each Province of the Moravian Church has a Secretary and Treasurer; the staff consists of a Moravian Missionary, his wife, and five assistant nurses; and all true Moravians are expected to support this holy cause. At this hospital, of course, the Missionary and his assistants come into the closest personal contact with the lepers. They dress their sores; they wash their clothes; they run every risk of infection; and yet not one of the attendants has ever contracted the disease. When Father Damien took the leprosy all England thrilled at the news; and yet if England rose to her duty the black plague of leprosy might soon be a thing of the past.

Again, the Moravian Church is united in her work in Bohemia and Moravia. At the General Synod of 1869 a strange coincidence occurred; and that strange coincidence was that both from Great Britain and from North America memorials were handed in suggesting that an attempt be made to revive the Moravian Church in her ancient home.

In England the leader of the movement was Bishop Seifferth. In North America the enthusiasm was universal, and the petition was signed by every one of the ministers. And thus, once more, the Americans were the leaders in a forward movement. The Brethren agreed to the proposal. At Pottenstein (1870), not far from Reichenau, the first new congregation in Bohemia was founded. For ten years the Brethren in Bohemia were treated by the Austrian Government as heretics; but in 1880, by an Imperial edict, they were officially recognized as the "Brethren's Church in Austria." Thus is the prayer of Comenius being answered at last; thus has the Hidden Seed begun to grow; thus are the Brethren preaching once more within the walls of Prague; and now, in the land where in days of old their fathers were slain by the sword, they have a dozen growing congregations, a monthly Moravian magazine ("Bratrske Litsz"), and a thousand adherents of the Church of the Brethren. Again, as in the case of the Leper Home, the Managing Committee meets at Herrnhut; each Province has its corresponding members; and all Moravians are expected to share in the burden.

Above all, the Moravian Church is united in the work of Foreign Missions. For their missions to the heathen the Moravians have long been famous; and, in proportion to their resources, they are ten times as active as any other Protestant Church. But in this book the story of Moravian foreign missions has not been told. It is a story of romance and thrilling adventure, of dauntless heroism and marvellous patience; it is a theme worthy of a Froude or a Macaulay; and some day a master of English prose may arise to do it justice. If that master historian ever appears, he will have an inspiring task. He will tell of some of the finest heroes that the Christian Church has ever produced. He will tell of Matthew Stach, the Greenland pioneer, of Friedrich Martin, the "Apostle to the Negroes," of David Zeisberger, the "Apostle to the Indians," of Erasmus Schmidt, in Surinam, of Jaeschke, the famous Tibetan linguist, of Leitner and the lepers on Robben Island, of Henry Schmidt in South Africa, of James Ward in North Queensland, of Meyer and Richard in German East Africa, and of many another grand herald of the Cross whose name is emblazoned in letters of gold upon the Moravian roll of honour. In no part of their work have the Brethren made grander progress. In 1760 they had eight fields of labour, 1,000 communicants, and 7,000 heathen under their care; in 1834, thirteen fields of labour, 15,000 communicants, and 46,000 under their care; in 1901, twenty fields of labour, 32,000 communicants, and 96,000 under their care. As the historian traces the history of the Moravian Church, he often finds much to criticize and sometimes much to blame; but here, on the foreign mission field, the voice of the critic is dumb. Here the Moravians have ever been at their best; here they have done their finest redemptive work; here they have shown the noblest self-sacrifice; and here, as the sternest critic must admit, they have always raised from degradation to glory the social, moral, and spiritual condition of the people. In these days the remark is sometimes made by superior critics that foreign missionaries in the olden days had a narrow view of the Gospel, that their only object was to save the heathen from hell, and that they never made any attempt to establish the Kingdom of God on earth. If that statement refers to other missionaries, it

313

may or may not be true; but if it refers to Moravians it is false. At all their stations the Moravian Missionaries looked after the social welfare of the people. They built schools, founded settlements, encouraged industry, fought the drink traffic, healed the sick, and cast out the devils of robbery, adultery and murder; and the same principles and methods are still in force to-day.

At the last General Synod held in Herrnhut the foreign mission work was placed under the management of a General Mission Board; the Board was elected by the Synod; and thus every voting member of the Church has his share in the control of the work. In each Province there are several societies for raising funds. In the German Province are the North-Scheswig Mission Association, the Zeist Mission Society, and the Fuenf-pfennig Verein or Halfpenny Union. In the British Province are the Society for the Furtherance of the Gospel, which owns that famous missionary ship, the "Harmony"; the Juvenile Missionary Association, chiefly supported by pupils of the boarding schools; the Mite Association; and that powerful non-Moravian Society, the London Association in aid of Moravian Missions. In North America is the Society for Propagating the Gospel among the Heathen. In each Province, too, we find periodical missionary literature: in Germany two monthlies, the Missions-Blatt and Aus Nord und Sued; in Holland the Berichten uit de Heidenwereld; in Denmark the Evangelisk Missionstidende; in England the quarterly Periodical Accounts and the monthly Moravian Missions; and in North America two monthlies, Der Missions Freund and the Little Missionary. In Germany the missionary training College is situated at Niesky; in England at Bristol. In England there is also a special fund for the training of medical missionaries. Of the communicant members of the Moravian Church one in every sixty goes out as a missionary; and from this fact the conclusion has often been drawn that if the members of other churches went out in the same proportion the heathen world might be won for Christ in ten years. At present the Mission field contains about 100,000 members; the number of missionaries employed is about 300; the annual expenses of the work are about -L-90,000; and of that sum two-thirds is raised by the native converts.

There are now fourteen Provinces in the Mission field, and attractive is the scene that lies before us. We sail on the "Harmony" to Labrador, and see the neatly built settlements, the fur-clad Missionary in his dog-drawn sledge, the hardy Eskimos, the squat little children at the village schools, the fathers and mothers at worship in the pointed church, the patients waiting their turn in the surgery in the hospital at Okak. We pass on to Alaska, and steam with the Brethren up the Kuskokwim River. We visit the islands of the West Indies, where Froude, the historian, admired the Moravian Schools, and where his only complaint about these schools was that there were not enough of them. We pass on to California, where the Brethren have a modern Mission among the Red Indians; to the Moskito Coast, once the scene of a wonderful revival; to Paramaribo in Surinam, the city where the proportion of Christians is probably greater than in any other city in the world; to South Africa, where it is commonly reported that a Hottentot or Kaffir Moravian convert can always be trusted to be honest; to German East Africa, where the Brethren took over the work at Urambo at the request of the London Missionary Society; to North Queensland, where the natives were once so degraded that Anthony Trollope declared that the "game was not worth the candle," where Moravians now supply the men and Presbyterians the money, and where the visitor gazes in amazement at the "Miracle of Mapoon"; and last to British India, near Tibet, where, perched among the Himalaya Mountains, the Brethren in the city of Leh have the highest Missionary station in the world.

As the Moravians, therefore, review the wonderful past, they see the guiding hand of God at every stage of the story. They believe that their Church was born of God in Bohemia, that God restored her to the light of day when only the stars were shining, that God has opened the door in the past to many a field of labour, and that God has preserved her to the present day for some great purpose of his own. Among her ranks are men of many races and many shades of opinion; and yet, from Tibet to San Francisco, they are still one united body. As long as Christendom is still divided, they stand for the great essentials as the bond of union. As long as lepers in Palestine cry "unclean," they have still their mission in the land where the Master taught. As long as Bohemia sighs for their Gospel, and the heathen know not the Son of Man, they feel that they must obey the Missionary mandate; and, convinced that in following these ideals they are not disobedient to the heavenly vision, they emblazon still upon their banner the motto encircling their old episcopal seal:—

"Vicit Agnus noster: Eum sequamur."
(Our Lamb has conquered: Him let its follow.)

Footnotes

1. De Ecclesia.

2. Calixtine = Cup-ite, from the Latin, calix, a cup. Utraquist = in both kinds, from the Latin, utraque.

3. Pronounced: Kelchits. The ch is a guttural like the Hebrew kaph, or like ch in the word loch.

4. A common saying in Peter's day.

5. Pronounced Rockitsanna.

6. This outbreak made a great sensation, and was frequently quoted by the Brethren in their writings.

7. Rockycana's character is rather hard to judge. Some of his sermons have been preserved, and they have the ring of sincerity. Perhaps, like Erasmus in later years, he wished to avoid a schism, and thought that the Church could be reformed from within.

8. These settled, not at Kunwald, but close by.

9. For many years there has been a tradition that the Moravian Church was founded on March 1st, 1457; but this date is only a pious imagination. We are not quite sure of the year, not to speak of the day of the month. If the Moravian Church must have a birthday, March 1st, 1457, will do as well as any other; but the truth is that on this point precise evidence has not yet been discovered.

10. This division into three classes is first found in a letter to Rockycana, written in 1464.

11. De Schweinitz (p. 107) says that the Brethren now took the title of "Fratres Legis Christi," i.e., Brethren of the Law of Christ. This is a mistake. This title is not found till towards the close of the sixteenth century, and was never in general use; see Mueller's "Boehmische-Brueder" in Hauck's Real-Encyclopaedie.

12. The best way to understand the Brethren's attitude is to string together their favourite passages of Scripture. I note, in particular, the following: Matthew xviii. 19, 20; Jeremiah iii. 15; John xx. 23; Revelation xviii. 4, 5; Luke vi. 12-16; Acts iv. 32.

13. And this raises an interesting question: If the lot had decided against the Brethren, what would they have done? They have given us the answer themselves. If the inscribed slips had remained in the vase, the Brethren would have waited a year and

then tried again. The final issue, in fact, did not depend on the use of the lot at all. They used it, not to find out God's will, but simply to confirm that faith in their cause which had already been gained in prayer.

14. It is here stated by De Schweinitz (p. 137), on Gindely's authority, that the members of the Synod were now re-baptized. The statement is not correct. It is based on a letter written by Rockycana; but it is unsupported by any other evidence, and must, therefore be rejected. As the Brethren have often been confounded with Anabaptists (especially by Ritschl, in his Geschichte des Pietismus), I will here give the plain facts of the case. For a number of years the Brethren held that all who joined their ranks from the Church of Rome should be re-baptized; and the reason why they did so was that in their judgment the Romanist baptism had been administered by men of bad moral character, and was, therefore, invalid. But in 1534 they abandoned this position, recognised the Catholic Baptism as valid, and henceforth showed not a trace of Anabaptist views either in theory or in practice.

15. 1. The "Six Commandments" are as follows:—(1) Matthew v. 22: Thou shalt not be angry with thy brother. (2) Matthew v. 28: Thou shalt not look upon a woman to lust after her. (3) Matthew v. 32: Thou shalt not commit adultery, or divorce thy wife. (4) Matthew v. 34: Thou shalt not take an oath. (5) Matthew v. 39, 40: Thou shalt not go to law. (6) Matthew v. 44: Thou shalt love thine enemy. 2. Moravian Episcopal Orders.—For the benefit of those, if such there be, who like a abstruse historical problems, and who, therefore, are hungering for further information about the origin, maintenance and validity of Moravian Episcopal Orders, I here append a brief statement of the case:—(1) Origin.—On this point three opinions have been held: (a) For many years it was stoutly maintained by Palacky, the famous Bohemian historian, by Anton Gindely, the Roman Catholic author of the "Geschichte der Boehmischen Brueder," and also Bishop Edmund de Schweinitz in his "History of the Unitas Fratrum," that Stephen, the Waldensian, was made a Bishop at the Catholic Council of Basle, and that thus Moravian Episcopal Orders have a Roman Catholic origin. But this view is now generally abandoned. It is not supported by adequate evidence, and is, on the face of it, entirely improbable. If Stephen had been a Romanist or Utraquist Bishop the Brethren would never have gone near him. (b) In recent years it has been contended by J. Mueller and J. Koestlin that Stephen was consecrated by the Taborite Bishop, Nicholas von Pilgram. But this view is as improbable as the first. For Nicholas von Pilgram and his rough disciples the Brethren had little more respect than they had for the Church of Rome. Is it likely that they would take their orders from a source which they regarded as corrupt? (c) The third view—the oldest and the latest—is that held by the Brethren themselves. They did not believe that Bishop Stephen had any connection, direct or indirect, with the Church of Rome. They believed that he represented an episcopate which had come down as an office of the Church from the earliest Christian days. They could

not prove, of course, up to the hilt, that the Waldensian succession was unbroken; but, as far as they understood such questions, they believed the succession to be at least as good as that which came through Rome. And to that extent they were probably right. There is no such thing on the field of history as a proved Apostolic succession; but if any line of mediaeval Bishops has high claims to historical validity it is, as Dr. Doellinger has shown (in his Beitraege zur Sektengeschichte des Mittelalters), the line to which Waldensian Stephen belonged. (2) Maintenance.— We now come to another question: Has the Church of the Brethren maintained the succession from the time of Stephen to the present day? Here again the historian has a very tight knot to untie. At one point (if not two) in the history of the Brethren's Church, 1500 and 1554, there is certainly the possibility that her Episcopal succession was broken. For the long period of eleven years the Brethren had only one Bishop, John Augusta; and Augusta was a prisoner in Purglitz Castle, and could not, therefore, consecrate a successor. What, then, were the Brethren to do? If John Augusta were to die in prison the line of Bishops would end. Meanwhile the Brethren did the best they could. As they did not wish the office to cease, they elected Bishops to perform Episcopal functions for the time being. Now comes the critical question: Did John August, some years later, consecrate these elected Bishops or did he not? There is no direct evidence either way. But we know enough to show us the probabilities. It is certain that in 1564 John Augusta came out of prison; it is certain that in 1571 two Bishops-elect, Israel and Blahoslav, consecrated three successors; it is certain that Augusta was a stickler for his own authority as a Bishop; it is not certain that he raised an objection to the conduct of Israel and Blahoslav; and, therefore, it is possible that he had consecrated them himself. If he did, the Moravian succession is unbroken; and, at any rate, it is without a flaw from that day to this. (3) Validity.—Is the Moravian Episcopacy valid? The answer depends on the meaning of the word "Validity." If the only valid Bishops in the Church of Christ are those who can prove an unbroken descent from the Apostles, then the Brethren's Bishops are no more valid than the Bishops of any other Church; and all historians must honestly admit that, in this sense of the word "Valid," there is no such thing as a valid Bishop in existence. But the word "Validity" may have a broader meaning. It may mean the desire to adhere to New Testament sanctions; it may mean the honest and loyal endeavour to preserve the "intention" of the Christian ministry as instituted by Christ; and if this is what "Validity" means the Moravian Episcopate is just as valid as that of any other communion. Meanwhile, at any rate, the reader may rest content with the following conclusions:—(1) That Gregory the Patriarch and his fellow Brethren were satisfied with Bishop Stephen's statement. (2) That they acted honestly according to their light, and desired to be true successors of the Primitive Church. (3) That the Waldensian Episcopate was of ancient order. (4) That no break in the Brethren's Episcopal succession has ever been absolutely proved. (5) That, during the whole course of their history the Brethren have always endeavoured to preserve the Episcopal office intact. For a further discussion of the whole question see "The Report of the Committee appointed by the Synod of the Moravian Church in Great Britain for the purpose of inquiring into the possibility of more friendly relations on the part of this Church with the Anglican Church"; see also, in German, Mueller's "Bischoftum," where the whole evidence is critically handled.

16. For the later history of the Brethren's Church this entrance of German-speaking Waldenses was of fundamental importance; of far greater importance, in fact, than is recognised either by Gindely or de Schweinitz. As these men spoke the German language, the Brethren, naturally, for their benefit, prepared German editions of their Confessions, Catechisms, and Hymn-books; and through these German editions of their works they were able, a few years later, to enter into closer contact with the Reformation in Germany. But that is not the end of the story. It was descendants of this German branch of the Church that first made their way to Herrnhut in 1722, and thus laid the foundations of the Renewed Church of the Brethren.

17. A Brother, e.g., might take the oath to save another Brother's life.

18. We are, therefore, justified in regarding the year 1495 as a turning-point in the history of the Brethren. The revolution was thorough and complete. It is a striking fact that Luke of Prague, whose busy pen was hardly ever dry, did not back up a single passage by appealing to Peter's authority; and, in one passage, he even attacked his character and accused him of not forgiving an enemy.

19. And here I beseech the reader to be on his guard. It is utterly incorrect to state, with de Schweinitz, that at this period the Brethren held the famous doctrine of justification by faith, as expounded by Martin Luther. Of Luther's doctrine, Luke himself was a vigorous opponent (see p. 69).

20. Taine, History of English Literature, Book II. cap. V. For a good defence of Alexander's character, see Cambridge Modern History, Vol I. p. 241.

21. This tract, however, was probably a later Waldensian production.

22. So called because the Diet opened on St. James's day (July 25th, 1508).

23. A corruption of Beghard. The term, however, appears to have been used very loosely. It was simply a vulgar term of abuse for all who had quarrelled with the Church of Rome. John Wycliffe was called a Picard.

24. Jednota Rimska.

25. Jednota Lutherianska. For the Church Universal they used another word: Cirkey, meaning thereby all those elected by God.

26. I desire to be explicit on this point. It is, of course, true enough that when the Brethren in later years began to use the Latin language they used the term "Unitas Fratrum" as the equivalent of Jednota Bratrska, but in so doing they made an excusable blunder. The translation "Unitas Fratrum" is misleading. It is etymologically correct, and historically false. If a Latin term is to be used at all, it would be better to say, as J. Mueller suggests, "Societas Fratrum," or, better still, in my judgment, "Ecclesia Fratrum." But of all terms to describe the Brethren the most offensive is "sect." It is inconsistent for the same writer to speak of the "sect" of the Bohemian Brethren and of the "Church" of Rome. If the Roman Communion is to be described as a "Church," the same term, in common courtesy, should be applied to the Brethren.

27. De Schweinitz. (p. 126) actually sees in this passage the doctrine of justification by faith. I confess that I do not.

28. This letter was probably written by Luke of Prague.

29. Mueller's Katechismen, page 231.

30. This was actually reported to the Pope as a fact by his agent, Henry Institoris. See Mueller's Katechismen, p. 319.

31. From the German edition of 1522; printed in full in Mueller's "Die deutschen Katechismen der Boehmischen Brueder."

32. Compare our Queen Elizabeth's view:—Christ was the Word that spake it, He took the bread and brake it, And what that Word did make it, That I believe, and take it.

33. Letter to the Brethren, 1523.

34. There is no doubt whatever on this last point. If the student will consult any standard work on the history of the early Christian Church, he will see how closely the institutions of the Brethren were modelled on the institutions of the first three centuries as pourtrayed, not only in the New Testament, but also in such documents as the Didache, the Canons of Hippolytus, and the Apostolic Constitutions. For English readers the best guide is T. M. Lindsay's The Church and the Ministry in the Early Centuries; and the following references will be of special interest: (1) For the Brethren's conception of priesthood, see p. 35; (2) for their rule that the clergy should learn a trade, p. 203; (3) for their ministry of women, p. 181; (4) for their contempt of learning, p. 182; (5) for their preference for unmarried ministers, p. 179; (6) for the term "Brotherhood" (Jednota) a synonym for "Church," p. 21; (7) for Acoluths and their duties, p. 355; (8) for their system of discipline, Matthew xviii. 15-17; (9) for Beginners, Proficients, and Perfect—(a) Heb. v. 13, (b) Heb. v. 14, vi. 1, (c) 1 Cor. ii. 6, 2 Cor. vii. 1, Rom. xv. 14, Philipp iii. 15.

35. There is a beautiful copy of this "Confession" in the Moravian Theological College at Fairfield, near Manchester.

36. An important point. It shows that the scheme which Augusta afterwards sketched in prison was a long-cherished design, and not a new trick to regain his liberty. (See Chapter XI.)

37. It is perfectly clear from this prayer that the Brethren tried to reconcile their loyalty to Ferdinand with loyalty to their faith. The prayer is printed in full in J. Mueller's "Gefangenshaft des Johann Augusta."

38. Gindely's narrative here is quite misleading. For no reason whatever he endeavours to make out that the Brethren were the chief authors of the conspiracy against Ferdinand. For this statement there is not a scrap of evidence, and Gindely produces none. It is not often that Gindely romances, but he certainly romances here, and his biting remarks about the Brethren are unworthy of so great an historian! (See Vol I., p. 293.)

39. Gindely's naive remark here is too delightful to be lost. He says that the rich Brethren had not been corrupted by their contact with Luther's teaching, and that, therefore, they still possessed a little of the milk of human kindness for the refreshment of the poor. (See Vol. I. p. 330.)

40. The Unitarians were specially strong in Poland.

41. The letter, that is, in which the Brethren had pleaded not guilty to the charge of treason.

42. The fallacy underlying this argument is well known to logicians, and a simple illustration will make it clear to the reader:—

All Hottentots have black hair.

Mr. Jones has black hair.

Therefore, Mr. Jones is a Hottentot.

43. I must add a brief word in honour of Jacob Bilek. As that faithful secretary was thirteen years in prison (1548-61), and endured many tortures rather than deny his faith, it is rather a pity that two historians have branded him as a traitor. It is asserted both by Gindely (Vol. I., p. 452) and by de Schweinitz (p. 327) that Bilek obtained his liberty by promising, in a written bond, to renounce the Brethren and adhere to the Utraquist Church. But how Gindely could make such a statement is more than I can understand. He professes to base his statement on Bilek's narrative; and Bilek himself flatly denies the charge. He admits that a bond was prepared, but says that it was handed to the authorities without his knowledge and consent. For my part, I see

no reason to doubt Bilek's statement; and he certainly spent his last days among the Brethren as minister of the congregation at Napajedl.

44. It had been presented in 1564.

45. Confessio Bohemica; there is a copy in the archives at 32 Fetter Lane, E.C.

46. This was doubtless an exaggeration, but it shows that the Brethren were more powerful than the reader would gather from most histories of the Reformation.

47. A copy of this may be seen in the College at Fairfield. The copy is a second edition, dated 1596. There are two columns to a page. The "title page," "preface," and "contents" are missing in this copy.

48. This point is ignored by most English historians, but is fully recognised by Count Lutzow. "It can be generally stated," he says, in his "History of Bohemian Literature," p. 201, "that with a few exceptions all the men who during the last years of Bohemian independence were most prominent in literature and in politics belonged to the Unity."

49. "The Imprisonment of John Augusta," translated into German by Dr. J. T. Mueller. An English translation has not yet appeared.

50. J. Mueller puts the estimate still higher. He thinks that at this time at least half of the Protestants in Bohemia were Brethren; and that in Moravia their strength was even greater.

51. Prepared 1609; published 1616; republished in Latin, 1633; and translated and published in England in 1866, by Bishop Seifferth. There is one point in this treatise to which special attention may be drawn. It contains no allusion to the fact that among the Brethren the ministers had to earn their living by manual labour. The reason is obvious. The practice ceased in 1609, as soon as the Charter was granted, and from that time the Brethren's ministers in Bohemia (though not in Moravia and Poland) stood on the same footing as the other evangelical clergy.

52. Printed in full in J. Mueller's "Katechismen."

53. Ranke, "History of the Popes." Book VII. cap. II., sect. 3 note.

54. In his "Labyrinth of the World."

55. I commend this book to the reader. It has recently been translated into English by Count Luetzow, and is included now in Dent's "Temple Classics."

56. Surely a poetic exaggeration.

57. Succeeded in 1629 by Andreas Wengierski; known commonly to historical students as Regenvolscius, the author of an admirable "History of the Slavonic Churches."

58. It is stated in most biographies of Zinzendorf that Spener stood sponsor at his baptism; but Gerhard Wauer, in his recent work, Beginnings of the Moravian Church in England, says that Spener's name is not to be found in the baptismal register. And this, I imagine, should settle the question.

59. Hymn No. 851 in the present German Hymn-book.

60. Collegia pietatis.

61. Ecclesiolae in ecclesia.

62. Ante is to be construed as an adverb.

63. In his classic Geschichte des Pietismus (Vol. III. p. 203), Albrecht Ritschl says that Zinzendorf's unwillingness to be a missionary was due to his pride of rank. The statement has not a shadow of foundation. In fact, it is contradicted by Zinzendorf himself, who says: "ihre Idee war eigentlich nicht, dieses und dergleichen selbst zu bewerkstelligen, denn sie waren beide von den Ihrigen in die grosse Welt destiniert und wussten von nichts als gehorsam sein." I should like here to warn the student against paying much attention to what Ritschl says about Zinzendorf's theology and ecclesiastical policy. His statements are based on ignorance and theological prejudice: and his blunders have been amply corrected, first by Bernhard Becker in his Zinzendorf und sein Christentum im Verhaeltnis zum kirchlichen und religioesen Leben seiner Zeit, and secondly by Joseph Mueller in his Zinzendorf als Erneuerer der alten Bruederkirche (1900).

64. For further details of Zinzendorf's stay at Wittenberg I must refer to his interesting Diary, which is now in course of publication in the Zeitschrift fuer Bruedergeschichte. It is written in an alarming mixture of Hebrew, Greek, Latin, German, and French; but the editors have kindly added full explanatory notes, and all the student requires to understand it is a working knowledge of German.

65. This picture is now in the Pinakothek at Muenich. It is wonderful how this well-known incident has been misrepresented and misapplied. It is constantly referred to now in tracts, sermons, and popular religious magazines as if it was the means of Zinzendorf's "conversion"; and even a scholar like the late Canon Liddon tells us how this German nobleman was now "converted from a life of careless indifference." (Vide Passiontide Sermons. No. VII., pp. 117, 118.) But all that the picture really accomplished was to strengthen convictions already held and plans already formed. It is absurd to talk about the "conversion" of a youth who had loved and followed Christ for years.

66. The phrase inscribed upon her tombstone at Herrnhut.

67. The Smalkald Articles were drawn up in 1537; and the clause to which Zinzendorf appealed runs as follows: "In many ways the Gospel offers counsel and help to the

sinner; first through the preaching of the Word, second, through Baptism, third, through the Holy Communion, fourth through the power of the keys, and, lastly, through brotherly discussion and mutual encouragement, according to Matthew xviii., Where two or three are gathered together.'" The Count, of course, appealed to the last of these methods.; For some reason, however, unknown to me, this particular clause in the Articles was always printed in Latin, and was, therefore, unknown to the general public.

68. In his treatise, "The German Mass," published in 1526 (see Koestlin's "Life of Luther," p. 295; Longmans' Silver Library).

69. August, 1738.

70. See page 58.

71. Not to be confounded with Kunwald in Bohemia.

72. It is probable that the Neissers were descendants of the Brethren's Church, but we cannot be quite certain about it. About the third band, that arrived in 1724, there is no doubt whatever. (See the next chapter, p. 200.)

73. "Hutberg"; i.e., the hill where cattle and sheep were kept secure. The name "Hutberg" was common in Germany, and was applied, of course, to many other hills. For the payment of a small rent the landlords often let out "Hutbergs" to the villagers on their estates.

74. Ps. lxxxiv. 3. The spot where David felled the first tree is now marked by a monument, inscribed with the date and the text; and the date itself is one of the Brethren's so-called "Memorial Days."

75. Zinzendorf's expression.

76. These "Injunctions and Prohibitions" are now printed for the first time by J. Mueller, in his Zizendorf als Erneuerer der alten Bruder-Kirche (1900). They must not be confounded with the "Statutes" printed in the Memorial Days of the Brethren's Church.

77. Here again Ritschl is wrong. He assumes (Geschichte des Pietismus, III. 243) that when Zinzendorf drew up his "Injunctions and Prohibitions" and "Statutes" he was already acquainted with the Ratio Disciplinae. But the "Injunctions" and "Statutes" were read out on May 12th, and the "Ratio" was not discovered till July.

78. There was, however, no community of goods.

79. I am not exaggerating. In one of his discourses he says: "I regard the Augsburg Confession as inspired, and assert that it will be the creed of the Philadelphian

Church till Christ comes again." See Mueller, Zinzendorf als Erneuerer, p. 90, and Becker, p. 335.

80. As I write these words a copy of the first Text-book lies before me. It has only one text for each day, and all the texts are taken from the New Testament.

81. It is often referred to in the English Congregation Diaries. It was abandoned simply because it was no longer valued; and no one was willing to take part.

82. For striking examples see pages 230, 236, 266, 302, 394.

83. Luke xxii. 17.

84. The whole question is thoroughly discussed by J. Mueller in his "Zinzendorf als Erneuerer der alten Brueder-Kirche."

85. Was this true to Luther, or was it not? According to Ritschl it was not (Geschichte des Pietismus, III. 248); according to J. T. Mueller, it was (Zinzendorf als Erneuerer, p. 40). I agree with the latter writer.

86. It is not clear from the evidence who suggested the use of the Lot. According to Zinzendorf's diary it was the Brethren; but I suspect that he himself was the first to suggest it. There is no proof that the Brethren were already fond of the Lot; but there is plenty of proof that the Pietists were, and Zinzendorf had probably learned it from them. (See Ritschl II., 434, etc.)

87. And here I correct a popular misconception. It has often been stated in recent years that the first Moravian missionaries actually became slaves. The statement is incorrect. As a matter of fact, white slavery was not allowed in any of the West Indian islands.

88. E.g., Dr. George Smith's Short History of Christian Missions, Chapter XI.

89. See Book I., pp. 74-5.

90. For details about this interesting point, see La Trobe's Letters to My Children, pp. 13-25.

91. The first number appeared in 1790, and the first editor was Christian Ignatius La Trobe.

92. The vessel referred to was the Harmony. It belonged to the Brethren's "Society for the Furtherance of the Gospel," and carried their missionaries and goods to and from Labrador.

93. For proof see Th. Bechler's pamphlet: Vor hundert Jahren und heut (pp. 40-47).

94. See 1 Peter i. 1: "Peter to the strangers scattered." The Greek word is diaspora; this is the origin of the Moravian phrase, "Diaspora Work."

95. i.e. By the Lot.

96. i.e. By the Lot. This is what Zinzendorf's language really means.

97. But this applied to Europe only. In America Bishop Spangenberg was still Chief Elder; and Christ was not recognized as Chief Elder there till 1748. What caused this strange incongruity? How could the Brethren recognize a man as Chief Elder in America and the Lord Christ as Chief Elder in Europe? The explanation is that in each case the question was settled by the Lot; and the Brethren themselves asked in bewilderment why our Lord would not at first consent to be Chief Elder in America.

98. See Benham's Memoirs of James Hutton, p. 245, where the papers referring to Bishop Wilson's appointment are printed in full.

99. It was a little green book, with detachable leaves; each leaf contained some motto or text; and when the Count was in a difficulty, he pulled out one of these leaves at random.

100. Matthew xi. 25. "Little Fools" (Naerrchen) was Zinzendorf's rendering of naypeeoee (spelled in greek: nu, eta, pi, iota (stressed), omicron, iota}.

101. For want of a better, I use this word to translate the German "Laemmlein"; but, in common justice, it must be explained that "Laemmlein" in German does not sound so foolish as "Lambkin" in English. In German, diminutives are freely used to express endearment. (See James Hutton's sensible remarks in Benham's Memoirs, p. 563.)

102. Cross-air—soaring in the atmosphere of the Cross.

103. See Chapter XIV., p. 384.

104. See Chapter III., p. 208.

105. It has often been urged, in Zinzendorf's defence, that he did not know what was happening at Herrnhaag. But this defence will not hold good. He was present, in 1747, when some of the excesses were at their height; and during the summer of that year he delivered there a series of thirty-four homilies on his "Litany of the Wounds."

106. See, e.g., Kurtz's Church History. Dr. Kurtz entirely ignores the fact that the worst features of the "Sifting Time" were only of short duration, and that no one condemned its excesses more severely than the Brethren themselves.

107. Canon Overton's sarcastic observations here are quite beside the point. He says (Life of John Wesley, p. 55) that Spangenberg subjected Wesley to "a cross-examination which, considering the position and attainments of the respective parties, seems to an outsider, in plain words, rather impertinent." I should like to know where this

impertinence comes in. What were "the position and attainments of the respective parties?" Was Spangenberg Wesley's intellectual inferior? No. Did Spangenberg seek the conversation? No. "I asked his advice," says Wesley, "with regard to my own conduct."

108. Thus Overton, e.g., writes: "If John Wesley was not a true Christian in Georgia, God help millions of those who profess and call themselves Christians." Life of John Wesley, p. 58.

109. "And forthwith commenced the process of purging," adds Overton. Witty, but untrue. Boehler did nothing of the kind.

110. See, e.g., Overton, Evangelical Revival p. 15; Fisher, History of the Church, p. 516; Wakeman, History of the Church of England, p. 438.

111. This clause is omitted by John Wesley in his Journal! He gives the fundamental rules of the Society, but omits the clause that interfered most with his own liberty. See Journal, May 1st, 1738.

112. Precise date uncertain.

113. What did the Brethren mean by this? We are left largely to conjecture. My own personal impression is, however, that the Brethren feared that if Wesley took Communion with them he might be tempted to leave the Church of England and join the Moravian Church.

114. Mr. Lecky's narrative here (History of England, Vol. II., p. 67, Cabinet Edition) is incorrect. He attributes the above two speeches to Moravian "teachers." No Moravian "teacher," so far as I know, ever talked such nonsense. John Bray was not a Moravian at all. I have carefully examined the list of members of the first Moravian congregation in London; and Bray's name does not occur in the list. He was an Anglican and an intimate friend of Charles Wesley, and is frequently mentioned in the latter's Journal. It is easy to see how Lecky went wrong. Instead of consulting the evidence for himself, he followed the guidance of Tyerman's Life of John Wesley, Vol. I., p. 302-5.

115. Cur religionem tuam mutasti? Generally, but wrongly, translated Why have you changed your religion? But religio does not mean religion; it means Church or denomination.

116. I believe I am correct in stating that the Watch-Night Service described in this chapter was the first held in England. As such services were held already at Herrnhut, where the first took place in 1733, it was probably a Moravian who suggested the service at Fetter Lane; and thus Moravians have the honour of introducing Watch-Night Services in this country. From them the custom passed to the Methodist; and from the Methodist to other Churches.

117. This letter was first discovered and printed by the late Rev. L. G. Hasse, B.D., in 1896. See Moravian Messenger, June 6th, 1896.

118. Cennick described these incidents fully in his book, Riots at Exeter.

119. See Moravian Hymn-book, No. 846.

120. A nickname afterwards applied to John Wesley.

121. Now called Bishop Street.

122. The congregations which owe their existence to the labours of Cennick are as follows:—In England: Bristol, Kingswood, Bath, Devonport, Malmesbury, Tytherton, Leominster; in Wales: Haverfordwest; in Ireland:—Dublin, Gracehill, Gracefield, Ballinderry, Kilwarlin, Kilkeel, Cootehill.

123. There was no real truth in these allegations.

124. See Boswell's "Johnson," April 10, 1772; April 29, 1773; and April 10, 1775.

125. Regarded then as one of the wonders of England. (See Macaulay's History of England, Chapter III., Sect. Fashionable part of the capital.)

126. The case of Gomersal may serve as an example. The certificate of registration runs as follows: "14th June, 1754. These are to certify that the New Chapel and House adjoining in Little Gumersall, in the Parish of Birstall, in the County and Diocese of York, the property of James Charlesworth, was this day Registered in the Registry of his Grace the Lord Archbishop of York, for a place for Protestant Dissenters for the public worship of Almighty God. "ROB. JUBB, "Deputy Registrar."

127. Consolatory Letter to the Members of the Societies that are in some connection with the Brethren's Congregations, 1752. I owe my knowledge of this rare pamphlet to the kindness of the late Rev. L. G. Hasse.

128. Contents of a Folio History, 1750.

129. The Representation of the Committee of the English Congregations in Union with the Moravian Church, 1754.

130. His other works were: (a) A Solemn Call on Count Zinzendorf (1754); (b) Supplement to the Candid Narrative (1755); (c) A Second Solemn Call on Mr. Zinzendorf (1757); (d) Animadversions on Sundry Flagrant Untruths advanced by Mr. Zinzendorf (no date).

131. Indignantly denied by James Hutton, who was present at the service in question.

132. At one time I could not resist the conviction that Frey had overdrawn his picture (see Owens College Historical Essays, p. 446); but recently I have come to the

conclusion that his story was substantially true. My reason for this change of view is as follows:—As soon as the settlement at Herrnhaag was abandoned a number of Single Brethren went to Pennsylvania, and there confessed to Spangenberg that the scandals at Herrnhaag were "ten times as bad" as described by Frey. See Reichel's Spangenberg, p. 179. Frey's book had then appeared in German.

133. Their chief apologetic works were the following: (1) Peremptorischen Bedencken: or, The Ordinary of the Brethren's Churches. Short and Peremptory Remarks on the Way and Manner wherein he has been hitherto treated in Controversies (1753), by Zinzendorf. (2) A Modest Plea for the Church of the Brethren (1754), anonymous. (3) The Plain Case of the Representatives of the Unitas Fratrum (1754), anonymous. (4) A Letter from a Minister of the Moravian Branch of the Unitas Fratrum to the Author of the "Moravians Compared and Detected," (1755), probably by Frederick Neisser. (5) An Exposition, or True State of the Matters objected in England to the People known by the name of Unitas Fratrum (1755), by Zinzendorf. (6) Additions, by James Hutton. (7) An Essay towards giving some Just Ideas of the Personal Character of Count Zinzendorf (1755), by James Hutton. (8) A Short Answer to Mr. Rimius's Long Uncandid Narrative (1753), anonymous.

134. And yet Tyerman says that in 1752 the Moravian Church was "a luscious morsel of Antinomian poison." Life of John Wesley, II., 96.

135. See Gerhard Reichel's admirable Life of Spangenberg, Chapter X. (1906. J. C. B. Mohr, Tuebingen.)

136. Translated by Samuel Jackson, 1838.

137. Zinzendorf's Robe.—At a conference at Friedberg Zinzendorf suggested (Nov. 17th, 1747) that a white robe should be worn on special occasions, to remind the Brethren of Rev. vii. 9, 13; and, therefore, the surplice was worn for the first time at a Holy Communion, at Herrnhaag, on May 2nd, 1748, by Zinzendorf himself, his son Renatus, two John Nitschmanns, and Rubusch, the Elder of the Single Brethren. This is the origin of the use of the surplice by the modern Moravians.

138. Referred to hereafter as U.E.C.

139. A rule repeatedly broken by the rebellious British. It is frequently recorded in the Synodal Minutes, "the British deputies turned up without having had their election ratified by the Lot."

140. E.g., in Labrador, where it is regularly read at week-night meetings.

141. But this was not the case in England. Only a few children were educated at Broadoaks, Buttermere, and Fulneck; and the parents of the children at Fulneck were expected to pay for them if they could. I am indebted to Mr. W. T. Waugh for this information.

142. For a fuller discussion of this fascinating subject see Bernhard Becker's article in the Monatshefte der Comenius Gesellschaft, 1894, p. 45; Prof. H. Roy's articles in the Evangelisches Kirchenblatt fuer Schlesien, 1905, Nos. 3, 4, 5, 6; and Meyer, Schleiermachers und C. G. v. Brinkmanns Gang durch die Bruedergemeine, 1905.

143. For the poet Goethe's opinion of the Brethren, see Wilhelm Meister (Carlyle's translation), Book VI., "Confessions of a Fair Saint."

144. At the special request of the Fulneck Conference an exception was made in the case of Fulneck School, in Yorkshire.

145. John Wesley, in his Journal, does not tell the story properly. He makes no mention of the Love-feast, and says it was not the Moravian custom to invite friends to eat and drink. The facts are given by Hegner in his Fortsetzung of Cranz's Bruedergeschichte, part III., p. 6.

146. The cause in Ayr was started in 1765 by the preaching of John Caldwell, one of John Cennick's converts. It was not till 1778 that Ayr was organized as a congregation; and no attempt was ever made to convert the other societies into congregations.

147. At the special invitation of William Hunt, a farmer.

148. For complete list of the Brethren's societies in Scotland, see the little pamphlet, The Moravian Church in Ayrshire, reprinted from the Kilmarnock Standard, June 27th, 1903; and for further details about abandoned Societies, see Moravian Chapels and Preaching Places (J. England, 2, Edith Road, Seacombe, near Liverpool).

149. In all this, the object of the Brethren was to be true to the Church of England, and, to place their motives beyond all doubt, I add a minute from the London Congregation Council. It refers to United Flocks, and runs as follows: "April 11th, 1774. Our Society Brethren and Sisters must not expect to have their children baptized by us. It would be against all good order to baptize their children. The increase of this United Flock is to be promoted by all proper means, that the members of it may be a good salt to the Church of England."

150. The certificate was as follows: "This is to certify, that the Bearer, ——, of ——, in the Parish of ——, in the County of ——, is a Member of the Protestant Episcopal Church, known by the name of Unitas Fratrum or United Brethren, and such is entitled to the Privileges granted by an Act of Parliament 22 Geo. II. cap. 120. in the year 1749; and also by an Act of Parliament 43 Geo. III. cap 120. in the year 1803, exempting the members of the said Church from personal Military Services. Witness my Hand and Seal this —— day of —— One Thousand Eight Hundred ——
—."

151. See History of Fulneck School, by W. T. Waugh, M.A.

152. For a fine appreciation of the Brethren's music, see La Trobe, Letters to my Children, pp. 26-45.

153. P.E.C. = Provincial Elders' Conference—i.e., the Governing Board appointed by the U.E.C.; known till 1856 as Provincial Helpers' Conference.

154. P. 431. See the transactions of the Synod of 1818.

155. N.B.—The Moravians in America are not to be confounded with another denomination known as the "United Brethren," founded in 1752 by Philip William Otterbein (see Fisher's "Church History," p. 579). It is, therefore, quite misleading to call the Moravians the "United Brethren." The term is not only historically false, but also leads to confusion.

156. This is necessary in order to fulfil the requirements of German Law.

157. It was also settled in 1899 that the Advocatus Fratrum in Anglia and the Secretarius Fratrum in Anglia should no longer be ex-officio members of the General Synod.

158. See Goll, Quellen und Untersuchungen, II., pp. 78 and 85, and Mueller, Die deutschen Katechismen der Boehmischen Brueder, p. 112.

159. In the Moravian Church the rite of Confirmation is generally performed, not by a Bishop, but by the resident minister; and herein, I believe, they are true to the practice of the early Christian Church.

160. See preface to Moravian Tune Book, large edition.

161. Burkhardt: Die Bruedergemeine, Erster Theil, p. 189.

Made in the USA
Las Vegas, NV
21 March 2024

87471888R00184